Chasing Ghosts

Also by John Mueller and Mark G. Stewart:

Terror, Security, and Money: Balancing the Risks, Benefits, and Costs of Homeland Security

JOHN MUELLER

MARK G. STEWART

Chasing Ghosts

The Policing of Terrorism

OXFORD
UNIVERSITY PRESS

Oxford University Press is a department of the University of
Oxford. It furthers the University's objective of excellence in research,
scholarship, and education by publishing worldwide.
Oxford is a registered trademark of Oxford University Press in the UK
and in certain other countries.

Published in the United States of America by
Oxford University Press
198 Madison Avenue, New York, NY 10016, United States of America

Cataloging-in-Publication Data is on file at the Library of Congress.
ISBN 978–0–19–023731–8

9 8 7 6 5 4 3 2 1
Printed in the United States of America
on acid-free paper

To Judy and Xiaoli

CONTENTS

Chasing Ghosts

INTRODUCTION | Counting Ghosts

I N *DECISION POINTS*, a memoir of his time as president of the United States, George W. Bush recalls a briefing he received from the director of the Federal Bureau of Investigation a few weeks after the terrorist tragedy of September 11, 2001. The director informed him "that there were 331 potential al-Qaeda operatives inside the United States."

Bush says his routine at the time was to pepper such reports with questions: "How credible was each threat? What had we done to follow up on a lead?"[1] However, when writing his book nearly a decade later, he apparently did not feel it useful to reflect critically (or ironically) on the director's impressive and remarkably precise number. If he had, he would likely have concluded that all of the 331 envisioned terrorists—or virtually all of them depending on how one weighs the words *potential* and *operative*—turned out to be ghosts.

Over the next year, the official ghost count rose considerably. Intelligence sources were soon telling rapt and uncritical reporters—and presumably the president of the United States—that the number of trained al-Qaeda operatives in the United States was between 2,000 and 5,000.[2] Terrorist cells, they confidently disclosed, were "embedded in most U.S. cities with sizable Islamic communities," usually in the "run-down sections," and were "up and active"—electronic intercepts had found some of them "talking to each other."[3]

At it happens, however, scarcely any al-Qaeda operatives have ever been unearthed in the United States. The government, as it happens, has been far better at counting them than at finding them.

Impelled by such extravagant perceptions of threat, there have been great increases in spending on policing and intelligence to chase (and count) terrorists in the United States. As Dana Priest and William Arkin have documented in their remarkable book, *Top Secret America*, by 2009 there were something like 1,074 federal government organizations and almost 2,000 private companies devoted to counterterrorism, homeland security, and intelligence spread over more than 17,000 locations within the country. A simple listing of the government's "Special Operations Programs" runs to 300 pages. Collectively this apparatus has launched far more covert operations in the aftermath of 9/11 than it had during the entire forty-five years of the cold war.[4]

A particular comparison might be useful. At least 263 of the agencies devoted to counterterrorism were created or reorganized after 9/11.[5] Since 9/11, as arrayed in appendix A in this book, some 62 cases have come to light of Islamist extremist terrorism, whether based in the United States or abroad, in which the United States itself has been, or apparently has been, targeted. (As will be discussed in chapter 3, almost none of the people in the plots in this array who were based in the United States had any connection to al-Qaeda.) The total number of real terrorists, would-be terrorists, and putative terrorists populating this set of cases, excluding FBI and police undercover operatives, is around 100. Thus, the United States has created or reorganized *more than two entire counterterrorism organizations* for every terrorist arrest or apprehension it has made of people plotting to do damage within the country.

Central to this massive enterprise is what in the FBI has often come to be called "ghost-chasing" or the pursuit of "ghost leads."[6] Agencies like theirs, redirecting much of their effort from organized crime and white-collar embezzlement, have kept their primary focus on the terrorist threat. In a process assessed in more detail in chapter 1, the government reportedly each day follows up on more than 5,000 tips or leads—or "threats," as they are (rather preposterously) called internally.[7] If each of these takes an average of two days to investigate, the United States has followed up on 915,000 "threats" per year, or well over 10 million since 2001. Even under very generous assumptions about how many of these contain true grist, only one alarm in 10,000 fails to be false—the rest all point to ghosts. And the vast majority of the leads deemed worthy of pursuit seem to have led to terrorist enterprises that were either trivial or at most aspirational. But the chase will continue, of course, because no one wants to be the one whose neglect somehow leads to another catastrophe—or in the hyperbole of an official at the FBI's National Threat Center, "it's the one you don't take seriously that becomes the 9/11."[8]

Chasing ghosts is an expensive, exhausting, bewildering, chaotic, and (as chapter 1 will suggest) paranoia-inducing process. At times, in fact, it seems to be an exercise in dueling delusions: a Muslim hothead has delusions about changing the world by blowing something up, and the authorities have delusions that he might actually be able to overcome his patent inadequacies to do so.

This book is devoted to exploring and systematically evaluating the rather amazing process of ghost-chasing. It is an extension and further development of our earlier book, *Terror, Security, and Money: Balancing the Risks, Benefits, and Costs of Homeland Security*, which was published in 2011. That book concentrated primarily on evaluating security measures devoted to protecting infrastructure—buildings, bridges, and the airlines. These constitute about 46 percent of overall homeland security expenditures. This book focuses on policing and intelligence, which account for another 44 percent.[9]

To put the perspective of this book into a broader context, it may be useful at the outset to examine a couple of precedents for present-day ghost-chasing. These involve hunts for witches (rather than for ghosts): real ones in one case, and metaphorical ones in the other.

Witches

Between about the years 1480 and 1680, tens of thousands of people—the vast majority of them women—were executed in Europe as witches, very often by being burned at the stake. This method was preferred because, although obviously excruciatingly painful, it was considered morally and/or religiously superior, in that it did not involve the visible shedding of blood. Accused witches routinely confessed, generally under torture, to such crimes as, in Steven Pinker's enumeration, "eating babies, wrecking ships, destroying crops, flying on broomsticks on the Sabbath, copulating with devils, transforming their demon lovers into cats and dogs, and making ordinary men impotent by convincing them that they had lost their penises."[10]

In a book about what he calls the "witch-craze," historian Hugh Trevor-Roper notes that one square in a German town "looked like a little forest, so crowded were the stakes," and that over an eight-year period, one prince-bishop "burnt 900 persons, including his own nephew, nineteen Catholic priests, and children of seven who were said to have had intercourse with demons." Torturers became so professionalized that they developed exquisite Latin monikers for the various methods. Most successful, they found, was *tormentum insomniae*, or sleep deprivation. Even those capable of resisting *estrapade* (described as "a pulley which jerked the body violently in mid-air") would yield, says Trevor-Roper, "to a resolute application of this slower but more certain torture, and confess themselves to be witches." However, he suggests, the campaign against the witches failed to reduce their actual (or at least their perceived) number: "The more fiercely they were prosecuted, the more numerous they seemed to become."[11]

In Scotland, officials discovered and executed fifty witches each year on average, whereas the number in England was only five.[12] *Macbeth*, William Shakespeare's play about witches (and ghosts), was written when the witch hunts were in full rampage. It may be that his London audiences thought that, since more witches were executed in Scotland, there must simply be more of them up there—perhaps, one might tentatively surmise, it's because its special climate is somehow more conducive to broomstick riding, cauldron bubbling, and dark orgies.

However, there is a less theatrical, if more prosaic, reason for the discrepancy: torture was used to inspire confessions in Scotland, but not in England. Nonetheless, it is impressive that in England, without using torture at all, authorities were able to get an average of five people a year to confess, at the known consequent loss of their own lives, to the standard litany of impossible crimes. A considerable number of these (and other) people probably did actually imagine they were witches.

At various times during the witch craze, a few people tried to debunk the process. But their attacks were ineffectual, not only because they were sometimes tortured and executed themselves for such heresy but also because their argument took place at what Trevor-Roper calls the "periphery" of the justification for the executions. That is, the critics went after the consequences of the system, not its premise, as they railed "against the cruelty of torture, against the implausibility of confessions, against the identification of witches."[13] For example, an Italian judge killed his mule, accused his servant of the murder, and had him tortured, causing the man to confess to the crime, even refusing to recant on the gallows out of fear of being tortured again.[14]

However, this approach left intact the "central doctrine" of the witch craze holding that Satan was waging war on humanity with the assistance of corporal associates: witches. The critics lacked a substitute for this doctrine. By contrast, notes Trevor-Roper, "If the witch-craze were to be attacked at its centre, not merely doubted at its periphery, it was necessary to challenge the whole conception of the kingdom of Satan."[15]

In consequence, the witch craze, with its tremendous human, societal, and material costs, only died out, he argues, when theologians eventually were able to sell a re-evaluation of the premise that formed the engine for the craze. In this, the notion of "the duel in Nature between a Hebrew God and a medieval Devil was replaced by the benevolent despotism of a modern, scientific 'Deity.' "[16] In addition, it appears, they were able to convince people that, although the devil was indeed out there, he didn't actually need corporal assistants to carry out his nefarious handiwork.[17]

Domestic Communists

Some three centuries later, the United States held something of what Trevor-Roper might call a "communist craze" during the cold war against international communism. By that time, any perceived menace from witches had dwindled considerably. Modern polls—ones usually published around Halloween time—do find that 24 percent of American adults still continue to profess a belief in witches (an additional 7 percent say they are "unsure" about their beliefs on the matter).[18] But even those who believe in witches do not appear to hold that, in league with the devil, witches are a central cause of dismal happenings and therefore need to be expunged.

However, during the cold war, few Americans—perhaps none at all—would have denied the existence of another internal enemy: domestic communists. Though communism was long considered by many to be a potential danger, fears about domestic communists were greatly enhanced after two spectacular trials: that of Alger Hiss, who was convicted in 1950 of perjury in denying that he had supplied the Soviet Union with classified State Department documents a decade earlier; and that of Julius and Ethel Rosenberg, who were convicted in 1951 of being at the center of a ring of domestic communists who supplied secrets about the atomic bomb to the country's then-ally, the Soviet Union, during the Second World War.[19]

The fear of domestic communism much impelled the hasty expansion of a costly anti-communist surveillance and policing system that persisted for decades. Extravagant alarmist proclamations about the degree to which domestic communists—"masters of deceit" and "enemies from within"—presented a threat to the republic found a receptive audience. Thus, J. Edgar Hoover, the highly respected, even revered, director of the FBI, divulged in a 1958 book that the American Communist Party was working "day and night to further the communist plot in America" with "deadly seriousness"; that a "Bolshevik transmission" was in progress that was "virtually invisible to the non-communist eye, unhampered by time, distance, and legality"; that it was "creating communist puppets throughout the country"; and that it had for "its objective the ultimate seizure of power in America."[20]

To a degree, the dynamic is suggested by Trevor-Roper in an observation about the witch phenomenon: "When a 'great fear' takes hold of society, that society looks naturally to the stereotype of the enemy in its midst; and once the witch had become the stereotype, witchcraft would be the universal accusation." Moreover, "the stereotype, once established, creates, as it were, its own folk-lore, which becomes in itself a centralizing force."[21]

Although no real or accused communists were burned at the stake during the communist craze (there were only two executions), those in quest of the enemy within, like Hoover, spent a prodigious amount of time and public money in pursuit. For example, in 1972, the FBI in full perpetual motion mode opened 65,000 new files as part of its costly quest to ferret out communists in the United States.[22] Trevor-Roper's observation about the witch craze—"The more fiercely they were prosecuted, the more numerous they seemed to become"—appears to resonate.

In a fascinating book, German literature specialist Alexander Stephan describes the U.S. government's surveillance of a group of German émigré writers during and after World War II. None was found to pose much of a subversive threat, and the surveillance never led to real persecution—indeed, few of the writers noticed they were being watched. Instead, what impresses Stephan is the essential absurdity of the situation—the "high efficiency and gross overkill" as hundreds of agents were paid to intercept and catalog communications, to endlessly record goings and comings, and to sift enterprisingly through trash bins in a quest for incriminating information. For example, there is something profoundly ludicrous about the fact that dozens of government employees spent their time in the middle of a world war monitoring pillow talk between Bertolt Brecht and his Danish co-worker, Ruth Berlau—all this, notes the amazed Stephan, "at taxpayers' expense."[23]

Nevertheless, critics of this costly, extravagant process focused almost entirely on the potential for civil liberties violations in what, as it happens, they routinely labeled a "witch hunt." In this, they were in line with their predecessors during the actual witch craze: "To the last," notes Trevor-Roper, "the most radical argument against the witch-craze was not that witches do not exist, not even that the pact with Satan is impossible, but simply that the judges err in their identification."[24] In like manner, it appears that no one during the cold war attacked the premise of the system: that domestic communists posed a threat severe enough to require an elaborate and expensive policing effort. Substantially, it seems, Hoover's dire exaggerations were accepted.

There seem to have been few, if any, instances in which domestic communists actively engaged in anything that could be considered espionage after World War II, and at no time did domestic communists commit much of anything that could be considered violence in support of the cause. Yet it appears that during the cold war no one ever said this in public: "Many domestic Communists adhere to a foreign ideology that ultimately has as its goal the destruction of capitalism and democracy and by violence if necessary; however, they do not present much of a danger, are actually quite a pathetic bunch, and couldn't subvert their way out of a wet paper bag. Why are we expending so much time, effort, and treasure on this issue?" It is astounding that this plausible, if arguable, point of view—a proposition that, unlike witch denial during the Middle Ages, was unlikely to prove to be fatal to the proposer—seems never to have been publicly expressed by anyone during the lengthy cold war, whether by politician, pundit, professor, or editorialist. Instead, the essential premise of the system was generally accepted: there are a lot of dangerous and capable communists in the country.

Thus, the fear of domestic communism, and the consequent costly anti-communist surveillance system it spawned, flourished for decades. The communist craze died out only when international communism obligingly collapsed at the end of the cold war, when any machinations by domestic communists no longer had a threatening foreign referent: although espionage continued to be of concern, there no longer existed a hostile foreign power to whom domestic communists could relay secrets, nor was there a prominent, threatening ideology stressing subversion and violent revolution for them to serve.[25]

Terrorists

Switching now from witches to ghosts, it might be pointed out that, although only 24 percent of the adult population in the United States currently professes to believe in witches, a full 34 percent acknowledge a belief in the existence of ghosts.[26] Indeed, that number advances to 49 percent when the query is expanded somewhat: "Do you believe in ghosts, or that the spirits of dead people can come back in certain places or situations?" And nearly half of those questioned responded in the affirmative when asked, "Have you, personally, ever seen or believed yourself to be in the presence of a ghost?"[27]

There seem to be no comparable data on whether Americans have ever seen or believed themselves to be in the presence of a terrorist. However, as chapter 2 will document, although the yearly chance an American will be killed by a terrorist within the country is about one in 4 million under present conditions, around 40 percent of Americans have professed, in polls taken since late 2001, that they worry they or a family member will become a victim of a terrorist.

Like witches, actual or presumed terrorists have been around for centuries, even millennia.[28] Terrorism has often commanded far more attention than it probably has deserved, but for the most part it seems to have been deemed a limited and manageable phenomenon. Over the course of the terrible morning of September 11, 2001, however, concerns in the United States about the threat terrorists present and the damage they might inflict escalated dramatically, becoming cosmic and existential to many—or even to most. And, as this book will seek to demonstrate in the next couple of chapters, that initial attitude continues substantially to prevail among officials and among the public more than a dozen years later—even though, unlike during the crazes over witches and communists, there has been at least a bit of commentary (virtually none of it coming from officials) suggesting that domestic terrorists don't actually present all that much of a threat.

As a result, there has been that almost mind-boggling expansion of the apparatus designed to counter the terrorist enemy within. Tallying the expenditures on domestic homeland security and adding opportunity costs—but leaving out related overseas costs such as those entailed by the terrorism-induced wars in Iraq and Afghanistan—we find that the increase in expenditures on domestic homeland security since 9/11 easily exceeds $1 trillion.[29] This has not been enough to move the country into bankruptcy—arch-terrorist Osama bin Laden's stated goal after 9/11—but it clearly adds up to real money, even by Washington standards. As Alexander Stephan might amazedly suggest, taxpayers really ought to take note.

As part of this, the policing and intelligence agencies, like their predecessors during the quests to quash witchery and domestic communism, have dutifully and laboriously assembled masses of intelligence data and have pursued an astoundingly extensive array of leads. Moreover, as will be discussed much more fully in chapter 1, it certainly appears that Trevor-Roper's dictum about witches holds for the current spooky adversaries: the more fiercely they are persecuted, the more numerous they seem to become.

The Road Ahead

A central concern in this book is that, as with the hunts for witches and communists, the chief challenge for the domestic counterterrorism system has been at what Trevor-Roper calls the "periphery." In some important respects, the risk presented by terrorism has only very rarely been explained, or even systematically examined, by those who are appalled at the system those exaggerations have spawned. Instead, there are worries about invasions of privacy, about prosecutorial or investigative misconduct, about the potential entrapment or misidentification of suspects, about the legality of imprisonment at Guantanamo. Entirely legitimate concerns, of course, but ones likely to be ineffective in front of judges anxious to set deterring sentences and before juries composed of frightened citizens.

Former Vice President Dick Cheney has been fond of asserting that security measures put into place after 9/11 have saved thousands of lives, and by 2009 he had escalated this to "perhaps hundreds of thousands of lives." There have been few efforts to refute or even examine such extravagant and evidence-free claims—for the most part, they are simply allowed to lay there.[30]

However, no defense of civil liberties is likely to be terribly effective if people believe that infringements have saved huge numbers of lives and that the threat from terrorism is massive, even existential. Civil liberties concerns and cost excesses can be reduced only if the internalized anxiety about terrorism is substantially dampened: if Americans have come to believe that their chance every year of being killed by a terrorist is dangerously high, rather than one in 4 million, they are unlikely to be moved by concerns about civil liberties infringements or about counterterrorism expenditures that are designed to keep, or to make, them safe. Thus to undo, or even modify, the vast security system that has expanded so greatly since 2001, one must directly assess not simply the costs and consequences of the system but also the premises that furnish its essential engine.[31]

This book takes on that task. It seeks to evaluate—or, better, to put into sensible context—the premises that drive the vast policing and intelligence venture to counter terrorism within the United States. Among these are the notions that terrorism presents a dire, existential, or at least significant threat to national security; that we can never be safe enough; that most (or many, or at least a considerable number of) terrorists are diabolically clever and resourceful, and that some are "masterminds"; that the terrorist success on September 11, 2001, not only "changed everything" but also demonstrates that the terrorists can and would readily do it again or even amass and use weapons of mass destruction, including especially nuclear ones.

As part of this effort, the book will evaluate key components of domestic counterterrorism policing measures, particularly those of the FBI, the National Security Agency, the Department of Homeland Security, and local policing agencies like the New York City Police Department. It also assesses public opinion stemming from iconic or "Black Swan" events like 9/11—a key driving force for counterterrorism efforts. And it concludes by setting out a perspective about what responsible policy making should look like under the circumstances.

Many of those accused of witchcraft probably did believe they had copulated with the devil and had somehow gained special powers to shape events in his service. And dedicated communists and Islamist terrorists have been committed to violent actions that they hope will somehow advance the historical revolutionary process or Allah's will. However, it is vital for those who seek to counter such people to consider not only the dreams and desires of their adversaries but their capacities as well.

Few of those who believe today in witchcraft hold that witches ever presented much of a practical danger, and at least in retrospect, few once-fervent anti-communists today insist that any threat presented by domestic communists justified the alarm. There may be a lesson in that for the vast ghost-chasing industry that has burgeoned since September 11, 2001.

We do not argue that there is nothing for the ghost-chasers to find—the terrorist "adversary" is real and does exist. The question that is central to the exercise, but one the ghost-chasers never really probe, is an important and rather straightforward one to which standard cost-benefit procedures can be applied: Is the chase worth the effort? Or is it excessive, given a serious evaluation of the danger that terrorism actually presents?

PART ONE | The Ghosts

| Official Perceptions
The Threat Matrix

T HIS CHAPTER DEALS with the fear among officials in the wake of 9/11 that terrorists were everywhere and all-powerful, with the vast increase in policing and intelligence measures that took place as a result, and with the perpetuation of the costly enterprise even after initial fears were demonstrated to be overwrought. It also examines the illusions and delusions that have accompanied, or been impelled by, the process, and it evaluates the costs incurred.

Throughout this chapter, and throughout the remainder of this book, there will be references to a collection of terrorism cases that is available separately on the web. This collection consists of detailed studies, each organized in a similar manner, of the 62 cases that have come to light since 9/11 of Islamist extremist terrorism, whether based in the United States or abroad, in which the United States has been—or apparently has been—targeted. A listing of these cases is included in appendix A of this book.

The 9/11 Atmosphere: Consequences and Persistence

In the immediate aftermath of the September 11 attacks, recalls Rudy Giuliani, who was mayor of New York City at the time, "anybody, any one of these security experts, including myself, would have told you on September 11, 2001, we're looking at dozens and dozens and multiyears of attacks like this." As journalist Jane Mayer observes, "[T]he only certainty shared by virtually the entire American intelligence community" in the months after September 11 "was that a second wave of even more devastating terrorist attacks on America was imminent." President George W. Bush recalls that "it seemed almost certain that there would be another attack" and that "we believed more attacks were coming, but we didn't know when, where, or from whom." Or, in the words of deputy CIA director John McLaughlin, "There was a pervasive feeling that 9/11 was not the end of the story." Staffer Dean McGrath recalls that "There was a real, almost fatalistic concern that we were going to be hit again." In the words of analyst Philip Mudd: "There was a pervasive sense that an event of unimaginable magnitude had happened, but there was also an overwhelming dread that we had witnessed only the start of a series of events." John Poindexter saw the attacks as "an opening salvo, not a final shot."[1]

At the time, Michael Morell was the CIA agent in charge of briefing the president, and he later became the agency's deputy director. In a book published in 2015, he recalls the atmosphere vividly. "We were certain we were going to be attacked again." There was "an avalanche—literally thousands—of intelligence reports in the months following 9/11 that strongly indicated that al Qa'ida would hit us again," and some of these indicated that the terrorists might use chemical or biological weapons or "even crude nuclear devices"—a suggestion Morell says he found to be "believable."[2]

Such fears and concerns were, of course, reasonable extrapolations from the facts then at hand. As journalist Peter Baker puts it, "It would take weeks, months, and even years to tighten security for a country as large and as open as the United States, and it seemed implausible that terrorists would not mount follow-up attacks."[3] However, that *every* "security expert" should fervently embrace such alarmist—and, it turned out, erroneous—views, and that the intelligence community should be *certain* about them, is fundamentally absurd. It was also an entirely plausible extrapolation from facts then at hand that 9/11 could prove to be an aberration rather than a harbinger.[4]

Yet it appears that no one in authority could even imagine that proposition to be true—effectively, they dismissed it out of hand—even though it could have been taken to fit the available information fully as well as the passionately embraced alarmist perspective. Even fourteen years later, Morell does not pause to reflect on why or how those "thousands" of alarming intelligence reports could have been so hopelessly and so spectacularly wrong.

Similarly, in a 2007 book, CIA Director George Tenet says "it was inconceivable to us that Bin Laden had not already positioned people to conduct second, and possibly third and fourth waves of attacks inside the United States." Under the circumstances it was certainly sensible to use that as a working assumption, but it is patently absurd and irresponsible, and perhaps even dangerous, to completely reject the possibility that the assumption might be wrong. Tenet goes on to assert that "getting people into this country—legally or illegally—was no challenge before 9/11," and he proclaims that "nothing I had learned in the ensuing three years ever let me to believe that our initial working assumption that al-Qa'ida had cells here was wrong."[5] But by the time he wrote his book, the FBI, after exhaustive and frantic investigation, had been unable to find a single true cell in the country, and the chief architect of the 9/11 attacks had repeatedly confessed under various forms of interrogation that the most difficult part of the scheme had been to infiltrate operatives into the United States.[6]

The process, or syndrome, has a substantial pedigree. For example, historian John Lewis Gaddis observes that *no one* at the summit of foreign policy in 1950 anticipated most of the major international developments that were to take place in the next half-century. Among these: "that there would be no World War" and that the United States and the Soviet Union, "soon to have tens of thousands of thermonuclear weapons pointed at one another, would agree tacitly never to use any of them."[7] However, the potential absence of a further world war, whether nuclear or not, was compatible with the fairly obvious observation that those running world affairs after World War II were the same people or the intellectual heirs of the people who had tried desperately to prevent that cataclysm. It was entirely plausible that such people, despite their huge differences on many issues, might well manage to keep themselves from plunging into a self-destructive repeat performance.[8] Although this perspective was not, of course, the only possible one, there was no definitive way to dismiss it, and it should accordingly have been on the table. But it seems not to have been.

Operating under their apparently unanimous alarmist mentality after 9/11, U.S. intelligence came extravagantly to imagine by 2002 that, as noted in this book's introduction, the number of trained al-Qaeda operatives in the United States was between 2,000 and 5,000.[9] An imaginative account from London relayed the view of "experts" that Osama bin Laden was ready to unleash an "11,000 strong terrorist army" operating in more than sixty countries, an army "controlled by a Mr. Big who is based in Europe," while noting rather unhelpfully that intelligence had "no idea where thousands of these men are."[10]

The alarm of the early years is perhaps best illustrated by the saga of Cofer Black, head of the CIA's Counterterrorism Center, who, says a colleague, was "acting wilder and wilder." Black insisted that unless his staff was increased by hundreds, or even thousands, "people are going to die," and that Western civilization hung in the balance. When he went home, according to his wife, he would turn off the lights and sit in the dark with a drink and a cigar, sunk in an apocalyptic gloom.[11]

Morell says that, "aware of all the intelligence," he and CIA Director Tenet "would routinely ask each other, 'Is this the day we get hit again?'" So fearful was Morell of a nuclear detonation that he told his wife that "if such an attack were to happen in Washington to put the kids in the car and start driving west and not stop. It was surreal."[12]

In that "surreal" atmosphere, authorities were looking everywhere, often with considerable imagination, to locate and break up all those terrorist cells they were convinced must be out there somewhere. No one, it appears, was given to question the enterprise or its essential premise. In 2006, the PBS *Frontline* series telecast an assessment of some terrorism arrests that had taken place the previous year in Lodi, California. Christine Biederman, who was in the fray as an assistant U.S. attorney (AUSA) in the years after 9/11, wrote to the program recalling, "I cannot begin to describe the pressure prosecutors face to produce convictions to justify the massive expenditures in the 'war on terror.' Most AUSAs are, like the one interviewed, good soldiers who believe in the 'war' the way they believe in God and family and apple pie—because they were raised that way and always have, because these form the core of their belief system and because questioning the mission would trigger all kinds of crises: moral, political, professional and, in the end, financial."[13]

That sort of dark perspective seems to have been internalized and institutionalized over the years in a great many ways, and it has proved to be notably resistant to counter-information. For example, in early 2005, Richard Clarke, counterterrorism coordinator for the Clinton administration, issued a scenario that appeared as a cover story in the *Atlantic*. In the article, he darkly envisioned terrorist shootings at casinos, campgrounds, theme parks, and malls in 2005, bombings in subways and railroads in 2006, missile attacks on airliners in 2007, and devastating cyberattacks in 2008.[14]

In his 2005 reflections on post-9/11 fears, Rudy Guiliani added, "It hasn't been quite that bad"—a bit of an understatement considering that not only had none of the "dozens and dozens" of attacks like 9/11 that he and fellow "security experts" unanimously anticipated failed to come about, but there hadn't been a successful attack of any magnitude in the United States at all. Nor, of course, in the ensuing years did *any* of the fanciful scenarios spun out by expert Richard Clarke—or anything remotely like them—materialize. A poll in 2006 of more than 100 of "America's top foreign-policy experts"—nearly 80 percent of whom had worked in the government—found 79 percent unfazed by the good if unexpected news, declaring it certain or likely that "a terrorist attack on the scale of 9/11" would occur in the United States by the end of 2011.[15]

In the summer of 2007, a National Intelligence Estimate (NIE) produced an official report warning that, as Morell summarizes it, the leadership of al-Qaeda had now established a "safe haven" in Pakistan and, as a consequence, had become "less concerned about its own security." This meant that it had more time to scheme and "had regenerated key elements of his homeland attack capability" including "the development of capable operational lieutenants" and was "in the process of planning high-impact attacks on the US homeland." Those "capable operational lieutenants" seem to have failed utterly in this mission, though Morell suggests this is because, duly alarmed by the NIE, the administration launched more aggressive counterterrorism operations. The only case he can come up with to illustrate the danger about "high-impact attacks on the US homeland" that the NIE warned about is the Zazi case that took place a full two years later, to be discussed more fully later in this chapter.[16] It concerned a former donut peddler who had wandered into the area with the intent to fight for the Taliban in Afghanistan. Al-Qaeda opportunistically convinced him to return to the United States to bomb the New York subway system, an operation that proved to be a fiasco and, once arrested, Zazi helpfully supplied his captors with detailed information about the terrorist group.

The threat of terrorism in the country obviously proved to be far more limited than has persistently been feared. The number of al-Qaeda operatives actually in the country has held at zero or nearly so, and the FBI's inability to find sleeper cells has persisted to the present day—the ghostly terrorists espied in the thousands by the intelligence community in 2002 either never existed or afterward obligingly vanished.

Accordingly, there might have been some judicious re-evaluations, and perhaps even some cutbacks to the funds devoted to dealing with chasing them. However, the FBI will continue to engage, perhaps forever, in the exhaustive, and exhausting, pursuit. Thus, FBI Director Robert Mueller declared: "I'll fight tooth and nail for more criminal agents, but I'll never at the end of the day take an agent out of counterterrorism and national security."[17] In the meantime, those agents in the counterterrorism business were creatively, and presumably soberly, warning Americans to be on the alert for people walking around bearing almanacs, because these might, for example, contain information about the location of bridges.[18]

At times, the Obama administration that assumed office in 2009 took some pains to downplay the rhetoric of war as it deals with terrorism. However, some months later, in October 2009, one of the advisers to the new administration, Bruce Riedel, was publicly maintaining that the al-Qaeda threat to the country continued to be "existential."[19]

And at a 2011 press conference, Homeland Security chief Janet Napolitano opaquely, if creatively, announced that, although the likelihood of a large-scale organized attack had diminished, the continued danger of a small-scale disorganized attack meant that there was a "sense" in which it could be said that the terrorist threat was higher than at any time since 9/11.[20] This extraordinary contention failed to prompt a skeptical query from her rapt auditors. And a senior Obama administration analyst implied in 2012 that the situation remained bad: al-Qaeda "lacks the ability to plan, organize and execute complex, catastrophic attacks, but the threat persists."[21]

In a speech in 2013, President Obama did express some distaste for what he called the "boundless" global war on terror.[22] But in some important respects, his vision of the enterprise seemed even more extravagant—and boundless—than before. In part, perhaps, this is because his desire to use the weapons and methods of war such as missile and drone attacks against terrorists required him to plunge into the rhetoric of war and in the process to hype the threat that terrorism presents.

At any rate, he began the speech by confirming that the United States had indeed been at "war" ever since 9/11. He deemed that war to be going rather well, but concluded that it must necessarily continue because "our nation is still threatened by terrorists." Then, musing on the "future of terrorism," he argued that the threat had "shifted and evolved" somewhat—a common assertion by officials, but one that is banal because that can be said about almost any aspect of human affairs. Obama insisted that a war against this shifting and evolving threat would be required as long as there are al-Qaeda affiliates out there, as long as there are threats to diplomatic facilities and businesses abroad, and as long as there are "homegrown extremists" willing to set off bombs or shoot people. Whether there will always be violent groups saying they are affiliated with al-Qaeda is uncertain. But it seems fair to suggest that there will always be people who threaten American diplomatic facilities or businesses abroad, and that there will always be extremists at home—however trivial and pathetic—who will try from time to time to do violence to other people to advance a political cause. Consequently, the war will continue forever.

But there was more. In one of the more arresting passages in the speech, Obama pointed out that the present terrorism threat is much like the one of the 1980s and 1990s, listing a number of terrorist outrages during those decades; therefore, he seemed to suggest that the United States must have been at war with terrorism in those decades as well, even if nobody exactly noticed. And, of course, a similar litany of terrorist excesses could be brought out for just about any decade in U.S. or world history. Consequently, not only had the United States been at war with terrorism for "over a decade," not only would it be at war with it for eternity, but also it has been at war with it for the whole of time. Sounds pretty boundless.[23]

The Threat Matrix

Important in all this—and central to the issues examined in this book—have been increases in expenditures on intelligence and policing as the ghost-chasing enterprise continues to be expanded. And central to that enterprise is the "Threat Matrix," an itemized catalog of all the "threats"—or more accurately, "leads"—needing to be followed up.[24] In Philip Mudd's description, it is "a synopsis of the threats that had rolled in that day, or significant threats from previous days or weeks that required steady follow-up."[25] The Threat Matrix, or selected excerpts from it, forms the centerpiece of the briefings on terrorism the FBI director undergoes each day, and it also undergoes scrutiny at the daily 5 P.M. briefing presided over by the director of the CIA attended by a group numbering over thirty.[26] And every morning, it would be used to brief the president.[27]

According to journalist Garrett Graff, the Threat Matrix "tracks all the unfolding terrorist plots and intelligence rumors" and is "filled to the brim with whispers, rumors, and vacuous, unconfirmed information."[28] Baker calls it "a compendium of potential horrors" from which "almost nothing, it seemed, was left out."[29] Impelled by what some have called "the 9/11 Commission Syndrome"—an obsession with the career dangers in failing to "connect the dots"—it is in no one's interest to reduce the length of the list "because it was possible you'd cull the wrong threat and end up, after the next attack, at the green felt witness table before the next congressional inquiry."[30] As a result, "claims that ordinarily wouldn't have made it past the intake agent, claims that wouldn't even be written down weeks earlier, suddenly became the subject of briefs to the President in the Oval Office."[31] Or, as Mudd puts it, it comprises "threats, fabrications, half-truths, vague warnings, and spurned poison-pen lovers." Included is

> everything from unvetted walk-ins around the world—people who simply walked into an Embassy, for example, and volunteered information—to nuts who wrote into U.S. government websites, to second-rate sources who made up tales to earn a paycheck. All this was read by the president, in a document intended initially to serve as a working-level draft. What was initially a simple, almost inevitable way of tracing threats—it had to be done somewhere—became a means by which senior policymakers reviewed raw material that many of us, myself included, thought was "below threshold" for them.[32]

Graff supplies an example. One entry in the Threat Matrix is crisply cited as "a threat from the Philippines to attack the United States unless blackmail money was paid." It turns out that this entry was based on an email that said, "Dear America. I will attack you if you don't pay me 99999999999999999 9999999999999999999999999 dollars. MUHAHAHA." Graff reports that the FBI dutifully traced the email's author and sent information to Philippine police, who then paid a visit to the would-be extortionist's parents.[33]

It was in August 2008, in its hundredth year, that the FBI celebrated (or acknowledged) the receipt of its two millionth terrorism tip from the public.[34] All told, concludes Graff, the government pursues "upwards of 5,000" leads every day,[35] a process that has led to, at the very most, a few hundred prosecutions, most of them on quite minor charges.[36] As former TSA director Kip Hawley notes, intelligence briefings can become thrilling, elaborate story-time breaks for government executives, albeit ones "that rarely result in action."[37] Yet all have been dutifully scrutinized under the admonition of Director Robert Mueller that "No counterterrorism lead goes uncovered."[38]

There is also something ghostly about the experience. "Threats" appear on the Matrix only when they are first uncovered and then, later, when new information about them is generated.[39] Consequently, they are like specters: constantly popping up and then vanishing.

The enterprise can be summarized, perhaps, in Hawley's reminiscence of his last morning in office in 2009, shortly before Barack Obama's inauguration, when he dutifully waded through intelligence reports in quest of possible "threat streams." At the time, he notes, intelligence "had already highlighted threats to mass transit"—without bothering to note, of course, that none of those "threats" ever materialized. One report that morning particularly caught his eye: the corpses of four young men had recently been found at a small, remote "training camp" in Algeria, possibly killed by poison or by "some sort of biochemical accident." This set Hawley into wondering, "[H]ad they maybe been practicing for today on the mall?" This creative, if rather extravagant, exercise in globalized dot-connecting is, says Hawley, a "perfect metaphor for how I had spent nearly the last four years of my life."[40] Even with a few years of hindsight, he never bothers to tell us, or even muse about, how the Algerian story turned out. Nor does it express curiosity about what may have been behind it. Probably, one is led to suspect, nothing.

And it is hardly a "metaphor." Rather, it is a clear example of fruitless (and perhaps mindless) ghost-chasing, of needless anguish, and of creative extrapolation. The Algerian corpse "threat" was only one of hundreds Hawley examined on his last morning. With the swelling intelligence apparatus pitchforking ever more "threats" onto the haystack to be pawed through by people paid to be imaginative, we will always be in an "emergency." It appears, then, that the title of Hawley's book, *Permanent Emergency*, is not, as might at first appear, an oxymoron.

This is also suggested by a more recent development. Around 2013, some twelve Threat Matrix–filled years after 9/11, the FBI finally tried to put together a mechanism to deal with, or at any rate order, the blizzard of tips (though it continued to hold to its resolution to follow up every tip or "threat"). It instituted something called the Threat Review and Prioritization (TRP) process to be used in conjunction with a Consolidation Strategy Guide (CSG) by Threat Mitigation Teams (TMTs). Applying the TRP and the CSG, the TMTs are supposed to identify and prioritize "national threat issues" and then act on those in the top "bands." However, in 2015, a review commission instituted by Congress sharply criticized the procedure because it might neglect "threats" that do not currently exist— "over-the-horizon threats," it calls them. It went on to point out helpfully that the terrorist enterprise (not unlike life itself) is constantly "emerging" and "evolving" and "growing" while the terrorism problem is becoming "increasingly complex and more dangerous," as well as more "globally dispersed" even as terrorists become "more adaptive and sophisticated" in strategy and "more advanced" in the use of technology.[41]

Institutionalized Paranoia and Its Consequences

"Much of the material in the matrix was trash," notes Mudd, and the people reading it "were looking at material not worth their time." However, he continues, "they saw it differently." In consequence, the Threat Matrix "took on a life and legend of its own."[42] Moreover, whatever the ratio of needle to hay, living with the Threat Matrix also seems to take a psychological toll on its daily readers: as presidential adviser Condoleezza Rice recalls, "it had a huge effect on our psyches."[43] Henry Kissinger stresses that, "Historians rarely do justice to the psychological stress on a policy-maker."[44] One can only imagine what happens when this rather natural hazard of office is exacerbated every day or week by multiple fusillades of undifferentiated, yet seemingly dire, threats.

As Graff vividly describes the process, the Threat Matrix could become "all-consuming and paralyzing" and comes off as "a catalogue of horrors," as the "daily looming prognoses of Armageddon," and as "a seeming tidal wave of Islamic extremist anger that threatened to unhinge American society."[45] Jack Goldsmith, an avid consumer of the Threat Matrix when he was in the Bush administration, stresses that "[i]t is hard to overstate the impact that the incessant waves of threat reports have on the judgment of people inside the executive branch who are responsible for protecting American lives." He quotes Tenet: "You simply could not sit where I did and read what passed across my desk on a daily basis and be anything other than scared to death about what it portended." This, writes Goldsmith, captures "the attitude of every person I knew who regularly read the threat matrix."[46] *Every* person.

And it commonly has the effect, by its sheer magnitude, of terrifying them. President Bush recalls that "for months after 9/11, I would wake up in the middle of the night worried about what I had read," a recollection confirmed by his wife: "I could see the lines cut deeper into his face and could hear him next to me lying awake at night, his mind still working."[47] Mudd notes that "the backdrop was always threat. It shadowed us every day." The "voluminous and dominating" threat information "contributed to a pervasive sense that every day might bring a new attack."[48] As another reader puts it, "Your mind comes to be dominated by the horrific consequences of low-probability events."[49] Another has arrestingly offered a vivid comparison: "Reading the Threat Matrix every day is like being stuck in a room listening to loud Led Zeppelin music," and "after a while, you begin to suffer from sensory overload and become paranoid about the threat."[50] The process even led to suicide in one case: obsessed by the implied imminence and certainty of doom, one overworked reader, Special Agent Brad Doucette, was led to kill himself in 2003.[51]

In essence, it appears to be like being barricaded in an apartment and listening only to the police radio for information about what is going on outside. Or repeatedly giving one's full attention to scary ghost stories spun out around a late-night campfire. According to Jim Comey of the FBI (who became its director in 2013), it causes you to "imagine a threat so severe that it becomes an obsession."[52]

Adam Garfinkle characterizes the effect as "institutionalized paranoia."[53] The consequences of the process are considerable.

SEEING GHOSTS

Goldsmith quotes a Threat Matrix veteran who rather explicitly envisions the process as one of seeing ghosts. "Think of the goalie at a soccer game who must stop every shot, for the enemy wins if it scores a single goal. The problem is that the goalie cannot see the ball—it is invisible. So are the players—he doesn't know how many there are, or where they are, or what they look like."[54] Hawley, too, says the work involved the constant "scrambling and unscrambling" of what he calls "invisible threats."[55] To Mudd, it was "the pursuit of endless ghost leads."[56]

So primed, officials often seem to live in what might be called "I think, therefore they are" denial.

Thus, on February 11, 2003, a year and a half after 9/11, FBI Director Robert Mueller assured (or spooked) the Senate Intelligence Committee by insisting that "the greatest threat is from al-Qaeda cells in the United States that we have not yet identified." He somehow judged the threat from those unidentified entities to be "increasing" while claiming to know that "al-Qaeda maintains the ability and the intent to inflict significant casualties in the United States with little warning," and had "developed a support infrastructure" inside the United States that would allow the network to mount another terrorist attack on U.S. soil.[57]

Later in that year, Homeland Security Secretary Tom Ridge divined that "extremists abroad are anticipating near-term attacks" that they believe will "rival or exceed" those of 2001.[58] And in 2004, Attorney General John Ashcroft, with FBI Director Mueller at his side, announced that "credible intelligence from multiple sources indicates that al Qaeda plans to attempt an attack on the United States in the next few months," that its "specific intention" was to hit us "hard," and that the "arrangements" for that attack were already 90 percent complete. Within days, intelligence insiders were telling the press that the extravagant 70 and 90 percent figures were issued by a largely discredited group with a website that had claimed credit for power blackouts and for just about everything else except, noted one, the 2004 "cicada invasion of Washington"—something that, unlike Ashcroft's touted terrorist events, actually happened as predicted.[59] (Oddly, Ashcroft fails to mention this memorable headline-grabbing episode in *Never Again*, his 2006 memoir of the period.)

The next year, on February 16, 2005, the FBI's Mueller related the ultimate ghost story in testimony before Congress. He remained, he said, "very concerned about what we are not seeing," a sentence rendered in bold lettering in his prepared text. However, in a report from the time that was kept secret for some (or no) reason, the FBI and other investigative agencies reported that, after years of well-funded sleuthing, they had been unable to uncover a single true al-Qaeda sleeper cell anywhere in the United States.[60] And Director Mueller did acknowledge that, although his top concern was "the threat from covert operatives who may be inside the U.S.," and although he considered finding them to be his top priority, the bureau actually had, well, not been able to find any.[61] Nonetheless, some in the FBI remained unmoved: one person told *Fox News* that "just because there's no concrete evidence of sleeper cells now, doesn't mean they don't exist."[62]

Not only was the director of the CIA by his own testimony "scared to death" for much (or all) of his tenure in office, but he was apparently hearing voices, or seeing ghosts. In 2007, he announced that his "operational presumption is that they infiltrated a second wave or a third wave into the United States at the time of 9/11. Can I prove that to you? No. It's my operational intuition."[63] Or, "I know one thing in my gut: al-Qaeda is here and waiting."[64] Thus, one of the key people in charge of keeping the American people safe was also prominently scaring them, based, by his own admission, on nothing. Later, in a 2012 book, Kip Hawley, too, insisted without supplying coherent evidence that al-Qaeda networks currently exist in the United States.[65] Presumably, both are still waiting for that ghostly, and aging, second wave to leap into action.

ENVISIONING THE THREAT TO BE EXISTENTIAL

The ultimate extension of such thinking is to characterize the terrorist threat as "existential," routinely asserting that terrorists somehow threaten to expunge the United States, the modern state, or even civilization itself. Rather amazingly, this extreme expression, which, if accepted as valid, can close off all judicious evaluation of the problem, has only rarely been called into question.[66] When he was Homeland Security Secretary, Michael Chertoff went one step further, proclaiming the "struggle" against terrorism to be a "significant existential" one—carefully differentiating it, apparently, from all those insignificant existential struggles Americans have waged in the past.[67]

In like manner, a former CIA official insisted, in a best-selling book in 2004, that our "survival" is at stake and that we are engaged in a "war to the death."[68] Such extravagant rhetoric of alarm has continued at a high pitch. In 2008, the *New York Times* editorial board proclaimed that "the fight against al-Qaeda is the central battle for this generation," and Republican presidential nominee John McCain repeatedly labeled the struggle against radical Muslim extremism the "transcendental challenge of the 21st century," one that can affect "our very existence."[69] And in his 2012 book, Hawley joined the chorus by declaring without explanation that our "survival" is at stake.[70]

It is just possible that things began to change in 2014, however. In a speech at Harvard University in October, Vice President Joseph Biden offered the thought that "we face no existential threat—none—to our way of life or our ultimate security."[71] Then, after a decent interval of three months, President Barack Obama reiterated this point at a press conference, and then expanded it in an interview a few weeks later, adding that the United States should not "provide a victory to these terrorist networks by over-inflating their importance and suggesting in some fashion that they are an existential threat to the United States or the world order."[72] Later, his national security adviser, Susan Rice, echoed the point in a formal speech.[73] It is astounding that these utterances—"blindingly obvious" as security specialist Bruce Schneier puts it—appear to mark the first time any officials in the United States have had the notion and the courage to say so in public.[74]

Whether that development, at once remarkable and absurdly belated, will have some consequence, or even continue, remains to be seen. Thus, General Michael Flynn, who had recently retired as head of the Defense Intelligence Agency, was given in 2015 to insist that the terrorist enemy is "committed to the destruction of freedom and the American way of life" while seeking "world domination, achieved through violence and bloodshed." It was reported that his remarks, to an audience of "special operators and intelligence officers," evoked "many nods of approval," "occasional cheers," and "ultimately a standing ovation."[75]

Thus even the most modest imaginable effort to rein in the War on Terror hyperbole may fail to gel.

BELIEVING THERE IS NO ROOM FOR ERROR

A slightly modified version of the existential, our-survival-is-at-stake argument is reflected in an assertion by George W. Bush: "To stop the enemy, we had to be right 100 percent of the time. To harm us, they had to succeed only once."[76] The implication is that any blow by the terrorists will be entirely devastating. The same extravagant sense of threat lies behind the essentially deranged notion quoted earlier: "Think of the goalie at a soccer game who must stop every shot, for the perpetrator wins if it scores a single goal."

This is a fanciful, if empty-headed, derivation from the dictum of the Irish Republican Army that, in repeatedly trying (and failing, as it turned out) to assassinate British Prime Minister Margaret Thatcher, they only had to get it right once, while her defenders need to get it right every time. But killing a single person is not the same as destroying a state.

NEGLECTING PLAUSIBLE COUNTER-HYPOTHESES

There seems to be no capacity to accept or retain, even as a hypothesis, that the threat has been exaggerated and may, actually, not really exist; or if it is "considered" in some sense, it is immediately rejected to err on the side of doing something.[77] Thus, Goldsmith's account suggests that the sheer number of "threats," combined with the fact that these scarcely ever led to anything, never inspired analysts and policy makers to consider the rather plausible, if arguable, conclusion that there was little or nothing out there to fear. Rather, it caused them—exclusively, it seems—to embrace the dead opposite. "The want of actionable intelligence combined with a knowledge of what *might* happen," he says, "produced an aggressive, panicked attitude that assumed the worst about threats."[78] George Tenet agrees when he talks about "the palpable fear that we felt on the basis of the fact that there was so much we did not know."[79]

The phenomenon is also seen in another observation by Tenet. He begins by musing in his 2007 autobiography that "[i]t would be easy for al-Qaeda or another terrorist group to send suicide bombers to cause chaos in a half-dozen American shopping malls on any given day." He then asks, "Why haven't they?" One plausible answer, obviously, is that, in Schneier's words, "Terrorists are much rarer than we think, and launching a terrorist plot is much more difficult than we think." Schneier acknowledges that "this conclusion is counterintuitive, and contrary to the fearmongering we hear every day." But, although it is "what the data shows" (as will be demonstrated later in this book), Schneier's plausible proposition seems never to enter Tenet's mind. Instead he says he believes the remarkable absence of a big al-Qaeda attack on the United States "is because they have set for themselves a bigger goal."[80]

In part, the problem emerges from what Marc Sageman, after years of experience in the intelligence community, calls "a bias for alarming interpretations." In particular, he finds that when raw intelligence is worked into reports, "much is lost in the transcription." Often, he says, "the reports read like a prosecutor's brief, with the worst interpretation given full attention and potentially disconfirming evidence casting doubt on the gist of the report is neglected." Commonly, they "look only for confirmatory evidence and do not bother searching for disconfirmation." Sageman also suggests that this approach renders the report more "worthy of attention" and can aid in "personal promotion."[81] Robert Jervis agrees in his assessment of "why intelligence fails." Probing for "alternative explanations of what was happening" is, he finds, "very rare," pointing out that before the Iraq War of 2003, intelligence had little to say about how difficult, or easy, it would be to deter a nuclear Iraq—something that was particularly "unfortunate because this was a central part of the justification for war."[82]

NEGLECTING PROBABILITIES

Also neglected is a consideration of probabilities.[83] For example, at no point does Hawley, in his laudable desire to make airlines safer from terrorism, suggest that he has troubled to dope out an answer to the question that is fundamental to the issue: "How safe are we?" At present rates, a passenger's chance of boarding an airliner in the United States that is subsequently attacked by terrorists is something like one in 22 million.[84] Maybe for some that's not safe enough, but as will be discussed much more fully in chapter 5, it's where the conversation should start.[85]

Probability neglect is also evident in former CIA Director George Tenet's observation of the Threat Matrix that "[y]ou could drive yourself crazy believing all or even half of what was in it." Or, "At each session, we went over the next day's matrix, recognizing that many, perhaps most, of the threats contained in it were bogus. We just didn't know which ones."[86] The suggestion that anything like half the leads in the Threat Matrix, or even that "many" of them, might be valid would mean that literally millions of the leads had actually led to something. Nothing remotely like that has happened.

Overall, observes Sageman, intelligence analysts "have little understanding of probability and suffer from low base rate neglect for very rare events."[87] Sometimes—indeed, commonly—the probability assessment essentially is, "Because 9/11 was improbable, anything that is improbable is probable." This certainly seems to be the methodology that George W. Bush applied when he talks about a terrorist case from 2002:

> Some claimed the Lackawanna Six and others we arrested were little more than "small-town dupes" with fanciful plots "who had no intention of carrying out terrorist acts." I always wondered how they could be so sure. After all, in August 2001, the idea that terrorists commanded from caves in Afghanistan would attack the World Trade Center and the Pentagon on U.S. commercial airplanes would have seemed pretty far-fetched.[88]

Probability neglect is also continually found in the media. For example, on the December 28, 2009, PBS NewsHour Gwen Ifill, in introducing a segment on the then-recent underwear bomber's attempt to down an airliner, happened to note that the number of terrorist incidents on American airliners over the previous decade was one for every 16.5 million flights. This interesting bit of information was never brought up again, either by Ifill or by the three terrorism experts she was interviewing. Nor, of course, did anyone think of suggesting that, at that rate, maybe the airlines are safe enough.

Or, to put it more broadly, the continual question, "Are we safer?" is never answered with: "At present rates, your chances of being killed by a terrorist are about one in 4 million per year; how much safer do you want to be?"

EXAGGERATING TERRORIST CAPACITIES

In 2009, the Department of Homeland Security (DHS) issued a lengthy report on protecting the homeland. Key to achieving such an objective, it would seem, should be a careful assessment of the character, capacities, and desires of potential terrorists targeting that homeland.

Although the report does contain a section dealing with what its authors call "The Nature of the Terrorist Adversary," it devotes only two paragraphs to this important concern, and both are decidedly one-dimensional and fully preoccupied with the dire end of the spectrum of terrorist threat. Within that section, it devotes but two sentences to an assessment of the actual nature of the "adversary" it is so concerned about:

> The number and high profile of international and domestic terrorist attacks and disrupted plots during the last two decades underscore the determination and persistence of terrorist organizations. Terrorists have proven to be relentless, patient, opportunistic, and flexible, learning from experience and modifying tactics and targets to exploit perceived vulnerabilities and avoid observed strengths.[89]

Kip Hawley also professes to be impressed by those "adversaries," never finding them to be less than "innovative" and "quick moving." These qualities, he says, require the TSA to be "lightning-fast" in connecting thought to action (lots of luck on that one).[90]

An examination of the capacities of the terrorist "adversary" and of the degree to which "masterminds" are included in their number will be conducted in chapters 3 and 4. For now, however, it might be useful to array the descriptors of terrorists and would-be terrorists that have tended to dominate the case studies as summarized in appendix A: incompetent, ineffective, unintelligent, idiotic, ignorant, inadequate, unorganized, misguided, muddled, amateurish, dopey, unrealistic, moronic, irrational, foolish, and gullible.

The inability of the DHS to consider this fact even parenthetically in its fleeting discussion is really quite amazing—and perhaps delusional in its single-minded preoccupation with the extreme.

EXTRAPOLATING MASSIVELY: THE ATOMIC

The greatest exaggeration of terrorist capacities is their supposed capacity to develop nuclear weapons or devices. Concerns about these escalated greatly after the September 11 attacks. Brian Jenkins has run an Internet search to discover how often variants of the term *al-Qaeda* appeared within ten words of *nuclear*. There were only seven hits in 1999 and eleven in 2000, but this soared to 1,742 in 2001 and to 2,931 in 2002.[91]

However, to observe that terrorists were able, mostly by thuggish means, to crash airplanes into buildings, and then to conclude from that observation that they might therefore be able to construct an atomic bomb is an extrapolation of cosmic proportions. But it happened, and by 2008 Defense Secretary Robert Gates was assuring a congressional committee that what keeps every senior government leader awake at night is "the thought of a terrorist ending up with a weapon of mass destruction, especially nuclear."[92]

Few of the sleepless, it seems, found much solace in the fact that an al-Qaeda computer seized in Afghanistan in 2001 indicated that the group's budget for research on weapons of mass destruction (almost all of it focused on primitive chemical weapons work) was some $2,000 to $4,000.[93]

In the wake of the killing of Osama bin Laden, officials now had many more al-Qaeda computers, and it appears that nothing in their contents suggested the miserable little group had the time or inclination, let alone the money, to set up and staff a uranium-seizing operation, as well as a fancy, super-high-tech facility to fabricate a bomb. It is a process that requires trusting corrupted foreign collaborators and other criminals, obtaining and transporting highly guarded material, setting up a machine shop staffed with top scientists and technicians, and rolling the heavy, cumbersome, and untested finished product into position to be detonated by a skilled crew, all the while attracting no attention from outsiders.[94]

EXTRAPOLATING MASSIVELY: BIOLOGICAL, CHEMICAL, RADIOLOGICAL, AND CYBER

By 2003, John Negroponte, the U.S. ambassador to the United Nations, had come to the conclusion that "[t]here is a high probability that within two years al-Qaeda will attempt an attack using a nuclear or other weapon of mass destruction."[95] However, the miscreants in the cases in appendix A were never anywhere remotely close to fabicating nuclear weapons or to creating biological, radiological, or chemical ones. In fact, with perhaps one exception, no one ever seems to even have dreamed of the prospect. The exception is Jose Padilla, arrested in 2002, who apparently mused at one point about creating a dirty bomb—a device that would disperse radiation—or even possibly an atomic one. His idea about isotope separation was to put uranium into a pail and then to make himself into a human centrifuge by swinging the pail around in great arcs.[96]

Even if the weapons were made abroad and then imported, their detonation would require that there be people in-country with the capacity to receive and handle the complicated weapons, and then to set them off. Thus far, the talent pool appears to be, to put it mildly, very thin. The same goes for the increasingly popular concerns about cyberterrorism.[97] Many of the people in the cases did use the Internet for communication and for information, but none showed much ability at, or interest in, committing cyberterrorism.

EXPANSIVELY REDEFINING WMD

Many of those arrested for terrorism in the United States have been charged with planning to use "weapons of mass destruction" (WMD), even though they were working, at most, on small explosives or contemplating planting a hand grenade or two in a trash bin. This is the result of a bizarre legal expansion of the concept of "weapons of mass destruction." The expanded definition does, however, help make would-be terrorists seem more impressive and threatening.

The concept had once been taken to be simply a dramatic synonym for nuclear weapons, or was meant to include nuclear weapons and weapons yet to be developed that might have similar destructive capacity. The phrase came increasingly into vogue after the cold war, at which point it was expanded to embrace chemical, biological, and radiological weapons, even though those weapons for the most part are simply incapable of committing destruction that could reasonably be considered "massive," particularly in comparison with nuclear ones.

Then in 1992, the phrase was explicitly rendered into American law to include those weapons. In this process of codification, the definition was extended far further to include any bomb, grenade, or mine; any rocket having a propellant charge of more than four ounces; any missile having an explosive or incendiary charge of more than one-quarter ounce; and any projectile-spewing weapon that has a barrel with a bore of more than one-half inch in diameter. Included as well, it certainly appears, would be a maliciously designed toy rocket or potato gun even if it doesn't have a warhead, and a missile-propelled firecracker if its designers intended it to be a weapon.[98]

It turns out, then, that Francis Scott Key was exultantly, if innocently, witnessing a WMD attack in 1814; that the "shot heard round the world" by revolutionary war muskets was the firing of a WMD; and that Iraq was chock full of WMDs when the United States invaded in 2003—and *still is*, just like virtually every other country in the world.[99]

CREATING TERRORISTS

One approach to the problem of the near-dearth of domestic terrorists is to create them—to make, in a sense, the invisible visible; and the police seem increasingly to be getting better at this enterprise.[100] The process involves finding some Muslim hothead and linking him with an informant who encourages the hotheadedness and eventually reveals that he just happens to have an unused truck bomb available in his garage. When the hothead takes possession of the weapon or, more commonly of late, plants it near his target and then presses a phony detonator button, he is arrested.[101] In 2008, restrictions on domestic intelligence gathering were eased, making such sting operations easier.[102] In fact, in the following years, police operatives embedded in terrorist plots in the United States have considerably outnumbered actual would-be terrorists.

Overall, operatives and informants have been crucial to the development and disruption of over half of the plots—those identified as case type 3 in appendix A.[103] There are also instances in which the plot seemed to be disintegrating and was kept going largely by the efforts of the insider operative.[104] The FBI maintains some 15,000 official informants—ten times the number it had during the 1970s to deal with internal communism and other concerns—and it also has as many as 45,000 unofficial informants, tipsters in the community known as "hip pockets."[105]

Most of these people were trained and experienced in such matters, and often the process seems to be one in which an able con man is set among the gullible. Interestingly, the operative often appears to have been considerably older than the informed-upon, and there is frequently a pattern in which a police operative becomes something of a father figure to young, insecure men, many of whom grew up mostly without one.[106] Another relevant concern is that informants often receive what the FBI calls "performance incentives"—which can run to six figures—if the object of their labors is convicted.[107]

Left to their own devices, some of the gulled would-be terrorists—often hate-filled but generally pretty lost and incompetent—might eventually have done something violent on their own. It seems likely, however, that most would never have gotten around to doing much of anything without the creative, elaborate, and costly sting efforts of the police.[108] And, given their natural incapacities, even those who did attempt to inflict violence on their own were likely either to fail in their efforts or to commit destruction of quite limited scope. As Jenkins notes, "[W]hile America's jihadist terrorists have lethal intentions, they have trouble getting their act together on their own," and the stings sometimes seem to have acted as a "psychological accelerant" for would-be terrorists.[109]

In imposing the minimum sentence allowed by law (25 years) on those convicted in the Bronx synagogues plot of 2009, the judge, while acknowledging that the men were "prepared to do real violence," also noted that they were "utterly inept" and on a "fantasy terror operation," and that "only the government could have made a 'terrorist'" out of the plot's leader, "whose buffoonery is positively Shakespearean in its scope."[110] She also said, "I believe beyond a shadow of a doubt that there would have been no crime here except the government instigated, it, planned it, and brought it to fruition," adding, however, "that does not mean there is no crime."[111]

There are no accusations in any of the cases that the authorities used torture to create terrorists. Plea bargaining is not, technically speaking, a form of torture. But with the vagueness of such central concerns as "material support for terrorism," and with the huge sentences that can be imposed for plotting, or envisioning, terrorism, the police are in a good position to exact confessions and guilty pleas. The law defines "weapons of mass destruction" very broadly, as discussed earlier, and heavy penalties are associated with it. Because it can be applied even when defendants have imagined the use of hand grenades, in many cases it has greatly added to the prosecution's plea bargaining arsenal. Also on the side of the prosecution are judges who, in fear of terrorism, are anxious to set deterring examples. Moreover, as Jenkins puts it, "[J]uries comprised of frightened citizens do not always reach unbiased verdicts."[112]

EXAGGERATING THE IMPORTANCE AND POTENTIAL DESTRUCTIVENESS OF FOILED PLOTS

The American cases seem to suggest that a *New York Times* article in 2009 was engaging in considerable understatement when it observed, "Since the terrorist attacks of Sept. 11, 2001, senior government officials have announced dozens of terrorism cases that on close examination seemed to diminish as legitimate threats."[113] And Garrett Graff considers as "almost routine" a pattern in which "a breath-taking high-profile announcement of a terrifying scheme against the United States" is "gradually downgraded as more information trickle[s] out afterward."[114] Examples include two instances in 2011 in which the New York Police Department prominently announced terrorism arrests of people even the FBI did not think worth pursuing—while taking the opportunity to request more counterterrorism funds from Washington.[115]

In this spirit, the bumbling efforts of the Times Square bomber of 2010 are blithely held to have "almost succeeded," according to John Yoo and Ali Sofan.[116] However, the bomb was reported from the start to be "really amateurish," with some analysts charitably speculating when it was first examined that it might be "some sort of test run" created by "someone who's learning how to make a bomb and will learn from what went wrong with this [one]." Apparently because it is difficult to buy explosive fertilizer, the bomber purchased the nonexploding kind instead. It is not clear why he didn't use dirt or dried figs for his explosive material, as these are cheaper, easier to find, and will fail to explode with the same alacrity as nonexplosive fertilizer. He also threw in some gasoline—which doesn't explode, either, though it does burn— and some propane, which will explode only when it is mixed precisely with the right amount of air—the latter a bomb-design nicety he apparently never learned in his weeks of training. The crudely wired contraption was to be triggered by a cheap-looking alarm clock tied to a can of fireworks that sputtered and smoked for a while, attracting the attention of people nearby who then alerted the police.

Similarly, former Deputy Secretary of Homeland Security James Loy has argued that in 2006, terrorists "nearly succeeded in blowing up seven planes crossing the Atlantic."[117] And, on the day of the arrests, Homeland Security Secretary Michael Chertoff repeatedly characterized it as "a very sophisticated plan and operation. . . . The conception, the large number of people involved, the sophisticated design of the devices that were being considered, and the sophisticated nature of the plan all suggest that this group that came together to conspire was very determined and very skilled and very capable. . . . [T]his was a plot that is certainly about as sophisticated as any we've seen in recent years, as far as terrorism is concerned."[118]

However, the London-based terrorist group planning the attack was under constant and extensive police surveillance, including all their international communications, and it could be closed down at any time. Moreover, it is not clear that, when authorities did close the plot down, the conspirators had anything near sufficient materials or effective bombs. And the bomb-making was in the hands of a twenty-eight-year-old dropout who is described by analyst Bruce Hoffman as "a loser with little ambition and few prospects."[119] The notion that none of the bombs created by this "loser" would prove to be duds is, to say the least, questionable, as is the notion that all of the amateurs (few, if any, of which had undergone any training at the time) would be successful in detonating them, particularly given the failed efforts by the shoe and underwear bombers of 2001 and 2009. Moreover, in the evaluation of the CIA, the bombs were too small to bring down the airliners anyway.[120]

There is also the almost impossible problem of simultaneity. If one bomb were to go off in one airliner restroom (the detonation venue decided on by the plotters), all other airliners aloft and on the ground would likely be immediately alerted in the post-9/11 and post–shoe bomb era. This would render replications nearly impossible. Moreover, an airliner does not necessarily crash when its fuselage is breached.[121] In addition, the plot required two terrorist bombers per plane, and at the time the inner circle contained only three people—though, of course, more could eventually have been brought in from those on the periphery of the plot. As this suggests, there was nothing imminent about the plot, a conclusion that is reinforced by the facts that no tickets had been bought, that no dry runs had been made, that no bombs had been tested, and that many of the conspirators did not possess the passports that would have allowed them to board the planes—and it routinely takes six weeks to obtain a passport in the United Kingdom. Finally, the widely promulgated notion that thousands would be killed on the ground if the planes were blown up over cities does not survive sensible analysis—for example, an Airbus jetliner that crashed into heavily populated Queens, New York, in 2004 killed five on the ground.[122]

There were also exaggerated claims about potential destruction when a terrorist cell led by Najibullah Zazi was foiled in its plans to detonate four suicide bombs on the New York subway in 2009. Thus, the attorney general of the United States held that the planned attack had the potential to be "even larger" than the Madrid train bombings in 2004 that killed nearly 200 people.[123] And experts estimated that the attack could have killed anywhere between 200 and 500 people if all four explosives had been successfully detonated.[124] These estimates ignored the experience in July 2005, when two sets of terrorists each attempted to set off four bombs on the crowded transit system in London. The first set killed 52, while the second killed none because the bombs were ill constructed. The killing of 52 is a tragedy, but not of the same order of magnitude as the prospective 200 to 500 fatalities of the "expert" estimates. Presumably, the London bombers could have killed more if, in the first case, the bombs had been placed differently; or in the second, if they had been constructed properly. But because the number of dead is known, it is that number, not an imagined one, that ought to be the basis of comparison. The train bombings in Madrid in 2004 were very destructive, killing 191. However, this was accomplished by detonating ten bombs, not four, as planned in the New York subway case—and even this death toll is lower than the attorney general's lowest estimate. Extravagant death tallies have also been imagined for the amazingly inept would-be Times Square bomber of 2010.

Interestingly, however, the plot dreamed up since September 11 that could potentially have caused the most damage was the one in 2006 that aspired to topple the Sears Tower in Chicago. Even if the toppling failed to create the planners' hoped-for tsunami, thousands would have died—perhaps even tens of thousands—and the damage to the neighborhood would have been as monumental as that to the building. The plotters had no capacity to carry out this colossal deed, however, so their expressed desire is not taken seriously, even though the case is generally known as the Sears Tower plot. Analysts should apply this kind of reasonable reticence more broadly for aborted or foiled plots.

MISIDENTIFYING TERRORIST MOTIVATIONS: THE CONCEPT OF "RADICALIZATION"

Terrorists can also be made to seem more threatening by suggesting they have grand ideological plans to radically change Western society—to establish grand "caliphates" and to spread and then rigidly enforce an extreme version of Sharia law. The "radicalization" syndrome plays nicely into this narrative.

Thus in a segment on the PBS NewsHour in 2015 called "What Can the U.S. Do to Stop Radicalization at Home?" a former FBI counterterrorism analyst was asked about why people are drawn to violent extremism. He stressed that there are "ideological issues" as well as "local grievances" including "access to education and job opportunities" and whether one feels that one is fully accepted in society.[125] And speakers at a formal White House summit on Countering Violent Extremism (CVE), conducted at the time to discuss "concrete steps" to "counter hateful extremist ideologies that radicalize, recruit or incite to violence," typically found the "root causes" of terrorism to lie in ideology, the ministrations of propagandists, the influence of the Internet, poverty, inadequate job opportunities, and alienation from society.[126]

This approach conveniently, but misdirectingly, ignores the most prominent motivating force. Terrorism specialist and former CIA officer Marc Sageman points out that "radicalization" principally happens because of perceived injustice against one's group—a perspective the Washington Post's David Ignatius considers to be "worth a careful look," but calls "contrarian."[127]

The authors of the case studies summarized in appendix A were specifically asked to assess the motivations driving the people in those cases. The results strongly supported Sageman's view.

There were a few cases in which it could probably be said there was no notable motivation at all.[128] However, in almost all the other cases, the overwhelming driving force was simmering, and more commonly boiling, outrage at American foreign policy—the wars in Iraq and Afghanistan in particular, and also the country's support for Israel in the Palestinian conflict. Religion was a key part of the consideration for most, but it was not that the plotters had a burning urge to spread Islam and Sharia or to establish caliphates—indeed, few would likely be able to spell either word. Rather, it was the desire to protect their religion and religious heritage against what they commonly saw as a concentrated war upon it in the Middle East by the U.S. government and military.[129] None seemed to remember (or perhaps in many cases ever knew) that the United States strongly favored the Muslim side in Bosnia and in Kosovo in the 1990s—as well as, of course, in the war against the Soviet Union in Afghanistan in the 1980s.

In stark contrast, there was remarkably little hostility to American culture or society, or to its values, or to democracy. Almost none of the terrorist characters in the cases had any problem with American society—indeed, a number of them showed a deep and quite nuanced appreciation for American girls. This is particularly impressive because many of the people under examination (though certainly not all) were misfits, suffered from personal identity crises, were friendless, came from broken homes, were often desperate for money, had difficulty holding jobs, were on drugs, were petty criminals, experienced various forms of discrimination, and were—to use a word that pops up in quite a few of the case studies and fits even more of them—losers.

In our discussion we have included only instances in which the United States was, or apparently was, targeted by terrorists. We have not dealt with those concerning people who have sought to go abroad to fight against American interests there by joining the insurgencies in Iraq and Afghanistan or to defend Somalia against Ethiopian invaders. Hostility to American foreign and military policy was obviously the primary motivator for those individuals.

Thus, although it is common to assess the process by which potential terrorists become "radicalized," it is not at all clear that this is a good way to look at the phenomenon, at least for the disclosed American domestic cases.[130] The concept tends to suggest that there is an ideological motivation to the violence. However, these guys are not set off so much by anything theoretical but rather by intense outrage at American and Israeli actions in the Middle East and by a burning desire to seek revenge, to get back, to defend, and/or to make a violent statement expressing their hostility to what they see as a war on Islam. As one radical Islamist intellectual puts it, the "root causes" are the "occupation of the Muslim land," the "torture of Muslims," and the "foreign policy of governments like Britain and America."[131]

Although many of the people discussed in the cases were not terribly religious, some of them did become increasingly steeped in and devoted to Islam. However, what seems primarily to have driven them to contemplate violence is not an increasing religiosity but, instead, an increasing desire to protect the religion and its attendant way of life against what they saw as a systematic attack upon it abroad.

An object lesson on the issue is supplied by early information put out by officials when two men were picked up for planning to machine-gun and lob grenades at a local military processing center in Seattle in 2011. According to news reports, the perpetrators said they were motivated by a desire to retaliate for crimes by U.S. soldiers in Afghanistan and that they wanted to kill military personnel to prevent them from going to Islamic lands to kill Muslims. The official Department of Justice press release on the case, however, merely says that the men were "driven by a violent, extreme ideology."[132]

In a similar manner, in its discussion of an embryonic plot to bomb Herald Square in 2004, an important New York Police Department report includes a great deal of material about "extremist literature" and "jihadi ideology."[133] However, there is almost nothing to suggest that, as even the prosecutors in the case had contended, the perpetrators were driven by anger over American foreign policy in the Middle East, the war in Iraq, and abuse by American soldiers of Iraqi prisoners at Abu Ghraib.[134]

And after the (incredibly inept) effort by a terrorist to bomb Times Square in 2010, New York Mayor Michael Bloomberg was quick to conclude that "[t]here are some people around the world who find our freedom so threatening that they're willing to kill themselves and others to prevent us from enjoying it."[135] Far from warring against freedom, however, the would-be bomber was primarily motivated by (or radicalized by) a desire to be "part of the answer to the U.S. terrorizing Muslim nations and the Muslim people," and he was particularly angered by America-led drone strikes in Pakistan and Afghanistan.[136]

It should be stressed that, although hostility toward American policy is a primary motivator in these cases, there are a huge number of people who have also been strongly opposed to American policy in the Middle East—including for most of the time a very large percentage of Americans who identify themselves as Democrats.[137] Although the tiny number of people plotting terrorism in the United States display passionate hostility toward American foreign policy, there is a far, far greater number of people who share much of the same hostility but are in no sense inspired to commit terrorism to express their deeply held views.[138]

INCREASINGLY ENVISIONING THREAT FROM THE HOMEGROWN

In the early years after 9/11, as discussed earlier, the context for the authorities was one of massive, even overwhelming, alarm about al-Qaeda operatives either functioning within as sleeper cells or invading from abroad.

However, this perspective eventually changed, at least somewhat. To begin with, the secret finding (or nonfinding) by the FBI in 2005 that there appeared to be, after all, no al-Qaeda sleeper cells whatsoever in the United States was publicly acknowledged in 2007. Thus, in testimony on January 11 of that year, Director Mueller, while maintaining that "we believe al-Qaeda is still seeking to infiltrate operatives into the U.S. from overseas," stated that his chief concern within the United States had now become homegrown groups. Then, later in the year, the officer who drafted that year's National Intelligence Estimate told the press "we do not see" al-Qaeda operatives functioning inside the United States.[139]

Over the ensuing years, the fear of the homegrown escalated to fill the gap and soon became standard. It was endorsed by Obama's Secretary of Homeland Security, Janet Napolitano, in 2009, and Attorney General Eric Holder let it be known in 2010 that the threat of homegrown terror was keeping him up at night.[140] Then, in the 2011 press conference noted earlier, even as Napolitano joined other counterterrorism officials in announcing that the "likelihood of a large-scale organized attack" had been reduced, she worried that the rise of the homegrown was part of the reason the terrorist threat "in some ways" was now the highest it had been since September 11.[141] Later in the year, two top terrorism analysts, Peter Bergen and Bruce Hoffman, were concluding that, although the terrorists appeared to be incapable of launching a mass-casualty attack in the United States, local terrorists would still be able to carry out "less sophisticated operations," a "trend" they somehow deemed to be "worrisome."[142]

But even a very quick assessment of the domestic terrorism cases suggests that homegrown terrorism is hardly new—and there has scarcely been anything like a "trend." There may have been a few, a very few, al-Qaeda operatives or associates working in the country in the first years after 9/11.[143] And there have been several instances of terrorists abroad planning attacks in—or mostly on airplanes bound for—the United States.[144] However, any real or imagined threat from terrorism within the country has been almost entirely "homegrown" from the beginning.[145] What changed was not a new appearance of the homegrown, but the evaporation, or the discrediting, of the notion that there were a bunch of non-homegrown terrorists abroad in the land.

INCREASINGLY FEARING THE LONE WOLF

There has been another, related development. Public officials have also publicly expressed alarm that the "greatest concern" has now become the "lone wolf" terrorist. As Leon Panetta put it in 2011 when he was the director of the CIA, "It's the lone wolf strategy that I think we have to pay attention to as the main threat." And a DHS departmental pronouncement of May 31, 2011, concludes: "Our review of attempted attacks during the last two years suggests that lone offenders currently present the greatest threat."[146] Then in June 2014, Attorney General Holder, citing an "escalating danger from self-radicalizing individuals within our own borders," revived a domestic terrorism "task force" within the Justice Department, though he cited no specific domestic threat and did not provide data indicating that any danger was "escalating."[147]

This concern may be a valid one—and, indeed, it is only lone wolves (or in the case of the 2013 Boston marathon bombings, two brothers acting in secret, lone wolf–like concert) who have managed to kill anyone at all in the United States since 9/11.[148] By definition, they can't be uncovered by tips from accomplices or acquaintances, much less by advertising their intentions on Facebook. However, those who find this situation to be especially "worrisome" should also note that terrorists operating entirely alone are unlikely to be able to commit major damage. As Max Abrahms notes, "[L]one wolves have carried out just two of the 1,900 most deadly terrorist incidents over the last four decades."[149]

Among the lone wolf failures in the cases listed in appendix A are those of a guy who tried, and failed, to run over people with a rented SUV at the University of North Carolina in 2006; the supremely inept effort of another to set off a car bomb in Times Square in New York in 2010; the bone-headed nighttime shootings by a third at the Pentagon and other government buildings in 2011; and the shooting attack by two others at a cartoon exhibit in 2015. These attacks resulted in little or no damage except to the perpetrators, who are now serving very long prison sentences or were killed in their attempt.

INCREASINGLY FEARING RETURNEES

There has also been a growing concern that homegrown terrorists would go abroad for training and then return to the United States to wreak violence.

That this fear is overwrought is suggested by an examination of the cases in appendix A. Six of these involve Americans who went abroad and then returned, or may have considered returning, with an eye toward committing terrorism. In all, they have inflicted one death in the United States.

Two involve American citizens who went abroad to obtain terrorism skills with the aim of returning to the United States to ply their trade.

In one case, the would-be terrorist seems never actually to have managed to obtain any training at all. Increasingly outraged at U.S. foreign policy, he came to yearn for martyrdom and ventured to Yemen to get training to do damage at home. But he was instead incarcerated by authorities there for various infractions and then deported back to the United States. It is possible he picked up a few tips in jail. If so, however, they scarcely did him much good.

Questing for targets to attack on his return to the United States, he conducted Google map searches related to "Jewish entities," a Baptist church, Times Square, a child-care facility, a U.S. post office, and military recruiting centers in six different cities. In 2009, he decided to kill rabbis in Little Rock, Arkansas, and in Memphis and Nashville, Tennessee, after which he planned to attack army recruitment centers in several cities (as he put it later, he wanted "to kill as many people in the Army as he could"). He first tried to kill a rabbi in Nashville by throwing a Molotov cocktail at the rabbi's house. It is not clear how setting fire to one part of a house would kill people inside, as they would have various ways to exit the building. However, the effort failed miserably even on its own terms. The weapon bounced off the window and, regardless, failed to explode. Moreover, he had the wrong house. He then decided to shoot up a military recruitment center in Florence, Kentucky (chosen because "it was near an interstate highway and bordered Ohio"), only to find that the office was closed.

Finally, he went home to Little Rock and, with no plan at all, shot at a recruiting center three miles from his apartment, killing one soldier who was on a smoke break and wounding another. After making a wrong turn in his getaway car, he was captured by police twelve minutes after the shooting.

In the other instance, the perpetrator, a native of Pakistan who had received U.S. citizenship, actually did receive quite a bit of training abroad. Motivated by hostility toward America's wars in the Middle East and by the plight of the Palestinians, he abandoned his American-born wife and children in the United States to travel to Pakistan. His anger escalated by an American drone strike on the border area between Pakistan and Afghanistan, he went to a terrorist camp run by the Pakistan Taliban, where he underwent a full forty days of training between December 1, 2009, and January 25, 2010. Training, however, does not necessarily lead to successful bomb-making skills.[150]

Working on his own back in the United States, he put together a car bomb to be detonated in Times Square in New York, the craftsmanship of which was discussed earlier. After his "bomb" fizzled, the authorities traced the vehicle mostly—perhaps entirely—by applying standard police work, taking advantage of the would-be bomber's many blunders of planning and execution, such as leaving his keys in the car's ignition. They didn't even have to rely on the many security cameras that cover the very public area he chose to target. The culprit was apprehended within two days.

One case involves an American citizen who had joined al-Qaeda before 9/11 and was arrested when he returned to the United States.

In 2002, the American Jose Padilla returned from Pakistan with over $10,000 cash and a cellphone with telephone and email addresses for al-Qaeda members. The government had information concerning his involvement with al-Qaeda operatives and with plots to do damage in the United States, and agents arrested him as he disembarked at O'Hare Airport in Chicago. Al-Qaeda may have been seeking to use its singular American recruit to hit its far enemy. He was dedicated to the cause and violence-prone; a former Chicago street thug, he had kicked a fellow gang member to death as a teenager. However, there seem to have been no specific terrorism plans afoot, and Padilla's skills and mental capacity seem to be quite limited.

One case involves an American who may have plotted abroad to do damage in the United States, but was arrested long before he could do so.

The American, Abu Ali, was arrested in Saudi Arabia by Saudi authorities in 2003, in connection with a recent terrorist attack in that country. A few months later he confessed to involvement with local al-Qaeda members. He said he had discussed various jihad plans, including one to assassinate President Bush, and had attended a training camp where he learned, among other things, forgery techniques. Never formally charged by the Saudi government, he was returned to the United States at his family's insistence and was tried in American courts for receiving funds from a terrorist organization and for conspiring to assassinate the president. He claimed that his confession was extracted under torture and that it was entirely false. He was convicted on all counts, receiving a sentence of thirty years in prison followed by thirty years of probation. After losing an appeal, he was resentenced to life.

Finally, two cases involve Americans who went overseas with the intention of joining the groups fighting Americans, but then they returned, or considered returning, to the United States to carry out terrorist violence back home.

In one, Bryant Neal Vinas was increasingly incensed at America's support for Israel and at what he saw as America's war on Islam in the Middle East. He made his way to Pakistan and eventually into the ranks of al-Qaeda, where he was given training. The terrorist group apparently was impressed by Vinas's palpable and clearly sincere enthusiasm for the cause, by his equally sincere anti-American vitriol, and by the recommendations of people who had seen him in operation. He must have seemed an asset of considerable potential value to them. For one thing, he had intimate knowledge of Penn Station in New York City and might be highly useful for setting off a bomb in that venue, a venture he enthusiastically helped them plan. American intelligence had been monitoring him all along, and when, for reasons that seem oddly foolish, al-Qaeda allowed its prize asset to leave the training camp in 2008 for Peshawar in Pakistan, he was arrested by the Pakistanis and then turned over to the United States. There is no evidence to indicate that the plot against Penn Station was anything but a gleam in the eye of a few dreamy conspirators ten thousand miles away.

In the other, Najibullah Zazi and two other Afghan Americans went abroad with the goal of fighting with the Taliban against the United States in Afghanistan. As recalled by his step-uncle affectionately, Zazi was "a dumb kid, believe me." A high school dropout, Zazi mostly worked as a doughnut peddler in Lower Manhattan, barely making a living.[151] The men were recruited in Pakistan by al-Qaeda, and they eventually agreed to return to carry out a "martyrdom operation" in the United States, setting off bombs on the New York transit system.[152] In preparation, Zazi received explosives training and emailed nine pages of bomb-making instructions to himself. FBI Director Robert Mueller asserts that this training gave Zazi the "capability" to set off a bomb.[153] That, however, seems to be a substantial overstatement because, upon returning to the United States, Zazi spent the better part of a year trying to concoct the bombs he had supposedly learned how to make. In the process, he purchased bomb materials reportedly using stolen credit cards, a bone-headed maneuver that all but guaranteed that red flags would go up about the sale and that surveillance videos in the stores would be maintained rather than routinely erased.[154] Moreover, even with the material at hand, Zazi *still* apparently couldn't figure it out, and he frantically contacted an unidentified person overseas for help several times. Each of these communications was "more urgent in tone than the last," according to court documents.[155] Communications between Zazi and al-Qaeda leaders were being monitored even before he began to try to construct his bombs, and the plot was closed down in 2009.

Besides these cases, the Lackawanna experience may be relevant. Before 9/11, a handful of adventurous guys were persuaded to attend al-Qaeda training camps abroad. However, all but one of them returned thoroughly disillusioned, and they successfully persuaded another group of young men against going over before being arrested in 2002.

When Barack Obama came to office in 2009, he was warned by Director of National Intelligence Dennis Blair that 100 Westerners, including many with American passports or visas, were being trained in Pakistan safe havens to return to commit major terrorism mayhem back home. CIA Director Michael Hayden issued a similar warning: "Al-Qaeda is training people in the tribal areas who, if you saw them in a visa line at Dulles, you would not recognize as potential terrorists."[156] Over the intervening years, however, the only ones to return with malevolent intent to the United States have been the hapless Zazi who received inadequate training from al-Qaeda, and the even more hapless Times Square bomber who received training from a non-al-Qaeda group that was even more inadequate.

Thus experience suggests that overseas training is of questionable value—none of those who received it and then returned to the United States managed to do any damage. This also holds for the shoe bomber of 2001 and the underwear bomber of 2009, each of whom completely bungled his mission.

In addition, there appears to be a special problem, from al-Qaeda's perspective, with taking in, and seeking to benefit from, American interlopers.

After 9/11, the group became exceedingly wary of taking on American recruits even if they seemed to be genuinely devoted. This presumably reflects the sensible concern that the recruits might actually be agents of the CIA or other such forces. As it happens, however, it does not appear that the CIA has ever been able to infiltrate an operator into al-Qaeda ranks—a rather interestingly impressive nonachievement given the amount of effort the agency presumably has devoted to the effort.

However, maybe it hasn't been necessary. Vinas and Zazi—Americans acting on their own and genuinely dedicated to the Muslim extremist cause—were able to do what the CIA has apparently been unable to do: join up with, and be accepted by, the organization. From al-Qaeda's perspective, however, this proved to be disastrous. Both were eventually captured and, although previously "radicalized," they almost immediately abandoned their former comrades once they were in captivity and fully cooperated with authorities. Effectively, they acted as if they had been CIA plants from the beginning. Vinas even helped with the disruption of a terrorist plot in Belgium that required his betraying some of the people he had met in an al-Qaeda training camp.

Others also cooperated. The Lackawanna boys told everything they knew as soon as they were arrested, and Iyman Faris, who had apparently cased the Brooklyn Bridge for al-Qaeda, not only talked freely in 2003 even before he was formally arrested but also was contemplating writing a tell-all book about his experiences.[157]

Police and prosecutors are also aided by the fact that they can enlist the help of friends and family members in the United States, and also by the fact that they can sometimes credibly threaten to indict the friends and family for variously providing aid to terrorism. This is also seen in the case of a non-American, the underwear bomber of 2009, who spilled all sorts of helpful information after being arrested. In this, he was partly yielding to the importuning of a couple of family members from whom he had apparently been rebelling—it was his concerned father, after all, who alerted authorities to his son's association with extremists. Thus, as in the Vinas and Zazi cases, not only did international terrorism lose a dedicated, if inept, asset but the asset deployed was effectively converted after the fact into a spy for its enemies.

The terrorist returnees in these cases were motivated by hostility to American foreign policy and yet they were ineffective. It seems possible that returnees motivated by concerns other than hostility to Western foreign policy will be even less dangerous if and when they return.

Daniel Byman and Jeremy Shapiro have assessed the returnee issue as it has played out in Europe. They, too, generally find only limited reason for concern. They point out that European and American fighters attracted to insurgencies abroad, contrary to repeated fears, do not have much of a history of returning home to wreak violence there. Instead, they tend to be killed (they are among the first picks for suicide missions), to be disillusioned by infighting in the ranks and other unanticipated miseries, or to be arrested by authorities who find them fairly easy to track, in part because of their reckless and foolhardy use of social media.[158]

INCREASINGLY FEARING AFFILIATED GROUPS: LINKAGES, CONNECTIONS, TIES, THREADS

Terrorism alarmists often find themselves explaining that, although al-Qaeda has been weakened, it still manages to present a grave threat. Various techniques honed over the years are applied to support this claim. If they are accepted as valid, al-Qaeda will cease to exist or be "defeated" only when we run out of tiny groups or individual nuts operating with al-Qaeda–like aspirations.

Although al-Qaeda Central has done little since 9/11, it has gotten better at issuing videos, and sometimes this talent is tallied as an indicator of the threat.[159] However, it has been more common to focus on al-Qaeda's role as an inspiration to individual would-be terrorists around the world and to variously affiliated groups that have been willing to adopt or adapt its moniker. Thus, an array of "linkages" or "connections" or "ties" or "threads" between and among a range of disparate terrorists or terrorist groups has been espied. On closer examination, most of these appear rather gossamer and of only limited consequence.

Thus, we've been told that al-Qaeda's "ideology of the global jihad" still "survives" and that the group is "making provisions for the long term," is "poised to survive," "is regrouping," is "not entirely isolated," might work with Iran because "they share a common enemy," has been "embraced" by a Nigerian group with purely local concerns, has provided "strategic advice," has "inspired" a number of inept would-be amateur terrorists here and there, and has been thinking about plotting the assassination of Barack Obama.[160] A common ploy in such discussions is for an "al-Qaeda–inspired" terrorist group in one sentence to become an "al-Qaeda–linked" one in the next.[161]

Related has been a tendency to exaggerate the importance and effectiveness of the "affiliated groups" linked to al-Qaeda Central. In particular, alarmists point to the al-Qaeda affiliate in chaotic Yemen, proclaiming it to be the "deadliest" and the "most aggressive" of these and a "major threat."[162] Insofar as it threatens the United States, the Yemen group has been elevated by two or three efforts at international terrorism, all of which failed abysmally.

It apparently supplied the 2009 underwear bomber with an explosive that he was unable to detonate—one that, a test by the BBC concludes and Kip Hawley confirms, would not have downed his plane even if it had gone off.[163] And other failures are a foiled effort to set off bombs contained within laser printers on cargo planes bound for the United States in 2010, and a similar effort in 2012.[164] With that track record, the group may pose a problem or concern to the United States, but it scarcely presents a "major threat." The capacities of the Yemen group, and especially of its "master" bomb maker, are discussed and evaluated more fully in chapter 4.

Moreover, the degree to which the United States is really threatened by these groups is considerably bounded by the scope of their ambition. As a recent report concludes, "The bulk of terrorist activity in the world is accounted for by militant actors that pursue relatively limited goals in local or regional contexts."[165]

INCREASINGLY FEARING NONAFFILIATED GROUPS

In 2014, a militant group calling itself the Islamic State, or ISIL, but more generally known as ISIS, burst into official and public attention with some military victories in Iraq and Syria in the middle of the year. Former NSA and CIA head Michael Hayden was quick to stoke alarm by proclaiming that "[t]his is quite a dangerous thing that we're seeing unfold here" and applying the predictable comparison: "It's probably not 9/11, but it's certainly in the same area code."[166] And Senators John McCain and Lindsey Graham proclaimed the group to present an existential threat to the United States.[167]

That cry escalated after ISIS performed and webcast several beheadings of defenseless Western hostages a few months later. Democratic Senator Dianne Feinstein was soon insisting that "[t]he threat ISIS poses cannot be overstated"—effectively proclaiming, as columnist Dan Froomkin suggests, hyperbole on the subject to be impossible. Meanwhile one of her Senate colleagues, Republican Jim Inhofe, born before World War II, was doing his best by extravagantly claiming that "we're in the most dangerous position we've *ever* been in" and that Islamic State is "rapidly developing a method of blowing up a major U.S. city."[168] And Defense Secretary Chuck Hagel soared ever skyward, saying, "[W]e've never seen a threat" like this before, a "comprehensive threat" with sophistication, armaments, strategic knowledge, funding, capacity, and ideology.[169] Because he found it "beyond anything we've seen," and "an imminent threat to every interest we have," he modestly proposed that "we must prepare for everything."[170] By the next year, an alarmed David Brooks was reporting that financial analysts have convinced themselves that the group has the potential to generate a worldwide "economic cataclysm."[171]

However, ISIS had actually separated itself from al-Qaeda (or had been summarily kicked out of the al-Qaeda area code by al-Qaeda itself) because, instead of focusing on doing damage against the far enemy, the United States in particular, the new group was mainly devoted to killing and terrorizing fellow Muslims and neighboring Christians that it doesn't like.[172] "In contrast to al-Qaeda," notes one report, the group "is fully mired in the regional context."[173]

The vicious group is certainly a danger to the people under its control, and it is conceivable it *might* come to be tempted to strike abroad.[174] However, Middle East specialist Ramzy Mardini notes that "the Islamic State's fundamentals are weak"; that "it does not have a sustainable endgame"; that its "extreme ideology, spirit of subjugation, and acts of barbarism prevent it from becoming a political venue for the masses"; that its foolhardy efforts to instill fear in everyone limits "its opportunities for alliances" and makes it "vulnerable to popular backlash"; that "its potential support across the region ranges from limited to nonexistent"; and that the group "is completely isolated, encircled by enemies."[175]

Moreover, to the degree that Islamic State, unlike the more wary al-Qaeda Central, welcomes fighters from abroad, the group is likely to be penetrated by foreign intelligence operatives. And actually controlling and effectively governing wide territories is likely to become a major strain.[176] It is possible it will become vulnerable to airstrikes aided by an increasingly alienated population under its control.

Nor do American and foreign intelligence agencies embrace the hype that has engaged the attention of the public (and thereby boosted television news ratings). They have concluded that ISIS poses no immediate threat to the United States. As for the notion that the group will use its foreign fighters to attack the West, some observe that "ISIS has no ability to attack inside the United States." Indeed, they find it not at all clear "that the group even wants to." And some officials and terrorism experts "believe that the actual danger posed by ISIS has been distorted in hours of television punditry and alarmist statements by politicians." Daniel Benjamin, a top counterterrorism adviser during Obama's first term, characterizes the public discussion about the ISIS threat as a "farce," with "members of the cabinet and top military officers all over the place describing the threat in lurid terms that are not justified."[177]

The fear has centered on the potential return of people with Western passports who have joined ISIS. In June 2014, for example, UK Prime Minister David Cameron chose to ignore ISIS videos showing its foreign fighters burning their passports and reports that foreign fighters were common candidates to become suicide bombers. Instead, Cameron announced unequivocally that ISIS was "planning to attack us here at home in the United Kingdom," and he promised to do "absolutely everything we can" to protect Britain from the threat of fighters returning from Iraq and Syria. Similar concerns, as noted, have been expressed for the United States. As Cameron spoke, Frank Gardner, a BBC security correspondent, noted that "there are no details available of any actual attack planning." However, he went on humbly to suggest that "there are bound to be things that the intelligence agencies pick up that they share with the National Security Council but not with us, the public."[178]

However, there are also bound to be politicians who make grand proclamations based on nothing while hiding behind official secrecy to avoid exposing the baselessness of their pronouncements.

In May 2015, an audio message, apparently from the leader of ISIS, exorted "every Muslim in every place" either to emigrate to join the fight in his territory or to "fight in his land wherever that may be." There was nothing about training people to return home to wreak havoc.[179]

Institutional Interest in Delusion

It should be pointed out that once engaged in the counterterrorism enterprise, officials have a strong personal interest in keeping it churning along. Indeed, much of the official reaction to the September 11 attacks discussed in this chapter calls to mind Hans Christian Andersen's fable of delusion, "The Emperor's New Clothes," in which con artists convince the emperor and his court that they can weave fabrics of the most beautiful colors and elaborate patterns from the delicate silk and purest gold thread they are given (and promptly squirrel away). These fabrics, they further convincingly explain, have the wonderful property that they will remain invisible to anyone who is (a) unusually stupid or (b) unfit for (profitable) office. The emperor finds this all quite appealing: not only will it furnish him with splendid new clothes, but it will allow him to discover which of the officials in his empire are unfit for their posts—or in today's terms, have lost their effectiveness. All the courtiers consequently have a great professional incentive to proclaim the fabrics on the loom to be excellent, very beautiful, absolutely magnificent: "What a splendid design! What glorious colors!"

The process can be seen in an episode in New York City. In a 2008 book, Michael Sheehan, the city's former deputy director for counterterrorism, recalls a 2003 conversation in which he told his bosses, Raymond Kelly and David Cohen, that "I thought al-Qaeda was simply not very good. . . . Under the withering heat of the post-9/11 environment, they were simply not getting it done. I said what nobody else was saying: we underestimated al-Qaeda's capabilities before 9/11 and we overestimated them after." Journalist Christopher Dickey describes what happened next:

> He could see that they were taken aback. It was not so much that they disagreed. . . . They all understood only too well the way the public and politicians would react if headlines started to read "Commissioner disses Qaeda." Support for counterterrorism would start to crumble. . . . And then, if the bad guys got lucky . . . Kelly, Cohen, and Sheehan agreed it would be better if Sheehan kept his estimate to himself for a while.[180]

And so, it seems, Sheehan kept his views rather quiet for several years, and all three officials continued to pretend in public that terrorists were everywhere. Thus, support for counterterrorism did not "crumble" and the newspapers were kept from revealing an unconventional—or inconvenient—truth that all three agreed upon. Moreover, had there actually been an attack in New York in the meantime, various bureaucratic backs would have been strategically covered. (They need not have worried: when Sheehan's book did appear in 2008 with that statement in it, it had no discernible impact.)

Another example (among many possible) of the process of calculated and self-interested deception was supplied by National Security Agency chief Keith Alexander when he forcefully insisted in 2014 that, because the number of terrorist deaths had increased between 2012 and 2013, there were "a lot more coming our way." He did not bother to note that the increase had occurred almost entirely in Iraq, Pakistan, Afghanistan, and Nigeria and not in the West—or "our way."[181]

Kelly, Cohen, Sheehan, and Alexander are members in top standing of what might be called the terrorism industry.[182] In his 2014 book *Pay Any Price*, James Risen, a reporter for the *New York Times*, skewers what he calls the "homeland security-industrial complex."[183] American leaders, he notes, "have learned that keeping the terrorist threat alive provides enormous political benefits" by allowing "incumbents to look tough" and lending them "the national attention and political glamour that comes with dealing with national security issues."[184] More generally, "fear sells." Thus "a decade of fear-mongering has brought power and wealth to those who have been the most skillful at hyping the terrorism threat" and this "is central to the financial well-being of countless federal bureaucrats, contractors, subcontractors, consultants, analysts, and pundits."[185]

In a generally favorable review of Risen's book in the *New York Times*, Louise Richardson lauds Risen's criticism of "the profligacy of government agencies and the 'over-sight free zone' they operated," as well as of "self-appointed terrorism experts" who promote fear "while drawing lucrative consulting contracts for themselves." She is troubled, however, that Risen "makes no mention of the press," which she considers a key member of the terrorism industry and "at least as guilty as others in his book of stirring up public anxiety for public gain."[186] For example, as noted earlier, it was in 2008 that the *New York Times* editorial board found it useful extravagantly to assure its readers that "the fight against al-Qaeda is the central battle for this generation."[187] And it was on the fifth anniversary of 9/11 that Charles Gibson intoned in an *ABC News* program that "[n]ow putting your child on a school bus or driving across a bridge or just going to the mall—each of these things is a small act of courage. And peril is a part of everyday life."

Politicians and bureaucrats may feel that, given the public concern on the issue, they will lose support if they appear insensitively to be downplaying the dangers of terrorism. In contrast, the media like to tout that they are devoted to presenting fair and balanced coverage of important public issues. However, a cynical aphorism in the newspaper business holds that "if it bleeds, it leads." There is an obvious, if less pungent, corollary: if it doesn't bleed, it certainly shouldn't lead and, indeed, may well not be fit to print at all.

Another problem concerns follow-up. When a major political figure makes some sort of fear-inducing pronouncement or prediction about terrorism, it tends to get top play in the media. But there have been almost no efforts, systematic or otherwise, to go back to people who have prominently made dire predictions about terrorism that proved to have been faulty (and, indeed, thus far almost *all* of them have been), to query the exaggerators and predictors about how they managed to be so wrong.[188] One journalist working on a daily newspaper said it was difficult to do stories that don't have a hard news component.

Moreover, as has often been noted, the media appear to have a congenital incapacity for dealing with issues of risk and comparative probabilities—

except sometimes in the sports and financial sections. In consequence, there are quite a few elemental aspects of the terrorism issue that have been almost entirely ignored in the media. For example, that an American's chance of being killed by a terrorist is one in 4 million, or that in almost all years the number of people killed annually by terrorists in the entire world outside war zones (where the last major attack took place in 2006) is only a few hundred at most.

Fearmongering by officials and by the media is politically (and economically) understandable, but it is also decidedly irresponsible. Especially when public safety is the concern, it is vital to get the threats right and to evaluate counterterrorism measures in a systematic and coherent manner. Money and effort spent on dealing with lesser threats is money unavailable for dealing with greater ones. This theme is expanded more fully in chapter 5 of this book and also in its conclusion.

Counterterrorism as Black Comedy

That some aspects of the terrorism enterprise can be envisioned as a form of dark, or black, comedy is suggested in the acts and actions of some of the would-be terrorist perpetrators—a phenomenon to be discussed more fully in chapter 3. However, dark comedy is also suggested by some of the official counterterrorism exercises, or antics, carried out by the authorities. Indeed, many of these resemble self-parody.

There is, for example, something comic in expanding the already-bloated concept of weapons of mass destruction so that it now includes potato guns. There is definitional comedy as well in the pompous concepts of "critical infrastructure" and "key resources" constantly applied to elements that, by any sensible criterion, are neither.[189] It is also in the childish way terrorists have been portentously labeled "the universal adversary" in counterterrorism plans and games. And there is the rather absurd labeling decision in which all leads and tips, including ones that are patently trivial, are designated to be, and therefore presumably constitute, "threats."

Or there is Secretary Napolitano's remarkable notion that, although the likelihood of a large-scale organized attack is diminished, the continued danger of a small-scale disorganized attack means that the terrorist threat is higher than at any time since 9/11.

Or there is the perpetual chant, or cant, holding that terrorism presents an "existential" threat to the United States—or even, in the words of Napolitano's predecessor, Michael Chertoff, "a significant existential" one. Even more impressive (or ridiculous) is that the people making such lavish claims seem almost never to be asked to explain what they could possibly mean by them.

Or there is the bland, head-nodding response to George W. Bush's preposterous post-9/11 admonition that his goal must be to "rid the world of evil." (However, one newspaper did modestly suggest that "perhaps the president over-promised."[190])

Comedy is also suggested when authorities—and the media—soberly take seriously the petty ramblings and ridiculous fulminations of pathetic schemers of the Sears Tower plot in 2006 about how they wanted to launch "a full ground war" against the United States, or when they uncritically relayed the childish jihadist drivel of one of the participants in the Fort Dix episode of 2007, or when they exultantly tally the number of tips they have received on their terrorism hot lines without disclosing that none of these has ever led to a terrorist arrest.

It is also ludicrous that, as will be discussed in chapter 3, a great many Americans profess that they worry about becoming a victim of terrorism when the likelihood is almost vanishingly small, or that authorities have almost *never* relayed that prosaic fact to the public. Or that no one ever answers the perennial query, "Are we safer?" with, as suggested earlier, "At present rates, your yearly chance of being killed by a terrorist is one in 4 million; how much safer do you want to be and how much money do you want to spend to achieve that level of safety?"

Although there was no evidence that the Vinas plot against Penn Station in 2008 was anything but a gleam in the eye of a few dreamy conspirators ten thousand miles away, warnings were issued in the United States that there might just possibly be an attack on the subway system in New York. It was further divined, or fantasized, that it might take place over the Thanksgiving weekend. Extra police patrols were instituted at taxpayers' expense, and seasoned counterterrorism provocateurs came out of the woodwork to soberly inform television viewers that "we're at critical times right now . . . terrorists are gearing up."[191]

Then there is the report that, although some officials privately doubt al-Qaeda's ability to launch another 9/11, they will say so only on condition of anonymity because they fear that "publicly identifying themselves could make them a target" of terrorists.[192]

As part of this, a sort of bitter comedy is present when the authorities, joined by legions of terrorism experts, continually proclaim there to be thousands of terrorists afoot and predict imminent disaster, and when they are never countered or even questioned when they make their proclamations or held to account later when these prove to have been so much hot air. However ironic the phenomenon, it is a deeply serious issue, as suggested elegantly by Brian Jenkins: "Needless alarm, exaggerated portrayals of the terrorist threat, unrealistic expectations of a risk-free society, and unreasonable demands for absolute protection will only encourage terrorists' ambitions to make America fibrillate in fear and bankrupt itself with security."[193]

And the media should not be excluded from blame for the fundamentally absurd process of hype and threat exaggeration as when ABC's Charles Gibson assures us that going to the mall constitutes "a small act of courage."

There are also instances when it all fades to black—there is no comedy at all. For example, when a study presents credible evidence that delays due to measures designed to make the public secure on airlines have caused many passengers to bypass planes on short-haul trips, driving instead in a more dangerous automobile, a shift that may result in hundreds of deaths on the highways each year.[194]

Or when funds diverted to counterterrorism and away from helping people during natural disasters result, as in the response to Hurricane Katrina in 2005, in thousands of unnecessary deaths.[195]

Or, because of the vagueness of the concept of "material support for terrorism," many Somali Americans were reluctant to aid in a catastrophic famine taking place in their home country, in areas partly occupied by a people officially designated as a terrorist group.[196]

The ultimate black (or in this case, red) joke in the counterterrorism enterprise, however, may be the one played on the taxpayers. Dana Priest and William Arkin pointedly note that intelligence spending has increased by 250 percent since September 11, 2001, "without anyone in government seriously trying to figure out where the overlaps and waste were"—an apt description of a delusionary process. After receiving a "steady diet of vague but terrifying information from national security officials," they continue, American taxpayers

> have shelled out hundreds of billions of dollars to turn the machine of government over to defeating terrorism without ever really questioning what they were getting for their money. And even if they did want an answer to that question, they would not be given one, both because those same officials have decided it would gravely harm national security to share such classified information—and because the officials themselves don't actually know.[197]

Or perhaps the taxpayers are playing the joke on themselves. That possibility will be explored in the next chapter.

| Public Perceptions

Perpetual Anxiety and War Wariness

A SSESSING THE PUBLIC reaction to the terrorist attacks of September 11, 2001, anthropologist Scott Atran muses, "Perhaps never in the history of human conflict have so few people with so few actual means and capabilities frightened so many."[1] Poll data suggest that much of that fright continues to linger more than a decade after the impelling event.

This chapter assesses the long-term response of the American public to 9/11. Even though other issues—particularly economic ones—crowded out terrorism as a topic of daily concern, the 9/11 event clearly has achieved perpetual resonance in the American mind. And as part of this, it appears to have resulted in a long-term, routinized, mass anxiety—or at least a sense of concern—that has shown little sign of waning over the years since 2001.[2]

At the time of the attacks, the common comment was "Everything has changed." That change, it appears, has been permanent or at least perpetual: the public has chosen to persist in engaging in what philosopher Leif Wenar has labeled a "false sense of insecurity."

However, even as the public continues to support the general "war on terror," it appears to have soured on one of its main tactics. Opposing the terrorist "adversary" remains important, and concerns about becoming a victim of terrorism and about likely future attacks have not notably waned since 2001. But the public has clearly lost much of whatever enthusiasm it ever had for the most extreme counterterrorism measure: lengthy armed ground conflicts in distant lands. To a considerable degree, it has come to favor withdrawal from such commitments and avoidance of that tactic, even if that means the terrorists might be advantaged.

Something similar happened during the cold war after the debacle in Vietnam, and it appears that the "Vietnam Syndrome" has been replaced (or reinforced) by the "Iraq Syndrome." However, it is more accurate to conclude that the public has gone back to levels of wariness about military involvement abroad that were established after Vietnam. These levels have generally held ever since then, except when responding to severe stimuli, the chief one being the 9/11 attacks. The experience of Vietnam can rather reasonably be taken to suggest that, although the willingness to use military measures short of ground troops to protect Americans and American interests abroad remains high, the studied reluctance to engage in extended ground combat abroad is unlikely to be effectively reversed.

The chapter also reflects on the process by which some objectively important, dramatic, and emotion-engaging events and episodes in the American experience have achieved lasting resonance, while other, seemingly similar events and episodes have not done so. The process appears to be remarkably fluid and is often unpredictable, filled with cognitive biases and with what often seems to be the capricious application of emotional and social whim. As part of this reflection, we compare the public reaction to 9/11 with the long-term response to two dramatic, emotion-grabbing events: Pearl Harbor (which achieved lasting resonance) and the Gulf War of 1991 (which did not). There is also a comparison of concerns about domestic terrorism with those generated during the cold war by the threat of domestic communism, a comparison suggesting that fears about the threat that terrorism presents at home are likely to wane only very slowly. The figures begin on p. 81.

All public opinion data in this chapter, whether shown in its figures or only mentioned in the text, are posted online.[3]

Public Opinion on Terrorism

As figure 2-1 demonstrates, the American public has come to pay less attention to terrorism as other concerns—the wars in the Middle East and, more lately, the economy—have dominated its responses to questions about the most important problem facing the country.[4] Moreover, after a bit of time following 9/11, much behavior returned to normal: people again boarded airliners, and property values in the targeted cities of New York and Washington continued upward.[5]

However, poll questions specifically focused on terrorism generally find little decline in the degree to which Americans voice concern about that hazard, although there have been various temporary ups and downs in these trends in response to specific events.

There are two patterns. On some questions, concerns soared at the time of the 9/11 attacks, dropped to lower levels in the subsequent few months, but then afterward failed to decline much further. On other questions, levels of concern reached at the time of the attacks continued to remain at much the same level in subsequent years.[6]

The first pattern is shown in the response to the vivid, clear, and personal question as displayed in figure 2-2. At the time of 9/11, those who professed to be very or somewhat worried that the respondent or a family member might become a victim of terrorism spiked to around 60 percent. This declined to 35 to 40 percent by the end of 2001, a level that has held ever since.

The second pattern is displayed in figure 2-3. The percentage holding "another terrorist attack causing large numbers of Americans to be lost" to be very or somewhat likely registered at over 70 percent in the immediate aftermath of 9/11, and it was still at that level in late 2013, the most recent time the question was posed. The same pattern holds for a question about which side was winning the war against terrorism (figure 2-4). Although that percentage has bounced around quite a bit, particularly in response to the wars in Afghanistan and Iraq, a decade later—even after the death of Osama bin Laden—it stood at almost exactly the same level as in October 2001.

The percentage maintaining that terrorists remain capable of launching "another major attack" was, if anything, higher in 2013 and 2014 than it had been in 2002 (figure 2-5). The portion concerned that their community will be attacked in the next several weeks, although relatively small, is also, if anything, a bit higher than it was in early 2002. In another poll, worries about flying on airplanes because of the risk of terrorism registered at about the same level in 2010 as in 2002.

As discussed earlier, the increase in spending on domestic homeland security since 9/11 has totaled well over $1 trillion, while efforts to chase down and eliminate terrorists abroad have cost trillions more. However, these extraordinary expenditures have utterly failed to make people feel safer: the percentage of people who profess to have confidence in the government's ability to prevent further terrorist attacks (figure 2-6) or to protect them from such attacks (figure 2-17) remained more than a decade later at about the same level as it was in 2001, and it is actually lower than it was in the immediate aftermath of 9/11—when something of a "rally 'round the flag" effect took place.[7] (These two figures also demonstrate the spike-like pattern that the impacts of some major events have. Although a very substantial boost was registered in the figure 2-6 rating in a poll conducted at the time of the bin Laden capture in May 2011, that boost soon evaporated—the data in figure 2-7 suggest it happened within a few months.)[8] In addition, in 2013 and 2014, more Americans considered the country to be less safe than before 9/11 than had said so a decade or so earlier and the rise of ISIS in 2014 pushed that feeling to new highs (figures 2-8 and 2-9). The startling revelations in June 2013 (two months after the Boston bombing) by Edward Snowden about the massive data-collection efforts of the National Security Agency (to be discussed at length in chapter 7) had some effect on concerns about invasions of privacy by the country's counterterrorism enterprise, but this change proved to be temporary (figure 2-10).[9]

These results suggest that the impact of 9/11 has been internalized, but this does not mean that people are simply offering unthinking, routinized responses—responses they deem to be socially required. Over time, the numbers on many questions have notably fluctuated (usually, however, only for short periods of time) in reaction to certain events, such as the beginning of the wars in Afghanistan in 2001 and in Iraq in 2003, the captures of Saddam Hussein and Osama bin Laden, the terrorist bombings in London in 2005, and the rise of ISIS in 2014.[10]

Here and there are glimmers—but only that—of what might be a bit of more change lately. The percentage professing to worry about becoming a victim of terrorism stood in 2013 at nearly a historic low for the post-9/11 period, although it rose again after the beheadings of American captives by ISIS (figure 2-2). A similar question about worry shown in figure 2-11 does show something of a decline—but not all that much since early 2005. Another glimmer can be seen in figure 2-3. Although the percentage holding it to be very or somewhat likely that "another major attack causing a large number of American lives to be lost in the near future" did not change much between 9/11 and 2013, the percentage within that sum may have shifted somewhat in more recent years from the "very likely" to the "somewhat likely" category. However, this change can be looked at differently. By late 2013, the tallies for the two middle lines had returned to where they were in the 2002–3 period after something of a shift toward the "very likely" category between 2006 and 2008. Meanwhile, the tiny percentage of perhaps heroic Americans who deem another large terrorist attack to be "not at all likely" in the "near future" has scarcely moved at all during the decade and more since 9/11.

A few of the questions on terrorism were asked before 9/11, stimulated by the vehicle bombing of a federal building in Oklahoma City in 1995 that resulted in the death of 168 people—at the time by far the most damaging terrorist attack in the United States and one of the most destructive in history.

In the aftermath of that bombing, over 40 percent of the public said it worried about becoming a victim of terrorism. However, this percentage declined considerably in the next few years (figure 2-2). The 9/11 events caused it to spike to 60 percent, after which it declined to around 35 or 40 percent, the level registered right after the Oklahoma City bombing. However, there has been little further decline in this percentage in subsequent years. The same pattern is suggested in figure 2-12. The decline in worry about terrorism between 1995 to 1997 that it documents would likely have continued over the next few years. Then, as in figure 2-2, worry soared to new highs at the time of 9/11, sharply dropping in the next weeks to levels from which it has subsequently failed to further decline.

It should be pointed out that these patterns were all in place before the rise in 2014 of the Islamic State, or ISIS, in the Middle East, a development that, as will be discussed more fully later, was accepted to be particularly threatening to the United States by Americans.

Tactical Shift: Rejecting Ground War

While expressed alarm, or at least concern, about terrorism has not notably declined since 2001, there has been a very substantial change in a related area of interest. Over the same period, the public has notably soured on the wars in Afghanistan and Iraq. These were substantially launched as extended efforts in counterterrorism, and they would likely not have been politically possible without the stimulus of 9/11. The public now seems to want to avoid such conflicts in the future, even, perhaps, if this might increase the terrorist danger to the country. There are notable parallels in this with earlier American wars, particularly with the one in Vietnam.

TRENDS IN SUPPORT FOR WARS IN KOREA, VIETNAM, AFGHANISTAN, AND IRAQ

Since World War II, the United States has engaged in four extended ground wars: in Korea from 1950 to 1953, in Vietnam from 1965 to 1975, and in Afghanistan starting in 2001 and Iraq starting in 2003. A broad assessment of the degree to which these wars have been supported is provided by a poll question asked in each of them, often known as the "mistake" question: "Do you think the United States made a mistake in sending troops to fight in [country], or not?" There are some variations in the exact wording of the question, but these are minor.

Figure 2-13 shows the trends in support for the four wars, tallying, for each of the conflicts, those thinking the wars were *not* a mistake as a percentage of those with opinions. The key issue for present purposes is that support dramatically declined as the wars wore on and as casualties mounted. This decline tended to be faster earlier in the wars than later.[11] Support from people who had only reluctantly or reticently embraced the wars at the start dropped off quickly, leaving support to the more hard core and less easily disillusioned.

The outsized effect of 9/11 is clearly seen at the left of the figure. Some 75 percent expressed support on this measure as troops were being sent into action in Korea, Vietnam, and Iraq. In contrast, over 90 percent supported the venture in Afghanistan when it started. That war, of course, began only a couple of months after 9/11, and it was widely seen as a necessary response to a direct assault on the homeland—rather like Pearl Harbor.

Also of interest is that, relative to American casualties, the war in Iraq was far less popular than the ones in Vietnam and Korea. After about two years, the number supporting each of these three wars dropped below the 50 percent level. However, by that time around 20,000 Americans had been killed in Vietnam and Korea, but only about 2,000 in Iraq. This suggests that the public has judged the stakes in Iraq to be far less significant than they had been for the two cold war conflicts.

The "mistake" question is somewhat flawed in its application to Afghanistan. To a considerable degree, that war has actually been two armed conflicts. The seeming success of 2001–2 was followed by a few years of apparent peace, and war was gradually reignited later. As can be seen in figure 2-13, polling agencies scarcely even asked the war-support question for several years after 2001. Thus, the respondent might read the question to pertain to the first war (when troops were sent in to get those responsible for 9/11), not to the second conflict. However, a decline in support for the war in Afghanistan parallel to that found by the "mistake" question is also recorded in other questions asking simply "Do you favor the war?" or "Do you think the war has been worth it?"[12]

TRENDS IN OPINIONS ON MILITARY INTERVENTION

Some commentators, including such unlikely soul mates as Andrew Bacevich, Robert Kagan, John Mearsheimer, Rachel Maddow, and Vladimir Putin, have variously maintained that there has been a rise in a new American militarism in the last decades or that Americans congenitally hail from Mars.[13]

But that perspective extrapolates far too much from the wars in Afghanistan and Iraq. In these cases, opinion was impelled not by a propensity toward militarism but, as with entry into World War II, by the reaction to a direct attack on the United States.[14] These ventures—the 9/11 wars—have proved to be aberrations from usual patterns in the post-Vietnam era, not indicators of change or portents of the future. Although they demonstrate that Americans remain willing to respond forcefully if attacked, they do not indicate a change in the public's reticence toward becoming militarily involved in other kinds of missions, particularly humanitarian ones.

This can be seen in an examination of the long-term trends in a set of poll questions designed to tap "isolationism." They do not suggest that there has been a surge of militarism. Three versions are mapped in figure 2-14.[15] They document something of a rise in wariness about military intervention by the end of the Vietnam War and then, thereafter, a fair amount of steadiness punctured by up and down spikes in response to current events, including 9/11 and its ensuing wars.

The poll question with the longest pedigree has been asked at least since 1945: "Do you think it will be best for the future of this country if we take an active part in world affairs, or if we stayed out of world affairs?" The question seems to have been fabricated to generate an "internationalist" response. In 1945, after all, the United States possessed something like half the wealth in the world and scarcely had much of an option about "taking an active part in world affairs," as it was so blandly and unthreateningly presented. The authors of the poll question got the number they probably wanted: so queried, only 19 percent of poll respondents in 1945 picked the "stay out" or "isolationist" option. As can be seen in the figure, to generate high levels of "isolationism," the query can be reformulated by asking respondents whether they agree or disagree that "[w]e shouldn't think so much in international terms but concentrate more on our own national problems and building up our strength and prosperity here at home." In that rendering, the option of staying out of world affairs is only implied, and measured "isolationism" consistently registers 30 or 40 percentage points higher.

In the years following 1945, the "stay out" percentage rose a bit to around 25 percent, but it had descended to 16 percent in 1965, in the aftermath of the 1962 Cuban missile crisis and as the war in Vietnam began. The experience of that war pushed it much higher—to 31 to 36 percent as part of what has been called the "Vietnam Syndrome."

The percentage has stayed at around that level ever since. There was a downward dip during the Gulf War of 1991, at the end of which the war's chief author, President George H. W. Bush, grandly concluded a speech by trumpeting, "By God, we've kicked the Vietnam Syndrome once and for all."[16] The first part of that statement was sound, but not the second. Within weeks, the "stay out" option had regained its previous attractiveness. There were also interesting spikes in wariness about military interventions abroad when troops were sent to Bosnia in 1995 and at the time of the Kosovo conflict in 1999. In these instances, the spikes were upward, even though no American troops were lost in either venture and even though both ventures were deemed successful, at least in their own terms, at the time.

In the current century, the "stay out" percentage dropped to 14, its lowest recorded level, in the aftermath of 9/11. It rose the next year, and then plunged downward again in 2003 and 2004—the first two years of the Iraq War. By 2006, however, it had risen again to post-Vietnam levels, where it remained through 2012, the last time the question was asked. A related question, asking whether the United States "should mind its own business internationally" while letting "other countries get along as best they can on their own," did, however, reach new—or almost new—highs in 2013.[17]

One popular explanation for the American public's palpable unwillingness to countenance military involvement in the wake of the wars in Iraq and Afghanistan is that the country has slumped into a deep isolationist mood. But the reaction scarcely represents a "new isolationism," or a "growing isolationism," or a "new non-interventionist fad."[18] Rather, there has always been a deep reluctance to lose American lives or to put them at risk overseas for humanitarian purposes.

In Bosnia, for example, the United States held off intervention on the ground until late 1995 after hostilities had ceased, and even then the public was anything but enthusiastic when American peacekeeping soldiers were sent in.[19] Bombs, not boots, were sent to Kosovo, and in Somalia, the United States abruptly withdrew its troops when nineteen of them were killed in the chaotic "Black Hawk Down" firefight in 1993. The United States, like other developed nations, has mostly stood aloof in many other humanitarian disasters, such as those in Congo, Rwanda, and Sudan.[20] The country did get involved in Libya in 2011, but the operation was strained and hesitant, and there was little subsequent enthusiasm to do much of anything about the conflict in neighboring Mali that was spawned by the Libyan venture or about the ensuing civil war in Libya itself.

The perspective is seen most clearly, perhaps, when Americans were asked in 1993 whether they agreed that "[n]othing the U.S. could accomplish in Somalia is worth the death of even one more U.S. soldier." Fully 60 percent expressed agreement.[21] This is not such an unusual position for humanitarian ventures. If Red Cross or other workers are killed while carrying out humanitarian missions, their organizations frequently threaten to withdraw, no matter how much good they may be doing. Essentially what they are saying is that the saving of lives is not worth the deaths of even a few of their service personnel.

Given the bland attractiveness of the "take an active part in world affairs" option, it is impressive that around a third or more of the public since Vietnam has generally rejected it to embrace the "stay out" option. However, this should likely be taken to be more nearly an expression of wariness about costly and frustrating military entanglements than as a serious yearning for full withdrawal from the world, or "isolationism." There is, for example, no real indication that Americans want to erect steely trade barriers.[22] And polls continually show that the public is far more likely to approve foreign ventures if they are approved and supported by allies and international organizations.[23] Real isolationism should be made of sterner stuff.

RESPONSE TO DEBACLE

In 2014, Iraq splintered and tumbled into civil chaos and effective partition, with the result that, as in Vietnam, just about everything the United States had fought and paid for went down in flames and explosions. It was a major debacle.

However, experience suggests that Americans are quite capable of taking foreign policy debacles in stride.[24] When sending policing troops to wartorn Lebanon in 1983, President Ronald Reagan grandly declared that the conflict there somehow was "a threat to all the people of the world, not just to the Middle East itself."[25] However, the venture sagged into debacle when a terrorist bomb killed 241 of those troops, after which the public supported—indeed, impelled—his decision to abruptly withdraw and then handily reelected him a few months later. Something similar happened to Bill Clinton when he withdrew troops from Somalia a few months after a firefight that killed nineteen U.S. soldiers: by the time the next election rolled around, people had largely forgotten the whole episode.

But the most remarkable instance, and the one most relevant to the situation in Iraq, is the way the public embraced debacle in Vietnam after 1975. That war's chief author, President Lyndon Johnson, had mused in the early 1970s,

> I knew that if we let Communist aggression succeed in taking over South Vietnam, there would follow in this country an endless national debate—a mean and destructive debate—that would shatter my presidency, kill my Administration, and damage our democracy. I knew that Harry Truman and Dean Acheson had lost their effectiveness from the day that the Communists took over in China. I believed that the loss of

China had played a large role in the rise of Joe McCarthy. And I knew that all these problems, taken together, were chickenshit compared with what might happen if we lost Vietnam.

He was particularly concerned because

> this time there would be Robert Kennedy out in front leading the fight against me, telling everyone that I had betrayed John Kennedy's commitment of South Vietnam. That I had let a democracy fall into the hands of the Communists. That I was a coward. An unmanly man. A man without a spine.[26]

But no such political disaster took place. There was a spectacular failure of the U.S. position in Vietnam in 1975 as the communists almost effortlessly took control of the country, a failure that was presided over by President Gerald Ford. However, far from suffering political damage from the episode, Ford actually tried to use this supreme foreign policy catastrophe to his advantage in his reelection campaign the next year, pointing out that, when he came into office the United States was "still deeply involved in the problems of Vietnam, [but now] we are at peace. Not a single young American is fighting or dying on any foreign soil tonight."[27] His challenger, Jimmy Carter, apparently did not think it good politics to point out the essential absurdity of Ford's declaration in defense of debacle.

Even more remarkable, and equally relevant to Iraq, was the bland, shrugging public response to communist gains around the world that took place after the Vietnam debacle. Johnson had confidently and vividly predicted disaster on this score as well:

> I was as sure as any man could be that once we showed how weak we were, Moscow and Peking would move in a flash to exploit our weakness. They might move independently or they might move together. But move they would—whether through nuclear blackmail, through subversion, with regular armed forces, or in some other manner. As nearly as anyone can be certain of anything, I knew they couldn't resist the opportunity to expand their control over the vacuum of power we would leave behind us. And so would begin World War III.[28]

Following the communist victories in 1975 in Vietnam and in Cambodia and Laos, international communism did pick up a series of new ideological allies: Angola in 1976, Mozambique and Ethiopia in 1977, South Yemen and

Afghanistan in 1978, and Grenada and Nicaragua in 1979. But after the disastrous war in Vietnam, the American public remained determined never to do another Vietnam. And, in fact, the country never ventured into "another Vietnam" during the cold war.

Impelled by the Vietnam Syndrome, Congress hampered the White House's ability to pursue even rather modest anti-communist ventures in Africa and, to a lesser extent, in Latin America—though there was bipartisan support for aiding, but not necessarily for sending troops to participate in, the anti-Soviet jihad in Afghanistan. Mostly, the public lapsed into its preferred condition: a studied inattention to foreign affairs.[29] Thus, the genocide in Cambodia perpetrated by the communists after their victory there in 1975 was ignored in part because of fears that paying attention might lead to the conclusion that American troops should be sent over to rectify the disaster.[30]

However, even as the public ceased to accept the use of American ground troops as a tactic, it does seem to have continued to support the cold war effort against international communism, including extensive spending on defense. And, as it happened, American ground troops were scarcely necessary to end the cold war. On the contrary.

Vietnam had been an extreme application of the policy of containment that sought to hold international communism in check, with the hope that in time it would rot from its internal contradictions. However, that policy was logically flawed. If the Soviet system really was as rotten and as destined to self-destruct as containment's chief architect, George Kennan, more or less accurately surmised, then the best policy would not have been to contain it but to give it enough rope to hang itself—to let it expand until it reached the point of terminal overstretch.[31]

And it turned out that what ultimately helped bring about the mellowing of Soviet expansionism was not containment's success but its failure. Partly out of fear of repeating the Vietnam experience, the United States went into a sort of containment funk and watched from the sidelines as the Soviet Union, in what seems in retrospect to have been remarkably like a fit of absentmindedness, opportunistically gathered that collection of Third World countries into its imperial embrace.

The Soviets at first were quite gleeful about these acquisitions—the "correlation of forces," they concluded, had decisively and most agreeably shifted in their direction.[32] However, almost all the new acquisitions soon became economic and political basket cases, fraught with dissension, financial mismanagement, and civil warfare; meanwhile, the situation in neighboring Afghanistan so deteriorated that the Soviets found it necessary to send in troops, descending into a long period of enervating warfare there.[33] As each member of their newly expanded empire turned toward the Soviet Union for maternal warmth and sustenance, many Soviets began to wonder if they would have been better off contained. Eventually, the Soviets were able, as Kennan had hoped, to embrace grim reality; and in the late 1980s, they decisively abandoned their threatening ideology under the leadership of Mikhail Gorbachev.[34]

LESSONS FROM VIETNAM FOR IRAQ AND AFGHANISTAN

The Iraq Syndrome, a later reflection, or application, of the Vietnam Syndrome, was in full flower in 2013 when President Barack Obama, initially supported by the Republican leadership in Congress, planned to bomb Syria for its apparent use of chemical weapons in the costly civil war being waged there—something he had previously (and ominously) declared would be a "game changer."[35] The bombing idea, however, was met with intense hostility by a public determined not to be dragged into another war in the Middle East, even though no American lives were likely to be lost in the exercise and even though Obama's secretary of state insisted that the bombings would be "unbelievably small."[36]

The Iraq Syndrome was next applied, as it happens, in Iraq itself. However, that the Iraq War would spawn a "let's not do that again" attitude had been rather predictable for quite some time. For example, a poll in relatively hawkish Alabama in 2005—before things got really bad in the war—found only a third of the respondents willing to agree that the United States should be prepared to send troops back to Iraq to establish order if a full-scale civil war erupted there after a U.S. withdrawal.[37]

Something like civil war did erupt in Iraq in 2014. Although on one poll some 42 percent of the American public did think the United States had a responsibility to "do something" about the violence in Iraq, only 19 percent favored sending ground troops to do so.[38] In another poll, 64 percent opposed sending in ground forces—two-thirds of them saying they felt strongly that way.[39]

Supporters of "doing something" militarily in Iraq tried to convince people that some sort of intervention was necessary to prevent a direct attack on the United States—although, wary of the Iraq Syndrome, they avoided advocating "boots on the ground." Thus, Senator Lindsey Graham insisted that a takeover by Islamist extremists would provide terrorists with a "staging area" from which they would carry out "another 9/11," and former Ambassador Ryan Crocker issued a comparable warning. President Obama issued similar statements, and the *Washington Post*'s David Ignatius ominously, if vaguely, insisted that a newly established terrorist "safe haven"—as opposed to ones that have existed in the area for years—"could soon be used to attack foreign targets."[40]

Meanwhile, Senator John McCain opined that having Syria and Iraq in extremist hands would represent an existential threat to the United States.[41] That is, if Syria and Iraq acquire reprehensible leaders different from the ones they have had in the past, the United States would somehow cease to exist.

This sort of extravagant threat inflation, as detailed in chapter 1, has been applied frequently since 9/11, and it has gone amazingly unchallenged.[42] However, in 2013 and in early 2014, the rhetoric worked neither for Syria nor for Iraq.

Of particular importance for present purposes is that, as with the advance of communism after the Vietnam debacle, Americans may prefer allowing advances for terrorism to happen if the alternative is to send ground troops to deal with it. Thus, in a July 2014 poll, fully 42 percent said they felt "the situation in Iraq affects the national security of the U.S. a lot," but only 19 percent said they wanted "more involvement" with the civil war there while 44 percent wanted less.[43] In a June poll, 44 percent said they felt that a result of the violence in Iraq would be that "the threat of terrorism against the United States would increase," and 80 percent held "what happens in Iraq" to be important to American interests. However, only 19 percent favored sending in American ground troops to deal with the problem, and extrapolating more broadly, only 37 percent felt the United States should even take "the leading role" in trying to solve such international conflicts.[44]

The calm with which the public watched a considerable set of countries slide into the communist camp after the Vietnam debacle suggests that Americans will now respond to further terror attacks after the Iraq debacle in a much milder manner than they did to the one in 2001: there might be a strong reaction, but there would be a great reluctance to wage a ground war. These results further suggest that, even if another major terrorist attack, or set of attacks, were to take place in the United States, the reaction is unlikely to be as (self-destructively) severe as it was after 9/11.

The brutal beheadings of defenseless Americans carried out and then posted on the Internet by the ISIS group in Syria in August and September 2014 was seen by many to be something of a direct attack on the United States, and it did bolster support for using military force, but far less so for sending in ground troops. By the spring of 2015, strong majorities had come to view ISIS as a "major threat" to the "security of the United States," but the percentage willing to use American ground troops to fight the threatening group was much lower.[45] The effect of the beheadings is suggested in figures 2-1, 2-2, 2-8, 2-10, 2-12, and 2-13.

There is another potential lesson from the Vietnam debacle. The studied inattention to genocide in Cambodia after the collapse in the area suggests that, even if great disasters befall lands in the Middle East that have been abandoned to their fate (such as in Syria), American armed intervention, especially on the ground, is unlikely unless Americans come to see the disaster to be directly threatening the United States.[46]

THE ROLE OF "OPINION ELITES"

The public response in all this suggests that people, contrary to a large literature, are not readily manipulable by opinion elites.[47] Thus, in 2013, the Obama administration dramatically proposed military action in response to chemical weapons use in Syria, and leaders of both parties in Congress rather quickly fell into line. Moreover, these bipartisan "leadership cues" were accompanied by disturbing photographs of the corpses of Syrian children apparently killed in the attack. Nonetheless, the American public was decidedly unwilling to support even the limited punitive bombing of Syria. However, news about the beheadings of Americans by Islamic State (ISIS) in 2014 did stir a pronounced popular reaction, and it caused some in the elite to urge military action, although (rather reluctantly in some cases) they did not include direct ground combat in their demands.

Leaders may propose, but that doesn't mean public opinion will move in concert—that people will necessarily buy their message. And on the occasions when they do, it is probably best to conclude that the message has struck a responsive chord, rather than that the public has been manipulated.[48] Ideas are like commercial products. Some are embraced by the customers while most, no matter how well packaged or promoted, fail to ignite acceptance or even passing interest. It is a process that is extremely difficult to predict and even more difficult to manipulate. This phenomenon will be discussed more fully in the conclusion to this book.

Reasons to Have Expected a Decline in Concerns About Terrorism

In July 2014, on the tenth anniversary of the 9/11 Commission report, the commission's chair and vice-chair voiced concern that "complacency is setting in," with Americans exhibiting "counterterrorism fatigue" about the "evolving," "grave," and "undiminished" danger that, they insisted, terrorism continues to present—that there has been a "waning sense of urgency."[49]

As detailed earlier, however, there is little evidence from the polls to support such a conclusion. Americans had clearly become decidedly wary about getting involved in extended ground wars in the quest to counter terrorism (something the politically attuned commissioners did not recommend), and public opinion seems to be poised to accept debacle in the Middle East if there are no direct attacks on Americans. But there has been little or no decline in the public's concern about the threat to the United States presented by international terrorism. As figure 2-15 suggests, although the percentage of those holding international terrorism to be a "critical threat" skyrocketed at the time of, and in the immediate aftermath of, 9/11, it has been very high ever since pollsters started asking about it in 1994, and it has remained that way.[50] And at no time has more than 4 percent of the public deemed international terrorism to be "not an important threat at all."

This is rather surprising because there are quite a few reasons (we count 13) to have expected that, however traumatic the initial experience of 9/11, concerns and anxieties about terrorism would have begun to wear off over time.

1. **Low objective likelihood of harm from terrorism.** As noted several times, the objective probability that an American will be killed by a terrorist in the United States, with the events of 2001 very much included in the count, stands at about one in 4 million per year. If one concentrates just on the period since 2001, it is about one in 110 million each year (see table 5-2 on p. 138). By comparison, an American's chance of being killed in an automobile crash is about one in 8,000 a year, while the chance of becoming a victim of homicide is about one in 22,000, and the chance of drowning in a bathtub is one in 1 million. Yet, as shown earlier, polls indicate that some 40 percent of the public continues to maintain on polls that they worry about the prospect that they or a family member will become a terrorist victim, a number that has scarcely changed since late 2001. And the percentage holding that the country is less safe than before 9/11 has not moved much either in the decade after the 9/11 Commission issued its report.

It was on television's *60 Minutes* on February 16, 2003, that filmmaker-provocateur Michael Moore happened to remark that "[t]he chances of any of us dying in a terrorist incident is very, very, very small." His interviewer, Bob Simon, promptly admonished, "But no one sees the world like that." Remarkably, both statements were true then and continue to be so today.

2. **Absence of large attacks in the United States.** As discussed at length in the previous chapter, there was a great concern that the 9/11 attack would prove to be a harbinger. That anticipation has, of course, fortunately failed to be realized: there has been no really sizable terrorist attack in the country.

3. **Absence of al-Qaeda attacks on the United States.** Al-Qaeda has failed entirely to consummate any attack of any magnitude whatever on American soil—or, for that matter, in the air around it. This, despite the overwhelming early fears about a "second wave," as discussed in chapter 1, and the threats to do so repeatedly spun out by Osama bin Laden and other al-Qaeda operatives. It was in October 2002, for example, that bin Laden raved, "Understand the lesson of New York and Washington raids, which came in response to some of your previous crimes. . . . God is my witness, the youth of

Islam are preparing things that will fill your hearts with fear. They will target key sectors of your economy until you stop your injustice and aggression or until the more short-lived of us die."[51]

4. Absence of al-Qaeda cells in the United States. Despite extensive fears to the contrary in the aftermath of 9/11, no true al-Qaeda cell (nor scarcely anybody who might even be deemed to have a "connection" to the diabolical group) has been unearthed in the country.

5. Near absence of terrorist attacks from any source in the United States. Since 9/11, Islamist extremist terrorists (none of them linked to al-Qaeda Central) have managed to kill a total of some nineteen people in the United States.[52] And deaths from terrorism of all sources have been tallied for the period at thirty-three (see table 5-2). Considerably more people have been killed by deranged nonterrorists in various individual shootings at schools and theaters.[53] Indeed, virtually all terrorist violence within the United States has taken place in television dramas.[54]

6. Modest interest in the attacks that have taken place. The largest terrorist attack in the United States, the killing of thirteen at Fort Hood in 2009, scarcely stoked wide alarm. In fact, with the possible exception of the Boston Marathon case in 2013, none of the often rather interesting and colorful plots that have been uncovered have inspired much lasting interest. The media seem to have decided that the newsworthiness of such episodes is, for the most part, limited and declining. The decline of attention is also reflected in the data in this chapter: polling agencies have substantially reduced the frequency with which they have polled on the terrorism issue over the years since 9/11.

7. Incompetence of the plotters apprehended in the United States. As will be discussed much more fully in the next chapter, the homegrown "plotters" who have been apprehended, while perhaps potentially somewhat dangerous at least in a few cases, have mostly been amateurish and almost absurdly incompetent.

8. Absence of sizable attacks anywhere in the developed world since 2005. Major terrorist attacks were visited upon domestic transportation systems in Madrid in 2004, killing 191, and in London in 2005, killing 52. The London attack seems to have caused an upward spike in concerns about terrorism on some of the public opinion trend lines in the United States (figures 2-2, 2-4, 2-5, 2-9). However, there have been no attacks of that magnitude anywhere in the developed world since then—though two much smaller attacks in Paris in January 2015 did inspire considerable reaction.

9. The damage committed worldwide by al-Qaeda and al-Qaeda types outside war zones has been rather limited. As will be discussed more fully in chapter 4, al-Qaeda Central has done little of consequence since 9/11 anywhere in the world, and the total number of people killed worldwide by al-Qaeda types, al-Qaeda maybes, and al-Qaeda wannabes outside of war zones since 9/11 stands at some 300 or so a year—smaller than the yearly number of bathtub drownings in the United States.[55]

10. **Decline of official and media alarmism on the issue.** As documented in chapter 1, U.S. government officials have maintained their willingness and ability to stoke fear. However, official alarmism has actually tapered off in recent years, and explicit predictions that the country must brace itself for a large imminent attack, so common in the years after September 11, are rarely heard.[56] As part of this, extravagant assertions that terrorism presents a threat that is "existential," though still heard, have declined. It seems possible—though it is difficult to be certain—that there has also been something of a decline in concern that terrorists will get weapons of mass destruction, or at least nuclear ones, a major preoccupation for several years after 9/11.

Yet public anxiety about terrorism as tapped by the polls has not similarly waned, further suggesting that poll respondents are not simply responding to leadership cues. As noted, the phenomenon seems, then, substantially to be a bottom-up one rather than one inspired by policy makers, risk entrepreneurs, politicians, and members of the media who seem more nearly to be responding to the fears (and exacerbating them) than creating them.[57] Since it appears that official alarmist hype was not necessary for the alarm, a decline in the official and media hype has not led to much of a decline in alarm.

11. **Huge increases in counterterrorism efforts and spending.** One might have expected that the trillions of dollars spent on protecting Americans from terrorists since 9/11 might have comfortingly reduced anxieties about the hazard. That certainly was the goal: Michael Hayden recalls a dictim he issued two days after 9/11 when he was director of the National Security Agency: "We are going to keep America free by making Americans feel safe."[58] America does seem to have remained free, but polls strongly suggest it is not because Americans have come to feel safe. Actually, as noted in chapter 1, there is some reason to believe that, although noticeable security items like armed guards, high walls, and barbed wire make people feel less vulnerable to crime, these same devices make people feel tense, suspicious, and fearful when they are instituted in the context of dealing with the threat of terrorism.[59]

12. **Death of bin Laden.** In May 2011, Osama bin Laden, the prime author of the 9/11 attacks, and one of the most vilified villains in history, was found and killed by American commandos. It might have been anticipated that such a dramatic and memorable event would form something of a closure moment, allowing the public to relax a bit on the terrorism issue. However, little if any of that has taken place. As noted, figure 2-6 shows that there was an abrupt increase in the percentage of those having confidence in the government's ability to prevent

further terrorist attacks at the time of bin Laden's killing. But that gain had evaporated by the time the question was next asked.

13. Ease of registering change in the polling instrument. Most of the questions give those polled a response range with gradations that should make it fairly easy to register a degree of change if one is so inclined. For example, respondents are not obligated to choose between deeming another terrorist attack to be either likely or unlikely. Rather, they can go from "very likely" to "somewhat likely" or from "somewhat likely" to "not too likely." For the most part, they have declined to take the opportunity to do so, at least in the aggregate.

Assessing the Absence of Decline in Concern About Terrorism

The war in Iraq and then economic woes pushed terrorism down on the list of immediate concerns, and some polls found that anxieties about the threat presented by terrorism declined in the few weeks after the 9/11 attack (while other polls showed no decline whatever). However, people clearly continue overwhelmingly to deem international terrorism to be a threat—or even, as documented in figure 2-15, a "critical" one—and the substantial absence of further erosion in the years after 2001, as registered by poll data, is quite impressive given the multitude of reasons just arrayed to expect it.

Whatever the genesis, Americans seem to have internalized their anxiety, or concern, about terrorism; and politicians and policy makers have come to believe that they can defy it only at their own peril. Anxiety about terrorism may prove, then, to be perpetual, and the public will likely remain broadly supportive of official counterterrorism efforts even as it says it feels no safer from the efforts and even as it sours on the use of ground troops as a tactic to deal with the problem.

The persistence of anxieties about terrorism among Americans presumably stems importantly from the peculiar, outsized trauma induced by the September 11 attacks themselves: in the words of Fawaz Gerges, it "instilled disproportionate fear in their psyche."[60] And it is possible that initial alarm was importantly reinforced by the (unrelated) anthrax attacks that followed shortly after: fears about being harmed by terrorists, as tallied in figure 2-2, began to decline in the days after 9/11 and then were pushed to their highest levels ever when the anthrax story came out.[61]

Two other events that took place in late 2001 may also have reinforced alarm. One was an airliner crash in New York on November 12 that was at first commonly assumed to be due to terrorism, a conclusion that turned out not to be true. The other was the bungled effort of the shoe bomber on a flight from Paris to Miami on December 22.[62] If, however, September 11 has failed to be a harbinger, as it increasingly appears, it would seem to follow that the experience could be taken to be a tragic aberration, not one that should fundamentally determine consequent perceptions. But that has not happened.

Also relevant might be the continued resonance of the extrapolation discussed in chapter 1 that, because the 9/11 terrorists were successful with box cutters, they might soon be able to turn out weapons of mass destruction and then detonate them in an American city.[63]

The seemingly constant, if pointillistic, stream of well over 100 small-time terrorism cases that have come to light since 9/11 may have kept the pot boiling. These include terrorist plots, or proto-plots, in which Islamists, whether based in the United States or abroad, have planned, or appear to have planned, to attack targets in the United States, as arrayed in appendix A. In addition, there have been an equal or somewhat larger number of cases in which individuals have been apprehended in the process of seeking to go abroad to fight against America or American interests, particularly in Iraq or Afghanistan. Although, as noted, few of these cases have generated much in the way of lasting media interest, the almost relentless drumbeat of these small cases may have had its effect in continually reminding people there are still terrorists out there.[64]

The stress on what these failed (and mostly bone-headed) plotters hoped to do (destroy the Brooklyn Bridge, topple the Sears Tower, blow up the Capitol Building), rather than on what they were actually likely to be able to do, may also have contributed. As noted in the previous chapter, foiled plots can seem, or be made to seem, scarier than successful ones because the emphasis is on what the terrorist plotters hoped to do or might have been able to do, not on what they were likely to do.[65] However, it is also possible that the fact that these cases have overwhelmingly involved plots that were mindless fantasies could have set up a calming "cry wolf" effect.

Special fear and anxiety may also be stirred by the fact that Islamist terrorism seems to be part of a large and hostile conspiracy and network that is international in scope and rather spooky—not unlike, perhaps, the one posed by witches and international communism in earlier eras, as discussed in this book's introduction.[66]

Noting that the scale of the September 11, 2001, attacks has "tended to obliterate America's memory of pre-9/11 terrorism," Brian Jenkins reminds us (and we clearly do need reminding) that

> measured by the number of terrorist attacks, the volume of domestic terrorist activity was much greater in the 1970s. That tumultuous decade saw 60 to 70 terrorist incidents, mostly bombings, on U.S. soil every year—a level of terrorist activity 15 to 20 times that seen in the years

since 9/11.... [Terrorists] hijacked airliners; held hostages in Washington, New York, Chicago, and San Francisco; bombed embassies, corporate headquarters, and government buildings; robbed banks; murdered diplomats; and blew up power transformers, causing widespread blackouts.

However, unlike attacks by Muslim extremists, these were mainly domestic in apparent origin and scope. For the most part, they did not have a significant foreign or external referent.[67]

Anxiety may also derive from the perception that, unlike terrorists who seem mainly out to draw attention to their cause (in Jenkins's assessments, only 72 people perished in the hundreds of bombing incidents during the decade of the 1970s),[68] Muslim extremist terrorists like those of 9/11 (but like Timothy McVeigh in the 1995 Oklahoma City bombing) seem out to kill as many people as possible and to do so more or less at random.

At any rate, it appears that not only did 9/11 "change everything" but also that time has been slow to mellow the effect. Thus, in 2005, more people opined that 9/11 had permanently changed their life than had expressed that thought in 2002.

Comparisons with the Reactions to Other Events

As this exercise suggests, explaining why people are more impressed by some events than by others is not easy. Related research on why people fear some hazards, but not others, has come up with a laundry list of suggestions that is anything but tidy. On that list are such qualities as recent experience and the uncontrollability of the hazard; the dread (or fear) the hazards inspire; their involuntary nature or catastrophic potential; whether the hazards can be preventively controlled, are certain to be fatal, can easily be reduced, result in an inequitable distribution of risk, threaten future generations, or affect one personally; whether they are increasing or not observable, unknown to those exposed, new or unfamiliar, and unknown to science; and whether they have immediate impact and affect a large number of people.[69]

Moreover, applying these explanations can be tricky. For example, people who say they don't like flying because they have no control over the aircraft nevertheless seem to have little difficulty boarding trains, buses, and taxicabs. Psychologist Daniel Gilbert concludes that people are less afraid of global warming than of terrorism because climate change is unintentional, doesn't violate moral sensibilities, looms in the unseen future, and happens gradually.[70] But much the same could be said for nuclear reactor accidents, and the one that took place at Fukushima in 2011 has had a huge impact around the world, even though the accident, caused by a rare tsunami, has thus far resulted in no deaths.

And if it is difficult to explain which hazards will inspire special concern or anxiety, it is even more difficult to explain how long the phenomenon will linger. As detailed earlier, there is considerable reason to expect that concerns about terrorism in the United States would decline or at least erode in the years after 9/11 and that people would come to feel safe. But, for the most part, that hasn't happened.

To assess this phenomenon further, it may be useful to compare the public reaction to 9/11 with its reactions to three other dramatic and emotion-grabbing events. The first is an event that continues to resonate: Pearl Harbor. The second is an event that at the time seemed to have attributes that might cause it to achieve long-term resonance, but failed to do so: the Gulf War of 1991. And the third comparison is with concerns about an earlier persistent internal security threat that was seen to be connected to foreign enemies, the one presented by domestic communists during the cold war.

PEARL HARBOR

To the degree that 9/11 has been emblazoned on the public consciousness, it has from the beginning invited comparison with another dramatic and emotion-engaging experience, that of the Japanese attack on Pearl Harbor.[71]

There are important differences between the two events, of course. One was a large-scale, sophisticated attack on military targets by an important state, followed by formal declarations of international war that marked the beginning of a conflict resulting in the deaths of millions of people. The other was an attack on civilians by a small substate group with highly limited resources and capacities, triggering a cascade of consequences that, however dire, were far less destructive than the war in the Pacific. Thus, large forces are not necessarily required to cause or to impel lasting fear and anxiety: a national army did so in 1941, while a small band of terrorists did so in 2001—though the destruction wreaked by the 9/11 conspirators is exceptional in that it far surpassed that of any other terrorist event before or since.

Pearl Harbor and 9/11 were similar in their impetus: without really thinking about how it would come about, the planners of these attacks sought to deliver a blow that would move American opinion and policy against intervention in distant lands. However, both attacks proved to be wildly counterproductive in that respect and they culminated in substantial disaster for the perpetrators.[72]

The events were also similar in that they inspired a lasting moralistic, inchoate, never-again rage, as well as a demand for revenge regardless of costs or length of the struggle; they were taken to demand measures that irrationally ignored consideration of alternative and less extreme policy responses; they were initially taken to be far more destructive than was actually the case;[73] they generated exaggerated perceptions of enemy capacities and the degree to which there was a direct threat to the country;[74] and they were routinely, and wrongly, taken to be harbingers of future attacks, not aberrations—a reaction that evoked, in particular, unchallenged if unfounded fears of a near-term, even more destructive repetition.[75]

The events also inspired dedicated efforts to expand and to centralize intelligence gathering; led to greatly elevated and remarkably lingering approval ratings for the presidents in charge at the time, making their policies politically difficult to attack for years;[76] and became politically potent battle cries that resonated for decades. In addition, they were taken to present or imply existential threats to national security, even though the direct physical damage in the attacks, while terrible, scarcely justified such an extreme characterization; they invoked extravagant moralistic rhetoric about righteous might and ridding the world of evil, which was widely accepted without challenge; they evoked much exaggerated, and lingering, concerns about an enemy within; and they facilitated the efforts of policy entrepreneurs who wanted to include other enemies in the response, enemies essentially irrelevant to, but assumed to be somehow complicit in, the triggering event.

A comparison also suggests that whether an event resonates or not is determined primarily by the character of the event itself, not by political exploitation. After Pearl Harbor, officials sought to downplay the damage. Furthermore, gripping pictures and real-time media coverage were scarcely necessary to create anxiety: neither was present for Pearl Harbor, and when pictures did become available, they were vastly less dramatic than the collapsing of skyscrapers.[77] In neither case did people need guidance about how to react.

The initial impact of the events was probably reified by a succession of events in their immediate aftermath. Just as a plane crash in New York, the shoe bomber, and especially the anthrax attacks reified the 9/11 experience in the public's mind, the successful Japanese drive to the south in the weeks after the Hawaiian attack probably reified the Pearl Harbor experience, as did news about the brutal Japanese occupation of the Philippines and its attendant "death march."

And there's one final similarity. Although it was predictable that the Pearl Harbor and 9/11 attacks would generate alarm, the degree to which the experiences would generate great reaction was not so predictable. It is difficult to imagine Americans shrugging off either Pearl Harbor or 9/11, but the reaction to those events could conceivably have been more moderate. Because we know what actually happened in each case, it is difficult to recall important elements in the American mindset in the period before the events happened.

For instance, in 1941 there was a strong antiwar movement in the United States, generated in particular by the experience of the U.S. entry into World War I, which many took to have been the result of crafty European manipulation. As part of this, many considered American opposition to Japanese expansion in the Far East—mainly in China—to be ill-advised, potentially sucking the United States into a distant, opaque conflict that had nothing to do with American security (trade at the time with Japan was four times greater than that with China).[78]

With this as background, a plausible position after Pearl Harbor would have been to argue that the attack that killed 2,300 did not necessarily require a directly confrontational war in the Pacific, during which tens, perhaps hundreds, of thousands of Americans would be lost. An alternative policy might have been to shore up the protection of U.S. territory and to engage in a patient, far less costly cold war–like harassment of the much under-resourced and over-extended Japanese empire.[79] That such a policy option was not even broached in 1941 (nor scarcely in the many decades thereafter) is testimony to how much the attacks changed everything. However, that clear lapse in the evaluation of plausible alternative policies in one of the most important decisions ever made by American officials—a lapse, therefore, in rational decision making—was not necessarily predictable beforehand.

In 2001, there was a strong wariness about sending American troops abroad in costly "nation-building" exercises, and George W. Bush had campaigned in 2000 on the desirability of having a "humble" foreign policy. Moreover, as noted earlier, the United States had responded to terrorist or terrorist-like losses in the past with withdrawals that had proved to be politically acceptable, as when Ronald Reagan withdrew from Lebanon in 1984 and Bill Clinton retreated from Somalia in 1993. The official response to the December 1988 bombing of a PanAm airliner over Lockerbie, Scotland, which resulted in the deaths of 187 Americans, was to obtain compensation for the victims, while applying meticulous police work to tag the culprits—a process that bore fruit only three years later, and then only because of an unlikely bit of luck.[80] That cautious, deliberate response proved to be entirely acceptable politically.

With this as background, a plausible position after 9/11 would have been to argue that the attack that killed nearly 3,000 did not justify the invasion of Afghanistan—which, judging from recent and not-so-recent history, might well cost far more American lives. An alternative policy might have been to expand police and intelligence work and to work with sympathetic allies, including particularly Saudi Arabia and Pakistan, to pressure the Taliban (who seem to have had no connection to 9/11) to turn over al-Qaeda members in the country.[81] That such a policy option (which a number of Afghan experts think would have worked) was not even considered in 2001 (or scarcely in the years thereafter) is testimony to how much the attacks changed everything. As with Pearl Harbor, there was a clear lapse in rational decision making—that is, a failure to consider plausible alternative policies—and that lapse was not necessarily predictable beforehand.

THE GULF WAR OF 1991

It may be instructive to compare 9/11 (and Pearl Harbor) with an event that, in many respects, *should* have become resonant, but rather spectacularly failed to do so: the Gulf War of 1991.

When launching that war to turn back the 1990 invasion and occupation of Kuwait by Saddam Hussein's Iraq, President George H. W. Bush proclaimed that it would "chart the future of the world for the next 100 years," even as a front-page article in the *New York Times* speculated it might "change the face of domestic politics, the map of the Middle East, the realities of great-power relationships, and the world economy for years or decades to come." Moreover, the prospect of that war clearly engaged the emotions of the American public: shortly before the war began, 27 percent of poll respondents said they thought about it at least once an hour, while another 22 percent said they thought about it every few minutes (only 10 percent were so blasé as to say that they thought about it only once a day or less).[82]

When the war they were worrying about was launched, victory was achieved in short order and at an extraordinarily low cost—U.S. casualties came out far lower than just about anyone had expected. To a considerable degree, this result was because the enemy was far smaller and far more inept than expected, and because it lacked much of anything in the way of strategy, tactics, training, leadership, defenses, or morale.[83] But no one was in the mood to critically examine a victory that looked so tumultuous and unalloyed. Instead, great energies were expending on organizing massive victory parades for returning troops—the only American war since World War II for which that has happened.

Literally within days of the victory, however, the public was indicating that it wanted now to talk about the troubled U.S. economy.[84] And there was little flag-waving enthusiasm in 1992 for the chief, and perhaps nearly only, author of the war who, contrary to common expectations at the end of the war, went down to defeat in his reelection campaign. In speeches, Bush found that his successful war scarcely stirred resonance, even among politically sympathetic groups.[85]

DOMESTIC COMMUNISM DURING THE COLD WAR

Another potentially instructive comparison is with concerns about domestic communists during the cold war. In the few years after World War II, alarm about the threat presented by such people ("enemies within") grew with two spectacular espionage cases noted in the introduction to this book. First, a respected former State Department official, Alger Hiss, was accused of having sent huge quantities of classified documents to the Soviets before World

War II. Then a former communist, British physicist Klaus Fuchs, admitted that he had sent atomic secrets to the Soviets, and the trail from Fuchs soon led to the arrests of various co-conspirators and ultimately to the celebrated trial of two Americans, Julius and Ethel Rosenberg, who were convicted, and then executed, as atomic spies. This experience was then set into high relief with the invasion of South Korea by forces from communist North Korea in 1950, bolstered later in the year by hordes of troops from communist China. The war was a limited, opportunistic, and quite cautious military probe at a point of perceived vulnerability in a peripheral area. However, almost everyone simply assumed that the war was being directed from Moscow and was part of a broad, militarized quest for "world domination," a threatening venture impelled by its acquisition the year before of nuclear weapons that was assumed to have been facilitated by the atomic spies.[86]

Press and political concern about the communist enemy within probably peaked in 1954, when some 40 percent of the population deemed domestic communists as presenting a great or very great danger. As with 9/11, the attention of the press and the public turned to other matters, but concern about domestic communists, like that about domestic terrorism after 9/11, seems to have been internalized: the percentage considering communists a danger declined almost not at all in the ensuing ten years, even though media interest fell greatly (figure 2-16). When last tapped, in the mid-1970s, some twenty years after its probable peak, concern about the communist danger had declined only to 30 percent at a time when press attention to that internal enemy had fallen literally to zero.

This pattern might be extrapolated to anxieties and concerns about domestic terrorism. It would suggest that, although one shouldn't expect there to be much decline during the first decade after 9/11, there might be a notable, if still fairly modest, erosion in alarm during the second decade. However, it should probably be kept in mind that, unlike international terrorism, anxieties about domestic communists were not routinely jiggered by small-scale, notable arrests of violent plotters, arrests that were routinely, if briefly, covered in the media. Nor was there fear that domestic communists might contrive to set off a nuclear weapon within the country; concern that the Soviet Union might launch one from abroad was a different matter.

Becoming or Not Becoming Resonant: Four Processes

There seem to be four patterns by which important events and episodes that engage public emotions have subsequently continued to generate a perpetual resonance in the public mind—or have failed to do so.[87]

1. *Some important, emotion-engaging events and episodes resonate from the start and continue to do so.* Episodes like World War II and the Great Depression of the 1930s are examples, as are events like Pearl Harbor and 9/11.

2. *Some important, emotion-engaging events and episodes, while not technically "forgotten," are at first pushed from active consideration and only later become resonant.* A key case in point is the American Civil War. Although it was likely the most cataclysmic and emotion-engaging experience in their country's history, Americans essentially sought to put it out of their mind once it was over and continued to do so for nearly thirty years. As Gerald Linderman points out, there were scarcely any books written about it (because there seemed to be no market) and few, if any, memorials were constructed. That was reversed by the 1890s, however, and monuments began to spring up everywhere, library shelves soon began to groan with books on the subject, and Civil War reenactment eventually became a substantial industry.[88] Something similar happened with the Vietnam War. Like the painful Civil War, it faded from consideration after 1975. By the 1980s, however, it began to achieve resonance, and books and movies about it began to enjoy significant sales.

3. *Some important, emotion-engaging events and episodes maintain a considerable resonance for a while and seem to be on the way to becoming perpetually resonant, but then fade from recall.* The Korean War, arguably the most important event of the cold war and by far the most costly armed conflict since World War II, continued to resonate through the 1950s. In the 1960s, for example, Americans spontaneously listed Dwight Eisenhower's apparent ability to end the war in 1953 as his most important accomplishment as president.[89] Something similar happened with the War of 1812, which remained a major force in American politics for a couple of decades. Both conflicts then faded, and both have inspired books which have the word *forgotten* in their titles.[90] The Korean War Memorial in Washington was erected mainly as an embarrassed afterthought to the Vietnam War Memorial, and 2012 moved along quite well without reference (except perhaps in Canada) to the once-significant war that had begun precisely 200 years earlier.

4. *Some important emotion-engaging events and episodes rather quickly sink from sight once they are over, and then stay that way: they never achieve any sort of resonance.* The cold war is surely the most monumental experience in international history since 1945. Yet a very few years after its end, as anyone who taught about it at the time can attest, college students responded as if it was probably something that took place during the reign of Louis XIV. The Gulf War of 1991 has undergone a similar process—2001 turned out to be a memorable year, but not because that spring marked the tenth anniversary of what was popularly considered at the time to be one of the most amazing and satisfying triumphs

in U.S. military history. (This might be called the Super Bowl effect: *CBS Sports* once found in a December poll that less than 39 percent of self-described football fans could remember which team had won the passionately embraced contest that had taken place a mere eleven months earlier.[91])

Extrapolations and Further Considerations

Although the focus here has primarily been on major international events in American history, the query might be extended to other areas as well. For example, why have certain prominent personalities like Marilyn Monroe or Michael Jackson become icons, while other once-renowned celebrities, even ones who died suddenly and unexpectedly, have not? Why does the sinking of the *Titanic* continue to resonate, but not the historically far more important sinking of the *Lusitania*?

There are also puzzles about opinion trends concerning domestic policy. For decades, the "war on drugs" continued to be supported even though it could objectively be said to have failed miserably.[92] But then, only quite recently, popular support seems to have significantly waned. There has been a similar experience with gay rights. There was very little increase in popular support over several decades.[93] But then what appears to be a very substantial change of opinion occurred in quite recent years.

One final note in the comparison of post-9/11 opinion on terrorism with that on Pearl Harbor and domestic communists might be made. Both Pearl Harbor and 9/11 have had perpetual and long-lasting impacts on perceptions and perspectives.[94] Careful policy analysis has been, and perhaps always will be, impeded or even persuasively undercut by metaphorical (or even irrelevant) assertions that we can't have "another Pearl Harbor" or "another 9/11."

However, the post–Pearl Harbor war against Japan could definitively and unambiguously end, and concerns about the loyalty of Japanese people in the United States could vanish. Similarly, fears about the danger presented by domestic communists could be alleviated by the collapse of the perceived grand international communism conspiracy.

By contrast, the war on terror cannot be so logically ended, and in consequence, it could be with us for a very long time. Not only is there as yet no light at the end of the tunnel, but this tunnel might have no end at all: terrorism, like murder, has always existed in some form or another and always will. And, because of the special formlessness, even spookiness, of terrorism's hostile foreign referent in this case, it may be exceptionally difficult to get people to believe that the threat has really been extinguished—or at least that it no longer is particularly significant. Thus, public fear was stoked anew in 2014 with some beheadings of Americans by ISIS, a hostile and vicious group that had scarcely even been known to exist a year earlier. It is true that people did eventually cease to fear witches, the most spooky of adversaries, but the process took 200 years.

And, to the degree that the public remains terrorized, it seems likely to continue demanding that its leaders pay due deference to its insecurities. In the process the public will likely uncritically approve extravagant counterterrorism expenditures, including incessant security checks, civil liberties intrusions, and expanded police powers, as well as militarized forays overseas—if not necessarily full-scale ground assaults—if they can convincingly be associated with the quest to stamp out terrorists who might have America in their sights. Support for such policies, as Clem Brooks and Jeff Manza put it, "may become relatively enduring, persisting beyond the initial context in which political leaders offered their original justifications."[95]

Politicians, officials, and the media have routinely (and irresponsibly) played to and exacerbated these popular anxieties out of a sense of both duty and self-interest. But, as will be discussed more fully in this book's conclusion, the essential impetus is more nearly bottom-up than top-down.

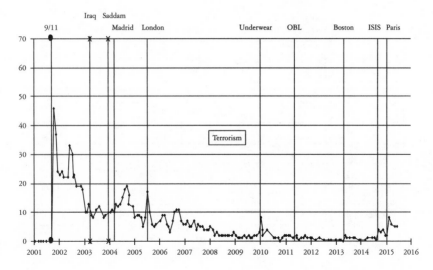

FIGURE 2-1 What do you think is the most important problem facing this country today?
Gallup

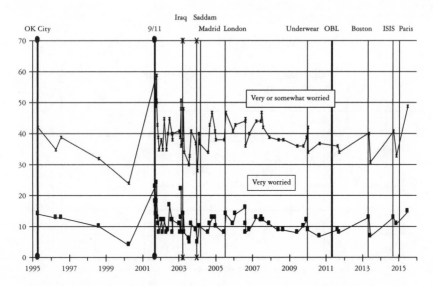

FIGURE 2-2 How worried are you that you or someone in your family will become a victim of terrorism? Very worried, somewhat worried, not too worried, or not worried at all?
USA Today/Gallup and CNN/Opinion Research Corporation

OK City:	Terrorist bombing in Oklahoma City	Underwear:	Underwear bomber
9/11:	Terrorist attacks of September 11	OBL:	Killing of Osama bin Laden
Iraq:	Beginning of the Iraq War	Boston:	Terrorist bombings at the Boston
Saddam:	Capture of Saddam Hussein		Marathon
Madrid:	Terrorist bombings in Madrid	ISIS:	First beheadings of Americans by ISIS
London:	Terrorist bombings in London	Paris:	Terrorist shootings in Paris

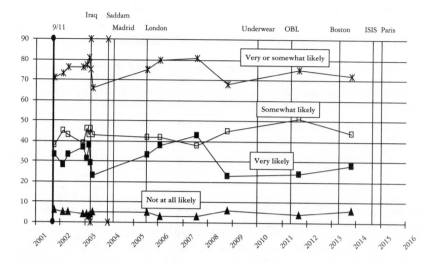

FIGURE 2-3 How likely do you think it is that another terrorist attack causing large numbers of American lives to be lost will happen in the near future? Very likely, somewhat likely, not very likely, or not likely at all?
Fox/Opinion Dynamics

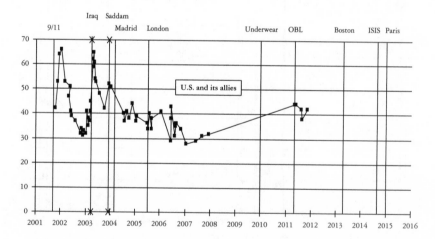

FIGURE 2-4 Who do you think is currently winning the war on terrorism? The U.S. and its allies, neither side, or the terrorists?
Gallup/CNN/*USA Today* and CBS/*New York Times*

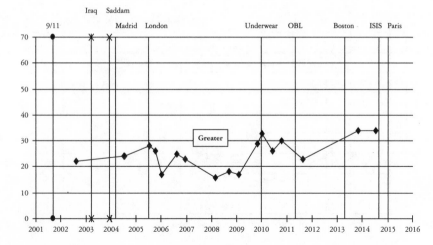

FIGURE 2-5 Overall, do you think the ability of terrorists to launch another major attack on the U.S. is greater, the same, or less than it was at the time of the September 11th terrorist attacks?
Pew

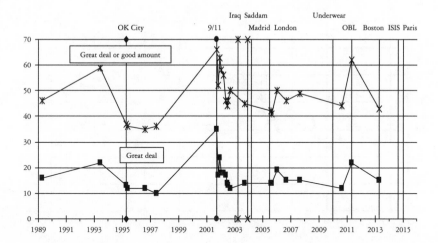

FIGURE 2-6 How much confidence do you have in the ability of the U.S. government to prevent further terrorist attacks against Americans in this country? A great deal, a good amount, only a fair amount, or none at all?
ABC/*Washington Post*

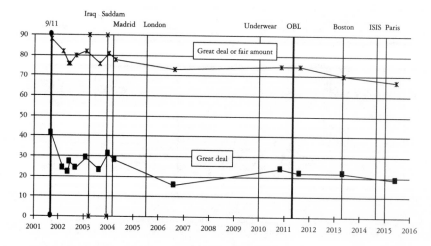

FIGURE 2-7 How much confidence do you have in the U.S. government to protect its citizens from future acts of terrorism? A great deal, a fair amount, not very much, or none at all?
Gallup

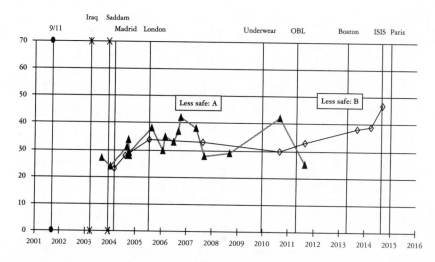

FIGURE 2-8 A: Compared to before September 11, 2001, do you think the country today is safer from terrorism or less safe from terrorism?
ABC/*Washington Post*

B: Do you think the United States is safer or less safe today than before 9/11?
Fox/Opinion Dynamics

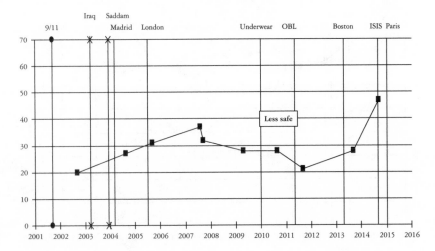

FIGURE 2-9 Do you think that as a country we are more safe, about as safe, or less safe than we were before September 11?
NBC/*Wall Street Journal*

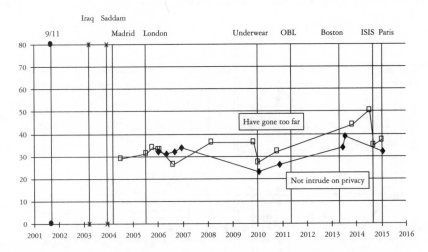

FIGURE 2-10 What concerns you more about the government's antiterrorism policies? That they have not gone far enough to adequately protect the country or that they have gone too far in restricting the average person's civil liberties?
Pew

What do you think is more important right now? For the federal government to investigate possible terrorist threats, even if that intrudes on personal privacy; or for the federal government not to intrude on personal privacy, even if that limits its ability to investigate possible terrorist threats?
Options rotated ABC/*Washington Post*

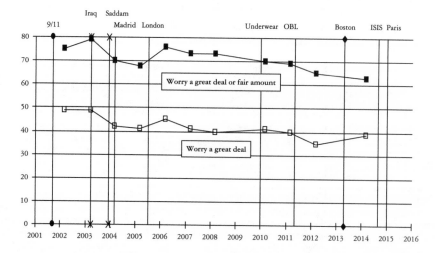

FIGURE 2-11 I'm going to read a list of problems facing the country. For each one, please tell me if you personally worry about this problem a great deal, a fair amount, only a little, or not at all. First, how much do you personally worry about [read in random order]: . . .

. . .The possibility of future terrorist attacks in the U.S. . . .
Gallup

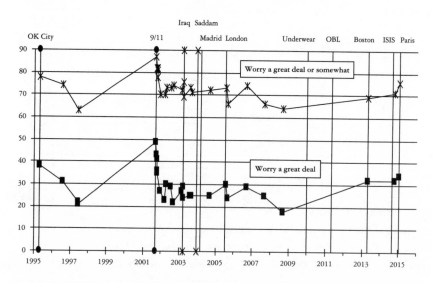

FIGURE 2-12 How concerned are you about the possibility that there will be more major terrorist attacks in the United States? Is that something that worries you a great deal, somewhat, not too much, or not at all?
ABC/*Washington Post*

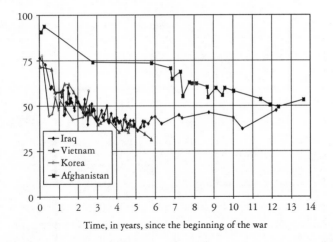

FIGURE 2-13 Percentage of those with an opinion thinking the wars were not a mistake.

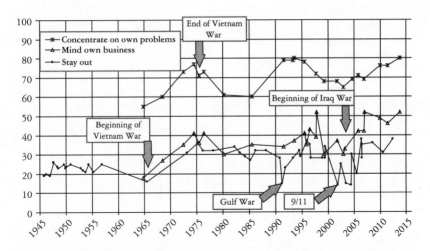

FIGURE 2-14 We shouldn't think so much in international terms but concentrate more on our own national problems and building up our strength and prosperity here at home.

The United States should mind its own business internationally and let other countries get along as best they can on their own.

Do you think it will be best for the future of this country if we take an active part in world affairs, or if we stayed out of world affairs?

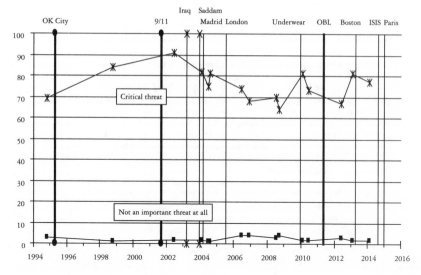

FIGURE 2-15 I am going to read you a list of possible threats to the vital interests of the United States in the next ten years. For each one, please tell me if you see this as a critical threat, an important but not critical threat, or not an important threat at all: . . . International terrorism . . .

Gallup/Worldviews/Globalviews/Chicago Council

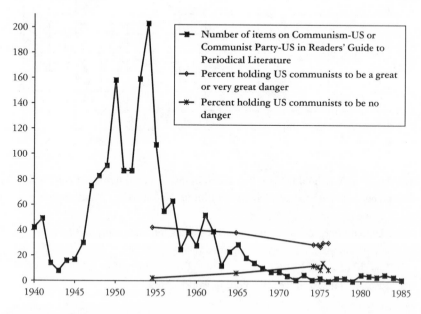

FIGURE 2-16 Domestic communism: press coverage and public fears, 1940–1985.

| Terrorism and the United States

O N NOVEMBER 22, 1963, Lee Harvey Oswald, a little man with grandiose visions of his own importance, managed, largely because of luck, to
assassinate President John F. Kennedy. For decades after that, many people
contended that such a monumental event could not have been accomplished by
such a trivial person—the proportions seemed all out of whack—and elaborate
efforts have been made to uncover a bigger conspiracy behind the deed.[1]

On September 11, 2001, a tiny group of men, members of al-Qaeda, a
fringe group of a fringe group with grandiose visions of its own importance,
managed, again largely because of luck, to pull off a risky, if clever and carefully planned, terrorist act that became by far the most destructive in history—scarcely any terrorist act before or since has visited even one-tenth as
much destruction, even in war zones where terrorist groups have space and
time to plot.[2] As with the assassination of President Kennedy, there has been
great reluctance to maintain that such a monumental event—however counterproductive to al-Qaeda's purpose—could have been carried out by a fundamentally trivial group, and there has been a consequent tendency to inflate
al-Qaeda's importance and effectiveness. At the extreme, as discussed in
chapter 1, the remnants of the group have even been held to present a threat
to the survival—to the very existence—of the United States or even of the
world system.

Finally, on May 1, 2012, nearly ten years after the September 2001 terrorist attacks, the most costly and determined manhunt in history culminated in Pakistan, when a U.S. Navy Seals high-tech hit squad killed
Osama bin Laden, a chief author of the attacks and one of history's most
storied and cartooned villains. Taken away with bin Laden's bullet-shattered

body, which was soon to be ceremoniously dumped at sea, were written documents and masses of information stored on five computers, ten hard drives, and one hundred or more thumb drives, DVDs, and CD-ROMs. This, it was promised, was a "treasure trove" of information about al-Qaeda—"the mother lode," said one U.S. official eagerly—that might contain plans for pending attacks.[3] And some terrorism specialists ominously and confidently predicted that "we can certainly expect acts of retribution, vengeance, frustration and punishment directed against the U.S. in the coming weeks and perhaps months," and "watch for more small strikes in the weeks and months ahead, launched around the world," even as former Senator Joseph Lieberman confidently predicted "an attack within the United States in the coming days or weeks."[4]

Poring through the material with great dispatch, however, a task force soon discovered that al-Qaeda's members were primarily occupied with dodging drone missile attacks, complaining about the lack of funds, and watching a lot of pornography.[5] And the predicted spate of revenge attacks never materialized. As Brian Jenkins puts it, the killing of bin Laden "produced plenty of bellicose rhetoric, but no explosions of violence."[6]

Except for the pornography, it proved to be a Wizard of Oz moment. However, although the mysterious and much quested-after bin Laden has been exposed mostly as a thing of smoke and mirrors, and is now as dead as the wicked witch, and although al-Qaeda has never been able to do much of anything again in the United States, the terrorism/counterterrorism saga persists determinedly and doggedly onward. As discussed in the previous two chapters, both American officials and public opinion continue to profess fear of another attack, and funds therefore continue to be expended massively to protect the country and to chase ghosts, all in the name of the fabled tragedy of 9/11. To say the least, there has been no closure.[7]

This chapter and the next assess the terrorist threat that American officials and the American public are so worried about and are spending so much money and effort to counter. This chapter assesses the characteristics and the capabilities of those Islamist terrorists who seek, or seem to seek, to do damage within the United States—people who constitute (or generate) the chief terrorism fear for Americans, people who the ghost-chasers and their confederates often portentously label the "universal adversary."[8]

It begins by looking at the sixty-two cases that been disclosed since 9/11 in which Islamist terrorists or would-be terrorists, whether based abroad or within the United States, have targeted, or apparently have targeted, the United States itself. Capsule summaries of each case are arrayed in appendix A. We then assess the threat actually or potentially presented by terrorists whose exploits or potential exploits have *not* been disclosed. These include those whose efforts have allegedly been disrupted without being made public; those who are suspected of harboring terrorist intentions but who have been arrested only on minor charges; and those who may thus far have been deterred by security measures or other concerns from actually committing terrorist violence.

The next chapter expands the focus to look more generally at the threat presented by Islamist terrorist groups throughout the world, including the Islamic State group, or ISIS, that exploded into notice in 2014. It also includes an examination of those international terrorist "masterminds" whose exploits and capacities, like those of the less masterly terrorism foot soldiers discussed in this chapter, seem to have been substantially exaggerated.

The Disclosed Terrorist Adversary

As noted in chapter 1, the Department of Homeland Security officials who put together a 2009 Department of Homeland Security report generally describe terrorists with adjectives like relentless, patient, opportunistic, flexible, while Kip Hawley adds innovative and *quick-moving.* Some of these words may apply to some terrorists somewhere, including at least a few of those involved in the September 11 attacks. However, they hardly apply to the vast majority of those individuals picked up on terrorism charges in the United States since those attacks.

The authors of the case studies of terrorists or would-be terrorists who were, or seemed to be, focusing on committing damage in the United States (as listed in appendix A) were specifically asked to explain what the nature of the terrorist "adversary" in their case was like. There were cases in which words like *determination, persistence, relentless, patient, opportunistic,* and *flexible,* and maybe even *quick-moving* were appropriate. As noted in chapter 1, however, far more common were words like *incompetent, ineffective, unintelligent, idiotic, ignorant, inadequate, unorganized, misguided, muddled, amateurish, dopey, unrealistic, moronic, irrational,* and *foolish.*[10] And for just about all of the cases where an FBI informant was plying his often well-compensated trade (case type 3, in appendix A), the most appropriate descriptor would be *gullible.*

In many instances, however, it may perhaps be a bit better to view the perpetrators or would-be perpetrators not so much as stupid or foolish as underdeveloped or incompetent or emotionally inadequate. Regardless, it seems that Jenkins has aptly summarized the overall situation when he concludes, "their numbers remain small, their determination limp, and their competence poor."[11]

Evidence concerning the capabilities of the vast majority of the disclosed terrorists will be on display throughout this chapter. In case after case, few seem incapable of doing much damage on their own. The conclusion of the judge in the Bronx Synagogues case of 2009 could be applied to a great many—though not all—participants in the other cases: she found them "utterly inept" and on a "fantasy terror operation," led by a man "whose buffoonery is positively Shakespearean in its scope."[12]

In all, as Shikha Dalmia has put it, to be effective, would-be terrorists need to be "radicalized enough to die for their cause; Westernized enough to move around without raising red flags; ingenious enough to exploit loopholes in the security apparatus; meticulous enough to attend to the myriad logistical details that could torpedo the operation; self-sufficient enough to make all the preparations without enlisting outsiders who might give them away; disciplined enough to maintain complete secrecy, and—above all—psychologically tough enough to keep functioning at a high level without cracking in the face of their own impending death."[13] The case studies certainly do not abound with people like that.

Suggestive of their capacities is the rather impressive inability of the terrorists in these cases to create and set off a bomb. In many instances, the only explosive on the scene was a fake one supplied by the FBI, and it is clear that many would-be terrorists generally lacked the capacity to create or acquire one on their own.[14] When they did try to create a bomb after extensive training abroad or were actually given one by a terrorist group abroad (cases to be examined more fully later), the plot was disrupted or the bomb failed.[15] As a result, the only method by which Islamist terrorists managed to kill anyone in the United States in the decade after 9/11 was through the firing of guns—in the El-Al case of 2002 and the Little Rock and Fort Hood cases of 2009.[16] Finally, in 2013, the Boston Marathon terrorists did manage to set off a pair of crude homemade bombs, killing three in a crowded area and bringing the total number of people killed by terrorists in the United States since 9/11 to nineteen, or less than two per year.[17]

This inability to fabricate bombs is impressive because, as discussed in chapter 2, small-scale terrorists in the United States in the past have been able to set off quite a few of them. As that discussion documents, terrorists in the United States (as well, of course, as those in other places in the developed world, like Northern Ireland, Great Britain, and Spain) have been fully able to create and set off bombs. Yet until 2013, no Islamist extremist terrorist was able to do so in the United States.

In principle, an improvised explosive device, or IED, is relatively simple to design and manufacture if done by well-trained personnel and results in reliabilities in excess of 90 percent.[18] However, analysis of the Global Terrorism Database shows that the probability that an IED will inflict damage is only 19 percent for terrorists in Western countries, where there is less opportunity for IED operational skills to be acquired. By contrast, the probability that a terrorist or insurgent IED attack will be successful is more than three times higher in the Middle East.[19] Kip Hawley notes that even world-class laboratories are able to get the explosive mixture right only one time in three when making hydrogen peroxide bombs.[20] This difficulty may help explain why no terrorist (however innovative, adaptive, masterly, and quick moving) has been able successfully to detonate a bomb of that sort in the United States since 2001, and why, except for the four bombs set off in London in 2005, neither has any in the United Kingdom. The low success rate in the West may explain why plotters there prefer either to source the explosives, detonators, and triggering mechanism from third parties, a process that increases the odds of detection, or else to try less ambitious attacks. And it may also explain why they are so grateful for assistance from FBI operatives posing as like-minded terrorists.

GOALS

The authors of the case studies did not characteristically have difficulty sorting out what chiefly motivated their subjects to proceed along the path to terrorist violence, nor was it usually difficult to describe their apparent plans and methods for committing violence—though for many there was a notable disconnect, sometimes even a preposterous one, between plans and capabilities.

Far more elusive was tying down what the would-be terrorists thought they would accomplish by their acts. Beyond expressing outrage (generally, as discussed in chapter 1, about American foreign and military policy), the actions very often seemed to have no purpose—that is, no goal—whatever. In a few cases, such as ones in Springfield, Illinois, in 2009 and Seattle, Washington, in 2011, they muttered something about how their acts might somehow be the "first domino" in an Islamic revolution or "wake the Muslims up," but the process by which this would come about characteristically went utterly unexamined.

TARGETING

After devoting two sentences in its description of "the nature of terrorist adversary" to an almost absurdly one-sided assessment of that nature, the 2009

DHS report concludes its discussion by shifting course and spinning out several sentences on terrorist targets:

> Analysis of terrorist goals and motivations points to domestic and international CIKR [critical infrastructure and key resources] as potentially prime targets for terrorist attacks. As security measures around more predictable targets increase, terrorists are likely to shift their focus to less protected targets. Enhancing countermeasures to address any one terrorist tactic or target may increase the likelihood that terrorists will shift to another, which underscores the necessity for a balanced, comparative approach that focuses on managing risk commensurately across all sectors and scenarios of concern. Terrorist organizations have shown an understanding of the potential consequences of carefully planned attacks on economic, transportation, and symbolic targets, both within the United States and abroad. Future terrorist attacks against CIKR located inside the United States and those located abroad could seriously threaten national security, result in mass casualties, weaken the economy, and damage public morale and confidence.[21]

The concepts of "critical infrastructure" and "key resources" do not seem to be completely felicitous ones. Applying commonsense English about what "critical infrastructure" could be taken to mean, it should be an empty category. If any element in the infrastructure is truly "critical" to the operation of the country, steps should be taken immediately to provide redundancies or backup systems so that it is no longer so. An official definition designates "critical infrastructure" to include "the assets, systems, and networks, whether physical or virtual, so vital to the United States that their incapacitation or destruction would have a debilitating effect on security, national economic security, public health or safety, or any combination thereof."[22] Yet vast sums of money are spent to protect elements of the infrastructure whose incapacitation would scarcely be "debilitating" and would at most impose minor inconvenience and quite limited costs.

And the same essentially holds for what DHS designates as "key resources." These are defined to be those that are "essential to the minimal operations of the economy or government."[23] It is difficult to imagine what a terrorist group armed with anything less than a massive thermonuclear arsenal could do to hamper such "minimal operations." The terrorist attacks of 9/11 were by far the most damaging in history, yet even though several major commercial buildings were demolished, both the economy and government continued to function at considerably above the "minimal" level.[24]

But the observation in the report that improving security at one target "may increase the likelihood that terrorists will shift to another" is certainly an apt one.[25] And in at least some of the cases examined the terrorists were indeed "opportunistic" in that they did seek out targets that are relatively easy to attack—though it is not clear that they usually gave it a great deal of thought.

However, in many of the cases it is a great stretch to suggest that any plotters showed much "understanding of the potential consequences of carefully planned attacks on economic, transportation, and symbolic targets," or that they could "seriously threaten national security, result in mass casualties, weaken the economy, and damage public morale and confidence." To be sure, some of them did harbor visions of toppling large buildings, destroying airports, setting off dirty bombs, or bringing down the Brooklyn Bridge.[26] However, these were nothing more than wild fantasies, far beyond their capacities, however much they may have been encouraged in some instances by FBI operatives.

Moreover, in many cases, target selection is effectively a random process, not one worked out with guile and careful planning. Often, it seems, targets have been chosen almost capriciously and simply for their convenience.[27] Thus, a would-be bomber targeted a mall in Rockford, Illinois, in 2006 because it was nearby. Terrorist plotters from the "JIS" cult in Los Angeles in 2005 drew up a list of targets that were all within a twenty-mile radius of their shared apartment, some of which didn't exist. And one of the Boston Marathon bombers of 2013 lived within three miles of the attack. Or there was the terrorist who, after several failed efforts, went home and, with no plan at all, shot at a military recruiting center three miles from his apartment.

As discussed in chapter 1, terrorist motivation seems mainly to arise from hostility to American foreign and military policy abroad, and not from some sort of broader philosophy or coherent ideology. Accordingly, military installations and personnel within the country were fairly common targets, even though they are not very good ones if one is seeking to do maximum damage and to inflict maximum shock. The easiest military targets to find are recruitment centers within cities, and would-be terrorists have frequently plotted to attack them.[28] As it happens, fourteen of the nineteen deaths caused by Islamist extremists since 9/11 were inflicted on or at military installations—and only one of the victims was a civilian.[29]

SUICIDE

Although there was sometimes talk of "martyrdom" or of a willingness to "die for jihad," and although all the people examined in the cases certainly knew they were following a path that entailed considerable danger, in only five cases was the plot clearly suicidal.[30] Moreover, two of these—the shoe and underwear bombers of 2001 and 2009—were hatched and carried out by foreigners. The suicidal plots from within included Zazi and his friends in 2009, who had been trained and motivated in an overseas camp. They apparently intended to die in the explosions they were planning to set off in New York City subway stations. There were also stings in which would-be terrorists sought to blow themselves up at the Capitol Building in 2012, the Federal Reserve Bank in 2012, the Wichita airport in 2013, and Fort Riley in 2015. With one exception, all the other plots involved remote-controlled explosions (mostly in the FBI stings) or shootings followed by hasty, if inadequately planned getaways. The exception is a case in Seattle in 2011, in which the plotters appear to have anticipated that they might well be "going down" in the process of shooting up a military recruiting center.

PRISON RADICALIZATION

Despite quite a bit of alarmed commentary to the contrary, prisons do not seem to have been hotbeds of recruitment. Very often prisoners do shop for religion as a way to get their lives back in order, and Islam has long had its attractions. But the vast majority of people who convert to Islam in prison do not become violent extremists. And for the few who do, it is not at all clear that the prison experience was a necessary part of their journey—they probably would have found that destiny in some other way.

As a Congressional Research Service report concludes about what it calls "jailhouse jihadism," the "threat emanating from prisons does not seem as substantial as some experts may fear."[31] And a criminologist who has intensely studied the issue both in the United States and abroad says he's found "spectacularly few" instances in which an inmate was led toward terrorism while in prison.[32]

THE SEDUCTIVE CLEVERNESS OF INSIDE OPERATIVES

Marc Sageman observes that in many cases abroad, the move toward terrorist violence was facilitated by an older man who took motivated and impressionable younger men and channeled their emotions.[33] There is an interesting parallel with many of the seducing FBI and police operatives in the American cases. These men have often been considerably older than their charges, and they are, almost by definition, smooth talkers—indeed, con artists. Over weeks or months, these men in many cases showered flattering attention on essentially trivial, insecure, inadequate, and unformed young men who had previously never really been taken seriously by anyone.[34]

The intellectual agility of some informants is seen in a case in Baltimore in 2010. When the would-be terrorist, Martinez, told the FBI informant that he was unsure about another undercover FBI agent working on the case, the informant cleverly told him that the other man had expressed his own doubts about Martinez and was thinking of canceling their operation. This agile ploy reassured Martinez. In the Sears Tower case of 2006, the inventive informant used for his purposes a fortuitous message to the world by Osama bin Laden. The statement said in part, "As for the delay in carrying out similar operations in America, this was not due to failure to breach your security measures. Operations are under preparation, and you will see them on your own ground once they are finished, God willing."[35] To nudge his often-recalcitrant buddies along, the informant flatteringly told them bin Laden was talking about them.[36]

Overall, the role of the informant is a delicate one. Informants are usually dealing with people who are at least contemplating murder, and a suspicion that there is a traitor in the plot could be dangerous—or, as in the Sears Tower case, cause the case to break apart. In addition, an empathetic friendship may sometimes develop during the weeks or months in which the informant is at work. In 2012, the informant was reported to have wept when he drove his friend, who was determined to end his life in a symbolic bombing of the Federal Reserve Bank, to his final rendezvous as a free man.[37]

SECURITY CAMERAS

Although a great deal of money has been spent on security cameras since (and before) 9/11, they appear to have been relevant only in the Boston Marathon case of 2013, where they facilitated the identification of the perpetrators, though they obviously did not prevent the bombings.[38] Police did look at what had been recorded in Times Square after a bombing attempt was made there in 2010, but information from the cameras does not seem to have been used in, or necessary for, affecting the arrest of the perpetrator.

ROLE OF THE INTERNET

Using the Internet may sometimes facilitate terrorism, but it scarcely appears to be required. In particular, it does not seem to be necessary for the process of stoking outrage at American foreign and military policy. For the most part, any stoking stems from information readily available in the evening news: the invasion of Iraq, abuse of Iraqi prisoners at Abu Ghraib, torture by the CIA, "collateral" damage from American air and drone strikes, the mounting body count in Iraq and Afghanistan, instances of American troop abuse of Muslim civilians, and Israeli bombings of Lebanon and Gaza.[39]

The people in many of the cases did go to the Internet for further information, and they frequently sought out the most radical sites of which there are a large number.[40] For example, as they searched for information congenial to their proclivities, several of the plotters in the cases were impressed by the works of the Yemen-based radical American cleric Anwar al-Awlaki. However, as Marc Sageman notes, such web searches "merely reinforce already made-up minds."[41] Indeed, for the most part the process simply supplied information that in earlier days might have been furnished by incendiary paper pamphlets—a relatively minor change. It is the message that is vital, not the medium for delivering it.

In many of the cases, the Internet helped plot participants communicate with each other, mainly through email. However, in the American cases, the bulk of the communication—and the most important—was face-to-face.

For the most part, the Internet played only a limited, or even perverse, role in plotting terrorism. There are many cases in which the would-be perpetrator used chat rooms or Facebook or Twitter to seek out like-minded souls and potential collaborators—and usually simply got connected to the FBI.[42]

The Internet could be useful in obtaining information about potential targets and other aspects of the plots. Except for the Boston Marathon terrorists in 2013, however, it clearly didn't convey enough information to build a successful bomb because none of the people in the other cases were able to do so—though one potential perpetrator in Texas in 2011 seemed to think he had acquired the relevant knowledge.

The popular notion that the Internet can be effective in providing useful operational information, particularly about making bombs, thus seems to be severely flawed. In one study, for example, Michael Kenney notes that the Internet is filled with misinformation and error and that it is no substitute for direct, on-the-ground training and experience.[43] Anne Stenersen is similarly unimpressed: the Internet manuals she has examined are filled with materials hastily assembled and "randomly put together," and contain information that is often "far-fetched" or "utter nonsense."[44]

Moreover, as David Benson points out, even if the information is valid, "it does not necessarily follow that one can actually carry out the task." Interaction with an instructor is often necessary. Thus, many are unable to prepare food correctly from Internet instructions, "let alone master gourmet cooking." No one seems to be contending that surgeons, arc-welders, explosives technicians, or combat soldiers be trained entirely from the web. And unlike failure at fudge-making, failure at explosive-making carries considerable danger.[45]

In addition, notes political scientist Louis Klarevas, "sophisticated explosives are nearly impossible to manufacture in the United States as the necessary precursor chemicals are not available to the general public." Would-be bombers incapable of getting around these restrictions need, then, to pursue simpler explosives like pipe bombs, which are, continues Klarevas, "least likely to inflict mass casualties."[46]

In at least two cases, including the Boston Marathon one in 2013 and the one involving the hapless, zombie-like Jose Pimentel in 2011, the terrorists were working from an article published in the Summer 2010 issue of *Inspire*, an English-language online "periodical magazine" issued by the al-Qaeda organization in Yemen. The article was written by someone calling himself "the AQ Chef" and is entitled "Make a Bomb in the Kitchen of Your Mom." The clumsy title is rendered in white lettering on a dark gray background in the magazine, but the words *bomb* and *Mom* are in light blue, presumably in an effort to highlight the author's cleverness at rhyme to his less perceptive, or more humorless, readers.

In the *Inspire* article, AQ Chef instructs the would-be bomber to paste nails to the outside of a pipe elbow joint, fill it with a mixture of crushed match heads and sugar, and then detonate it through a drilled hole with a contraption consisting of a broken Christmas tree light, a bit of wire, a small battery, and a clock with a nail pounded into its face. Although AQ Chef does note that one could use gunpowder extracted from "cartilages" rather than crushed match heads for the core "inflammable substance," he mainly focuses on the match head approach and suggests that eighty match heads per bomb would do the trick.

As Klarevas points out, however, experiments on the Discovery Channel's *Mythbusters* program indicate that AQ Chef was rather off the mark.[47] The television hosts first tried setting off 30,000 match heads in a bucket and did produce a colorful flameout, but no explosion, and the bucket emerged from the experiment singed but whole. They tried again with a million match heads, and got a flameout perhaps three times as impressive. The collected match heads in either experiment were far too voluminous to fit inside a standard pipe elbow joint.

In the day between the arrest of Pimentel and the press conference touting his arrest, the New York Police Department put together three pipe bombs of the sort he was striving to create. Presumably, they used gunpowder rather than match scrapings, and they detonated the three bombs *simultaneously*—a feat he was unlikely to be able to do—in a small four-door Mazda. A video recording of this effort was shown at the start of the press conference.[48] As Klarevas puts it, the explosion and fire shown in the video would probably have proved fatal to anyone who was sitting in the car and possibly to anyone who was standing outside very close to it. The limit of such bombs is suggested by the fact that two of them set off in a crowd at the Boston Marathon killed but three people. It would be quite possible and far easier, notes Klarevas, to kill more people with a single handgun.

For the most part, then, al-Qaeda's virtual army in the United States has, as Jenkins puts it, remained exactly that: virtual. "Talking about jihad, boasting of what one will do, and offering diabolical schemes egging each other on is usually as far as it goes." This "may provide psychological satisfaction" and "win accolades from other pretend warriors, but it is primarily an outlet for verbal expression, not an anteroom to violence."[49] To the degree that this has been done on the Internet, it seems mainly to have attracted the attention of the FBI. On balance, it appears that the Internet has mainly benefited the authorities.

THE AUTHORSHIP OF THE 9/11 ATTACKS

The belief is common around the world, especially within the Islamic world, that the 9/11 attacks were actually carried out by the U.S. government, Israeli intelligence, or both. However, with perhaps one or two exceptions, the terrorists or proto-terrorists populating the disclosed American cases accept that al-Qaeda was the source of the attack—some, in fact, are quite proud of the achievement. A blowhard Islamist bragged gleefully on Facebook (his favored medium) in 2010 about how "we" had "dropped the twin towers."

WMD AND CYBERTERRORISM

If the miscreants discussed in this book were generally unable by themselves to create and set off even the most simple conventional bombs, it stands to reason that none of them were very close to creating, or having anything to do with, nuclear, biological, radiological, or chemical weapons. In fact, with one exception, none ever even seems to have dreamed of the prospect. The exception is a former street thug, Jose Padilla, who apparently mused at one point before he was arrested in 2002 about creating a dirty bomb—a device that would disperse radiation—or even possibly an atomic one. As noted in chapter 1, his idea about isotope separation was to put uranium into a pail and then make himself into a human centrifuge by swinging the pail around in great arcs.

The same goes for the increasingly popular concerns about cyberterrorism.[50] As noted, many of the would-be terrorists in the case studies used the Internet for communication and to gather information, but none showed much ability at, or interest in, committing cyberterrorism—or even of being able to spell it.

CONNECTIONS BETWEEN THE CASES

There are few connections between the cases. Though often inspired by the violent jihadist movement, almost all were essentially planned in isolation from the others.[51]

The few interrelations are generally quite tenuous. The subjects in a couple of cases may have bumped up against each other in a mosque in Columbus, Ohio.[52] And there are some interconnections between the potential terrorists in a couple of others.[53] In addition, two of the plots were serviced by the same informant, and two of them have had, or appear to have had, some connections to the radical American cleric Anwar al-Awlaki, who hid out in Yemen from 2002 until his death by drone in 2011.[54] Several more were impressed by his writings—especially Pimentel in 2011.

RECRUITMENT

Although there are instances of tactical manipulation by informants, there do not seem to be very many instances of ideological manipulation by Muslim extremists. In almost all cases, potential terrorists were self-motivated—or, if you will, "self-radicalized." They sometimes sought out ever more radical companions, but their path was primarily chosen by themselves. A vivid instance in point is the case of Bryant Neal Vinas, who was arrested in 2008.

DIRECT RECRUITMENT BY AL-QAEDA WITHIN THE UNITED STATES

Although some Americans, on their own volition, have gone abroad to seek to join al-Qaeda, the organization has had almost no luck directly recruiting Americans in the United States.

In the early days, even before 9/11, there was some effort specifically to send recruiters to the United States to sign people up. The only instance of this in the case studies is the Lackawanna experience, when a smooth-talking al-Qaeda operative returned to an upstate New York town in early 2000 and tried to convert young Yemeni American men to join the cause. In the summer of 2001, seven agreed to go to an al-Qaeda training camp with him, and several more were apparently planning to go later. However, appalled at what they found there, six of the seven returned home and helped to waylay the plans of the next contingent. The total gain to al-Qaeda from this enterprise, then, was one man—who is apparently now in a Yemeni jail as his captors squabble over the reward money they will receive if they turn him over to the United States.

As Sageman notes, al-Qaeda generally does not have a top-down recruitment program.[55] It is possible that this early failure contributed to that policy.

INFILTRATION FROM CANADA AND MEXICO

Since 9/11, quite a bit of effort has been made to shore up the border with Mexico. Much of this, of course, has been to deal with illegal migration by people who want to work in the United States, or with those who want to bring in drugs that would then be willingly purchased by Americans. However, the counterterrorism quest has supplied an additional impetus. Crossing points with Canada have been tightened, and a costly requirement that Americans have passports to enter and return from Canada has been instituted.[56]

There is no evidence in any of the disclosed cases that this has been relevant. There has been some acceptance of the notion that all a terrorist has to do is arrive in Mexico, change his name to Mohammed Gonzales, and find a coyote to smuggle him into the United States. As Sageman points out, however, the foreign interloper will stand out in the crowd and his coyote is likely to report him to the border control to protect his smuggling business—or perhaps even to collect a reward.[57]

However, in a 2005 case, an American offered in a chat room to go to Canada to blow up pipelines to aid al-Qaeda, so it is perhaps the Canadians who should be alarmed. The primary danger for Canada, however, is not threats to their pipelines, but hysteria in the United States that could lead to a closing of the border, something that would be exceedingly costly to the United States, but an utter catastrophe for Canada.

OVERSEAS CONNECTIONS

For quite some time after 9/11—especially during the early years when it was thought that there were many sleeper cells in the country—authorities worried intensely that open messages sent by al-Qaeda Central might include coded signals to its operatives.[58] The worry, it turns out, was not required.

Four of the American-based cases in the early days did involve people who had had pre-9/11 connections to al-Qaeda, though none of these developed into much of anything that could be called a plot.[59]

In addition, there are a few instances in which Americans ventured abroad seeking to fight or to obtain training, and then were persuaded, or persuaded themselves, to return to the United States to inflict damage. These instances of "returnees" were discussed at length in chapter 1. As noted there, in total such returnees have been responsible for one terrorism death in the United States—and that was by someone who had failed in his quest to get training.

Almost all of the cases under consideration and arrayed in appendix A concern terrorists or would-be terrorists, whether based in the United States or abroad, who seek to do damage within the United States. There are, however, roughly a similar number of cases in which individuals have been waylaid for seeking to provide material support for terrorist groups abroad or to leave the United States to do damage to American interests overseas, including fighting against the American military in Iraq or Afghanistan.

One such effort is discussed in the Toledo case of 2006. Mostly it shows the difficulty would-be violent jihadists face. Despite several efforts, they were never able to find out how to join the fray overseas. This seems to be a fairly common problem. Indeed, it appears that the culprit in the Oregon case of 2010 initially wanted to go abroad to fight, but was unable to find out how to do so; only then did he turn his attention to domestic targets. The same phenomenon is found in the New York Stock Exchange episode of 2010, which is discussed at some length in chapter 7.

Although the FBI does expend a great deal of effort to deal with such cases, it is not particularly clear how a bit of money or an occasional American interloper would be of much benefit to anti-American combat forces in the Middle East.[60] This is surely so for the Taliban in Afghanistan, for ISIS in Syria and Iraq, and for al-Shabaab in Somalia, each of which has tens of thousands of combatants and military adherents already. At any rate, any resulting damage would, of course, occur abroad, and these cases are accordingly not included in the discussion here.

PLOTS HATCHED ABROAD, AIMED AT
THE UNITED STATES

Of the cases of threatened potential terrorist harm to the United States listed in appendix A, several were put together abroad by foreigners, or by foreigners working with Americans. Some of these had at least some direction from al-Qaeda or similar overseas groups. None resulted in any deaths.

Two of these cases involved efforts by foreigners to take down airliners traveling to the United States from Europe, with explosives implanted, in 2001, in the terrorist's shoes and, in 2009, his underwear. Both received overseas training (two years, in the case of the shoe bomber), each from a person who has been described in the media as a "master bomb maker." But each failed miserably in his mission.

Six other cases involved plots on the United States that were foiled abroad.

In 2003, a man who had been living in Baltimore, named Majid Khan, conspired with al-Qaeda to blow up some gas stations in the United States. However, he couldn't get back to the country because his visa had expired. In short order, all the participants were arrested. This case is discussed more fully in the next chapter.

Something similar happened with an American, Bryant Neal Vinas, who had managed to be accepted by al-Qaeda. In 2008, he was arrested abroad.

A group led by Dhiren Barot, apparently linked to al-Qaeda, worked in London until information surfaced in Pakistan in July 2004 that led to their arrests. They were planning to launch hugely destructive terrorist attacks on American financial buildings, probably by driving limousines full of explosives next to them or into their underground parking areas, and then setting them off. Curiously, even though not under surveillance by police or by informants, they seem never to have done anything about their dramatic plot except scout the buildings. An actual attack was never remotely imminent—indeed, the execution was never considered. In particular, during years of work they seem to have done nothing whatever about amassing the requisite operatives in the United States, and they do not seem ever to have explored the difficult issue of obtaining large amounts of explosives, nor to have considered in detail the likely effect of an explosion. Finally, no one in the group seems to have had any real expertise with explosives, a concern absolutely vital, obviously, to the successful carrying out of the grand plan. One analyst speculates that they temporarily shelved their plans because they were busy basking in the success of 9/11. But if their goal was to damage the American economy and spread terror, a quick sequel to 9/11 would seem to have been highly desirable from their point of view. Moreover, the longer they waited, the more likely the police would uncover the plot—which, in fact, is exactly what happened.

Then there is the case of a deeply religious, drug-addicted professor of economics at the Lebanese International University in Beirut (he taught business ethics and human resources), age twenty-eight, who plotted with seven people he met in virtual space to go to Canada, obtain explosives, and then journey south to set them off on a PATH commuter train as it traveled in a tunnel under the Hudson River to New York City. The conspirators never actually met in person, and while they were able to Google information on the tunnels in New York, none of them ever made it into the country to have a look at one in three dimensions. By 2005, the FBI had uncovered the plot—and possibly participated in it. It tipped the Lebanese police, and the professor was arrested in 2006. After twenty-six months in solitary confinement, he was released and then, on television, he denied all the charges against him. In 2012, he was convicted and sentenced to time served. As it happens, it was in the Lebanese government's interest at the time to curry favor with the United States by foiling a terrorism case, because Lebanon was seeking to gain leverage over Syria and Syria's Lebanese allies. The lead FBI official explained that the conspirators were "about to go into a phase" in which they would "attempt" to surveil the target, figure out "a regimen of attack," and acquire explosives. It was, he said, "the real deal." Other officials, however, anonymously suggested to reporters that the plot was essentially "aspirational" and characterized by "jihadi bravado." But, as one put it, "Somebody talks about tunnels, it lights people up." And, indeed, New York was quick to see the light: it immediately used the disclosure to try to get more funding from the federal government.[61]

There was also a plot in London to set off bombs more or less simultaneously on transatlantic airliners headed from Heathrow Airport to the United States. However, the group was under constant and extensive police surveillance throughout, including all their international communications that they foolishly continued to use. Accordingly, the plot could be closed down at any time, and the London police did so in 2006. The commonly promulgated view that the plot was "nearly successful" is assessed at some length in chapter 1.

And the sixth plot was the failed 2010 effort by the al-Qaeda affiliate in Yemen to blow up cargo planes headed from Yemen to Chicago, with bombs shipped within printer cartridges—making them difficult to detect but also difficult to detonate. The plot was disrupted by detailed information supplied by a member of the group who was either an informant for Saudi intelligence or a group member who had defected to the Saudi side. Putting the best face on the failure, the group later gloated that the caper cost them only $4,200 while causing airline security costs for their enemy to escalate by billions, and they inserted a copy of Charles Dickens' novel *Great Expectations* because the organization was "very optimistic" about the operation's success.[62] They also promised to "continue to strike blows against American interests and the interest of America's allies" and unveiled what they called a "strategy of a thousand cuts" with which they would "bleed the enemy to death."[63] The optimism, and thus far the promises, have gone unfulfilled. They did try again in 2012, but that effort also failed owing to the work of a Saudi agent on the inside. It is also not clear that bombing a cargo plane has all that much impact from the terrorists' perspective, as the bomb would kill few people.

The only plot hatched abroad that resulted in a real physical terrorist effort within the United States concerns that of Najibullah Zazi and his friends in 2009. As discussed at some length in chapter 1, the plotters bumbled at several levels and their efforts were rather quickly closed down.

There remains one final plot hatched abroad that is so bizarre it can scarcely be classified. In 2011, a sixty-six-year-old Iranian American with little ideological bent (he was mainly interested in expensive cars, alcohol, and women) found himself at the center of an Iran-inspired conspiracy to assassinate the Saudi Arabian ambassador in a Washington, D.C., restaurant. The man, who earned the name "Scarface" after he was knifed in the face in a Texas barroom brawl thirty years earlier, was quite possibly the least likely participant in a conspiracy. A repeated failure in business, he was friendly, but hopelessly unreliable and absent-minded, according to people who knew him. "His socks would not match," said one, and "he was always losing his keys and cellphone." He did, however, have a cousin who was a general in Iran and who offered the failed Texas businessman $1.5 million to arrange for the violent death of the Saudi ambassador in Washington. The idea was to hire gangsters in a Mexican drug cartel to carry out the deed. Scarface asked a woman he had once sold a car to whether she knew anyone who was familiar with explosives, and she referred him to one of her relatives, a member of such a cartel who also happened, as it turned out, to be an informant for the U.S. Drug Enforcement Agency. The two plotted for a while, and Scarface was able to get $100,000 wired to the presumed assassin as earnest money. It remains unknown how far up, if at all, the plot went in the Iranian hierarchy, and any foreign conspirators remain at large, and quiet, in Iran.

The Undisclosed Terrorist Adversary

The discussion thus far has dealt with an assessment of Islamist extremist terrorism, whether based in the United States or abroad, that has been directed at, or apparently directed at, doing damage within the United States since 9/11 and that has been disclosed on the public record. In general, any terrorist threat from these cases appears to be quite limited. However, there may be danger from others whose exploits have not been reported, who have been arrested but not as terrorism plotters, whose cases have been dropped, or who have thus far been deterred from attacking.

It is frequently argued by official ghost-chasers that many terrorist plots out there have been thwarted in addition to the ones that have entered the public record like those listed in appendix A. However, it is said, information about these cases cannot be disclosed for various reasons. In working on an extensive report about how U.S. intelligence efforts (and budgets) were massively increased after September 11, the *Washington Post*'s Dana Priest says that she frequently heard this claim. In response, she says she "asked them to share with us anything they could, plots that were foiled that we could put in the paper because we didn't have many examples. We said give us things, just in generalities." But "we didn't receive anything back."[64]

That such claims may be inflated is further suggested by the fact that when a terrorist plot has been uncovered, policing agencies generally seem to have been anything but tight-lipped about their accomplishments, instead parading their deeds and often, as noted in chapter 1, exaggerating the importance and the potential destructiveness of the threats presented by those detained.

Also relevant may be the effect of the "Threat Matrix" discussed at length in chapter 1. Huge numbers of leads are paraded daily before top decision makers and others, and it could well be this experience, or varieties of it at various levels, that has inspired the spooky and unsubstantiated claims like the ones Dana Priest often heard.

In addition, if undisclosed plotters have been so able and so determined to commit violence, and if there are so many of them, why have they committed so little of it before being waylaid? And why were there so few plots in the months and years following 9/11, before enhanced security measures could be effectively deployed? Policing efforts were massively increased after 9/11, and any sensible terrorist accordingly should have wanted to act as quickly as possible before being detected.

It may also be useful to point out that we have heard this story before. As discussed in the introduction, officials for decades exaggerated the degree to which domestic communists—"masters of deceit" and the "enemies from within"—presented a threat to the republic. In retrospect, claims like that clearly appear to have been extravagant, even fanciful.

Terrorism specialist Marc Sageman has had the relevant background (and clearances) to comment authoritatively on the matter: "As a member of the Intelligence Community, who kept abreast of all the plots in the U.S.," he says, "I have not seen any significant terrorist plots that have been disrupted and not disclosed. On the contrary, the government goes out of its way to take credit for non-plots, such as their sting operations."[65] Glenn Carle, who was deputy national intelligence officer for transnational threats at the CIA for several years before his retirement in 2008 after twenty-three years of service, is more terse. He characterizes the claim that there are a great many thwarted terrorist plots that have gone undisclosed in three (or six) words: "Bullshit. Bullshit. Bullshit."[66]

DISRUPTED MINOR OR EMBRYONIC PLOTS

As Sageman indicates, there do not seem to be any "significant terrorist plots" that have been broken up. However, there may have been a number of proto-plots or potential plots—ones that scarcely reach the point where one might call them "significant"—that have been disrupted. Some of these cases may be the basis for the claim about undisclosed thwarted terrorist plots.

To begin, authorities have encountered a number of loud-mouthed aspirational terrorists, and lacking enough evidence to convict on terrorism charges, they have levied lesser ones to put, or send, them away. Since this is the approach that was used with Al Capone, who was incarcerated for tax violations rather than for more serious but unprovable gangster activity, a Congressional Research Service report labels this the "Capone approach."[67] Attorney General John Ashcroft has called it the "spitting on the sidewalk" approach.[68] One FBI estimate is that only one terrorism case in four leads to actual terrorism charges, while simpler criminal charges, including lying to an FBI agent, are used to deal with other ones.[69] There have been suggestions that such statistics are exaggerated.[70] However, the number roughly resonates with one provided by Risa Brooks: between 2001 and 2010, only 32 percent of defendants in cases in which the word *terrorism* appears in indictments or press releases were actually charged on core terrorism statues.[71] Immigration violations appear to have been used in the bulk of cases to which the Capone approach was applied, allowing authorities to deport suspicious potential terrorists and creating something of a permanent solution to any threat they might present—at least as far as the United States is concerned. There also are some dozens or scores of cases in which the CIA has "rendered" people—turned them over to governments of other countries. Many of these may well take place out of counterterrorism concerns.[72]

For the most part, these plots or aspirations are even less likely than the disclosed ones to lead to notable violence—that is, they are even more embryonic than the ones that have led to terrorism trials. Clearly, if there were good evidence against them, the cases would have led to arrests and prosecutions on terrorism charges.

Of course, absent police intervention, some of these nascent plots *might* eventually have led to something significant. Indeed, policing agencies often argue that stopping a plot at a very low level is a more significant accomplishment than thwarting it at a higher one. However, as will be discussed more fully in the next chapter, the vast majority of even the craftiest terrorist conspirators—including those routinely labeled "masterminds"—fail to carry out their plots. This suggests that any policing effort that disrupts terrorist efforts and plans—whether disclosed or undisclosed—is likely to waylay impotent scheming far more than it prevents actual violence. It is also worth noting in this regard that few, if any, of the terrorist plots that have been consummated or that have been disclosed in the last dozen years remotely justifies panic. And it is difficult to believe that it is only the big ones that haven't come to light.

Also relevant is that fact that the bulk of people who are convicted in "terrorism-associated" prosecutions, and who are not deported or rendered, serve less than four years—and most of these less than one year.[73] Accordingly, these people are soon free to commit terrorism if they want to do so. It is thus impressive that, as will be discussed in somewhat different context in chapter 6, almost none of the individuals who had previously been arrested on terrorism charges, and then had been convicted and punished for lesser crimes, later show up in the domestic terrorism cases as arrayed in appendix A.

If the Capone approach has waylaid people plotting terrorism, then their enthusiasm was apparently permanently expunged by being convicted on lesser charges. However, if a violent jihadist is truly dedicated to committing violence, a previous unpleasant brush with the law, and the fact that he knows policing agencies are on to him, should not matter much. That is, if a would-be terrorist can be permanently dissuaded simply by being arrested or detained on relatively minor charges, his commitment to the cause would seem to be quite limited. This observation has additional ramifications that are explored at the end of chapter 6.

DROPPED INVESTIGATIONS

Agents frequently scope out suspects who have blustered about doing jihadist violence. The vast majority of these efforts determine the blusterer to be harmless, but one, of course, can never be completely sure.

In addition, a few of the blusterers seem to be more serious, and these will attract more direct attention, including the insertion of an operative into what seems to be a potential plot. However, it has become common, as noted in chapter 1, for the operatives repeatedly to ask the blusterer whether he is really sure he wants to commit violence, pointing out that there are plenty of peaceful ways to express discontent. If the blusterer backs away from the plot, he is generally not charged.[74]

The very fact that the person under investigation could be so readily dissuaded suggests a decided lack of sustained determination.

THE DETERRED

A similar line of thought holds for would-be terrorists who have never brushed up against the legal system but have been deterred—pulled back from actually committing violence—because they were intimidated by security measures.

There is evidence in the case studies that at least some of those seeking to do terrorist violence have sought easy targets, and in that sense, they have been deterred from attacking difficult ones. Thus, one terrorist in a 2003 case checked out the Brooklyn Bridge (supposedly by driving over it once) and decided against trying to bring it down because of the police presence there (and not so much, it appears, because of the implausibility of his scheme to take the bridge down on his own with a blowtorch).[75]

It seems reasonable to suggest in this regard that extensive and very costly security measures have taken one set of targets—commercial airliners—pretty much off the target list for just about all terrorists. It's rather in the way that extensive security measures seem to have made bank robberies an unattractive enterprise for ordinary criminals. Like banks, airliners may remain lucrative targets in principle. However, the difficulty of blowing them up—and particularly of hijacking them—likely provides an impressive deterrent to do so. In only two instances—the Bronx Synagogues case of 2009 and the Wichita case of 2013—did any of the U.S.-based plotters even envision attacking aircraft, and then it was only when their targets were parked on the ground and when the culprits received crucial aid with explosives from the FBI operatives.

Security measures have also likely deterred would-be terrorists from attacking military bases in the United States. In principle, these would be favored targets because a primary motivation for plotting terrorism has been outrage at U.S. military policy. As noted earlier, however, insofar as military installations have been targeted, these have usually been recruiting offices in cities or soldiers on the street, not full-blown military bases.

Nevertheless, although security measures may have complicated terrorism planning in some cases, and although destroying some specific targets may have become extraordinarily difficult, no dedicated would-be terrorist should have much difficulty finding other potential targets if the goal is to kill people or destroy property to make a statement. If someone is determined to rob for a living, the fact that banks have been effectively made into unproductive targets need not lead to seeking a new way of life—there are still plenty of sources of money out there, like convenience and liquor stores and little old ladies with handbags. Moreover, given the high recidivism rates for robbery, it appears that being arrested and serving time for the offense has scarcely been enough to cause robbers to go straight—to deter them from committing further robberies.

Similarly, a putative terrorist who is deterred by security measures from attacking a specific target like an airliner or military base should, if truly dedicated, easily be able to seek out another target.[76] Shooting up a mall or derailing a train, or setting a building or forest afire, or detonating a home-made bomb in a crowd may not have quite the same overall impact as destroying an airliner in flight, but experience suggests that such destructive acts, as with the Boston Marathon bombs of 2013 or the shootings in Paris in 2015, can still garner great attention and have substantial consequences. The same holds—even more so—for the coordinated attacks by small squads of gunmen on places of civilian congregation, as carried out in Mumbai, India, in 2008 and in Nairobi, Kenya, in 2013.

In addition, whereas the prospect of being killed or arrested in the process of committing a crime may often deter criminals (few liquor stores with police cars parked in front of them are held up), the same should not hold for terrorists—or at least for ones who are truly dedicated. Even if they are not specifically suicidal, they must surely be aware that they are very likely—probably sooner rather than later—to be arrested or killed in the process of committing terrorist destruction.

Thus, if security measures deter terrorism, they must primarily do so not because they are so effective but, rather, because the would-be terrorists are not very dedicated in the first place and are rather easily dissuaded. Relevant as well is John Horgan's observation that recidivism for terrorists "is notably lower than the rates commonly found in general offender populations."[77] This issue will be considered again, in a different context, in chapter 6.

There is also a related argument that maintains we have much to fear because we only catch the dummies, while all the smart ones get away to wait for the right opportunity to commit terrorist mayhem. But then why don't they eventually actually *do* something? They should know full well that the longer they wait, the more likely they are to be detected. Concern about the police should not dissuade them if they are truly dedicated, though it might make them more careful and lead to simpler plots involving fewer conspirators.

This consideration also holds for the argument that there are many more would-be terrorists lurking out there whom U.S. authorities have not yet discovered. As noted in chapter 1, people like former CIA head George Tenet have darkly suggested they must be out there.[78] Why do they wait? What are they waiting for?[79]

Actually, insofar as many people (smart or otherwise) are actually dissuaded from committing terrorism, it is likely that this dissuasion does not stem from specific measures designed to deter them, like the danger of disruption by the FBI. Rather, it comes from the realization that terrorism simply doesn't work: no matter how deeply felt their grievances and outrage, expressing them in random or semirandom civilian destruction is highly unlikely to be productive to their cause.[80] Accordingly, like just about everybody else, they embrace nonviolent means to express their beliefs.

Terrorism as Black Comedy

If post-9/11 counterterrorism in the United States, as suggested in chapter 1, can sometimes be envisioned as black comedy, so can the efforts of the adversaries whom the domestic counterterrorism enterprise is questing after.

Appearing finally in 2010 after considerable difficulty obtaining funding, the British film *Four Lions* is a dark comedy—if ultimately a desperately sad one—that looks at a set of Muslim would-be terrorists in the United Kingdom. Directed and co-written by Chris Morris, it is entirely fictional, although the leader of the terrorist cell does seem to resemble Abdullah Ahmed Ali, the leader of London's transatlantic airliner plot of 2006. Ringleaders as sharp as Ali appear in few, if any, of the plots detailed in the *Terrorism Since 9/11* book. However, the American terrorism enterprise finds resonance with other aspects of the film, even though none of the plots were (intentionally) comedic.

For example, when the terrorists in *Four Lions* accidentally kill a sheep, they justify it as an attack on the food infrastructure. But when their counterparts in the actual JIS plot of 2005 robbed gas stations to obtain funds to buy a gun, they envisioned the venture as a sort of mini-jihad against big oil as a political symbol of U.S. oppression. That they accidentally left a cellphone behind in their last robbery, allowing them to be found, and that their target list included a military base that didn't exist, is also the stuff of comedy. The efforts of one of the Four Lions to attach a small bomb to a crow (it ends badly for the bird) may be even more fanciful than those of the real-life would-be terrorist who was planning to implant bombs on model airplanes and them fly them into the Pentagon in 2011—but not greatly so.[81]

And the confident, if airy, prophecy of one of the fictional British terrorists that a Muslim uprising could be with a few explosions (they rise up "and it all kicks off") are surely no more ludicrously fanciful than those of the real-life one who believed in 2006 that setting off a grenade in a trash can in a mall in Rockford, Illinois, would be the "first domino," triggering a set of further attacks from Muslims that would ultimately lead to the fall of the government. (His idea that a grenade set off in a garbage can would create more shrapnel was also more than a bit flawed; since grenades are essentially made of shrapnel, it has been pointed out that his approach would be comparable to shooting somebody through a wooden board in hopes they would be impaled by flying splinters.) Equally deluded was the plan earnestly hatched by a man in jail in the JIS case of 2005 who orchestrated a plot by three men on the outside, one of them a confirmed schizophrenic, to use a few armed attacks to set off a revolution to establish a caliphate.

And there is the extravagant anticipation in 2004 of the real-life plotter who planned to enter the Herald Square subway station in New York (dressed "like a Jew" to waylay suspicion) and plant a small bomb. When set off, he imagined, it would destroy a major office and shopping building above it, even while killing few people (except for homeless ones sleeping in the station) if it were to be set off in the morning. Even more fantastic is the wild fantasy of the leader of the Sears Tower plot of 2006 that toppling the structure into Lake Michigan would create a tsunami, thereby allowing him to liberate prisoners from a Chicago jail from which he would form a vanguard for the establishment of a new Moorish nation.

We also have the adventure of the extremist in 2009 who (1) tried to kill a rabbi with a Molotov cocktail, only to go to the wrong house and, regardless, have the explosive bounce off the house's window and fail to explode; (2) tried to shoot up a military recruitment center, only to find that the office was closed; and (3) after actually firing at another recruiting center in Little Rock, Arkansas, made a wrong turn in his getaway car and was captured by police within twelve minutes.

Or there is the clever plotter in the transatlantic airlines plot of 2006 who thought that if his men carried pornographic magazines and condoms in their luggage they would be less suspicious.

Or the several plotters who divulged their violent plans (or fantasies), and often in addition tried to pick up co-conspirators, in FBI-haunted Internet chat rooms, on Facebook, or on Twitter.[82]

Or there is the guy who in 2011 took potshots at the Pentagon and three other military buildings in Washington in the middle of the night (video recording himself in action in one of the ventures), hoping to put out the lights while sending a message about the wars in Iraq and Afghanistan. He professed disappointment when no one got the message.

Or the man, known to police for having head-butted an infidel outside a Lady Gaga concert and whose troubles began when he tried to buy an al-Qaeda flag in a store run by an FBI informant. He aspired in 2012, among other things, to bomb bridges that link Tampa, Florida, to a neighboring county in order, he said, "to crush the whole economy" by cutting off city residents from their food supply and jobs and to bring terror to his "victims' hearts."

A conspiracy to blow up jet-fuel tanks at JFK airport in 2007 is notable not only for the daffy infeasibility of the plot, for the inability of the plotters to put it into motion, for the plotters' absence of practical knowledge, and for their apparent incomprehension of its essential absurdity, but also for their leader's justification: an attack on that airport would be like "killing the man twice," he sagely observed, because "anytime you hit Kennedy, it is the most hurtful thing to the United States. To hit John F. Kennedy, wow. . . . They love John F. Kennedy like he's the man. . . . If you hit that, the whole country will be in mourning."[83]

And there is a resonance with the common finding in the cases that few terrorists could scarcely be said to have figured out a credible goal to be serviced by their plot. This phenomenon is reflected in *Four Lions* by the response of one of the terrorists to a police query that he detail his demands: "I don't have any," he says dumbfoundedly.

The more clever terrorists in the film almost never actually explain what they are seeking, but at one point the leader does say that they are striking out at the materialism and "spiritual void" that characterize Western society. As noted earlier, such declarations are absent in the (nonfictional) cases as arrayed in appendix A. Almost none of the terrorist characters in the cases examined had any problem with Western society, but they had plenty of outrage at foreign policy in the Middle East—and this includes most decidedly the transatlantic airliner bombers plotting away in London in 2006.[84]

Although the terrorism efforts discussed often demonstrate the would-be perpetrators, like those in *Four Lions*, to be pathetic, even comical or absurd, the comedy remains a black one, of course. With a few possible exceptions (in the Albany case of 2004, for example), left to their own devices at least a few of the often inept and almost always self-deluded individuals under consideration might have been able to commit some serious, if decidedly less than cosmic, damage. Even those in *Four Lions* do manage to pull off at least some lethal mayhem—though the fact that all of their bombs actually explode, albeit usually in the wrong place, strains credulity.

And it is worth remembering in all this that Lee Harvey Oswald, the assassin of President John F. Kennedy, was pathetic and deluded in many ways. And so, as the FBI's John Miller points out, were the two snipers who terrorized the Washington, D.C., area for three weeks in 2002 and killed ten people.[85]

Trivial people sometimes are able to inflict nontrivial damage—mainly out of luck. However, although improbable things sometimes do happen, that doesn't mean that all improbable things are therefore probable. Nor does it follow that all trivial people are nontrivial—or masterminds.

| The Foreign Adversary
and the Myth of the Mastermind

THIS BOOK IS primarily devoted to evaluating the policing and intelligence efforts to deal with potential acts of Islamist terrorism since 9/11 that are focused on the United States—the chief concern of domestic ghost-chasers. In general, the capacities of those seeking, aspiring, or vaguely thinking about such terrorism, whether based in the United States or abroad, seem to be unimpressive, and any threat they present appears to be quite limited.

This chapter casts a wider look at the impact, effect, and character of Islamist terrorism worldwide.

The Foreign Adversary

For the most part, the basic conclusions about the threat presented to the United States and the West by the terrorist "adversary" do not change.

Words like *brilliant, crafty, imaginative*, and *ingenious*, not to mention *mastermind*, are notable for their absence in the case studies arrayed in appendix A. But they don't spring to mind all that much when one looks at the situation abroad, either.

TERRORISM ABROAD OUTSIDE WAR ZONES

Michael Kenney has analyzed court documents and interviewed dozens of government officials and intelligence agents in Europe and other Western locations. He finds that would-be terrorists there, like their counterparts in the United States, are operationally unsophisticated, short on know-how, prone to make mistakes, poor at planning, and limited in their capacity to learn.[1] For example, there was the neo-Nazi terrorist in Norway who, on his way to bomb a synagogue, took a tram going the wrong way and dynamited a mosque instead.[2] Another study documents the difficulties of network coordination that continually threaten the terrorists' operational unity, trust, cohesion, and ability to act collectively.[3] The lack of success of terrorists in the United Kingdom, Canada, Australia, and other Western countries mirrors that in the United States: the number of people killed by Islamist extremist terrorists in the UK is less than four per year, while for Canada and Australia, it is two in the last decade.

In all, extremist Islamist terrorism—whether associated with al-Qaeda or not—has claimed some 200 to 300 lives yearly worldwide since 2001 outside of war zones.[4] That's 200 to 300 too many, of course, but as can be seen in table 5-2 on p. 138, it is about the same number as deaths from bathtub drownings in the United States.

EXAMINING 9/11

As noted, the September 11 terrorist attacks were by far the most destructive in history—scarcely any terrorist act before or since, even in war zones, has inflicted as much as one-tenth the damage. However, the tragic event seems increasingly to stand as an aberration, not as a harbinger. Accordingly, it may well be that, as Russell Seitz put it in 2004, "9/11 could join the Trojan Horse and Pearl Harbor among stratagems so uniquely surprising that their very success precludes their repetition," and accordingly, that "al-Qaeda's best shot may have been exactly that."[5]

Although the 9/11 attacks were in many respects clever and well planned, their success was more the result of luck than of cleverness. In fact, it is not at all clear that the planners really appreciated why they might be successful. As pilot Patrick Smith points out, it was not because they "exploited a weakness in airport security by smuggling aboard box cutters." Rather, "what they actually exploited was a weakness in our mindset—a set of presumptions based on the decades-long track record of hijackings. In years past, a takeover meant hostage negotiations and standoffs; crews were trained in the concept of 'passive resistance.'"[6]

In earlier decades, and particularly between 1967 and 1972, nearly 200 commercial airline flights had been hijacked in American airspace. Most of these were diverted to Cuba where the hijackers disembarked and the plane was sent on its way back to the United States. In all this, there were almost no deaths and very little injury, and the total cost to the airlines was some $20,000 per hijacked flight at a time when industry profits were more than

$360 million per year. The most sensible policy seemed to be to play along with the hijackers, and crew members were sternly instructed that "it is much more prudent to submit to a gunman's demands than attempt action which may well jeopardize the lives of all on board," and pilots, no matter what their scheduled destination, were helpfully provided with charts of the Caribbean Sea and phrase cards in Spanish.[7] Some hijackers demanded sums of money rather than trips to Cuba, and the airlines continued to cooperate.

Things changed in late 1973, however. Three armed thugs hijacked a plane and demanded a huge ransom payment. Then, while the airline was scrambling to come up with the money, the extortionists downed forty small bottles of liquor on the plane and became increasingly erratic, even threatening to crash the plane into a nuclear reactor in Oak Ridge, Tennessee. This threat finally led to the institution of passenger screening which the airlines had previously opposed, fearing a drop in passenger traffic. This measure (combined with a change of policy by Cuba) very substantially reduced the numbers of hijackings. It did come, however, at a high cost: at the time, one study calculated that it cost $291,221 for every passenger spared the process of temporarily becoming a hostage. Policy, however, remained the same: crew members, notes Brendan Koerner in a fascinating study of the saga, "were still instructed to offer hijackers their complete cooperation."[8]

It was this policy, and experience, that made the 9/11 hijackings possible. However, the policy was obviously shattered by the 2001 hijackings as demonstated on the fourth plane in which passengers and crew, having learned of what had happened on the earlier flights, fought to overcome the hijackers. Nonetheless, apparently completely oblivious to this highly likely development, the 9/11 planners had also been working on a "second wave" hijacking in which the targets would be skyscrapers in Los Angeles, Seattle, Chicago, and New York.[9] This means they didn't appreciate the fact that the first attack would make a "second wave" vastly more difficult. As Smith continues, "Any hijacker would face a planeload of angry and frightened people ready to fight back."[10]

Moreover, the planners' mindset continued even *after* the 9/11 experience. Impressed by new airline security measures instituted by the Americans (but not, it appears, by the crucial change in mindset), they judged that the prospects for success in a second hijacking were low "at least for the short term," but they continued to keep the prospect in mind.[11]

Since that time, they have not again been able to do anything remotely that spectacular. Indeed, perhaps the only terrorist attack in which it does seem that the perpetrator successfully exploited holes in a security system was the shooting attack in Norway by an anti-Muslim terrorist, Anders Behring Breivik, in 2011. He created a crisis by setting off a bomb and then, dressed in police uniform, went to an unprotected island to carry out his shooting rampage.

In addition, there were many miscues in the execution of the 9/11 plot. Most impressively, Mohamed Atta, one of the ringleaders of the plot and the pilot of the plane that was crashed into the North Tower of the World Trade Center, almost missed his flight. For some unaccountable reason, he decided to go to Maine and take a commuter flight to Boston to connect. As it was, his luggage, filled with personal information, did not make the flight to Boston and was later delivered in pristine shape to investigators.[12]

As Kenney notes, "[L]ike Al Qaeda's previous attacks, 9/11 was characterized less by flawless execution than by steadfast, malleable militants practicing slipshod tradecraft." Indeed, "in spite of their training and experience in guerrilla warfare, several 9/11 perpetrators committed basic errors in tradecraft that nearly sabotaged their plans." Two were completely unprepared for their assigned roles of piloting the suicide aircraft and couldn't get training in the United States because they couldn't speak adequate English. One of them abruptly returned to Yemen to visit his family without permission, and the other befriended people with no connection to the plot, boasting to one that he would soon become famous.

Additionally, continues Kenney, two of them endangered the operation by receiving speeding tickets. One made no fewer than five trips abroad to visit his girlfriend and family. Another al-Qaeda trainee was so incompetent that two days into his aviation training his flight instructor reported him to the FBI as a potential hijacker. He called attention to himself by, among other things, insisting on receiving advanced training for flying large commercial aircraft, asking how much fuel a jumbo jet could carry and how much damage it would cause if it crashed into anything, and getting "extremely agitated" when asked about his religious background.[13]

Most important, it appears that Osama bin Laden's strategic vision for the attacks was, like that of the Japanese at Pearl Harbor, profoundly misguided. He was impressed in particular by the American reaction to losses in Lebanon in 1983 and in Somalia in 1993, concluding that this demonstrated "impotence," "weakness," and "false courage." Accordingly, he appears to have believed that the country would respond to a large direct attack at home by withdrawing from the Middle East.[14]

What he clearly failed to understand was that the United States withdrew from Lebanon and Somalia, not simply because of the losses, but because it did not value the stakes very much in those humanitarian ventures. As discussed in chapter 2, for Americans (and Canadians, Swedes, Belgians, the Red Cross, and so on), peacekeeping is simply not worth many of their own lives. By contrast, the American public concluded from 9/11 that the country's very survival was at stake in the conflict with bin Laden's form of terrorism. Accordingly, its willingness to confront the danger (and to exact revenge) was, as after Pearl Harbor, monumental. As Fawaz Gerges puts it, bin Laden had picked the "wrong yardsticks by which to measure the American response."[15] Popular support for chasing down the terrorists in Afghanistan, even though there was a prospect for considerable American losses, was exceedingly high—considerably higher, as is suggested in figure 2-13, than at the beginnings of the wars in Vietnam, Korea, or Iraq.

Initially there was panic in al-Qaeda at the unexpected ferocity of the American response.[16] Then bin Laden reformulated his theory after it was blown to shreds when the United States and its allies not only forced al-Qaeda out of its base in Afghanistan and captured or killed many of its main people but also toppled the country's accommodating Taliban regime. In a videotaped message in 2004, bin Laden mockingly asserted that it is "easy for us to provoke and bait. . . . All that we have to do is to send two mujahidin . . . to raise a piece of cloth on which is written al-Qaeda in order to make the generals race there to cause America to suffer human, economic, and political losses." His policy, he proclaimed, is one of "bleeding America to the point of bankruptcy," triumphally pointing to the fact that the 9/11 terrorist attacks cost al-Qaeda $500,000, while the attack and its aftermath inflicted, he claims, "a cost of more than $500 billion on the United States."[17] But that is more nearly a convenient rationalization than a fair representation of his goals when he had planned the attack—rather like that of his nemesis, George W. Bush, when he eventually argued that his invasion of Iraq was to establish democracy rather than to disrupt Saddam Hussein's supposed weapons of mass destruction program.[18] Initially, however, bin Laden apparently expected that the United States would essentially *under*react to the 9/11 attacks.

As discussed in chapter 2, the result of America's massive and self-destructive overreaction to 9/11 may well lead it to substantially withdraw from the Middle East. Thus, by luck, bin Laden's original goal may be eventually achieved, but not in the way he planned it.

Impressively, unlike the Wizard of Oz, bin Laden appears to have remained in a state of self-delusion, even to his brutal and abrupt end. The Wizard came to realize that he was a fraud but bin Laden never experienced a similar revelation, continuing to cling to the belief that another attack like 9/11, or even bigger, might force the United States out of the Middle East. He thus remained absurdly unfazed that the first such effort had proved to be spectacularly counterproductive in the respect that it triggered a deadly invasion of his base in Afghanistan and an equally deadly, long-term, determined pursuit of him and his operatives.[19]

Documents from bin Laden's lair, released in 2015, did show that he continued to harbor, in commentator David Ignatius's characterizarion, "big ambitions."[20] However, they also show him wallowing in delusion. Apparently abandoning his 2004 declaration that his goal was to bleed the United States into bankruptcy by sucking the country into expensive military ventures abroad, he now decided that the American losses suffered in these ventures (some 5,000 soldiers he estimates) had not been nearly sufficient to enrage the American people to force the politicians to withdraw from the Middle East. Consequently, he argued, al-Qaeda must concentrate on "large" operations within the United States—presumably killing many tens of thousands of people since he notes that even 57,000 deaths in Vietnam did not work. At the same time, he holds out some hope for targeting imported oil in order that "the income of the American citizen will be affected through the rise in his fuel bill," and he urges his tiny collection of terrorists to undertake "a large intensive media campaign" as well. He supplies no detail about how to carry out "this great feat," but he does rather unhelpfully suggest that the group "must mobilize the best efforts and capabilities" for the task. He also suggests that "the brothers in Somalia" need to take "maximum precautions" against drought and floods caused by climate change and that "brothers who have a good way of thinking" should be sent to college to learn Management Science and also Strategic Policies and Planning, a field that is "available at low cost."[21]

AL-QAEDA'S RECORD OUTSIDE OF 9/11

Before 9/11, al-Qaeda had launched several terrorist attacks, but even those that succeeded were laced with screw-ups. Thus, in picking when to bomb two American embassies in Africa in 1998, the plotters failed to note that the day chosen was a national holiday in one of the cities, thereby much reducing the casualty count.[22] An effort to send a bomb-loaded skiff to attack a U.S. destroyer when it refueled in Yemen failed when the skiff sank as it was launched.[23] A later attempt did damage another U.S. ship, though it failed to sink the ship as apparently was planned, and the video guy assigned to record the deed for posterity and propaganda fell asleep and missed the opportunity.[24] After 9/11, al-Qaeda Central has been holed up in Pakistan. However, its record of accomplishment has been rather meager, even taking into consideration that it has been isolated and under siege. It does not seem to have done much of anything except issue videos filled with empty, self-infatuated, and essentially delusional threats. Thus, it was in October 2002 that Osama bin Laden proclaimed,

> Understand the lesson of New York and Washington raids, which came in response to some of your previous crimes. . . . God is my witness, the youth of Islam are preparing things that will fill your hearts with fear. They will target key sectors of your economy until you stop your injustice and aggression or until the more short-lived of us die.

And in January 2006, he insisted that the "delay" in carrying out operations in the United States "was not due to failure to breach your security measures," and that "operations are under preparation, and you will see them on your own ground once they are finished, God willing."[25]

Bin Laden's tiny group of perhaps 100 or so does appear to have served as something of an inspiration to some Muslim extremists. They may have done some training, may have contributed a bit to the Taliban's far larger insurgency in Afghanistan, and may have participated in a few terrorist acts in Pakistan.[26] In his examination of the major terrorist plots against the West since 9/11, Mitchell Silber finds only two—the shoe bomber attempt of 2001 and the effort to blow up transatlantic airliners with liquid bombs in 2006—that could be said to be under the "command and control" of al-Qaeda Central (as opposed to ones suggested, endorsed, or inspired by the organization), and there are questions about how full its control was even in these two instances, both of which, as it happens, failed miserably.[27] Even under siege, it is difficult to see why al-Qaeda could not have organized attacks at least as costly and shocking as the shooting rampages (organized by other groups) that took place in Mumbai in 2008 or at a shopping center in Kenya in 2013. Neither took huge resources, presented major logistical challenges, required the organization of a large number of perpetrators, or needed extensive planning.

And ineptitude seems common, even rampant. Thus, around 2008 the group allowed an American member, Bryant Neal Vinas, to play a supporting role on an al-Qaeda propaganda video, a decision suggesting lack of clear thinking and certainly lack of cleverness. The video appearance might facilitate his identification by their ever-prying enemies, particularly if he were sent on an operation to the United States, as was the likely eventual intention. And communications between an American operative, Zazi, and al-Qaeda Central in 2009 naïvely used the word *wedding* as a code for their planned terrorist attack, even though authorities had long been on to that rather childish, and decidedly nonclever, Aesopian euphemism—indeed, the 9/11 attack had routinely been called "the big wedding," and it was a running joke among counterterrorists that they were lucky al-Qaeda couldn't dream up a better code word.[28]

This remarkably limited record, together with the *Wizard of Oz* conclusion of the ten-year quest for bin Laden, suggests that Glenn Carle was right in 2008 when he warned, "We must not take fright at the specter our leaders have exaggerated. In fact, we must see jihadists for the small, lethal, disjointed and miserable opponents that they are." Al-Qaeda "has only a handful of individuals capable of planning, organizing and leading a terrorist organization," and although they have threatened attacks, "its capabilities are far inferior to its desires."[29]

AFFILIATED AND OTHER GROUPS

Other terrorist groups around the world, affiliated or aligned, or otherwise "connected" to al-Qaeda, may be able to do intermittent damage to people and infrastructure, but nothing that is sustained or focused. Moreover, as Patrick Porter notes, al-Qaeda has "talent at self-destruction."[30] With the September 11 attacks and subsequent activity, bin Laden's agents and inspirees seem mainly to have succeeded in uniting the world, including its huge Muslim portion, against their violent global jihad.[31] These activities have also turned many radical Islamists against them, including some of the most prominent and respected.[32]

No matter how much threatened countries might disagree with the United States on other issues (most notably on its war in Iraq), there is a compelling incentive for them to cooperate in confronting any international terrorist problem emanating from groups and individuals connected to, or sympathetic with, al-Qaeda. Although these multilateral efforts, particularly by Muslim states including Iran, may not have received sufficient publicity, these countries have felt directly threatened by the militant network, and their diligent and aggressive efforts have led to important breakthroughs against al-Qaeda and its affiliates.[33]

This post-9/11 willingness of governments around the world to take on terrorists has been reinforced and amplified as they react to subsequent, if sporadic, terrorist activity in their own countries. Thus, a terrorist bombing in Bali in 2002 galvanized the Indonesian government into action and led to extensive arrests and convictions. When terrorists attacked Saudis in Saudi Arabia in 2003, the government became considerably more serious about dealing with internal terrorism, including clamping down on radical clerics and preachers. The main result of al-Qaeda–linked suicide terrorism in Jordan in 2005 was to outrage Jordanians and other Arabs. There were massive protests, and polls found that those expressing confidence in Osama bin Laden to "do the right thing" plunged from 25 percent to less than 1 percent. In polls conducted in thirty-five predominantly Muslim countries in 2008, more than 90 percent of those populations condemned bin Laden's terrorism on the basis of religious grounds.[34]

In addition, the mindless brutalities of al-Qaeda–affiliated combatants in Iraq—staged beheadings at mosques, bombing of playgrounds, the taking over of hospitals, execution of ordinary citizens, forced marriages—eventually turned the Iraqis against them, including many who had previously been fighting the U.S. occupation either on their own or in connection with the group.[35] In fact, they seem to have managed to alienate the entire population: data from polls in Iraq in 2007 indicate that 97 percent of those surveyed opposed efforts to recruit foreigners to fight in Iraq; 98 percent opposed the militants' efforts to gain control of territory; and 100 percent deemed attacks against Iraqi civilians to be "unacceptable."[36]

Overall, "al-Qaeda is its own worst enemy," notes Robert Grenier, a former top CIA counterterrorism official. "Where they have succeeded initially, they very quickly discredit themselves."[37] Grenier's improbable company in this observation is Osama bin Laden, who was so concerned about al-Qaeda's alienation of most Muslims that he argued from his hideout that the organization should take on a new name.[38]

Much of this may hold as well for the new concern, the Islamic State, most commonly known as ISIS. The group is not associated with al-Qaeda—indeed, as noted in chapter 1, it has withdrawn from, or been ceremoniously thrown out of, the al-Qaeda ranks in part because it does not primarily target the "far enemy." But it seems likely Islamic State will eventually be overcome by the same defects as the group from which it emerged, the al-Qaeda branch in Iraq.

Although it enjoyed some startling successes in Iraq in 2014, these were mainly because its opponent, the ill-led Iraqi army, disintegrated in northern Iraq. But ISIS seems to be led by millenarian crackpots.[39] Moreover, its counterproductive brutalities, such as staged beheadings of hostages, summary executions of prisoners, and the rape and enslavement of female captives have left it without allies and outside support—indeed, it is surrounded by enemies. As noted in chapter 1, its goal to control territory carries with it attendant difficulties of governing and of presenting a target. And, unlike al-Qaeda, ISIS has welcomed foreigners into its ranks, advancing the potential to be undermined by infiltrators.

Three Masterminds

Arthur Conan Doyle invented Moriarty to give his hero, Sherlock Holmes, an opponent worthy of the efforts of the great, if equally imaginary, detective. The counterterrorism establishment has been similarly inclined—as have those responsible for producing such imaginative products as television's *24* and *Homeland*. Early on, officials even invited Hollywood scriptwriters to spin out tales of what the "universal adversary" out there might be up to.[40] The enemy, all this implies, has generally been assumed to be clever, crafty, diabolical, resourceful, ingenious, brilliant, flexible, brutal, and equal—an opponent fully worthy of the stupendous and exceedingly expensive countering efforts being made.

Central to this exercise has been the identification of a few evil "masterminds" who were dominating the show. Since it made for good copy, journalists helped spread the word. We examine the distinctly unmasterly overall achievements of three of these masterminds.

KHALID SHAIKH MOHAMMED

In his book *Mastermind: The Many Faces of the 9/11 Architect, Khalid Shaikh Mohammed*, journalist Richard Miniter begins by listing his subject's admitted (or claimed) involvement with terrorist efforts in addition to 9/11. These include the 1993 World Trade Center and 2002 Bali bombings; plots on Heathrow airport, Big Ben, and the Panama Canal; plans to assassinate Bill Clinton, the Pope, and several prime ministers of Pakistan; two efforts to infiltrate agents into the United States; and the plan for a "second wave" of attacks by hijacked airliners on major U.S. landmarks including the U.S. Bank Tower in Los Angeles, the Sears Tower in Chicago, and the Plaza Bank Building in Seattle.[41]

Actually, Miniter does not do full service to his subject's claimed scheming. In addition, to the plots on Miniter's list, KSM declared himself to be the power behind the shoe bomber operation of 2001; an October 2002 attack in Kuwait; plots to attack oil tankers and U.S. naval ships in the Strait of Hormuz, the Strait of Gibraltar, and the port of Singapore; plans to assassinate Jimmy Carter; a plot to blow up suspension bridges in New York City; a plan to destroy the Sears Tower in Chicago with burning fuel trucks (an alternative, presumably, to the airline hijacking plan); plots to "destroy" Canary Wharf in London; a planned attack on "many" nightclubs in Thailand; Barot's plot, rolled up in 2004, to target the New York Stock Exchange and other U.S. financial targets with limousine-borne bombs; a plan to destroy buildings in Eilat, Israel; plans to destroy U.S. embassies in Indonesia, Australia, and Japan; plots to destroy Israeli embassies in India, Azerbaijan, Australia, and the Philippines; surveying and financing an attack on an Israeli El-Al flight from Bangkok; sending several agents into Israel to survey "strategic targets" with the intention of attacking them; a suicide bombing of a hotel in Mombasa, Kenya; the attempt to shoot down an Israeli passenger jet leaving Mombasa airport in Kenya; plans to attack U.S. targets in South Korea; providing financial support for a plan to attack U.S., British, and Jewish targets in Turkey; surveillance of U.S. nuclear power plants in order to attack them; a plot to attack NATO's headquarters in Europe; planning and surveillance in a 1995 plan (the "Bojinka plot") to bomb twelve passenger jets bound for the United States; a plot to blow up gas stations in the United States; plans to assassinate Pakistani President Pervez Musharraf; and an attempt to attack a U.S. oil company in Sumatra, Indonesia, that was "owned by the Jewish former Secretary of State Henry Kissinger." He also took pride in having personally beheaded the defenseless *Wall Street Journal* reporter Daniel Pearl.[42]

What is impressive is that, except for the Bali bombings, just about *all* of KSM's many schemes either failed or did not even begin to approach fruition. In addition, the role of the "mastermind" in the Bali case, according to Miniter and others, was simply to supply some money.[43] And KSM's entire role in the failed 1993 effort to bring down the World Trade Center was to wire $660 to one of the conspirators.[44] It is also noteworthy that KSM continued to work on the "second wave" hijacked airplane attack.[45] This suggests that, as discussed earlier, even after the fact, he understood neither the reason 9/11 worked nor the (rather obvious) lesson learned on the fourth plane.

Overall, as a terrorism planner, KSM has a fertile mind but a feeble record of accomplishment, one characterized by fanciful scheming and stunted execution. In this context, 9/11 clearly stands out as an aberration.

RAMZI YOUSEF

KSM's nephew, Ramzi Yousef, who was primarily responsible for the February 1993 truck bomb attack on the World Trade Center, is also widely considered to be a mastermind. Journalist Simon Reeve repeatedly uses the word to describe him, as do others.[46] Reeve also calls him an "explosives genius," a "genius bomb maker," a "master of explosives," and an "evil genius" possessed of "an obscene brilliance as a terrorist."[47] Asked if he considered himself to be a genius, Yousef obligingly responded strongly in the affirmative.[48]

The praise (and self-praise) seems to be excessive. As a bomb maker, he was given to splashing acid in his face and starting fires that drew the police.[49]

His attack on the World Trade Center in early 1993 did manage to kill six people, but for the most part it was a tragicomedy of errors. Indeed, notes Kenney, one of his main collaborators "became the poster boy for 'stupid' terrorists" by repeatedly trying to claim a $400 refund on the van he and his fellow conspirators had just blown up in their failed effort to topple one of the World Trade Center towers: he needed the cash for a plane ticket to Jordan.[50] Moreover, the bomb Yousef put together was not nearly big enough to topple the tower—which was his goal.[51] Obviously, if he wanted simply to kill six people, there were much easier ways to do so.

After that venture, Yousef engaged in a wide variety of terrorist efforts before his arrest two years later. These resulted in the deaths of twenty-eight more people. All but two of these deaths were inflicted by a bomb he created on hire for an Iranian rebel group that was detonated by the group in the women's section of a holy site in Iran. Thus, an examination of his record as a terrorist during this period suggests a continuing propensity for viciousness, but scarcely genius or mastermindhood.

In July 1993, a few months after the attack on the World Trade Center, Yousef was approached by a militant Islamic group to kill Pakistan's prime minister, Benazir Bhutto. With an accomplice, he tried to plant a bomb in a drain at her home, which would be detonated remotely. Police noticed the men scraping in the street and demanded to know what was going on. The pair said they were searching for keys they had dropped. Apparently fearing the police might return, Yousef tried to pull the bomb out of the drain, and its detonator (but not the bomb itself) went off in his face. Fragments damaged his fingers and one eye, and he was knocked unconscious. Friends got him to a hospital, where he was treated after explaining that a butane gas canister had exploded in his face.[52]

In September, he planned to assassinate Bhutto again by shooting her with a sniper's rifle as she talked at a meeting. However, the rifle did not arrive in time for him to use it.[53] It is not clear that he had any knowledge of, or skills with, firearms.

In March 1994, he created a bomb in Thailand that was placed in a truck after the driver had been strangled and killed by Yousef's accomplices. One of the men then drove the truck toward the Israeli embassy, accidentally crashed it, and fled. The owner of the truck later discovered the unexploded bomb and the decomposing body in the back of the truck.[54]

In June, the bomb created by Yousef for the Iranian rebel opposition group Mujaeddin-e-Khalq was set off by the group in the women's section at a holy Shiite site in Mashhad, in northeastern Iran. A wall toppled and twenty-six were killed.[55] Later in the year, seeking to kill a moderate Sunni leader in

Pakistan, Yousef bought a pistol and hired an assassin. Something went wrong with the attempt, and the contract was never fulfilled.[56]

In November, Yousef plotted to assassinate U.S. president Bill Clinton when he visited the Philippines. Yousef considered using a missile, explosives planted along Clinton's motorcade route, and an attack with phosgene gas. However, he abandoned the plot owing to the high security surrounding the visiting president.[57]

Working with some stolen textbooks, Yousef sought to develop a bomb that could be exploded by a timer on an airliner, bringing it down. He successfully tested a small prototype in Cebu City in the Philippines, and then one in a movie theater in Manila that inflicted light injuries on a nearby amorous couple. Next, he assembled a small bomb in the toilet of an airliner and planted it in the life vest under his seat. He disembarked when the plane landed, and the bomb went off as the plane proceeded on to Tokyo. One passenger, a Japanese businessman, was killed.[58]

In January 1995, he plotted to assassinate Pope John Paul II when the Pontiff was visiting the Philippines. Yousef apparently considered using plastic explosives and bombs dropped from a small plane onto the Popemobile. However, he abandoned the plot.[59]

While in the Philippines, Yousef plotted to load a small plane with chemical weapons and then have a friend who had some flight training fly it into, or spray the gas onto, CIA headquarters in Langley, Virginia, some 7,500 nautical miles to the east.[60] Nothing ever came of this plot.

Working on building bigger and better bombs to place on some eleven U.S.-bound airliners (a plot he labeled "Bojinka"), Yousef and a friend (the sole members of what Yousef grandly called a "Liberation Army") started a small fire in a cooking pot in his Manila apartment.[61] Both men fled when firefighters arrived. After the police and firefighters left, Yousef persuaded his accomplice to go back to the apartment to remove files, books, manuals, and a computer, but the accomplice was arrested when the police returned with a search warrant. From the chemical-stained apartment, the police seized books, manuals, containers of sulphuric acid, wires, timing devices, Bibles, priests' garments, and a large photograph of Pope John Paul II, as well as a Toshiba laptop containing plans for the Bojinka plot. Deleted files were still stored on the computer's hard drive. Yousef escaped.[62]

Now in Pakistan, Yousef plotted to kidnap the Philippine ambassador to Pakistan in order to put pressure on the Philippine government to free his arrested accomplice. Nothing came of this plot. Then, in Bangkok, Yousef assembled several bombs and put them in luggage to be checked as cargo on planes bound for the United States. However, his accomplice developed cold feet when sent to the airport to check the luggage.[63]

In Pakistan in February 1995, Yousef plotted to have a Qatari friend board a U.S.-bound plane in London with a luggage bomb, to pack bombs in toy cars to be exploded in Iran, and to send confederates on missions against the Israeli consulate in Bombay and the Israeli embassy in New Delhi. When he ordered another accomplice to take a mysterious parcel to a Shia mosque in Islamabad, the terrified accomplice called the U.S. embassy in hopes of receiving the $2 million reward for Yousef's capture and became a double agent. Yousef was arrested on February 7, and the accomplice became rich.[64]

In prison in 2007, Yousef claimed to have converted to Christianity.[65]

YEMEN'S IBRAHIM HASSAN AL-ASIRI

Hassan al-Asiri, Yemen's supposed master bomb maker, is considered an "evil genius" by House Homeland Security Committee Chairman Peter King, while the CIA's Michael Morell has proclaimed him to be a "mastermind," a "master at his craft," and perhaps "the most dangerous terrorist alive today."[66] Thus far, this mastermind's record is pretty miserable.

He was apparently responsible for the attempt, noted in chapter 1, by the Yemen al-Qaeda affiliate in 2010 to put bombs on cargo planes, as well as for a similar plot in 2012. Both of these were thwarted by insider intelligence work. He also seems to have furnished the underwear bomb used in a disrupted attempt to blow up a U.S.-bound airliner in 2009. That bomb suffered from a couple of rather unmasterly design flaws, according to the TSA's Kip Hawley: it could not be detonated and was too small to destroy the aircraft.[67] Yet, surveying this record of perfect failure on the *CBS Evening News* on March 23, 2015, Scott Pelley provocatively somehow managed to conclude that the Yemeni group was behind "three nearly successful attempts to bomb U.S. airlines."

The only one of al-Asiri's bombs to actually explode was placed on the body (probably in the rectum) of his brother, who was standing next to the target, a Saudi prince, when it was detonated remotely. Al-Asiri's brother was blown to pieces, but the prince escaped with only minor wounds.[68]

The Record

Overall, then, the record of accomplishment by homegrown terrorists, foreign adversaries, and those supposed "masterminds" abroad is, despite the 9/11 outlier, considerably less than awesome. For some, like Yemen's al-Asiri, it is pretty nearly one of unrelieved fiasco.

And there is a broader point. The persistent exaggeration of the mental and physical capacities of terrorists, as documented in this chapter as well as in chapters 1 and 3, has the perverse effect of glorifying the terrorist enterprise in the minds of many of its practitioners. Marc Sageman argues that to effectively counter terrorism, efforts should be made to reduce the glory from terrorism by treating terrorists more like common criminals—although this would mean, he points out, putting a stop to press conferences in which officials "hold self-congratulatory celebrations of their newest victories in the 'war on terror.'" He stresses that to allow officials to "exploit the issue of terrorism for political gain"—a phenomenon we called an "institutional interest in delusion" in chapter 1—"is counterproductive."[69]

To be sure, even knuckleheads can occasionally do damage. But there is something quite spooky about imagining terrorists to be everywhere, about extrapolating wildly from 9/11 to conclude that many are omni-competent masterminds, and about acting like their press agent by flaunting and exaggerating their often-pathetic schemes to do damage.

The remainder of this book turns its attention to an evaluation of the counterterrorists' chase of these people—an enterprise in which costs are high and benefits are often elusive.

PART TWO | The Chase

| Evaluating the Counterterrorism
Enterprise

I T SEEMS INCREASINGLY likely, earlier chapters have argued, that official
and public reaction to the terror attacks of September 11, 2001, has been
substantially disproportionate to the real threat al-Qaeda (and international
terrorism more generally) presents, either as an international menace in itself
or as an inspiration or model for homegrown amateurs.

However, unlike the emperor's new clothes, terrorism does exist, and therefore some degree of effort to deal with that hazard is certainly appropriate. The
issue, then, is a quantitative one: At what point does a reaction to a threat that
is real become excessive?

President George W. Bush says, "For me, the lesson of 9/11 was simple.
Don't take chances."[1] He is certainly right about the simplicity of the lesson
he managed to come up with. However, in applying it in response to a tragedy
that inflicted perhaps $200 billion in direct and indirect losses, he created
tragedies that were far greater: increases in domestic counterterrorism expenditures of over $1 trillion, and two wars that thus far have cost several trillion
dollars and have led to well over 100,000 deaths, including twice as many
Americans as died on September 11.[2]

Far overdue, clearly, are extensive, transparent, and less simplistic efforts
to evaluate the reaction to 9/11. Virtually none of this, it appears, has been
done by the administrators in charge.[3] Instead, under the daily barrage of the
Threat Matrix, initial, if clearly alarmist, perspectives have essentially been
maintained, and the vast and hasty increases in spending on homeland security have been perpetuated.

Thus in 2010, a careful assessment by a committee of the National Academy of Sciences concluded that counterterrorism funds have been expended without serious analysis of the sort routinely required in other areas of government, or indeed of the sort carried out by the Department of Homeland Security (DHS) itself for natural hazards—such as floods and hurricanes, which the committee deemed to be "near state of the art," "based on extensive data," "validated empirically," and "well suited to near-term decision needs." After searching for the better part of two years, the committee disclosed that it could not find "*any* DHS risk analysis capabilities and methods" adequate for supporting the decisions made. The committee noted that "little effective attention" was paid to issues that are "fundamental"; it was (with one exception) never shown "*any* document" that could explain "exactly how the risk analyses [were] conducted"; and it looked over reports in which it was not clear "what problem [was] being addressed."[4] As far as we can tell, the report, which essentially suggested that the DHS had spent hundreds of billions of dollars without knowing what it was doing, generated no coverage in the media whatsoever.

The question that should be key here is not "Are we safer?" but, rather, "Are any gains in security worth the funds expended?" Or, as this absolutely central question was posed shortly after September 11 by risk analyst Howard Kunreuther: "How much should we be willing to pay for a small reduction in probabilities that are already extremely low?"[5] That such questions are not asked and that standard methods of analysis are not applied to these enormous expenditures suggests denial at best and delusion at worst.

Applying Three Analytic Approaches

As noted earlier, U.S. expenditures since 9/11 on domestic homeland security alone—that is, excluding overseas expenditures like those on the wars in Iraq and Afghanistan—have expanded by a total of well over $1 trillion.[6] The question is: How much terrorist destruction must these expenditures have waylaid in order to justify the outlays?

To answer this, we apply standard cost-benefit and risk-analytic procedures of the sort called for by the National Academy committee. These have been developed, codified, and increasingly used as an aid in responsible decision making for the last few decades—or in some respects, for centuries.[7] Three specific analytic techniques central to this approach can be applied to evaluate the domestic counterterrorism spending that has taken place since 2001: the cost per saved life, acceptable risk, and cost-benefit analysis.[8] In later chapters, we will use this approach to evaluate specific policing and intelligence measures.

When regulators propose a new rule or regulation to enhance safety, they are routinely required to estimate how much it will cost to save a single life under their proposal. Table 5-1 supplies information about how this calculation comes out for dozens of government rules and regulations in the United States.

The results are anything but tidy, and they often reflect psychological and political aspects of risk perception or electoral and lobbyist pressures. However, some general tendencies and limits have been established over time. Regulators and administrators generally begin to become unwilling to spend more than $1 million to save a life, and they are quite reluctant to spend over $10 million, preferring instead to expend funds on measures that save lives at a lower cost.[9]

This approach can be, and has been, expanded to embrace deaths by terrorism. Following widely applied procedures, a study for the U.S. Department of Homeland Security by Lisa Robinson and her colleagues concluded that the best estimate of a value of a saved human life for homeland security analysis would be about $7.5 million in 2014 dollars.[10] Most studies focus on relatively common risks such as workplace or motor vehicle accidents, and the Robinson study goes on to suggest that "more involuntary, uncontrollable, and dread risks may be assigned a value that is perhaps twice that of more familiar risks," or some $15 million. This approach essentially adds into the analysis much of the substantial indirect and ancillary costs, including emotional ones, associated with a terrorist event.

In all, the United States spends about $115 billion per year on deterring, disrupting, or protecting against domestic counterterrorism.[11] If each saved life is valued at $15 million, it would be necessary for the counterterrorism measures to prevent or protect against between 7,000 and 8,000 terrorism deaths in the country each year—or twice that if the lower figure of $7.5 million for a saved life is applied.

These figures seem to be very high. As noted earlier, the total number of people killed by Islamist extremist terrorists in the United States since 9/11 is nineteen, or less than two per year—a far cry, of course, from 7,000 to 8,000 per year. A defender of the spending might argue that the number is that low primarily because of the counterterrorism efforts. Others might find that reasoning to be a very considerable stretch.[12]

An instructive comparison might be made with the Los Angeles Police Department, which operates on a yearly budget of $1.3 billion.[13] Considering only lives saved following this discussion, that expenditure would be justified if the police saved some 175 lives every year when each saved life is valued at

TABLE 5-1 Regulatory Expenditure per Life Saved

Regulation	Year	Agency	Cost per Life Saved in 2010 Dollars
Steering column protection standards	1967	NHTSA	140,000
Unvented space heater ban	1980	CPSC	140,000
Front seatbelt/air bag for autos	1984	NHTSA	140,000
Aircraft cabin fire protection standard	1985	FAA	140,000
Underground construction standards	1989	OSHA	140,000
Auto fuel system integrity	1975	NHTSA	710,000
Trihalomethane in drinking water	1979	EPA	850,000
Aircraft seat cushion flammability	1984	FAA	850,000
Alcohol and drug controls	1985	FRA	850,000
Aircraft floor emergency lighting	1984	FAA	990,000
Concrete and masonry construction	1988	OSHA	990,000
Passive restraints for trucks and buses	1989	NHTSA	1,100,000
Children's sleepwear flammability ban	1973	CPSC	1,400,000
Auto side impact standards	1990	NHTSA	1,400,000
Metal mine electrical equipment standards	1970	MSHA	2,400,000
Trenching and evacuation standards	1989	OSHA	2,600,000
Hazard communication standard	1983	OSHA	2,700,000
Truck, bus, and multipurpose vehicle side impact	1989	NHTSA	3,700,000
Grain dust explosion prevention	1987	OSHA	4,700,000
Rear lap/shoulder belts for autos	1989	NHTSA	5,400,000
Standards for radionuclides in uranium mines	1984	EPA	5,800,000
Ethylene dibromide in drinking water	1991	EPA	9,700,000
Asbestos occupational exposure limit	1972	OSHA	14,000,000
Benzene occupational exposure limit	1987	OSHA	15,000,000
Electrical equipment in coal mines	1970	MSHA	15,800,000
Arsenic emission standards for glass plants	1986	EPA	22,900,000
Cover/move uranium mill tailings	1983	EPA	76,100,000
Acrylonitrate occupational exposure limit	1978	OSHA	87,000,000
Coke ovens occupational exposure limit	1976	OSHA	107,400,000
Arsenic occupational exposure limit	1978	OSHA	180,800,000
Asbestos ban	1989	EPA	187,200,000
1,2-Dechloropropane in drinking water	1991	EPA	1,103,900,000
Hazardous waste land disposal ban	1988	EPA	7,084,000,000
Municipal solid waste landfills	1988	EPA	32,300,000,000
Formaldehyde occupational exposure limit	1987	OSHA	145,723,000,000
Atrazine/alachlor in drinking water	1991	EPA	155,640,000,000
Hazardous waste listing for wood-preserving chemicals	1990	EPA	9,635,870,000,000

Adapted by Mark Stewart from Viscusi, "Value of Life in Legal Contexts."

$7.5 million. (It makes sense to use the lower figure for the value of a saved life in this case, because police work is likely to have few indirect and ancillary costs—for example, a fatal car crash does not cause others to avoid driving.) At present, some 300 homicides occur each year in the city, and about the same number of deaths are inflicted by automobile accidents.[14] It is certainly plausible to suggest that both of those numbers would be substantially higher without police efforts, and accordingly it seems reasonable to conclude that local taxpayers are getting pretty good value for their money. Moreover, the police provide a great many other services (or "co-benefits") to the community for the same expenditure, from directing traffic to arresting burglars and shoplifters.

ACCEPTABLE RISK

Another way to approach the issue is to compare the annual fatality rates caused by terrorism with those caused by other hazards. Table 5-2 provides relevant information. It leads to a consideration of the central analytic issue of acceptable risk. Is the likelihood of being killed by the hazard unacceptably high, or is it low enough to be acceptable? That is, just how safe is safe enough?

We often say that there is nothing more important than the value of human life. Yet, obviously, we don't really believe this. Americans are clearly willing to sacrifice tens of thousands of lives each year to have automobiles, even though it is quite possible to move people without killing them: people killed in railroad accidents in a year can often be counted on the fingers of one hand. Many other social policies involve the same sort of consideration. As a society, we regularly and inescapably adopt policies in which human lives are part of the price.

A review of 132 federal regulatory decisions associated with public exposure to environmental carcinogens found that regulatory action never occurs if the individual annual fatality risk is lower than one in 700,000.[15] Variously, it appears, risks are deemed acceptable if the annual fatality risk is lower than that figure, or perhaps lower than one in 1 million or one in 2 million.[16]

These considerations, substantially accepted for years, even decades, by public regulatory agencies after extensive evaluation and considerable debate and public discussion, are designed to provide a viable, if somewhat rough guideline for public policy. Clearly, hazards that fall into the unacceptable range (traffic accidents, for example) should generally command the most attention and the most resources, while those hazards in the acceptable range (drowning in bathtubs, for example) would generally be deemed of little or even negligible concern—that is, they are risks we can live with—and further

TABLE 5-2 Comparison of Annual Fatality Risks

Hazard	Territory	Period	Total Fatalities for the Period	Annual Fatality Risk
World War II	Worldwide	1939–1945	61,000,000	1 in 221
Cancers	US	2009	560,000	1 in 540
War (civilians)	Iraq	2003–2008	113,616	1 in 1,150
All accidents	US	2007	119,000	1 in 2,500
Traffic accidents	US	2008	37,261	1 in 8,200
Traffic accidents	Canada	2008	2,431	1 in 13,500
Traffic accidents	Australia	2008	1,466	1 in 15,000
Homicide	US	2006	14,180	1 in 22,000
Traffic accidents	UK	2008	2,538	1 in 23,000
Terrorism	Northern Ireland	1970–2013	1,780	1 in 50,000
Industrial accidents	US	2007	5,657	1 in 53,000
Homicide	Canada	2008	611	1 in 55,000
Intifada	Israel	2000–2006	553	1 in 72,000
Homicide	Great Britain	2008	887	1 in 67,000
Homicide	Australia	2008	290	1 in 76,000
Terrorism	US	2001	2,982	1 in 101,000
Natural disasters	US	1999–2008	6,294	1 in 480,000
Drowning in bathtub	US	2003	320	1 in 950,000
Terrorism	UK	1970–2013	2,221	1 in 1,200,000
Home appliances	US	yearly average	200	1 in 1,500,000
Deer accidents	US	2006	150	1 in 2,000,000
Commercial aviation	US	yearly average	130	1 in 2,300,000
Terrorism	US	1970–2013	3,372	1 in 4,000,000
Terrorism	Canada	1970–2013	336	1 in 4,300,000
Terrorism	Great Britain	1970–2013	441	1 in 5,900,000
Peanut allergies	US	yearly average	50–100	1 in 6,000,000
Lightning	US	1999–2008	424	1 in 7,000,000
Terrorism	Australia (incl Bali)	1970–2013	120	1 in 8,000,000
Transnational Terrorism	World outside war zones	1975–2003	13,971	1 in 12,500,000
Terrorism	US	2002–2013	33	1 in 110,000,000

Source: Terrorism fatalities taken from START, Global Terrorism Database. It contains country-by-country information for more than 140,000 terrorist incidents that took place throughout the world between 1970 and 2013. The GTD has been updated since 2007 to include more terrorist incidents for the 1970–2007 period than were included in earlier editions of the compilation.

precautions would scarcely be worth pursuing unless they are quite remarkably inexpensive.

Overall, then, it is clear that governments have been able to set out, and agree upon, risk-acceptance criteria for use in decision making in regard to a wide variety of hazards, including ones that are highly controversial and emotive, such as pollution, nuclear and chemical power plant accidents, and public exposure to nuclear radiation and environmental carcinogens.

As can be seen in table 5-2, the annual fatality risks from terrorism in all its forms in the developed world are, in almost all cases, less than one in 1 million per year. For the United States from 1970 through 2013 (which includes, of course, the 9/11 attacks), they are one in 4 million per year. For the period from 2002 through 2013, they are one in 110 million per year.

Applying conventional standards, then, under current conditions terrorism presents a threat to human life in the Western world that is, in general, acceptable. And efforts, particularly expensive ones, to further reduce its likelihood or consequences are scarcely justified.[17] Indeed, a legitimate policy consideration might be to wonder whether expenditures designed to keep the terrorism risk that low have been excessive, and whether some of them might be better focused on dealing with hazards with higher risk, even if doing so increases the terrorism risk somewhat. Ignoring this policy option comes at the expense of considerable opportunity costs. Diverting even a few billion dollars from the $115 billion annual homeland security budget and toward more smoke alarms, tornado shelters, greater car safety, and other effective lifesaving measures would save hundreds of lives—far more than appear to have been saved by the mammoth homeland security expenditures.[18]

These calculations of the risk from terrorism are based on history, and there is, of course, no guarantee that the frequencies of the past will persist into the future: things could become worse. However, it has been shown in chapters 3 and 4 that terrorists are not really all that capable a bunch. Moreover, there seems to be little evidence that terrorists are becoming any more destructive, particularly in the West. In fact, at least outside of war zones, the level of terrorist activity and destruction seems to be diminishing, not expanding. Indeed, no major terrorist attack (one inflicting, say, more than twenty-five deaths) has occurred in the West since 2005.[19] Moreover, we include the 9/11 attacks in this count, and scarcely any terrorist attack before or since, even in war zones, has inflicted even one-tenth as much destruction. Not only is that tragedy standing out as an aberration, but, as noted in chapter 1, it has essentially become officially accepted that the likelihood of a large-scale organized attack like 9/11 has declined and that the terrorist attacks to most fear are ones that are small scale and disorganized. These can inflict painful losses, of course, as in the attacks in Paris in early 2015. But even if they do occur, they will not change the overall fatality risk very much. Those who wish to discount such arguments and projections need to demonstrate why they think terrorists will suddenly get their act together and inflict massively increased violence, visiting savage discontinuities on the historical data. Repeated warnings over the last decades that they would do so by developing nuclear weapons have proven to be empty.[20]

COST-BENEFIT ANALYSIS

Cost-benefit analysis brings this all together. A conventional approach to cost-effectiveness compares the costs of a security measure with its benefits, as tallied in lives saved and damages averted.

The benefit of a security measure is a multiplicative composite of three considerations: the probability of a successful attack absent all security measures; the losses sustained in a successful attack (these two, combined, constitute the risk); and the reduction in risk furnished by the specific security measure under consideration.[21] That is,

> (benefit of a specific security measure) = (probability of a successful attack absent all security measures) × (losses sustained in the successful attack) × (reduction in risk furnished by the specific security measure under consideration)

The interaction of these factors can perhaps best be seen in an example. Suppose there is a dangerous curve in a road that results in an automobile accident from time to time. To evaluate measures designed to ease this problem, the analyst would need to estimate (1) the probability of an accident each year if there were no safety measures in place, (2) the consequences of the accident (death, injury, property damage), and (3) the degree to which a proposed safety measure lowers the probability of an accident (such as erecting a warning sign) and/or the losses sustained in the accident (such as erecting a protective crash barrier). If the benefit of the risk-reduction measure—these three items multiplied together—outweighs its cost, the measure would be deemed to be cost-effective.

These considerations can be usefully adapted in a procedure known as "break-even analysis." In this, we seek to determine what the probability of a successful terrorist attack would have to be for a security measure to begin to justify its cost. Thus, we set the cost of the security measure equal to its benefit (the break-even point):

(cost of the specific security measure under consideration) = (probability of a successful attack absent all security measures) × (losses sustained in the successful attack) × (reduction in risk furnished by the specific security measure under consideration)

This becomes

(probability of a successful attack absent all security measures) = (cost of the specific security measure under consideration) / [(losses sustained in the successful attack) × (reduction in risk furnished by the specific security measure under consideration)]

This approach will now be applied to a specific security measure (or set of measures): the overall increase in homeland security spending in the United States (including for national intelligence) by federal and state and local governments. Specifically, we calculate how many terrorist attacks would have had to be deterred, averted, or protected by the increase in counterterrorism spending since 9/11 for that increase to begin to be justified. To do so, we need to estimate the three qualities on the right side of the equation—that is, (1) the cost of the security measure (or set of security measures), (2) the losses sustained in the successful attack, and (3) the reduction in risk furnished by the security measure.

1. **The increased cost in domestic counterterrorism expenditures.** Before the 9/11 attacks, domestic counterterrorism expenditures per year were about $40 billion in 2014 dollars. These increased by about $75 billion per year in the subsequent decade or so.

Although we will use this figure of $75 billion per year for the annual increase in spending on domestic counterterrorism, it should be viewed as a conservative measure of the degree to which homeland security expenditures have risen since 9/11. That is, the figure leaves out nearly $50 billion in various opportunity costs (like people's time spent in airport security lines), privacy issues, hidden and indirect costs of implementing security-related regulations, and $10 billion in costs per year incurred by the private sector.[22] We also exclude the costs of the terror-related (or terror-impelled) wars in Iraq and Afghanistan.

2. **The losses sustained in a successful terrorist attack.** For thinking about the possible losses—both direct and indirect—inflicted by a terrorist attack, we lay out a range of possibilities across the top of table 5-3. As noted earlier, deaths at the hands of terrorists are very often taken to be far more significant than those inflicted by other hazards; that study commissioned by the Department of Homeland Security suggests that, although human life is

TABLE 5-3 Evaluating the Increase in Counterterrorim Spending Since 2001

Risk Reduction Caused by Enhanced Counterterrorism Expenditures	Losses from a Successful Terrorist Attack						
	$100 million Ft. Hood shooting	$500 million Boston Marathon bombing	$1 billion Times Square bombing	$5 billion London bombing	$200 billion 9/11	$1 trillion nuclear port	$5 trillion nuclear Grand Central
10 percent	7,500	1500	750	150	4	.75	.15
25 percent	3,000	600	300	60	2	.30	.06
50 percent	1,500	300	150	30	.75	.15	.03
75 percent	1,000	200	100	20	.50	.10	.02
90 percent	833	167	83	17	.42	.08	.02
100 percent	750	150	75	15	.38	.08	.02

Note: The cell entries indicate the number of terrorist attacks that would need to occur each year in the absence of all counterterrorism measures in order to begin to justify a yearly counterterrorism expenditure of $75 billion. If the $75 billion expenditure is expected to reduce the risk (the likelihood of, and/or the damage caused by, a successful terrorist attack) by 50 percent, those expenditures would need to deter, disrupt, or protect against at least half of the attacks in each entry in the 50 percent line. For the boxed entries, that would be 150 Boston-type attacks per year, 15 London-type attacks each year, or one 9/11-type attack about every three years.

often taken to have a value of some $7.5 million, lives lost to terrorism should be valued at twice that amount. Others might suggest even higher multiples. In estimating the costs inflicted by a terrorist event, however, we prefer to value life at the lower figure and then, on a case-by-case basis, add in the indirect costs from economic, social, and psychological side effects.

As is developed more fully in appendix B, we see that terrorism mostly inflicts losses that are quite low—in general, terrorism is not only a low probability event but also a low consequence one. Indeed, the vast majority of terrorist attacks kill no one at all. However, at the low end of the scale in table 5-3, we start with events that impose a substantial loss of $100 million. An example would be the shootings at Fort Hood in Texas in 2009, in which thirteen people were killed. Although this has been by far the greatest loss of life inflicted in a terrorist act in the United States since 2001, almost all of the damage came in direct costs in the form of death and injury. It did not seem to cause additional substantial economic losses or widespread fear or anguish. At $7.5 million per life, the cost for the loss of life for that occurrence comes to $98 million. There would be additional costs for injuries and some for property damage, but any indirect losses are likely in this case to be fairly low: the event did not seem to traumatize many or cause economic shifts or tourism diversions.

Losses sustained in the Boston Marathon bombings of 2013 were quite substantial, even though the perpetrators appear to be fairly typical of those arrested in the United States, in that they were amateurs, devoid of much (if any) training, dependent on improvisation and luck, and poor at long-range planning.[23] In addition to three deaths and a considerable number of injuries, some of them very severe, the Boston Marathon terrorists inflicted considerable indirect costs on the region, not only through their actions but also through the costs of pursuing them during the several days they were on the loose.[24] Not only was the city effectively closed down for a day, but travel to Boston was canceled or deferred, a Red Sox baseball game was canceled, and the large crime scene forced the closure of many businesses. The daily GDP for Boston is close to $1 billion.[25] Thus, a reduction in economic activity of just 5 or 10 percent for three or four days easily reaches hundreds of millions of dollars. A reasonable estimate of the full losses inflicted by the Boston Marathon bombings would be in the vicinity of $500 million.

This would also be roughly the costs of the damage that might be inflicted in Times Square by a car bomb similar to the one a rather inept terrorist tried to detonate there in 2010. Adding in potential losses to business and tourism owing to the event, the total losses might come to $1 billion as an upper bound.

The losses sustained at the 2005 London and 2004 Madrid bombings that killed 52 and 191 commuters, respectively, are sometimes estimated to be $5 billion in direct and indirect losses, with most estimates around $2 or $3 billion.[26]

A number of studies have sought to assess the direct and indirect costs of the 9/11 terrorist attacks—far and away the most destructive single terrorist act in history, and one in which the indirect costs considerably outweigh the (obviously horrific) direct ones. The studies generally conclude that a fair, if somewhat high, estimate for the full losses sustained in the attack—lives lost, property damaged or destroyed, psychological trauma, and indirect losses from travel and tourism reductions, business interruptions, and economic shocks—would be some $200 billion, with loss of life valued at $20 billion, direct physical damage at $30 billion, and loss of GDP at $70 to $140 billion (equivalent to 0.5 to 1 percent of GDP).[27]

The potential losses if terrorists were able to set off an atomic bomb or device at an important port might reach $1 trillion.[28] And the losses for an atomic explosion in Grand Central Station in New York City could be $5 trillion.[29] However, the likelihood that terrorists could accomplish either seems to be extremely small.[30]

An additional consideration concerns what might be called extended (as opposed to indirect) costs. Thus, 9/11 not only led to considerable indirect costs as people avoided flying and traveling for a time, but the attacks also propelled the United States into expensive overseas wars. Few terrorist events trigger such extreme reactions, which can be considered as contributors either to the costs of the terrorist attack or to the costs of counterterrorism.[31] To the extent that extreme reactions like multitrillion-dollar wars are considered to be (a self-inflicted) part of the cost of the terrorist attack, they do far more damage to the attacked than the effort of the terrorists. To the extent that such reactions are considered to increase the costs of counterterrorism, they are likely to render almost any counterterrorism security measure cost-ineffective: if an increase in counterterrorism spending of $75 billion per year fails to be cost-effective, an increase of several times that amount will be even less so. We do not include extended costs in the basic analysis here, but they obviously can be significant in some cases. Indeed, in an important sense, the most cost-effective counterterrorism measure is to refrain from overreacting.

3. **The reduction in risk furnished by the enhanced security measures.** To evaluate the reduction in risk provided by this array of security measures we need to consider their effectiveness in deterring, disrupting,

or protecting against a terrorist attack. The rows of table 5-3 show various degrees of risk reduction.

In assessing the risk reduction attained by the increase in domestic counterterrorism expenditures since 9/11, it is important, first, to assess the risk-reduction effectiveness of security measures that were in place before that event. Police and domestic intelligence agencies have long had in place some procedures, techniques, trained personnel, and action plans to deal with bombs and shootings, and with those who plot them. Indeed, Michael Sheehan, former New York City Deputy Commissioner for Counterterrorism, contends that "[t]he most important work in protecting our country since 9/11 has been accomplished with the capacity that was in place when the event happened, not with any of the new capability bought since 9/11. I firmly believe that those huge budget increases have not significantly contributed to our post-9/11 security. . . . The big wins had little to do with the new programs."[32]

In addition, it should be kept in mind that the tragic events of 9/11 massively heightened the awareness of the public to the threat of terrorism, resulting in extra vigilance that has often resulted in the arrest of terrorists or the foiling of terrorist attempts—like those of the shoe and underwear bombers in 2001 and 2009.

In our analysis, we will assume that risk reduction caused by the security measures in place before 9/11 and by the extra vigilance of the public after that event together reduced risk by 45 percent. This is an exceedingly conservative estimate because security measures that are at once effective and relatively inexpensive are generally the first to be implemented—for example, one erects warning signs at a potentially dangerous curve in the road before rebuilding the highway. Thus, a study of security measures in shopping centers found that the least costly measures, suspicious package reporting, reduced risk by 60 percent, but the costly and inconvenient searching of bags at entrances achieved only 15 percent risk reduction.[33] Furthermore, as was discussed rather extensively in chapters 3 and 4, most terrorists (or would-be terrorists) do not show much intelligence, cleverness, resourcefulness, or initiative. Therefore, measures to deal with them are relatively inexpensive and are likely to be instituted first. Dealing with the smarter and more capable terrorists is more difficult and expensive, but these people represent, it certainly appears, a decided minority.

For our analysis, we will assume that the increase in U.S. expenditures on homeland security since 2001 has been dramatically effective at closing the gap. If the preexisting measures and the extra public vigilance reduce the risk by 45 percent, we will assume that the additional security expenditures put in place after 9/11 reduce the risk by another 50 percent. Thus, the total risk reduction supplied by all the security measures is assumed to be 95 percent.

Some measures advantage society in ways that are not particularly intended by their initiators, and therefore provide some "co-benefit" as a pleasant bonus or by-product. For example, there has been a decline in the number of deaths by lightning in the United States in recent years, caused among other reasons by the fact that people no longer use corded telephones nearly so much as they did in the past.[34] If expanded counterterrorism security measures reduced Americans' anxieties about terrorism, that effect might be seen as a social gain and accordingly be included when assessing the benefit of the security measures. As was seen in chapter 2, however, there does not seem to have been much decline in anxiety about terrorism, despite the truly impressive sums expended on counterterrorism since 2001. Thus, this consideration will not be included in our analysis.

RESULTS OF THE COST-BENEFIT ANALYSIS

In table 5-3, we evaluate the contribution of a security measure or set of measures that costs $75 billion per year. The cells show the number of successful attacks per year that would be required to take place in the absence of all counterterrorism measures in order to begin to justify that expense (the break-even point). This is shown for various attack scenarios and for various levels of risk reduction.

The boxed entries are for our rather generous assumption that the $75 billion increase in security expenditures reduces the risk of a terrorist attack (its consequences and/or its likelihood) by 50 percent. Under that assumption, in order for the yearly costs of a $75 billion security measure or set of security measures to begin to be justified, there would have to have been 300 attacks like the Boston Marathon bombing each year—or about one a day—in the absence of all security measures. Or thirty London-size attacks per year—more than one a week. Or about three 9/11 attacks every four years.

To begin to justify its expense, a $75 billion security measure that reduces risk by 50 percent would be expected to deter, disrupt, or protect against half of these—the 300 Boston Marathon–type attacks would be reduced to 150 per year, for example. In our case, that would be the task of the set of security measures added to those already in place in September 2001, while the existing security measures, combined with the added vigilance inspired by 9/11, would separately deter, disrupt, or protect against almost all of the rest.

To look at this another way, if the concern is that there might be one London-size attack every month, and if the enhanced security measures would reduce this risk by 50 percent, there would be a net loss of $45 billion per year. That is, $1 of cost would generate only 40 cents of benefit.

There are extreme scenarios that can be used to suggest that enhanced U.S. security expenditures could be cost-effective—if they routinely prevented a nuclear attack in a crowded city, for example. However, for those who find that outcome dangerously likely, the policy response would logically be to spend money on reducing the risk of nuclear terrorism by putting together international agreements to track stockpiles of nuclear material and to institute stings to undercut the illegal transfer of such material. The response would not be, for example, to spend tens of billions of dollars each year on protection measures that are scarcely likely to be effective against an atomic explosion.

Some homeland security spending is devoted to ventures other than counterterrorism, of course—to patrol and secure the borders, for example. However, it should be kept in mind that we are only assessing the *increase* in homeland security spending that has taken place since 9/11 and that has overwhelmingly been motivated by concerns about terrorism—an issue to be discussed more fully in later chapters. Moreover, our estimate that this increase has been $75 billion per year is decidedly on the low side. And, finally, even if one wishes to maintain that only half of the increase has been spent on counterterrorism measures, those expenditures would still need to deter, disrupt, or protect against seventy-five Boston Marathon–size terrorist acts per year—more than one a week—or the equivalent. As has been suggested in chapters 3 and 4, terrorists scarcely seem to be numerous, competent, and dedicated enough to carry out such a task.

Other Applications

Each security measure can be subjected to the methods of risk analysis we have applied in this chapter as a first cut toward evaluating them. In later chapters, we will do so for expenditures for various policing and domestic intelligence agencies and enterprises.

It should be pointed out that our findings should not be taken to suggest that *all* security measures necessarily fail to be cost-effective; there may be specific measures that are cost-effective. It appears, for example, that the protection of a standard office-type building would be cost-effective only if the likelihood of a sizable terrorist attack on the building is a thousand times greater than it is at present; something similar holds for the protection of bridges.[35] On the other hand, as will be discussed more fully in chapter 8, hardened cockpit doors and the federal flight deck officer program (which allows pilots, flight engineers, and navigators to volunteer for training so they can carry a firearm on flights) certainly appear to be cost-effective, even as the provision for air marshals on the planes decidedly is not and the cost-effectiveness of full-body scanners is questionable at best.

CHAPTER SIX

The Federal Bureau of
Investigation

I N THIS CHAPTER, we apply standard cost-benefit and risk-analysis procedures, as laid out in the previous chapter, in an effort to determine whether,
given all the other security, intelligence, and policing measures already in
place, the contribution of the Federal Bureau of Investigation to the counterterrorism effort reduces the terrorism risk enough to justify its cost. Specifically,
we determine the number of attacks the bureau would need to deter, disrupt,
or protect against to justify its counterterrorism budget.

Then, working from the discussion in chapters 3 and 4, we evaluate the
capacities and motivations of the terrorists and would-be terrorists who are the
FBI's focus and concern, and we apply this evaluation to estimate how many
terrorist acts might have been committed in the United States but for the
intelligence and policing efforts of the bureau.

Finally, we make some suggestions about the efficacy of policing efforts
in which simple, if forceful, warnings are delivered to putative terrorists early
on in their plotting. It seems quite possible that, given the capacities and the
mentalities of most would-be terrorists, this approach might well have waylaid
much terrorism at far lower cost than other policing methods, especially the
common one of implanting informants among the plotters.

The Costs of the FBI's Counterterrorism Program

To begin our evaluation, we need first to estimate the cost of the FBI's counterterrorism efforts.

The U.S. Department of Justice had frequently called upon Secret Service operatives to conduct federal investigations. Then in 1908 the department appointed a force of thirty-four special agents for the purpose, an action celebrated as the beginning of the FBI. The bureau was drastically reformed in 1924, becaming a "model of professionalism," according to its official history, under its new director, J. Edgar Hoover.[1] The bureau and its "G-men"—and notably Hoover himself—quickly rose to national prominence in the 1930s with the successful prosecution of Bruno Hauptmann for the Lindbergh kidnapping, the arrest of racketeer Al Capone, and the hunting down of Bonnie and Clyde, John Dillinger, "Baby Face" Nelson, and a raft of other colorful gangsters.

The FBI's workload—preventing sabotage at home and domestic counterintelligence—rose during World War II, when the 1940 staffing level of 2,000 increased nearly sevenfold to a peak of over 13,000 in 1944.[2] As figure 6-1 shows, the number of FBI employees dropped off after the war, but it increased rapidly again with the advent of the cold war, so that by 1955 staffing levels exceeded those reached during the height of the Second World War.

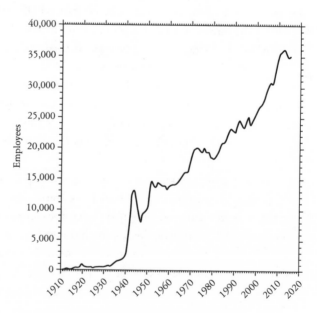

FIGURE 6-1 Federal Bureau of Investigation Employees.

Note: FY2014 and 2015 staffing levels are budget requests only.

Sources: Theoharis, *The FBI: A Comprehensive Reference Guide*, 4-5; FBI, *FBI Facts and Figures*, 9.

Although the 9/11 Commission noted that a "concern about the FBI is that it has long favored its criminal justice mission over its national security mission," the bureau did create separate counterterrorism and counterintelligence divisions two years before 9/11; and Dale Watson, the first head of the new Counterterrorism Division, recognizing an "urgent need to increase the FBI's counterterrorism strategy," developed a plan to bring the FBI to its "maximum feasible capacity" in counterterrorism by 2005.[3] Toward the end of 1999, the FBI reported that the "threat posed by extremists as a result of perceived events associated with the Year 2000 (Y2K) is very real," contending that "religious motivation" and conspiracy theories associated with the "New World Order" were "the two driving forces behind the potential for millennial violence." It was concerned that "biblical prophecy and political philosophy may merge into acts of violence by the more extreme members of domestic terrorist groups that are motivated, in part, by religion." Such a "volatile mix," it contended, "may produce violent acts aimed at precipitating the end of the world as prophesied in the Bible," and it urged law enforcement officers to be alert for "extremists willing to become martyrs."[4]

In this millennium alert of 1999, noted the 9/11 Commission, "the government as a whole seemed to be acting in concert to deal with terrorism" and "information about terrorism flowed widely and abundantly" while "the flow from the FBI was particularly remarkable." However, after the millennium alert (when not much of anything happened), "the government relaxed," and counterterrorism "went back to being a secret preserve for segments of the FBI, the Counterterrorist Center, and the Counterterrorism Security Group."[5]

Overall, then, before 9/11 the bureau most likely had modestly succeeded in reducing the terrorism risk—the consequences and/or the probability of an otherwise successful attack. Moreover, there was a strategic plan to increase that capacity by 2005—without, however, additional funding.[6] Also of benefit, the FBI has always had the ability to internally redeploy (or "surge") agents and resources to new or evolving threats in time of need—though surge officers may have little familiarity with counterterrorism issues.

By September 11, 2001, fully 1,351 agents, nearly 15 percent of its workforce, were assigned to counterterrorism tasks.[7] The tragic events of 9/11 showed that more needed to be done, and a report to FBI Director Robert Mueller in September 2001 argued that "the goal to 'prevent terrorism' requires a dramatic shift in emphasis from a reactive capability to a highly functioning intelligence capability which provides not only leads and operational support, but clear strategic analyses and direction."[8] In 2004, it was reported that after 9/11 the number of Special Agents working on terrorism had increased by

80 percent—from 1,351 to 2,398.[9] As can be seen in figure 6-1, the post-9/11 increase was exceeded in its rapidity only by the expansion in 1941 to deal with World War II. In 2002, fifty surveillance applications were sent to the courts; by 2003, the number had soared to 1,727.[10]

In the process, the FBI elevated counterterrorism to its highest priority.[11]

That mission comprises two elements: protecting the United States from terrorist attack and protecting the United States against foreign intelligence operations and espionage. The expansion of this dual mission since 9/11 has been dramatic. In 2001, the budget for counterterrorism and counterintelligence combined was $1.05 billion, or $1.4 billion in 2014 dollars.[12] This increased over threefold to $4.5 billion by 2014, making up just over half of the FBI's total budget of $8.3 billion.[13]

The FBI is not alone in substantial budget increases since 9/11: security services worldwide have also seen their budgets swell in the aftermath of 9/11.[14] Terrorism has become the highest priority for MI5 in the UK, for CSIS in Canada, for ASIO in Australia, and for other security and intelligence agencies around the world.[15]

The FBI operates field offices in 56 major U.S. cities and has over 360 "resident agencies"—satellite offices that support the larger field offices and allow the FBI to maintain a presence in a greater number of communities. FBI employees assigned to field offices and resident agencies perform the majority of the investigative and intelligence work for the FBI. The bureau also operates over 60 legal attaché offices and 14 suboffices in 67 foreign countries, coordinates and manages 103 Joint Terrorism Task Forces, and assigns staff to 55 Fusion Centers.[16] In the process, it has become the lead agency for 56 to 77 percent of terrorism convictions.[17]

The growth in FBI counterterrorism expenditures in 2014 dollars is evident in figure 6-2. The White House's Office of Management and Budget estimates that the FBI spent roughly $500 million to $600 million a year on counterterrorism prior to the events of 9/11. By separating yearly counterterrorism expenditures from those devoted to counterintelligence in the years since 9/11, we estimate an increase of approximately $2.5 billion.[18] In total, then, these expenditures accounted for close to $3 billion (36 percent) of FBI expenditures in 2014, with over 12,000 personnel dedicated to the task.[19]

Counterintelligence is the next largest expenditure category at $1.5 billion per year, while the budget for the rest—support for the administration of justice and combating civil rights violations and violent and organized crime—totals $3.7 billion.[20] The budget for its criminal division is $2.5 billion.[21]

As noted in chapter 1, since 9/11, the daily admonition from FBI Director Robert Mueller was "no counterterrorism lead goes uncovered."[22] Or, as the

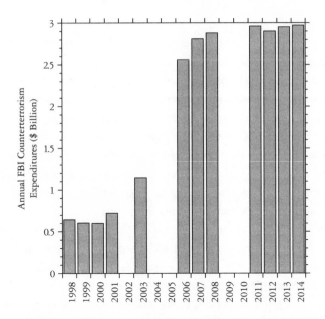

FIGURE 6-2 Annual FBI Counterterrorism Expenditures (in 2014 dollars).

Note: Includes enacted and supplemental/emergency expenditures. Funding levels for 2013 and 2014 are budget figures and do not represent actual expenditures. FBI budget data prior to 2006 do not distinguish between counterterrorism and counterintelligence expenditures. However, the OMB, Annual Report to Congress on Combating Terrorism, states that "Funding to Combat Terrorism (including Defense against WMD)" for the FBI in FY2001 was $547 million ($722 million in 2014 dollars). This will include some 9/11 costs in the last month of FY2001. FBI counterterrorism budgets in the three years prior to 2001 were roughly $450 million ($600 million in 2014 dollars). Data are not available for fiscal years 2002, 2004, 2005, 2009, and 2010.

Sources: 1998–2001: OMB, Annual Report to Congress on Combating Terrorism, Fiscal Years 2001 to 2003. 2003: OMB, Analytical Perspectives: Budget of the United States Government, Fiscal Year 2005. 2006–2014: Department of Justice, *FY2015—Authorization and Budget Request to Congress*.

FBI's special counsel puts it, "Any terrorism lead has to be followed up."[23] That costly perspective has continued to the present day.

CO-BENEFITS, AND OPPORTUNITY AND FOLLOW-ON COSTS

The cost of the security measure under consideration—the FBI's counterterrorism program—is thus $3 billion per year. However, there are some additional considerations in evaluating this figure.

On the one hand, there may be co-benefits that could be added to the benefit side of the ledger. Thus, the FBI, in the process of going after terrorists, may obtain valuable information about other crimes unrelated to terrorism, such as immigration violations, drug trading, and passport fraud, and this information may contribute to their disruption. Though not a central focus of the counterterrorism measures, this clearly is of benefit to society by reducing crime and reassuring the public.

In addition, although the FBI may not always be able to prevent attacks, its enhanced ability to apprehend terrorists quickly is a definite benefit. In particular, it reduces the costs of having suspects on the loose, scaring a risk-averse public. In 2013, the speedy identification of the Boston Marathon bombers quickly led to their apprehension, reassuring the public and allowing Bostonians to return to normalcy. Overall, however, as discussed in chapter 2, there is little indication that the public has come to feel safer by increased spending on counterterrorism measures since 2001.

On the other hand, there may be important costs of the FBI's counterter-rorism measures that have not been included. One of these involves oppor-tunity costs. There is little doubt, for example, that the increase in resources for counterterrorism has come at the expense of other FBI programs, such as combating corruption, organized crime, economic crimes, drugs, and violent crime.[24] As FBI Director Robert Mueller testified in 2011, after the September 11 attacks, the FBI immediately shifted 2,000 agents to new roles in coun-terterrorism, with 1,500 of those agents coming from drug enforcement pro-grams. And he noted as well that narcotics investigations had yet to recover from the loss of manpower: "We have not had anywhere near the footprint we had in addressing narcotics cases since 9/11."[25] Between 2000 and 2004, public corruption cases dropped from 2,491 to 1,438, violent crime cases from 32,535 to 17,299, organized crime cases from 7,678 to 3,685, and financial crime cases from 17,402 to 10,463, while fraud cases under $150,000 virtu-ally disappeared entirely, creating new categories of "risk-free crimes."[26] As an assistant U.S. attorney put it in 2002, "This is a great time to be a white-collar criminal."[27]

There are also follow-on costs. The FBI's counterterrorism efforts impose additional costs when arrested and indicted suspects enter the court system, and when those convicted are required to serve prison sentences that, in the terrorism area, are frequently very long, even when the convicted have actually committed no violence whatever: twenty-five years to life. Incarcerating a sin-gle prisoner costs multiple tens of thousands of dollars per year. This, of course, is a standard result of the policing system, and it is generally worthwhile from society's standpoint if it keeps dangerous people off the streets and helps deter others from committing crimes. It also satisfies the notion that those who break the rules should be punished. However, it will be argued later in this chapter that some, and perhaps many, of those arrested and prosecuted might have been effectively kept from perpetrating terror by simple, but pointed, warnings that they were being watched. To the degree that this is true, policing that leads to unnecessary court and incarceration costs has exacted additional outlays that do not particularly benefit society.

We exclude co-benefits and opportunity and follow-on costs from our cost-benefit calculations. However, we recognize that their inclusion could be warranted if their magnitude is determined to be significant. Throughout, it should be kept in mind that adding co-benefits will improve the cost-effectiveness of the FBI's counterterrorism measures (by increasing estimates of the benefit of the measures) while including opportunity and follow-on costs will lower it (by increasing estimates of the measures' cost).

Deaths from Terrorism Absent FBI Counterterrorism

One way to begin an evaluation of these counterterrorism expenditures is to assess how many deaths from terrorism the FBI would have to deter, prevent, or foil each year to justify its $3 billion counterterrorism budget.

Although it can be a morally difficult consideration, there is a long history of placing a monetary value on human life as discussed in chapter 5. As noted there, the concept has been expanded to embrace homeland security concerns, leading to an estimate valuing a saved human life to be about $7.5 million in 2014 dollars, with the suggestion that "more involuntary, uncontrollable, and dread risks" like terrorism might be assigned a value of some $15 million. This approach provides a useful overall first-cut assessment.

If the FBI spends $3 billion per year on policing terrorism, and if each saved life is valued at $15 million, it would be necessary for the FBI by its efforts to prevent some 200 terrorism deaths in the United States each year to justify such an expenditure. If the lower figure of $7.5 million for a saved life is applied, the number of terrorism deaths the FBI would have to prevent would be 400 per year.

As detailed in chapter 3, the total number of people killed by Islamist extremist terrorists within the United States since 9/11 is nineteen, or less than two per year—nowhere near, of course, 200 or 400 per year. A defender of FBI spending might well insist that it is that low primarily because of the counterterrorism efforts of the bureau. For instance, it could be argued that about 250 lives per year could have been saved as a result of thwarting planned terrorist attacks in the country in the period 2001–2007, assuming that each plot would have been successfully carried out.[28] As detailed in chapter 3, however, that assumption scarcely seems justified in light of the patent incompetence of many would-be terrorists. Defenders of the spending would also need to explain why there were no attacks in the West in the immediate aftermath of 9/11, or in the years that followed before enhanced homeland security measures, and spending, were put in place.

Another comparison might be useful. Between 2000 and 2013, "active shooters," defined by the FBI as individuals "actively engaged in killing or attempting to kill people in a confined and populated area," have murdered 468 people in the United States.[29] Only about 16 of these shooting deaths were inflicted by Islamist terrorists. The FBI does expend much more effort on terrorism than on the problem presented by "active shooters." However, the huge imbalance in the numbers may suggest that it is not FBI efforts that have been decisive in keeping the terrorism kill count so low. Rather, it is because there simply aren't very many terrorists out there.

Applying a Full Cost-Benefit Analysis

On its face, it seems implausible that the FBI has been able to save some 200 (or 400) lives every year from terrorism within the United States—particularly from Islamist extremist terrorism that is the chief concern and the one that has impelled, and continues to be used to justify, its impressive counterterrorism budget. However, terrorism causes losses beyond inflicting fatalities. A full risk and cost-benefit analysis of the FBI's counterterrorism efforts requires including these other costs in addition to those generated by a loss of life.

To do so we apply a version of the break-even approach, as set out in chapter 5, to FBI counterterrorism spending. In this case, we consider a conditional situation. Specifically, we evaluate how many terrorist attacks that were not deterred, disrupted, or protected against by other security measures would need to occur in the absence of the FBI's counterterrorism efforts in order to justify its yearly expenditure of $3 billion. The key equation is:

(probability of a successful attack absent the FBI's counterterrorism program) = (cost of the FBI's counterterrorism program) / (losses sustained in the successful attack) × (reduction in risk furnished by FBI's counterterrorism program)

The cells in table 6-1 show an array of break-even points: the annual number of successful attacks in the absence of the FBI's counterterrorism program that would need to take place to begin to justify a counterterrorism expenditure

TABLE 6-1 Evaluating the FBI's Counterterrorism Efforts

	Losses from a Successful Terrorist Attack						
Risk Reduction by FBI	$100 million / Ft. Hood shooting	$500 million / Boston Marathon bombing	$1 billion / Times Square bombing	$5 billion / London bombing	$200 billion / 9/11	$1 trillion / nuclear port	$5 trillion / nuclear Grand Central
5 percent	600	120	60	12	0.3	0.06	0.012
10 percent	300	60	30	6	0.2	0.03	0.006
25 percent	120	24	12	2.4	0.06	0.012	0.002
50 percent	60	12	6	1.2	0.03	0.006	0.001
75 percent	40	8	4	0.8	0.02	0.004	0.0008
90 percent	33	6.7	3.3	0.7	0.017	0.003	0.0007
100 percent	30	6	3	0.6	0.015	0.003	0.0006

Net Benefit

Net Benefit in billions of dollars for FBI counterterrorism expenditures of $3 billion, assuming one attack per year in the absence of FBI counterterrorism efforts and 90 percent risk reduction

| | -2.9 | -2.6 | -2.1 | 1.5 | 177 | 897 | 4,497 |

Each entry represents the benefit-minus-cost result for each loss. Entries that are positive would be considered to be cost-effective.

The cell entries indicate the annual number of otherwise successful terrorist attacks that would need to occur in the absence of the FBI's counterterrorism efforts and that were not deterred, disrupted, or protected against by other security or protective measures in order to begin to justify its annual expenditure of $3 billion, for attacks of various magnitudes and at various degrees of risk reduction.

of $3 billion per year. As in table 5-3, we display results for attacks at various levels of destruction and for various degrees of risk reduction.

REDUCTION IN RISK CAUSED BY THE FBI'S COUNTERTERRORISM EFFORTS

It is also essential to evaluate how much the FBI reduces the risk (the likelihood and/or the consequences) of terrorism. To do so, we need to consider its effectiveness in deterring, disrupting, or protecting against a terrorist attack. Because no one knows with any certainty how many attacks there might have been without the FBI's efforts (terrorism is characteristically a rare event), it is difficult to calibrate how large the risk actually is. However, whatever the magnitude of the risk of terrorism, the FBI probably has substantially reduced it. Table 6-1 applies a range of risk-reduction estimates, but in our discussion we will assume considerable success for the FBI because it is, as noted, the lead agency for investigating the crime of terrorism and because it has a great many agents assigned to the counterterrorism enterprise. Also, as noted earlier, it had likely already reduced the terrorism risk at least modestly by its reforms before 2001.

Relevant as well is the fact that the tragic events of 9/11 massively heightened the awareness of the public, as well as state and local police, to the threat of terrorism, resulting in extra vigilance that has often ended in the arrest of terrorists or the foiling of terrorist attempts. That's a change that would enhance the risk-reduction achievements of the FBI—all this well before additional funding was granted to these agencies. For example, there was the peddler in New York who reported the smoking vehicle bomb in Times Square in 2010. And, as will be discussed more fully in chapter 9, tip-offs have been important to prosecutions in many of the terrorism cases in the United States since 9/11. Thus, whatever the risk reduction provided by the FBI before 9/11, the extra, and free, vigilance of the public, and state and local police, together with reorganization of the bureau to direct more of its energies and expertise to counterterrorism (albeit at the expense of dealing with organized crime and other hazards), would boost risk reduction considerably.

Putting this all together, we posit that, if an attack is not deterred, disrupted, or protected against by other policing, security, or protective measures, then, with its expanded efforts and with the aid of tips from the public, the bureau has succeeded in reducing the remaining risk—the consequences and/or the probability of an otherwise successful attack—by a full 90 percent. This estimate, while not unreasonable, is likely to err on the generous side.

RESULTS

Central to our discussion, accordingly, are the entries that are boxed in table 6-1. They indicate how many very substantial terrorist attacks in the absence of the FBI's counterterrorism measures would need to occur each year to begin to justify the FBI's counterterrorism budget of $3 billion per year, assuming the bureau's efforts reduce risk—the consequences and/or the likelihood of such an attack—by an impressive 90 percent. Under this condition, the measures, to begin to be considered cost-effective, would have to deter, waylay, or protect against 90 percent of the number in each cell in the 90 percent row. Under that condition, there would have to have been six or seven Boston Marathon–type attacks each year that were not deterred, disrupted, or protected against by the DHS, NSA, state or local police, or other security measures to begin to justify the FBI's $3 billion budget. A security measure that reduces that residual risk by 90 percent would be expected to deter, disrupt, or protect against nearly all of these. Alternatively, the FBI's efforts would need to reduce by 90 percent the effect of one or two London-type bombings every two years—some six or seven over the course of a decade.

Or, again alternatively, the FBI budget would justify itself by reducing by 90 percent a huge attack with direct and indirect damage equivalent to that inflicted by 9/11 once every 60 years.[30] An extreme upper bound would be the detonation of a 10-kiloton nuclear device in New York City's Grand Central Terminal on a busy day, a nightmare scenario that, as discussed in chapter 5, might exact losses of up to $5 trillion. FBI counterterrorism expenditures would be cost-effective in this case only if, without them, such an extreme attack would have successfully been executed once every 1,400 years. The same thinking, roughly, would hold for another extreme scenario, one in which the terrorist attack triggers an expensive, multi-trillion-dollar war like the one in Iraq.

The table also discloses that the assumption about risk reduction in all this is quite significant. If the FBI's counterterrorism efforts only reduce the total risk of losses in a terrorist attack by 50 percent, rather than 90 percent, the number of terrorist events that would need to occur would nearly double.

Table 6-1 also shows the net benefit, or the benefit minus the cost. Note that even if the likelihood of a $100 million attack were 100 percent per year without FBI counterterrorism efforts, the money spent to prevent or protect against the attack would not be worth it: the costs of the security measure ($3 billion) would far outweigh its benefit ($100 million).

If we posit that a $5 billion attack would occur once per year, and would not be deterred, disrupted or protected against by other policing, security, and protective measures (a very conservative set of assumptions), the net benefit of FBI counterterrorism expenditures is $1.5 billion, assuming those expenditures reduce risk by an impressive 90 percent. However, a more plausible threat on the scale of the Times Square or Boston Marathon bombings results in a net loss of $2.1 billion or more per year—meaning that spending $1 buys less than 30 cents of benefits.[31]

Evaluating Prospective Terrorist Attacks in the United States

To evaluate these results from the cost-benefit analysis, it is necessary to consider how many terrorist attacks there would be in the United States, and what their likely consequences would be, in the absence of the FBI's counterterrorism efforts. That is, assuming the FBI is extremely effective at deterring and foiling terrorist attacks, would the bureau have been able to deter or foil six substantial attacks each year inflicting direct and indirect costs totaling $500 million? Or one or two attacks every two years like the one in London that may have inflicted as much as $5 billion in losses? Or one 9/11 every sixty-seven years?[32]

There are several ways to evaluate this issue.

TERRORISM LOSSES INFLICTED WORLDWIDE OUTSIDE WAR ZONES

As discussed in chapter 4 (p. 117) and earlier in this chapter, the total number of people killed worldwide in the several years after 9/11 by Islamist extremists outside of war zones comes to some 200 to 300 per year. This includes many areas of the world, of course, where counterterrorism measures are far less extensive than those in the United States. It considers violence committed both by domestic Islamist terrorists and by ones with international connections, and it includes not only attacks by al-Qaeda but also those by its imitators, enthusiasts, lookalikes, and wannabes, as well as ones by groups with little or no apparent connection to it. Included in the count would be terrorism of the much-publicized sort that occurred in Bali in 2002 and 2005; in Saudi Arabia, Morocco, and Turkey in 2003; in the Philippines, Madrid, and Egypt in 2004; in London and Jordan in 2005; and in Mumbai in 2008.

For comparison, during the same period more people—320 per year—drowned in bathtubs in the United States (see table 5-2).[33] Or there is another, rather unpleasant comparison noted in chapter 1. Increased delays and added costs at U.S. airports due to new security procedures provide incentive for many short-haul passengers to drive to their destination rather than fly, and since driving is far riskier than air travel, the extra automobile traffic generated has been estimated to result in something like 500 additional road fatalities per year.[34]

Of course, casualties from Islamist terrorist attacks have been higher in war zones like Iraq, Afghanistan, Syria, Yemen, and Pakistan, but that is not what Americans are alarmed about: they fear isolated terrorist attacks, not sustained warfare, and it is this concern that is the FBI's focus. For most Americans, the most resonant comparison would be with terrorism in the West: Europe, Canada, Australia, New Zealand, and Japan and a few other countries in East Asia. The last major attack (one exacting at least twenty-five deaths) in that wide area occurred in 2005, and there have been only a very few attacks there of any magnitude since.[35] Appendix B in this volume supplies additional information on this.

Obviously, terrorism casualties *could* have been higher in the United States. However, the notion that but for the FBI's efforts there would be several major terrorist attacks yearly in one country in the developed world appears to be highly questionable.

DISCLOSED AND UNDISCLOSED TERRORISM CASES RELEVANT TO THE UNITED STATES

Following the approach laid out in chapter 3, we can also try to add up information about cases, disclosed or undisclosed, that have threatened, or appear to have threatened, the United States—the area of concern for the FBI's counterterrorism efforts.

Some sixty-two cases have come to light in the fourteen years since September 11, 2001, that involve Islamist terrorists who were apparently planning to commit, or actually did commit, violence in the United States, whether they were based in the United States or were abroad. These are the kinds of attacks that most alarm Americans, of course, and appendix A provides a capsule summary of each.

This might be taken to suggest that the attack probability in the United States is about four or five attacks per year. The British experience, proportionate to population size, is not too dissimilar. The head of MI5, Andrew Parker, told a private audience at the Royal United Services Institute in 2013 that "[s]ince 2000, we have seen serious attempts at major acts of terrorism in this country typically once or twice a year."[36]

However, even if each of the plots focused on the United States, absent the FBI's efforts, resulted on average in a terrorist act inflicting $500 million in damage, there would only be a total of about four or five per year—fewer than the six or seven per year required to deem the FBI's efforts to begin to be cost-effective (applying the $500 million benchmark and the 90 percent risk reduction figures in table 6-1). In addition, it might be noted that fully nine of the cases originated overseas and thus were outside the general purview of the FBI.[37]

One might get around this fact by positing that some of the plotters might have been able to perpetrate several large attacks before being apprehended, or that at least a few of them would have been able to pull off attacks much more destructive than the Boston Marathon attack. However, the capacities and capabilities of the people who populate the cases do not, as suggested in chapter 3, lead one to anticipate that they would, even under the most generous assumptions, have been able to execute six or seven terrorist acts each year on the magnitude of the Boston Marathon attack.[38] And none of the American-based conspirators had anything vaguely resembling the capacity to inflict damage on the order of 9/11.[39]

Indeed, some of the plots being hatched did not envision casualties of substantial magnitude, as they involved, for example, setting off a grenade in a trash bin in a mall or taking some potshots at a military recruitment center. Although a few plots in the set did at least somewhat realistically envision committing major destruction, all but two of these were developed and instituted overseas, where the FBI is not particularly relevant.[40] Plotters in other cases did sometimes harbor visions of toppling large buildings, destroying airports, setting off dirty bombs, or bringing down the Brooklyn Bridge.[41] But these were far beyond the plotters' capacities. In fact, as discussed in chapter 1, it seems likely that many—probably most—would never have become operationally engaged in plotting terrorist attacks at all without the creative, elaborate, and costly sting efforts of the police.[42] Moreover, given their own natural incapacities, even those who did attempt to inflict violence on their own were likely either to fail in their efforts or to commit destruction of quite limited scope.

It is sometimes argued that would-be terrorists caught in a sting would otherwise have eventually been able to obtain the methods and weapons they were supplied by FBI operatives. As Trevor Aaronson notes, this argument probably makes sense for many drug stings—eventually those conned would likely have been able to buy or sell drugs on their own. However, an examination of the terrorism cases supports his conclusion that this pattern does not hold for terrorism: "[T]here has not been a single would-be terrorist in the

United States who has become operational through a chance meeting with someone able to provide the means for a terrorist attack."[43] Only the police have been able to provide that service. In addition, as observed in chapter 3, even if a would-be terrorist were to get help from a like-minded operative, there is evidence from some of the cases that this assistance might well be less than productive.

Any suggestion, then, that those in these case studies could have pulled off several very substantial attacks each year under more permissive policing conditions is highly questionable.[44]

The discussion in chapter 3 also assessed several other potential sources of terrorism. In addition to terrorist plots that have entered the courts and the public record, like those arrayed in appendix A, there are claims that many other potential terrorist plots—or proto-plots—have been thwarted. In particular, there are the "Capone" cases in which prosecutors, lacking enough evidence to convict on terrorism charges, have levied lesser ones, such as immigration violations, to put or send the potential terrorists away. And there are would-be terrorists who have never brushed up against the legal system but have been deterred—pulled back from actually committing violence—because they were intimidated by security measures.

As stressed at various points in this book, the vast majority of even the craftiest terrorist conspirators—including those popularly designated as "masterminds"—fail to carry out their plots, or even begin to put them into motion. Thus policing efforts that disrupt or deter their plans are likely mostly to interrupt scheming that never actually would have resulted in violence.

But setting that consideration at least partly aside, some might find the following to be a plausible speculation. Suppose that, without the FBI's efforts, plotters in some 20 percent of the disclosed cases in appendix A would have been able to carry out a Boston Marathon–style attack—about ten attacks in total over the period since 9/11. Suppose in addition that without the FBI's efforts, 10 percent of the perhaps 150 or 200 Capone cases over the period would have led to that kind of attack (15–20 in total). And suppose that, without the FBI's efforts, 5 percent of, say, 1,000 otherwise deterred attacks would have been carried to fruition (50 in total). That would come to some 75 attacks—about the number that the FBI would need to have prevented over the years since 9/11 to begin to justify its yearly counterterrorism budget of $3 billion. Such thinking might be persuasive to some people.

Or there is the finding from the analysis that, by its efforts, the FBI would have to prevent one attack of 9/11 magnitude every sixty-seven years for its counterterrorism budget to begin to be justified. There have been no terrorist attacks in the dozen years since 9/11 that remotely caused that much destruction, even in war zones like Iraq and Afghanistan where terrorists have space and leisure to plan. And there were also none in the previous decades—or even, probably, millennia. Nonetheless, some might argue that, although 9/11 continues to stand out as an aberration, the experience obviously demonstrates that terrorist destruction of that magnitude is possible, and they then might point out that sixty-seven years is a long time.

The analysis applied here is designed to represent the issue in a clear, understandable, and systematic manner. It supplies decision makers with a coherent perspective on the relevant parameters and how they interact, but it does not of itself make the decision. Overall, while it is not inconceivable that the FBI has deterred, disrupted, or protected against enough terrorist attacks to begin to justify its yearly $3 billion counterterrorism budget, we find, applying standard cost-benefit and risk-analysis approaches, and assuming that the FBI has been exceedingly successful in reducing the terrorism risk, this to be quite implausible.

This approach should not be seen as all or nothing. While it may tell us that a $3 billion expenditure on counterterrorism fails to be cost-effective, it does not automatically follow that spending nothing on counterterrorism is the best course of action. What is important is to determine what levels of expenditure and risk reduction furnish the greatest benefit and when the law of diminishing returns kicks in. The first dollars spent on counterterrorism measures are likely to be worthwhile, even if the last one is not. This approach is further developed in appendix C, where we find that FBI counterterrorism expenditures of up to $1.2 billion—the 2001 or 2003 levels of expenditure in 2014 dollars—seem to be optimal, while expenditures above this level are less likely to be worth it.

As we have seen, total expenditure on domestic homeland security efforts exceeds $115 billion per year. The FBI's counterterrorism efforts cost a very modest 3 percent of these expenditures and thus might be considered a prudent investment, given the FBI's proven track record since 9/11. Whatever in the end is decided about the cost-effectiveness of the FBI's counterterrorism efforts, however, they are certainly far closer to being so than many other security measures.

For example, the yearly cost for the Transport Security Administration's Federal Air Marshal Service is $1.1 to $1.2 billion, and so is the cost of its AIT/body scanner technology when fully deployed. Together, these aviation security measures are nearly as costly as the FBI's counterterrorism efforts, but as will be discussed in context in chapter 8, their risk reduction is negligible. Moreover, they only deal with specific threats associated with hijacking and body-borne bombs on aircraft. If this is the comparison, FBI expenditures would seem a preferable option: they deal with all terrorism threats, almost certainly do reduce the terrorism threat, and provide forces that can be rapidly deployed or redeployed as threats emerge or evolve.

An Alternative Approach to Policing Terrorism Cases

Some of the discussion earlier, as well as some in chapter 3, can be taken to suggest that there could be an alternative, and far less costly, approach to policing would-be terrorists, one that might generally (but not always) be effective without having to jail them.

The experience with a case from 2010 suggests the approach.[45] It involves a twenty-five-year-old Afghan American living in northern Virginia, who appears to have been as much a pre-terrorist or proto-terrorist as many of the others who have been arrested, convicted, and sentenced to very long terms on terrorism charges. An angry, frustrated, violent, and perhaps mentally unbalanced hothead, he made dramatic and intemperate threats of violence on Facebook to a female correspondent who lived in New Orleans. His profile there contained several photos showing him holding weapons (one an AK-47 rifle), as well as one of a tent full of explosives with a caption sardonically reading, "My family business." He gleefully bragged to her that "we" had "dropped the twin towers like a bad habit hahaha."

When he (correctly) suspected that his correspondent was telling the authorities about this, and therefore betraying him, he called her a "bitch" and said he was going to set off explosives on the DC Metro the next day. He made this explicit threat only a week after the FBI had found out about his ravings. Not wanting to take any chances, the FBI promply arrested him.

Not surprisingly, he did not actually have any explosives, but that hardly makes him unusual among the young hotheads that populate the American terrorism cases—many of whom have been sentenced to decades in prison for plotting murderous crimes. The difference seems to be that there never was time to employ a cool, calculating, older, and experienced FBI informant to worm his way into the hothead's confidence and to encourage, and to play on, his propensity to spew bravado. If there had been time to insinuate an informant—particularly a fatherly one, as he seems to have been fatherless or effectively so—it does seem quite possible the hothead could have been moved along the path to terrorism over a few months.

Since irresponsible bloviating is not illegal, the police could only charge him with a minor crime: making an interstate threat. He received a good scare, a penalty of time served, and two years of supervised release.

That approach appears to have worked. Although the FBI may be continuing to monitor him, he appears not to have committed terrorism or to have been arrested on terrorism charges.

Something somewhat similar happened in the Sears Tower case of 2006. A small group of men in Miami was apparently plotting some acts of terrorism, the most fanciful of which was toppling a famous skyscraper in Chicago, and an FBI informant had infiltrated the group. At one point, at the request of the plot leader, the FBI brought in a religion entrepreneur and convicted rapist from Chicago who called himself Sultan Khan Bey and who was accompanied by his wife, Queen Zakiyaah (we are not making any of this up). Upon arrival, Bey quickly fingered the informant as an informant, and this information immediately caused the plot to begin to break up.[46]

Relevant here is the Secret Service's response when it gets a tip that someone has ranted about killing the president. It does not insinuate an encouraging informant into the ranter's company to eventually offer crucial, if bogus, facilitating assistance to the assassination plot. Instead, agents pay the person a Meaningful Visit and find that this works rather well as a dissuasion device. Also, in the event of a presidential trip to the ranter's vicinity, the ranter is visited again.[47]

It seems entirely possible that this approach could productively be applied more widely.[48] In an important sense, plotting to do terrorism is much more like plotting to kill the president than it is like crime. Most crime is essentially a business in which one uses illegal methods to attain money to put food (or drugs) on the table.[49] There are legal ways to do the same thing, but the ultimate goal is a requirement of life.

This does not hold either for terrorism or for killing the president—neither is a requirement of life. And angrily ranting about killing the president may be about as predictive of future violent action as angrily ranting about using terrorism to deal with a political grievance.[50] The terrorism cases frequently involve such ranters—indeed, tips about their railing have frequently led to FBI involvement. It seems likely that, as apparently happened in the Metro bombing case, the ranter could often be productively deflected by an open visit from the FBI indicating that the police are on to him. By contrast, sending in a paid operative to worm his way into the ranter's confidence may have the opposite result—encouraging, even gulling, him toward violence.[51]

John Horgan has studied people once disposed to committing terrorism who later walked away from it. He points out that this happens all the time and that it does not require them necessarily to change their fundamental views or beliefs. They may well remain deeply religious, politically aggrieved, and/or deeply outraged at what they see as an attack on their religion or on their co-religionists in the Middle East. None of these emotions, he points out, is "an operationally useful predictor of terrorist behavior."[52]

Horgan's observation seems to have relevance for our discussion as well, especially in connection with an earlier observation. The FBI asserts that three times as many would-be terrorists are arrested or detained on minor Capone-like charges as are involved in the cases leading to explicit terrorism indictments. Effectively, the FBI has put these people on notice that they are being watched. As noted in chapter 3, after having served short sentences, almost none have later moved toward committing terrorist violence in the United States, suggesting that the warnings were sufficient to dissuade them.[53]

It seems difficult to scare street criminals straight; however, this may not be true for many would-be terrorists of the kind unearthed by the FBI. Indeed, the approach might well have worked with a large percentage of the people who have instead been visited, and conned, by undercover informants and then sentenced to long, expensive prison terms.

It is possible that the FBI is already doing this to some degree. If so, it has been a near-total success because there appears to be very few instances in which a man arrested for terrorism had previously received a Meaningful Visit from the FBI. There may be a danger, of course, that if the FBI warns a proto-terrorist it is on to him, this may impel him to move toward terrorism not only more carefully but also more quickly. The experience in one case on record, however, suggests this danger may not be terribly severe. The visit did not work to dissuade him, but any negative consequences were minor.

In a 2015 case, a twenty-year-old Kansas man was paid a visit by the FBI after he had posted his desire to die while waging violent jihad: "I will soon be leaving you forever so goodbye!" and "[G]etting ready to be killed in jihad is a HUGE adrenaline rush!!" He had enlisted in the Army and was scheduled soon to report for basic training, but his candid assertion to his visitors that he planned to shoot other soldiers on the firing range or slay them elsewhere on the base with "a small gun or a sword" appears to have rendered him undesirable, and he was "subsequently denied entry into the military," as court documents dryly put it. However, he continued to have urgings to carry out holy war, and "confidential sources" later gained his trust. He was eventually arrested as he sought to arm a phony FBI-created 1,000-pound ammonium nitrate bomb just outside the perimeter of Fort Riley.[54]

Another case, however, is more troubling. In 2015, two men drove from Arizona to Garland, Texas, and opened fire at a Prophet Mohammed cartoon exhibit and contest, which Muslims found to be extremely offensive. The men wounded one unarmed security officer at the heavily guarded event and then were killed by police. One of the men had previously been detained on terrorism issues: he had been visited by FBI agents in 2007, put under surveillance, arrested in 2010, found guilty of making a false statement to federal agents, and sentenced to three years' probation.[55] These earlier brushes with the law, obviously, did not keep him from going violent.

Nevertheless, the broader experience with the American cases suggests that the Meaningful Visit approach (while holding other, far costlier policing measures in abeyance) might well work with many of the muddled, aimless, gullible, and emotionally inadequate culprits who populate the U.S. terrorism cases in such profusion. At the same time, it is likely to work only part of the time, and experience suggests that some continued monitoring of warned suspects may make sense.

An additional relevant concern, discussed earlier, seems to have no basis in the American experience: the popular fear that if no encouraging police operatives are infiltrated into an embryonic plot, the proto-terrorists will eventually come across *real* terrorists to help them out.

One other, somewhat related, point might be put forward. There seems to be some pretty good evidence in a 2010 case in Oregon that the FBI was tipped off by the would-be terrorist's concerned father (though the police were watching even before they got the tip). It seems quite likely that the father may have hoped the FBI would simply keep a watch on his son, perhaps letting him know they were on to him and stopping him should his new radical passions ever lead to coherent plans for violence. Since the young man, a class clown in high school obsessed about basketball, girls, and writing rap songs, had no criminal record and no experience with explosives or guns, it was a reasonable presumption, or hope, that this approach would keep him under control until he outgrew his jihadist obsession—much as other teenagers generally abandon cults and other fanciful expressions of youthful rebellion, eventually moving on to such parent-pleasing enterprises as getting married and having children. Instead, the FBI launched a sting—essentially fabricating a kind of cult operation around the young man's current obsession that played to, and importantly facilitated, his violent fantasies in a manner that he would never have been able to carry out on his own. It then arrested him before he had time to outgrow his youthful fancies. As a result, he will spend three decades in jail, followed by lifetime supervision at taxpayer expense. Knowing this outcome, it might be wondered if other worried parents would turn in their radical sons.[56]

CHAPTER SEVEN | The National Security Agency

I N THE PANICKY aftermath of 9/11, the National Security Agency (NSA) has been greatly expanded—and that process continues. Just since 2004, its budget has grown by 53 percent to $10.8 billion—a budget considerably larger than that of the FBI—and NSA employs nearly 35,000 civilian and military personnel.[1] Moreover, there are plans to add another 10,000 workers by 2026, and the price tag for just the first phase of this expansion is $2 billion.[2] As of 2011, the floor space it occupied matched that of the Pentagon, and (a key indicator of bureaucratic majesty) its buildings are surrounded by 112 acres of parking space.[3]

As part of that expansion, the NSA has been secretly gathering and storing a truly prodigious amount of communications information as part of the country's massive 9/11-induced ghost-chasing quest. Dana Priest and William Arkin noted in 2011 that it was then intercepting and ingesting 1.7 billion communication elements every day, including "telephone calls, radio signals, cell phone conversations, emails, text and Twitter messages, bulletin board postings, instant messages, website changes, computer network pings, and IP addresses."[4] The cost of data collection, processing, and exploitation runs to $4.1 billion a year, while data analysis costs another $1.5 billion. Across all agencies of the intelligence community, the total bill for "data collection" totals nearly $24 billion, comprising 45 percent of that community's combined $52.6 billion budget.[5]

When Edward Snowden's revelations emerged in June 2013 about the extent to which NSA was doing its secret business, Barack Obama's administration immediately set in motion a program to pursue him to the ends of the earth in order to have him prosecuted to the full extent of the law for illegally exposing state secrets.

However, the president also said that the discussions about the programs these revelations triggered were actually a good thing: "I welcome this debate. And I think it's healthy for our democracy. I think it's a sign of maturity because probably five years ago, six years ago, we might not have been having this debate."[6] There may be something a bit patronizing in the implication that the programs have been secret because we weren't yet mature enough to debate them when they were put into place. Setting that aside, however, a debate is surely to be welcomed—indeed, it is much overdue.

In that debate, a number of questions have been raised about the civil liberties and privacy implications of NSA's massive surveillance efforts. However, in some important respects, the key issue is not so much a matter of law as one of costs and benefits. In this regard, the central question was set out in 2013 by the President's Review Group on Intelligence and Communications Technologies, a committee established to advise the president on the issue. It is not whether a surveillance program "makes us incrementally safer," the group's report points out, "but whether the additional safety is worth the sacrifice in terms of individual privacy, personal liberty, and public trust."[7] For his part, the president insists that the programs, which he acknowledges include what he calls "modest encroachments" on privacy, do actually "help us prevent terrorist attacks." Therefore, he concludes, "on net, it was worth us doing."[8]

However, it is worth us doing only if its benefit, on net, outweighs its privacy and other costs. Clearly, if it could be demonstrated that the computerized surveillance programs have saved thousands of Americans from being killed by terrorists, many people would be willing to pay a considerable price, both in money and in privacy invasion, to keep the programs in operation. If, on the other hand, they have provided little benefit—if they have failed to accomplish much in the campaign against terrorism—few would advocate continuing to pay the programs' costs.

Thus, NSA critic Glenn Greenwald, noting that the Fourth Amendment to the U.S. Constitution prohibits "unreasonable searches and seizures" by the government and that there must be "probable cause" for issuing warrants to do so, argues appropriately that

[b]y drawing the line at such actions, we knowingly allow for the probability of greater criminality. Yet we draw that line anyway, exposing ourselves to a higher degree of danger, because pursuing absolute physical safety has never been our single overarching societal priority.[9]

However, if a specific series of what Greenwald calls "suspicionless invasions" of privacy by the state do happen to net a great many terrorists about to do a great deal of damage, there will be a tendency to consider such searches and seizures to be entirely reasonable, while the success of the exercise, by itself, would be taken to suggest that there has been probable cause for searching and seizing. Thus, to be effective, critics of domestic policing and intelligence *must* engage the contention that such programs have saved, or will surely save, many lives. It is not enough simply to contend that they may be violations of the law.[10] And it is a calculation that should be explicitly made, not simply declared.

This chapter seeks to carry out that task. It evaluates the huge and controversial data-gathering efforts of the NSA, the secrecy surrounding them, and the apparently quite limited benefits they have generated.

The impact that cost-benefit considerations have on legal conclusions in this matter is evident in opposing judgments handed down in December 2013, regarding the legality of one of NSA's surveillance programs. The program's apparent effectiveness, or lack thereof, clearly figured importantly in the decisions. Thus, Judge Richard J. Leon, in finding the program was likely unconstitutional, noted that the government "does *not* cite a single instance" in which analysis of information collected under the program "actually stopped an imminent attack," that it failed to present "any indication of a concrete danger," and that it provided "no proof that the program prevented terrorist attacks."[11] But then, eleven days later, Judge William Pauley, in finding the same program to be legal, stressed in his first sentence that the world is "dangerous and interconnected," going on to insist that the effectiveness of the data-collection program "cannot seriously be disputed," and noting that "the Government has acknowledged several successes in Congressional testimony and in declarations."[12]

Although much of the discussion in this chapter can be extrapolated more widely, it focuses primarily—and for starters—on two surveillance programs revealed by Snowden. These programs have often been mixed in, or confused, with each other.[13]

One of them, commonly known from its section in the FISA Amendments Act of 2008 as 702, permits NSA to gather electronic communication information on email and telephone conversations after approval by a judge if the target is both outside the United States and not an American citizen, and if there is an appropriate and documented foreign intelligence purpose for the collection.

The other, named after its section number in the Patriot Act of 2001 as 215, authorizes the gathering in bulk of business and communication records in the United States. It has been used in particular to amass telephone billing records—numbers called, numbers received, and conversation length—potentially for every telephone in the country. In principle, the 215 data are only supposed to be collected if there are "reasonable grounds to believe" the records are "relevant" to a terrorist investigation of a "known or unknown" terrorist organization or operative.[14] Creatively expanding the word *relevant* to the breaking point, this stipulation has been taken in practice to mean that NSA can gather billing records for every telephone conversation in the country. If there might be a known or unknown needle in the haystack, the entire haystack becomes "relevant." As many, including Senator Patrick Leahy, have pointed out, this broad approach could also be applied to banking, credit card, medical, financial, and library records, all of which could be held as reasonably "relevant" to the decidedly wide-ranging quest to catch terrorists.[15] The information gathered by either program can be held for five years.

This chapter primarily deals with the 215 program, the more controversial of the two—the one that involves the massive gathering of telephone billing records, or "metadata," in the United States. Overall, it appears, any benefit of the 215 metadata program has been considerably outweighed by its cost, even assuming that the unknown, and perhaps unknowable, cost figure is quite small. If the issue is security versus privacy, in this case privacy wins. Moreover, some of the concerns about that program—particularly those concerning its effectiveness—may apply to the more focused 702 program.

Assessing the Costs of the 215 Program

If we are to have a debate about 215 that is "healthy for our democracy," it seems reasonable to suggest that the debaters should be supplied with information about how much the NSA's massive metadata program costs. This information would furnish a key starting point for any debate.

Presumably, that figure has thus far been classified because the program itself was classified. But now that we know only too well that the program did exist, it is far from clear why its cost should remain secret. It is certainly difficult to see how knowing that cost would help the terrorists—except perhaps to amaze them further. However, there is the danger that the cost of gathering and storing and evaluating huge amounts of metadata on the telephone conversations of all Americans might also amaze American taxpayers. Perhaps that's another reason the metadata and other programs been kept secret.[16]

PROGRAM, INVESTIGATORY, PRIVACY, AND OPPORTUNITY COSTS

The cost of storing metadata—billing records for a set of communications—as in the 215 program is minuscule compared to storing content data as in the 702 program. An Australian Internet service provider, when estimating the costs of a 2015 legislated metadata-collection program, concludes that the storage requirements for one month to be 10 gigabytes. In comparison, storing content data would soak up 100,000 times more space and would cost $130 million per year—and this is for a company with less than 10 percent of Internet market share in Australia.[17] Scaling up the telephone metadata requirements for the United States, then, would require an annual storage program of about 100 terabytes.[18] The cost of 100 terabytes of storage is trivial—about $10,000—and about the volume of several shoeboxes.

However, although data storage itself is relatively cheap, data-retention costs include those entailed in collating the data, securing the data to maintain integrity for both consumers and for agency investigative purposes, making the data available to agencies in a form that can be used for their investigations, and destroying the data after the retention period has expired.[19] According to one major U.S. carrier, "it would cost in the range of $50 million a year to maintain a five-year, searchable database."[20] The aggregate cost to all American telephone companies for doing so would easily exceed $100 million a year.

Moreover, a full accounting should include not only the actual cost of gathering, storing, and maintaining the surveillance data but also the costs of constantly sorting through it to generate and develop leads (or "threats"). According to the NSA's director of compliance, the agency queries its databases about 20 million times each month.[21] Presumably that involves a great deal of human interaction, all of which must be paid for.

As noted, the full cost to the NSA for data collection, processing, and exploitation runs to $4.1 billion. If we assume that the 215 program constituted one-thousandth of this traffic, this amounts to a cost of $4.1 million. Or, if it constitutes one-hundredth, to a cost of $41 million.

Costs should also include those involved in following up on the leads (mainly by the FBI) once they have been generated, a process considered at some length in the previous chapter. Notes journalist Garrett Graff, the personnel resources expended by the FBI to investigate tips "churned out endlessly from NSA's computers" have been "tremendous."[22]

There are privacy costs deriving from leads that don't go anywhere, and these can be very considerable. The very act of running the leads down, notes journalist Mattathias Schwartz, means that there will be a great number of "innocent people who have been placed on watch lists, questioned, or detained due to some insignificant correlation or phone call with a suspect." A determined quest to identify a small number of miscreants within a large haystack, he continues, will inevitably and of necessity generate a huge number of false positives and, in the process, deprive innocents of the ability to travel, pressure them to become informants, and sometimes wrongfully detain them.[23]

Also included in the tally should be the opportunity costs; that is, what else could the money have been used for? For example, as discussed in chapter 6, there has been a downgrading by the FBI and other agencies of other priorities, including the pursuit of white-collar crime like fraudulent banking practices, to focus on the pursuit of terrorists, the vast majority of whom, like ghosts, do not exist. To fully evaluate the costs of the NSA surveillance efforts, one would need to take this issue into account: how much do the leads supplied by the NSA contribute to this process?

INTIMIDATION COSTS: THE ISSUE OF TRUST

Some consideration should also be made for the less quantifiable costs of privacy invasion and for the potential misuse of the data. Although the program has built-in safeguards, its operation ultimately requires us to trust those in charge. Citing unpleasant historical precedents from the days of Richard Nixon and J. Edgar Hoover, and from the run-up to the Iraq War of 2003, Stephen Walt has arrestingly suggested, or warned, that the program could be used to intimidate or harass whistle-blowers, dissidents, and overly inquisitive journalists: "[O]nce someone raises their head above the parapet and calls attention to themselves by challenging government policy, they can't be sure that someone inside government won't take umbrage and try to see what dirt they can find."[24]

The government's credibility on the issue of whether it can be trusted not to abuse this system has already has been strained to the point that, in a Rasmussen poll in June 2013, 57 percent of the respondents deemed it likely that the government would use data dredged up by the NSA to harass political opponents.[25]

That officials have several times been caught in lies—or supreme exercises in Clintonian sophistry—about the NSA programs scarcely proves that NSA information will be abused. But it certainly enhances the wariness about the programs. The 215 program was first exposed in a *USA Today* story in 2006, and officials responded with evasive assertions, contending that "[t]here is no domestic surveillance without court approval."[26]

Then there is the response of NSA Director Keith Alexander to a March 2012 cover story in *Wired* magazine reporting the views of William Binney, a former NSA official. Binney left the agency in late 2001, when it launched its warrantless-wiretapping program. According to the article, Binney retained close contact with other agency employees for several years thereafter. "They violated the Constitution [in] setting it up," he says. "But they didn't care. They were going to do it anyway, and they were going to crucify anyone who stood in the way. When they started violating the Constitution, I couldn't stay." Binney contended that, without a warrant, the NSA was collecting "a vast trove of international and domestic billing records" from major American telephone companies and that "they're storing everything they gather."[27]

In the ensuing months, Alexander crisply denied Binney's contention. "To think we're collecting on every U.S. person . . . that would be against the law. . . . The fact is we're a foreign intelligence agency."[28] He also categorically insisted that "we don't hold data on U.S. citizens." This statement has been defended by the administration on the grounds that the NSA's internal definition of *data* does not include metadata—a language-stretching nuance Alexander neglected to mention when he made his statement. As it happens, however, the agency's actual internal definition of *data* specifically does include "call event records and other Digital Network Intelligence metadata."[29] In like manner, Alexander probably had a special private definition of *dossier* in mind when he vehemently stated in 2012 that the notion that the NSA has "millions or hundreds of millions of dossiers on people is absolutely false."[30]

Then, in March 2013, Director of National Intelligence James Clapper was asked by Senator Ron Wyden in a Senate Intelligence Committee hearing, "Does the NSA collect any type of data at all on millions or hundreds of millions of Americans?" Even knowing that Wyden, owing to his position on the committee, knew what the answer to that question was, Clapper blandly demurred: "No, sir. . . . Not wittingly." Wyden says he had sent the question to Clapper's office the day before and that Clapper was also given a chance later to amend his answer. After Snowden's revelations three months later spectacularly shattered Clapper's crisp denial (as well as Alexander's earlier ones), Clapper sent a letter to the committee stating that his answer had been "clearly erroneous" and that when responding, he imagined that the question referred to content, not metadata—which he somehow believes the NSA does not collect "wittingly." Clapper has also said that an honest response would have required his divulging secrets that were highly classified, and thus he came up with the "least untruthful" answer he could imagine at the time.[31] However, he could, of course, have simply dodged the question, asking that it be dealt with in executive session.

There is additional evidence of deception in the disclosure that the NSA illegally collected email content data on thousands, or tens of thousands, of Americans before that practice was closed down by the courts in 2011.[32] The court's opinion on this was classified, and the Obama administration fought a Freedom of Information lawsuit seeking to get it released.[33] In the wake of the Snowden disclosures, however, the opinion was finally declassified and released in heavily redacted form. In it, the judge specifically pointed out that he had previously been the victim of "a substantial misrepresentation regarding the scope of a major collection program" and that the information gathered had been "fundamentally different from what the court had been led to believe."[34]

Similar concerns were raised in a 2009 ruling that had originally been classified as top secret, dealing with the way the NSA probed phone numbers on an "alert list." When it was finally declassified under pressure in 2013, the ruling included declarations that the government had failed to comply with the court's orders, that it had compounded this by "repeatedly submitting inaccurate descriptions of the alert process" and that court-approved privacy safeguards had "been so frequently and systematically violated" that they "never functioned effectively." A senior official explained rather lamely, but entirely plausibly, that any violations were "unintentional" because "there was nobody at NSA who really had a full understanding of how the program was operating at the time."[35]

It might be wondered, then, what *intentional* violations, keeping Walt's admonition in mind, could lead to. Senator Dianne Feinstein, who has chaired the Senate Intelligence Committee, insists that her committee "has never identified an instance in which the NSA has intentionally abused its authority to conduct surveillance for inappropriate purposes." However, the agency's director of compliance has indicated that there have been a very small number (perhaps one every five years) of "willful errors."[36] In the meantime, the agency, apparently less willfully, has broken privacy rules or overstepped its legal authority thousands of times a year, according to an internal audit.[37]

Relevant as well to a discussion of credibility is the disclosure that in 2006 the NSA deliberately weakened an encryption standard accepted both nationally and internationally in a systematic effort to defeat privacy protections for Internet communications, a venture that compromised the National Institute of Standards and Technology in the process.[38]

In all this, an assessment of the costs attendant on the NSA's surveillance efforts should hold in mind, to the degree to which they apply, warnings about an intimidation factor suggested in this passage from George Orwell's novel *1984*:

> There was of course no way of knowing whether you were being watched at any given moment. How often, or on what system, the Thought Police plugged in on any individual wire was guesswork. It was even conceivable that they watched everybody all the time. But at any rate they could plug in your wire whenever they wanted to. You had to live—did live, from habit that became instinct—in the assumption that every sound you made was overheard, and, except in darkness, every movement scrutinized.[39]

Echoes can be seen, perhaps, in Glenn Greenwald's estimate that within a year of Snowden disclosures, most journalists contacting him used encryption technology.[40]

Assessing the Benefits of the 215 Program

Once there's an estimate of the cost of the 215 program as it existed until mid-2015, it is possible to weigh that figure against the benefit the program has generated and then to determine whether "on net" the program was "worth doing" in its central mission of countering terrorism. Although those opposed to the program are deeply concerned about privacy issues, they have also argued that the program failed to be "an effective counterterrorism tool," in the words of Senator Leahy.[41]

PIZZA HUT LEADS

When asked in June 2013 at Senate hearings if NSA's massive data-gathering programs were "crucial or critical" in disrupting terrorist threats, agency head Alexander doggedly testified that in "dozens" of instances the databases "helped" or were "contributing"—though he did seem to agree with the word *critical* at one point.[42] The key issue for evaluating the programs, however, given their costs and privacy implications, would be to determine not whether the huge databases were helpful or contributing, but whether they were necessary.[43] NSA operatives sometimes suggest the program "ultimately completes the picture" or, in the words of FBI Deputy Director Sean Joyce, "closes the gap" on information in a case.[44] These formulations ingeniously, if deceptively, create the impression that the information was necessary.

Later in the month, Alexander provided Congress with a list of terrorism cases, specifically testifying that "the information gathered from these programs provided the U.S. government with critical leads" to "help prevent" over fifty "terrorist events," an assertion echoed by President Obama and members of Congress.[45] The list reportedly numbers fifty-four—unsurprisingly, the list itself is classified.

On the surface, this seems to be an amazingly small number for many years of work. As discussed in chapter 3, there have been hundreds of terrorism cases within the United States since 9/11. Those listed in appendix A have led to apprehensions for plotting to attack, or executing attacks, on targets in the United States. In addition, there are dozens more that have led to prosecutions for sending, or plotting to send, support to terrorists overseas or to go abroad to fight. And a few hundred more may have involved terrorism investigations that led to prosecutions on lesser charges. There have also been hundreds—or perhaps even thousands—of terrorism cases overseas outside of war zones.

If the NSA intercepts were so valuable, one would think that investigators on just about every case would routinely have run their information by the NSA. The exercise would be helpful even if the NSA efforts came up blank because that would allow investigators to close off some avenues of potential investigation, which if pursued would have been a waste of time and effort.

Although some investigatory materials may not have been disclosed, information in the public domain on the American terrorism cases suggests that investigators and prosecutors have not done so. This could be taken to suggest, perhaps, either that they have only occasionally found the NSA to be a helpful ally or that they were afraid of being swamped with leads that would clutter and distract their investigation while also greatly increasing its costs. Another study of American cases specifically concludes that "the contribution of NSA's bulk surveillance programs" to the known cases "was minimal."[46]

The experience at the FBI with NSA leads may be suggestive here. Explains Walter Pincus, if operatives at NSA, sorting through their 215 metadata collection or other sources, uncover "a questionable pattern," such as "calls to other suspect phones," they send a report to the FBI for investigation.[47] In NSA, this process has sometimes been called "We Track 'Em, You Whack 'Em."[48]

The FBI, then, is routinely supplied with what Graff calls "endless lists of 'suspect' telephone numbers." When followed up, these "leads" almost never go anywhere: of 5,000 numbers passed along, only 10—two-tenths of 1 percent—"panned out enough for the bureau to bother" to get court permission to follow them up. At the FBI, the NSA tips are often called "Pizza Hut leads" because, in running them down, FBI agents "inevitably end up investigating the local pizza delivery guy." There is, in other words, not much of anything to "whack." At one point, the generally diplomatic director of the FBI, Robert Mueller, bluntly told NSA director Alexander: "You act like this is some treasure trove; it's a useless time suck." And an agent in the trenches put it a bit less delicately: "You know how long it takes to chase 99 pieces of bullshit?"[49] With that attitude, investigators, overwhelmed by the trivial, may well be disinclined to treat NSA tips with much seriousness.

This resonates with the experience of the CIA. Using its wealth of data, the NSA has been fond of presenting massive, even supreme, exercises in dot-connecting, in which hundreds or even thousands of people, places, and events are linked in what some call BAGs, or "big ass graphs." For all their (presumed) awesomeness, these have reportedly produced very few useful leads—in part, perhaps, because "lone wolf" attacks, by definition, leave no dots to connect. "I don't need this," said an exacerbated senior CIA official. Because the BAGs include people who are three layers removed from the putative terrorist of interest, the number of people in any one full picture could number in the tens of millions.[50]

Even before coming to the NSA, Alexander had applied such massive data networks in the Army. Detractors there say that there was an absence of data and of verifiable sources behind the leads, that a quarter of the people on the charts were already dead, and that about the only thing the people in the networks were connected to was, as it happens, "pizza shops."[51]

THE CASES

According to the testimony of an NSA official, of the fifty-four cases that were supposedly disrupted by NSA surveillance data, more than 90 percent involved information from the 702 program that allows the NSA to intercept communications to and from people under suspicion abroad after obtaining judicial approval.[52] Thus, the 215 program, in which metadata are accumulated and stored for all telephone calls within the United States, presumably played a role only in around five cases during the course of the program. According to General Alexander, only thirteen of the fifty-four cases on the classified list had a "homeland nexus," the others having occurred in Europe (twenty-five), Asia (eleven), and Africa (five).[53]

Four of the cases, all presumably from the small "homeland nexus" subset, were discussed in public on June 18, 2013, by Alexander and Joyce at the rather tendentiously titled Hearing of the House Permanent Select Committee on Intelligence on How Disclosed NSA Programs Protect Americans, and Why Disclosure Aids Our Adversaries. Insofar as NSA surveillance played any role in these cases, it seems in almost all instances that it was the 702 program, not the 215, that was relevant.[54] Although the full array of cases remains classified, Senator Patrick Leahy has said that the notion that these cases represent disrupted plots is "plainly wrong." Indeed, "they weren't all plots and they weren't all thwarted."[55]

Only one, it appears, relied on the 215 program in any significant way.[56] It is among the four disclosed ones, and it involves a San Diego cab driver from Somalia and three friends who were convicted of sending the decidedly non-princely sum of $8,500 to help a designated terrorist group in Somalia fight Ethiopians who, with U.S. support, had recently invaded the country.[57] The government had been tapping the cab driver's telephone for months, and Director Mueller appears to have singled out this case as the only one in which the collection of phone data had been "instrumental"—a word, of course, that is not as strong as *crucial* or *critical* or *necessary*.[58] Alexander, it appears, agrees with Mueller's assessment.[59]

Joyce said that an investigation of the potential case using 215 information that began in October 2007 "did not find any connection to terrorist activity," but that there was a breakthrough when NSA connected a San Diego number with a suspicious contact outside the country by using 215.[60] However, it is not clear that the investigators needed to sort through a mammoth data bank. According to Senator Ron Wyden, they had enough information to get a court order to investigate.[61] Similar conclusions were reached by the Privacy and Civil Liberties Oversight Board (PCLOB), a five-person independent bipartisan agency appointed by the president and confirmed by the Senate to investigate civil liberties issues in counterterrorism actions taken by the executive branch. Although an NSA tip did set the investigation in motion, PCLOB noted, it is not clear that the FBI needed it because the relevant telephone number "was a common link among pending FBI investigations." Moreover, because the tip came from monitoring a specific foreign number that was already being tracked, "it is not clear to us that bulk collection of telephone records was necessary to discovering the connection." That is, the cab driver "was not entirely unknown to law enforcement, but rather was the subject of a previous FBI investigation and was the user of a telephone number already linked to pending FBI investigations."[62]

A correspondent for *The Hill* breathlessly characterized the cab driver culprit as "a top terrorist financier in San Diego, who was supporting militant extremist groups in Somalia."[63] However, it certainly appears that the crime prosecuted at great effort and cost (1,800 phone intercepts and 680 pages of email traffic were handed over to the defense) was, overall, a rather trivial one.[64]

The second disclosed case concerns the New York Stock Exchange and was closed down in 2010. It seems even more trivial. It involves three Muslim men, all naturalized American citizens: one in Kansas City and two in New York. At the time of the American invasion of Iraq in 2003, they decided they needed to fight for their "faith and community," in the words of one of them. Four years later, one of the men was able to connect to two apparently experienced al-Qaeda operatives in Yemen. Hoping to join the fight in Iraq, Afghanistan, or Somalia, the American men sent money and equipment to their new friends in Yemen under the impression that these would be set aside for their military training. Over several months they sent around $93,000, as well as watches, cold-weather gear, some Garmin GPS units, and a remote-controlled toy car. However, the recipients divided the physical loot among themselves and spent the money on (real) cars and as awards to families of Islamic martyrs. In 2008, the scam artists requested further payments of $45,000, which one of them planned to use to open an appliance store. They also suggested that the Americans were better suited to an operation in the United States, and cajoled one of them into casing the New York Stock Exchange for a possible bombing—a "plot" that they never had any intention of carrying out, according to the testimony of one of them. The American did do a walk around the target, and then, several months later, submitted a one-page report on his adventure consisting of information that could have been gotten from Google maps and from tourist brochures. The gesture was apparently more to prove his seriousness about going abroad to fight than anything else. However, his handlers were unimpressed.[65]

In his June 2013 testimony, Joyce said identification in the case was made not through 215, but through "702 authority."[66] At the same time, he raised interest, and then eyebrows, by dramatically proclaiming this to be a case "that was in the very initial stages of plotting to bomb the New York Stock Exchange." Another official said, "It was, as Deputy Director Joyce states, in its nascent stages and could have progressed well beyond that if it wasn't for our ability to obtain FISA material." However, when asked whether the plot was "serious," Joyce deftly dodged the issue: "I think the jury considered it serious because they were all convicted."

As it happens, however, there were no jury trials: the three men all pleaded guilty and then only to providing support to terrorism, not to the NYSE plot (such as it was). According to the other official, FBI Deputy Director Joyce "misspoke."[67] Alexander nonetheless appears to have been delighted with Joyce's performance at the hearings. An open microphone reportedly captured him asking Joyce to tell his boss, FBI Director Robert Mueller, "I owe him another friggin' beer."[68] PCLOB concluded about the case that although 215 was used in the investigation, there is "no indication that bulk collection of telephone records was necessary to the investigation, or that the information produced by Section 215 provided any unique value."[69]

The third disclosed case involves an American who had done surveillance work (the value of which seems to have been fairly limited) for terrorist gunmen who killed 166 people in a suicidal rampage in Mumbai, India, in 2008. He was later arrested as he was engaged in a plot to do terrorist damage in Denmark, a plot that was beset by many planning and financial difficulties at the time. According to *ProPublica* reporter Sebastian Rotella, who has done extensive research and reporting on the case, British intelligence already had the American under surveillance—suggesting that the Danish enterprise would never have been allowed to be carried out. The arrest resulted from a tip from the British, not from NSA intercepts. It does appear, however, that previously stored NSA intercepts, presumably from the 702 program, aided in building the legal case against the man.[70]

Only the fourth disclosed case involves a serious potential for terrorism within the United States. This is the Zazi case of 2009, in which three Afghan Americans received training in Pakistan and then returned to the United States with a plot to set off bombs on the New York City subway system.

Joyce testified that a connection was made through "702 authority."[71] But, as Justin Heilman points out in a study of the episode, and as others have more recently noted, the plot in the United States does not appear to have been disrupted so much by NSA data-dredgers but by standard surveillance procedures implemented after the British provided a hot tip about Zazi based on his email traffic to a known overseas terrorist address that had long been under surveillance.[72] At that point, U.S. authorities had good reason to put the plotters on their radar, and as Senator Wyden has pointed out, in this case, as in the San Diego one, "the government had all the information it needed to go to the phone company and get an individual court order."[73] Having NSA's metadata collection might have been helpful, but it seems scarcely to have been required. As PCLOB concludes bluntly, that program "played no role in disrupting this attack. It made a minor contribution by providing corroborating information about one of the plot's already known co-conspirators, who was arrested months after the plot was disrupted. There is no reason to believe that bulk collection of telephone records was necessary for this minor contribution."[74] In an interview the next year, however, Alexander casually, if ambiguously, insisted that the Zazi episode was a "215 case."[75]

Actually, it is not clear that even the tip was necessary. Given the perpetrators' limited capacities, it is questionable, as detailed in chapter 3, whether the plot would have ever succeeded.[76]

A related justification for the data storage program holds that, if it had been in place in 2001, it could have led to finding the location of one of the 9/11 hijackers who was calling a safe house in Yemen from San Diego. This instance plays an important role in Judge Pauley's "Memorandum & Order" of December 2013, discussed early in this chapter, upholding the surveillance programs. However, insofar as this justification is valid, it would have been the 702 program that was relevant, not the 215. Moreover, the CIA was already tracking the man's communications and knew he had entered the United States. It also knew about the calls to the safe house but failed to trace the calls even though it had both the ability and the authority to do so. It did not need a vast data bank.[77] PCLOB concludes that the problem "stemmed primarily from a lack of information sharing among federal agencies, not of a lack of surveillance capabilities." That is, it "was a failure to connect the dots, not a failure to collect enough dots." In order to have identified the relevant telephone number, "it was not necessary to collect the entire nation's calling records."[78]

When presenting his cases at the congressional hearings in June 2013, Alexander explained that he couldn't make the details of all the cases on his secret list public because "[i]f we give all those out, we give all the secrets of how we're tracking down the terrorists as a community, and we can't do that."[79] The remaining fifty will remain shrouded in secrecy then, presumably because it is believed that discussing them publicly would result in damage, perhaps even grave damage, to national security. Accordingly, so protected, we will never be able to examine them in our "healthy debate" on the issue of NSA surveillance.

Absent such information, and keeping in mind the impressive record of dissembling that NSA has so far amassed, it does seem to be a reasonable suspicion—supported by the public comments of Senator Leahy—that the four cases discussed represent not a random selection from the list, but the best they could come up with. If that is so, the achievements of 215 do seem to be decidedly underwhelming.

In this regard, one could also examine that set of case studies of the post-9/11 plots that have come to light by Islamist terrorists to damage targets in the United States, as arrayed in appendix A. Since these have resulted in public arrests and trials, there is quite a bit of information available about them. Overall, where the plots have been disrupted, the task was accomplished by ordinary policing methods; the NSA programs scarcely come up at all. A similar conclusion has been reached by Peter Bergen and his colleagues at the New America Foundation in going over their extensive database of terrorism cases.[80] And, in an examination of plots that were actually executed, Mattathias Schwartz observes that "the authorities were not wanting for data." Rather, the problem was that they failed "to appreciate the significance of the data they already had."[81]

Actually, however, some people have been able to go through the entire set of cases and have reported on general patterns, if not on details. Thus, Senator Ron Wyden has said there is simply nothing much there.[82] PCLOB reaches a similar conclusion. In going over the remaining cases in the government's collection of "success stories," it found three in which 215 telephone records "simply mirrored or corroborated intelligence that the FBI obtained independently through other means" while supplying no "unique value" or altering the outcome of the case. There are also five cases in which 215 data helped "eliminate the possibility of a U.S. connection to a foreign terrorist plot."[83] Although NSA officials "put on a pretty strong defense for the program," recalls PCLOB chair David Medine rather bluntly, "their success stories didn't pan out."[84] Similarly, in reviewing the PCLOB report, Senator Leahy has noted pointedly, "This finding stands in stark contrast to initial claims by senior

NSA officials that the Section 215 program helped thwart dozens of terrorist plots."[85] Quite astonishing, then, is the bald pronouncement of Michael Leiter, former director of the government's National Counterterrorism Center: "I can't think of any terrorist investigation where the NSA was not a preeminent or central player."[86]

At the June 2013 hearings, one committee member, Representative Jim Himes of Connecticut, noting that his constituents were mainly concerned about 215, tried to get Alexander and Joyce to indicate how many plots would have been carried out except for that program: "How essential, not just contributing to, but how essential are these authorities to stopping which terrorist attacks?" Alexander irrelevantly responded that 702 contributed to 90 percent of the cases, and in half of these it was "critical." Further pressed about 215, the issue at hand, he said that just over ten of the cases had a "domestic nexus" and therefore 215 would apply, and that 215 "had a contribution" to the "vast majority" of these. Joyce then added more verbiage, proclaiming that every tool in the kit was both "essential" and "vital":

I think you ask an almost impossible question to say how important each dot was. . . . Our mission is to stop terrorism, to prevent it. . . . And I can tell you, every tool is essential and vital. And the tools [under discussion] have been valuable to stopping some of those plots. You ask, how can you put a value on an American life? And I can tell you, it's priceless.

Himes, out of time, ended by expressing his "hope" that "you'll elucidate for us specifically case by case how many stopped terrorist attacks" the 215 program was "essential to."[87] The evidence strongly suggests that the answer to that question is perilously close to zero.

In an interview months later, Alexander had become more modest, contending that the 215 and 702 programs merely "had some play" in his fifty-four trumpeted cases. He had, however, found a new dodge for the "critical" issue. He contended that "the best way to illustrate what the intelligence people are trying to do" is to look at the television game show *Wheel of Fortune*, where contestants seek to guess which letters to insert into a blank phrase.[88] It is true, of course, that each letter in the phrase is in some sense critical to the whole, but it is also true that phrases are generally correctly completed by contestants long before all the slots are filled. In addition, the contribution of the 215 program in the analogy seems at best to confirm that a letter already correctly guessed has indeed been correctly guessed.

Evaluating 215: Applying Cost-Benefit Analysis

It certainly appears, then, that any benefit of the 215 metadata program has been very limited at best, and it has been considerably outweighed by its cost, even assuming that the cost figure for the program is quite small. That is, the program would very likely fail a full cost-benefit analysis handily, even one that only minimally takes into consideration the costs of privacy, intimidation, and civil liberties infringements. Representative Adam Schiff has done his own "on net" assessment. Even if the program is "occasionally successful," he concludes, "there's still no justification that I can see for obtaining that amount of data in the first place."[89]

Some officials have in fact acknowledged that the case for 215 is "less compelling" and "harder to make."[90] In 2015, it was revealed that in the months before the Snowden leaks, some top managers at NSA had advocated scrapping the program on the grounds that its costs outweighed its benefits. The proposal had not yet reached Alexander's desk, and some officials say they doubt he would have approved it. However, when Alexander was strenuously defending the program after the Snowden leaks, neither he nor anyone else at NSA seems to have believed that the public would be served by revealing the existence of the internal debate.[91]

In December 2013, the special panel set up by the president to review the NSA programs, while dwelling mostly on legal issues, noted that information provided by the program "was not essential to preventing attacks and could readily have been obtained in a timely manner" otherwise; that "there has been no instance in which NSA could say with confidence that the outcome would have been different" without the program.[92] The same conclusion was reached a month later by the Privacy and Civil Liberties Oversight Board. It noted that it was unable to identify either "a single instance involving a threat to the United States in which the telephone records program made a concrete difference in the outcome of a counterterrorism investigation" or one "in which the program directly contributed to the discovery of a previously unknown terrorist plot or the disruption of a terrorist attack." The report continued, "an intelligence-gathering tool with significant ramifications for privacy and civil liberties cannot be regarded as justified merely because it provides *some* value in protecting the nation from terrorism." Rather, one should determine whether the benefit of the program is greater than its cost: "whether any unique value offered by the program outweighs its implications for privacy and civil liberties."[93]

If the 215 program is all cost and no benefit, a cost-benefit calculation becomes something of a no-brainer. However, if we bend over backward to assume that the program has had, or might eventually have, some benefit, then cost-benefit analysis—and specifically a variant of the "break-even" approach—can be used to calculate how much the program would have to cost for it to begin to be cost-effective under such assumptions.

Accordingly, following the approach put forward in chapter 5 to determine the "break-even point," we set the cost of the security measure equal to its benefit:

(cost of the security measure) = (probability of a successful attack absent all security measures) × (losses sustained in the successful attack) × (reduction in risk furnished by the security measure)

Then we estimate the parameters on the right side of the equation. To do this, we will first assess the last of these parameters—the reduction in risk furnished by the NSA's 215 program.

As discussed earlier, NSA testimony states that of the fifty-four cases that were supposedly disrupted by NSA surveillance data, 90 percent involved information from the 702 program. This implies that about five cases, or 10 percent, were disrupted by the 215 program. According to a 2010 study by the New York University School of Law, the number of terrorism-associated convictions in the United States in the eight years after 9/11 runs to 523. The effectiveness rate of the 215 program, then, could be taken to be 5 divided by 523, or 1 percent. There are also the undisclosed cases as discussed in chapter 3, of course, and these might boost this number. In addition, the NYU study revealed that 22 percent of cases indicate the "presence of classified information at some point in the investigation or prosecution," and this might include "conversations intercepted via FISA electronic surveillance and materials seized in FISA-authorized 'sneak and peek' searches."[94]

If we (rather heroically) assume that in these cases the gathering of intercepted communications was primarily responsible—that is, was crucial or necessary—for foiling or preventing a terrorist plot, and if we also assume that in 10 percent of these cases it was the 215 program that did the essential work, then a risk reduction of about 2 percent would be suggested (that is, about 10 percent of 22 percent). In addition, a well-founded suspicion that their telephone communications may be monitored may sometimes act as a deterrent to would-be plotters, or at least would be an inhibitor to their scheming; this would increase risk reduction. Bundling this together, we will assume that the 215 program provides a risk reduction—that it crucially deters, foils, or prevents—4 percent of plots.

This line of thinking is very generous to NSA. The United States has a vast array of counterterrorism measures to deter, disrupt, or protect against terrorist attacks in the homeland. The intelligence community comprises not only the NSA but also the CIA and fifteen other agencies. Added to this are the FBI, the Department of Defense, the Department of Homeland Security, the Transportation Security Administration, the Federal Air Marshall Service, the Secret Service, the Bureau of Alcohol, Tobacco, and Firearms, as well as state and local police, and—perhaps most important—an aware and alert public. As we saw in chapter 1, total expenditures on homeland security efforts exceed $115 billion per year. It is difficult to imagine that a single surveillance program in a single agency can be solely or crucially responsible for deterring or foiling 4 percent of attacks, or one in every twenty-five.

The cells in table 7-1 show the maximum yearly cost for the 215 program in millions of dollars required for it to be cost-effective. That is, the program fails to be cost-effective if it costs more than the amount indicated in the cell. These values are calculated for a range of attack frequencies, absent all security measures, from .05 attacks per year—or one successful attack every twenty years—to a high of ten successful attacks every year, and for the range of attack costs we have applied elsewhere in this book. Throughout, we assume, as noted, that the 215 program reduces risk—the consequences and/or the likelihood of such an attack—by 4 percent.

The boxed entry in table 7-1 gives the maximum the program can cost for it to be cost-effective if there would otherwise be one successful $1 billion attack each year—an attack that, if successfully carried out, would result in the detonation of an improvised explosive device much larger than the car bomb that failed to detonate in Times Square in 2010, or one inflicting extensive damage to life and property. As noted, the 215 program has never done so in the past.

Under these generous assumptions about its effectiveness, the program would be cost-effective only if its full price tag is no more than $40 million per year. (The full NSA budget, for reference, is about $10.8 billion.) If risk reduction from 215 is set at a much more realistic 2 percent, all the numbers in the table would be divided by 2, and the cost for the program in the boxed scenario would need to be no more than $20 million. However it is sliced, then, since the 215 program costs considerably more than $40 million per year, it pretty much fails a cost-benefit analysis, even when the assumptions are substantially stacked toward coming to the opposite conclusion.

As discussed earlier, the program's costs include not only expenditures involved in gathering, collating, storing, securing, and maintaining the metadata (estimated earlier to be over $100 million per year), but also those devoted to accessing, querying, indexing, managing, and exploiting the metadata and then following up on the many leads (including the "Pizza Hut" ones) it produces. If the FBI spends a full $3 billion a year in its counterterrorism quest,

TABLE 7-1 Evaluating the NSA's 215 Program

Annual Number of Successful Attacks Absent All Security Measures	Losses from a Successful Terrorist Attack						
	$100 million Ft. Hood shooting	$500 million Boston Marathon bombing	$1 billion Times Square bombing	$5 billion London bombing	$200 billion 9/11	$1 trillion nuclear port	$5 trillion nuclear Grand Central
0.05	0.2	1	2	10	400	2,000	10,000
0.1	0.4	2	4	20	800	4,000	20,000
0.25	1	5	10	50	2,000	10,000	50,000
0.50	2	10	20	100	4,000	20,000	100,000
1	4	20	40	200	8,000	40,000	200,000
2	8	40	80	400	16,000	80,000	400,000
5	20	100	200	1,000	40,000	200,000	1,000,000
10	40	200	400	2,000	80,000	400,000	2,000,000

Each cell entry indicates the maximum yearly cost in millions of dollars of the 215 Program to ensure that it begins to be cost-effective for terrorist attacks of various magnitudes and frequencies, assuming the program reduces the risk of an otherwise successful terrorist attack by 4 percent. An attack frequency of 0.05 per year is equivalent to an annual attack probability of 5 percent.

it could easily be that tens of millions of dollars of that figure are expended on chasing down the ghostly leads supplied by the very prolific NSA.

The cost would also need to include those involved in privacy invasion. It is difficult to quantify the value of privacy, but it seems likely that considerably more than 40 million Americans would value their privacy enough to pay $1 a year (or 10 million to pay $4 per year) to have their privacy shielded from the NSA's 215 surveillance. Many people are already paying considerably more than this for web encryption, a choice that has more than doubled in North America since the Snowden revelations while increasing fourfold in Europe and sixfold in Latin America.[95] Polls conducted in late 2014 indicate that 61 percent of Americans say they would like to do more to protect their privacy if they could figure out how to do it, while about 14 percent say they care enough about their privacy to willingly change their behavior to preserve it (the same percentage was also found in a 2012 poll, before the Snowden revelations).[96] It seems likely that most of the people these percentages represent would be quite willing to cough up a few dollars a year to evade NSA snooping.

A PRECEDENT FOR CLOSING DOWN SURVEILLANCE PROGRAMS

In the past, as it happens, NSA has actually closed down programs like 215—though not without characteristic dissembling. That is, it was persuaded to conclude that some tools in its kit were not necessarily all that "essential and vital." James Bamford reports that for years the agency had a nationwide program to store email and Internet metadata in bulk. This program was ended in 2011 for "operational and resource reasons," according to the director of national intelligence. But, notes Bamford, a statement issued in 2013 by Senators Ron Wyden and Mark Udall contends that

> the real reason the program was shut down was that the NSA was "unable" to prove the usefulness of the operation. "We were very concerned about this program's impact on Americans' civil liberties and privacy rights," they said, "and we spent a significant portion of 2011 pressing intelligence officials to provide evidence of its effectiveness. They were unable to do so, and the program was shut down that year." The senators added, "It is also important to note that intelligence agencies made statements to both Congress and the [FISA court] that significantly exaggerated this program's effectiveness. This experience demonstrates to us that intelligence agencies' assessment of the usefulness of particular collection programs—even significant ones—are not always accurate."[97]

The senators pointedly elaborate a bit:

> We believe that the broader lesson here is that even though intelligence officials may be well intentioned, assertions from intelligence agencies about the value and effectiveness of particular programs should not simply be accepted at face value by policymakers or oversight bodies.... It is up to Congress, the courts and the public to ask the tough questions and press even experienced intelligence officials to back their assertions up with actual evidence, rather than simply deferring to these officials' conclusions without challenging them.[98]

Actually, if the NSA was unable to demonstrate the usefulness of a program of email and Internet intercepts, the task would likely be even more difficult for justifying telephone intercepts. Alexander reportedly believed that, unlike the email program, there was still crucial value to maintaining the phone records program.[99] However, an assessment of the cases arrayed in appendix A certainly suggests that the terrorists or would-be terrorists discussed there were far more likely to communicate on the Internet than the telephone.

TERMINATING 215

It seems likely, then, that "on net" (as the president puts it), the highly controversial 215 program could also safely be retired for "operational and resource reasons" with little or no negative consequences to security. Risk analyst Howard Kunreuther's proposal about the key question continues to be pertinent: "How much should we be willing to pay for a small reduction in probabilities that are already extremely low?"[100] If the 215 program has done little (and probably nothing) special to prevent or disrupt terrorist attacks in the United States, and if we are now having a healthy debate about the NSA programs, it seems reasonable to suggest that, even without full information about how the program costs, we have been paying too much.

In December 2013, the president's special panel recommended terminating the 215 program as such, while transferring the storage of bulk telephone metadata to a system in which the data would be held instead "either by private providers or by a private third party." The government would be granted access to that data only with a court order.[101] A month later, PCLOB, finding that the "bulk telephone records program is not sustainable from a legal or policy perspective," recommended that the 215 program simply be terminated entirely.[102]

In response, President Obama moved to adopt the special panel's key recommendation, proposing to "end the Section 215 bulk telephony metadata program as it previously existed and establish a new mechanism to preserve the capabilities we need without the government holding this bulk metadata."[103] Under the president's proposal, phone companies would need to store the metadata, and the U.S. government could access, "absent an emergency situation," the data if a judge agrees based on national security concerns. In July 2014, Senate Judiciary Committee Chairman Patrick Leahy introduced the USA Freedom Act, which would end the government's collection and storage of phone metadata, and instead require phone companies to retain those records, which intelligence agencies could obtain only after earning court approval for their queries. However, Congress failed to enact this legislation, and the program continued unchanged and was routinely reauthorized every ninety days.[104]

In November 2014, a bill supported by the administration to cancel the 215 program received fifty-eight affirmative votes in the Senate.[105] That was two less than needed for passage under the circumstances, but it did suggest that a majority of Senate members had found the program to be somewhat less than "critical" or "crucial" to national security.

Finally, in mid-2015, the 215 program was substantially revamped by Congress following the Leahy approach. Telephone metadata would no longer be held by NSA, but only by the telephone companies and only (to their relief) for as long as it was useful for them to do so for business purposes. NSA could, with a court order, gain targeted access to the data.[106]

This change, however, may fail to render the program cost-effective even under the generous assumptions applied in our analysis. It does reduce the privacy costs as well as the rather minimal costs of simply storing the data. However, the costs of getting the database into searchable form and then querying it would still be there as could those entailed in following up the leads so generated—though the increased difficulty of accessing the database may reduce the frequency with which it is queried. And ultimately, of course, it is highly questionable whether a ghost-chasing program that has a history of supplying little benefit should be continued in any form.

Evaluating 702

Just possibly, there are other elements in the vast intelligence and policing empire that were spawned in panic and in unseemly haste after 9/11 that might now also be retired. It might be useful, for example, to perform a cost-benefit analysis of NSA's 702 program. It does get considerably higher marks than the 215 metadata-collection program from official evaluators. Thus, both the

President's Review Group on Intelligence and Communications Technologies and the PCLOB put the program under scrutiny, and both recommended keeping it. The program, they conclude, has had significantly more success in aiding terrorism investigations than the 215 program.

The president's group reviewed details supplied by NSA about over four dozen counterterrorism investigations since 2007 that resulted in the prevention of terrorist attacks overseas and in the United States. In all but one of these, the group noted, "information obtained under section 702 contributed in some degree to the success of the investigation." Even while acknowledging that "it is difficult to assess precisely how many of these investigations would have turned out differently without the information learned through section 702," the group was "persuaded that section 702 does in fact play an important role in the nation's effort to prevent terrorist attacks across the globe."[107]

For its part, PCLOB was favorably impressed by the fact that, unlike 215, the 702 program does not involve "collecting wide swaths of communications and then combing through them for those that are relevant to terrorism or contain other foreign intelligence." That is, it "is not based on the indiscriminate collection of information in bulk"—a key constitutional and civil liberties issue, of course. Instead, if a "specific non-U.S. person located outside the United States" becomes suspect, that person's communications, including those with Americans and with people in the United States, can be collected. PCLOB also concludes that the "702 program has proven valuable in enabling the government to prevent acts of terrorism within the United States and abroad, and to pursue other foreign intelligence goals"; that it "has helped the government to learn about the membership and activities of terrorist organizations, as well as to discover previously unknown terrorist operatives and disrupt specific terrorist plots"; and that it is more flexible than other surveillance authorities.[108]

Counterterrorism is but one component of the 702 program. The global collection of signals intelligence, argues PCLOB, is essential for other foreign intelligence purposes, such as anti-proliferation, counterintelligence, and economic and foreign policy deliberations.[109] An evaluation of the 702 program would have to take these benefits into account, which in many cases are considerable and wide ranging. Nearly all Western countries have foreign-signals collection programs, and some share their intelligence, the most powerful being the Five Eyes intelligence alliance among the United States, United Kingdom, Canada, Australia, and New Zealand. This could be taken to be an endorsement of the benefits of such programs for national security.

At the same time, 702 is likely to be considerably more expensive than 215. For one thing, it collects content, not simply metadata. Moreover, while comparatively selective, it is still a vast enterprise: in 2013 alone, nearly 90,000 people were targeted and had their communications data recorded. And "hundreds of reports per month concerning terrorism that include information derived from Section 702" are written, disseminated, and evaluated.[110]

In addition, the section on the successes of 702 in the PCLOB report is short and less than fully impressive. The only specific examples it mentions are plots concerning Zazi and the New York Stock Exchange, discussed earlier in this book.[111] As noted, the second of these is trivial, while in the first, it scarcely seems that 702 was needed because the key email address that was surveilled was already well known, owing to a tip from British intelligence. The report does note that in cases like these (if not in these specific cases), the 702 program provides more flexibility and speed in obtaining approval for such surveillance.[112] However, that may suggest modifying current procedures rather than supplanting them with a new program. Less specifically, the report observes that in some twenty cases, 702 was used "in support" of a "counterterrorism investigation" that already existed, and in some thirty cases it provided "the initial catalyst that identified previously unknown terrorist operatives and/or plots." Together, in the cases it examined there were well over 100 arrests on "terrorism-related offenses." In other cases, 702 "appears to have been used to provide warnings about a continuing threat or to assist in investigations that remain ongoing." Overall, some fifteen of these cases "involved some connection to the United States," and about forty "exclusively involved operatives and plots in foreign countries." A footnote adds that there are other cases for which 702 had "proven useful."[113]

Keeping in mind the rather evasive observation of the president's group that 702 has "contributed in some degree" to successful investigations, one might be led to wonder whether the surveillance program has provided enough value to justify spying on 90,000 people every year, while supplying information included in hundreds of reports each month—all of which must then be read and evaluated by somebody or other. All this, as Alexander Stephan would pointedly stress, is "at taxpayers' expense."

Why Were the Programs Secret?

One additional question on NSA concerns the issue of why the programs were kept secret. Under Executive Order 135256, a classification of "secret" is permitted if "disclosure of the information reasonably could be expected to result in damage to the national security, which includes defense against transnational terrorism." The order continues: "If there is significant doubt about the need to classify information, it shall not be classified."[114] As defined in Executive Order 12356, the classification level of "top secret" should only be "applied to information, the unauthorized disclosure of which reasonably could be expected to cause exceptionally grave damage to national security."[115]

It is difficult to see how earlier exposure of the NSA surveillance programs' existence would have damaged national security, exceptionally gravely or otherwise. No one seems to be saying that the Snowden documents put undercover intelligence operatives, or operations overseas or elsewhere, in danger of being exposed, or that they revealed military secrets about weapons, or that they compromised U.S. strategy or tactics. Instead, we got vague, atmospheric pronouncements to the press as that from outgoing FBI Director Robert Mueller in August 2013: "Mueller said that leaks by former NSA contractor Edward Snowden 'have impacted, and [are] in the process of impacting, capabilities around the world,' but when asked to expand on this, he said simply, 'No details.'"[116] Even less helpful has been the expression of "belief" promulgated by NSA chief Alexander: "Based on what we know to date, we believe these disclosures have caused significant and irreversible harm to the security of the nation."[117]

Mark Young is more specific, arguing that terrorist groups will change how they conceive, plan, and execute attacks.[118] However, terrorists have surely known at least since the 1990s (when Osama bin Laden ceased talking on a satellite phone) that U.S. intelligence is searching communications worldwide to track them down.[119] Year after year, we have heard about "chatter" that has been picked up by official agencies, and one certainly has to conclude that it has dawned on the chatterers that there are extensive efforts to listen in. The terrorists may not know the precise number, but they are likely to be at least dimly aware—and are unlikely to be surprised—that NSA, in its tireless quest to conduct its very global war on terror, might well be on their case.[120] It is possible that the current revelations will impress the terrorists even further about the extent of the surveillance effort. But even if that is so, the main effect of the revelations would not be to facilitate communications but, rather, to make efforts at communication even more difficult and inconvenient. Moreover, although they don't always seem to have followed the instructions, it is quite clear that international jihadists have for over a decade had manuals and handbooks containing detailed information about how to keep communications secure.[121] The 9/11 attackers were very restricted in their use of electronic communication, and Osama bin Laden was informed of the date of the attack by courier.[122]

Conceivably, as some maintain, there exist some exceptionally dim-witted terrorists or would-be terrorists who are oblivious to the fact that their communications are less than fully secure. Indeed, it almost seems that the "chatter" must consist primarily either of deliberate misinformation or of the ramblings of hapless amateurs. But such supreme knuckleheads are surely likely to make many mistakes—like advertising on Facebook or searching there or in chatrooms for co-conspirators.[123] It scarcely seems necessary to maintain sophisticated and costly communications data banks to track them down.

Moreover, as noted earlier, NSA surveillance programs had already essentially been outed in May 2006 in a lengthy story in *USA Today*, and there was also exposure in an article in *Wired* in 2012 that was based on information supplied by a former NSA official. Although the program's existence was firmly denied by people in charge, any sensible terrorist would likely be inclined to wariness. The later release of the Snowden materials simply settled the matter.

Some defenders of the program have creatively argued that exposure of the 215 program has aided terrorists because they now know that NSA is gathering only metadata on telephone calls in the United States, not their content. Thus, said General Michael Hayden: "What I fear al-Qaeda learns about this program is not what we're *allowed* to do but they learn what we're *not* allowed to do, and they learn the limits of the program."[124] But if terrorists read past the first paragraph in discussions about the 215 program, they surely can also note that, if information gathered is deemed suspicious, investigators can apply for legal authority to record the content of the communications. And they can do that readily as well in the 702 program, which gathers and monitors not only metadata but also content. Moreover, like many others, terrorists are likely to suspect that, despite prominent denials to the contrary, considerably more than metadata is gathered even under the 215 program.[125]

Far less concerned is Director of National Intelligence James Clapper. In retrospect, he says, it would have been wiser from the beginning to have been open and transparent about the program with the American people and with Congress. Although he has condemned the Snowden revelations as harmful to national security in the past, he now seems to think that the benefits of disclosure would have trumped any harms.[126]

It has also been contended that the revelations will "diminish national security by degrading U.S. foreign relations," noting, for example, that "European Union officials have expressed outrage over the Snowden disclosures" while Brazil's president postponed a state visit.[127] But surely the outrage stems from the fact that the United States has been extensively, even exhaustively, spying on them, not from the revelation of that fact.

There is an old adage in diplomacy: gentlemen don't read other gentlemen's mail. Although it sounds rather prissy, the adage has a steel spine: people who do read the mail of others will inspire distrust and even rejection if that other gentleman finds out, while mutually beneficial cooperation and civility will decline. It is a rule with consequences, and one disobeys it at one's peril. Something similar holds for the argument that public confidence in intelligence organizations—and the willingness to fund them—will diminish when the scope of the spying is revealed.[128] That people will be outraged if they learn they are being spied on is not a valid reason for making the spying programs secret in the first place.

There is also the notion that the programs needed to be kept secret to protect the private communications companies, like AT&T, Verizon, and Sprint, which were dutifully supplying, or being forced to supply, the NSA with private data.[129] If their customers found out that their billing records are routinely being handed over to the government, it is said, they might drop their service and migrate to a company that doesn't send its data to the NSA. However, the potential embarrassment of businesses, although a reasonable concern, is not usually deemed to constitute a threat, grave or otherwise, to national security, and it would therefore seem to fail to be a legitimate reason for classification. Moreover, it seems elemental that customers be informed about what businesses are doing with their confidential information. In addition, although communications companies sensibly do worry about a backlash overseas, the concern certainly appears to have been overwrought at least for their U.S. base: the Snowden disclosures do not seem to have led to mass customer defections from cooperating companies. In part, perhaps, this is because it is difficult to find out which companies do not hand over the data.[130] And, even if one could find out, the company to which the customer defects could at any time be forced to turn over its data anyway. And enrolling with a foreign carrier would likely not work either, because such companies and their governments are strongly inclined, even bound, to cooperate with American intelligence agencies.

As a practical matter, businesses that betray the trust of their customers and business partners, even unwillingly or under government compulsion, will—and should—suffer if that betrayal becomes known. Indeed, it is an important goal for governmental regulators to increase the transparency of business practices for the benefit of the consumer.

Also relevant is consideration of an elemental axiom of good policing: treating everyone as a criminal reduces the incentive not to act like one.

If the public believes that only suspected criminals are spied upon, then only criminals will expend effort to maintain their privacy from government invasion. The massive, undifferentiated coverage of the 215 bulk data-collection program violates a key axiom of good government: the one enshrined in the United States in its constitutional stipulation against unreasonable search and seizure.

Unkind people might suggest that the real reason these programs were kept secret actually stems from the administration's fear that public awareness of their "modest encroachments" on privacy would make further efforts to encroach more difficult. Thus, Reuters notes that a former Air Force secretary ominously warns that a "growing unease about domestic surveillance could have a chilling effect on proposed cyber legislation that calls for greater information-sharing between government and industry." And it also noted that, after the revelations, more lawmakers signed on to legislation that would strengthen the privacy protections in the 1986 Electronic Communications Privacy Act.[131] Perhaps, then, the programs were kept secret not so much to protect people from terrorism but to protect the government from the annoying and inconvenient public and congressional outcry that, as it happens, constitutes the untidy stuff of democracy.

Assessing the Snowden Contribution

In a major speech on the NSA controversy in January 2014, President Obama stated, "One thing I'm certain of. This debate will make us stronger."[132] However, his speech contained no suggestion that he might be thinking of honoring the man responsible for getting the debate going—and therefore for strengthening the United States.

Nonetheless, if Snowden's debate leads to systematic efforts to reevaluate the huge, even preposterous, increases in spending on homeland security that have taken place since 2001, it will prove to be a most desirable development. His revelations do raise justifiable concerns about the potential for governmental invasions of privacy.

However, they also provide a window into a process of ghost-chasing gone rampant, a process that raises the counterterrorism enterprise to the level of self-parody. Thousands of people are at work gathering unbelievable quantities of information, or hay, simply because it has become technologically possible to do so in a process that has netted scarcely any terrorists—or needles at all. Mark Young thinks that we, and Snowden, should ask ourselves "if the transparency that he has forced onto the system is worth the diminishing of

American security."[133] It's a good question, and the answer to the implied cost-benefit assessment appears to be yes. Indeed, it is far from clear that security has been diminished at all.

In the meantime, the man whose revelations "make us stronger" is scheduled, as of this writing, to remain in effective exile abroad, even as American politicians fancifully spin conspiracy theories that his revelations were all part of an elaborate Russian plot.[134]

CHAPTER EIGHT

The Department of Homeland
Security

L ESS THAN A month after the tragic events of 9/11, President George
W. Bush established the Office of Homeland Security within the White
House. Its mission was "to develop and coordinate the implementation of a
comprehensive national strategy to secure the United States from terrorist
threats or attacks."[1] Although originally opposed to the idea, Bush proposed
in June 2002 that the Office of Homeland Security be elevated to cabinet level,
establishing the Department of Homeland Security (DHS) to "ensure greater
accountability over critical homeland security missions and unity of purpose
among the agencies responsible for them."[2]

DHS soon became the third largest federal department and brought together
twenty-two federal agencies with homeland security missions, including the U.S.
Coast Guard, the Customs Service, the Immigration and Naturalization Service,
the Federal Emergency Management Agency, and the newly created Transport
Security Administration (TSA). It started with a budget of $31.2 billion ($40.4
billion in 2014 dollars) with 180,000 employees, and by 2014 it had been increased
to $60.7 billion with 240,000 employees.[3] A decade and more after its creation,
however, the DHS is still sometimes characterized as a "work in progress."[4]

Although the DHS was established primarily to protect the United States
from terrorism, it has other responsibilities as well. Its five core missions are
to prevent terrorism and enhance security, secure and manage the country's
borders, enforce and administer immigration laws, safeguard and secure
cyberspace, and ensure resilience to disasters.[5] Activities related to homeland
security account for 55 to 65 percent of the total DHS budget. Response to

natural disasters, emergency management, Coast Guard search-and-rescue activities, and citizenship and immigration services constitute the bulk of its non–homeland security activities.[6] As figure 8-1 shows, DHS expenditures related to homeland security have grown since 2002 by nearly 60 percent, totaling $35.6 billion in 2014.

As required by the 2002 Act, homeland security activities are divided into three broad categories: prevent and disrupt terrorist attacks; protect the American people, our critical infrastructure, and key resources; and respond to and recover from incidents. As table 8-1 shows, in 2014, DHS devoted 75 percent of its effort to the first of these, with yearly expenditures of $26.9 billion and nearly 143,000 personnel assigned to the task.

Two elements in the table involve policing and intelligence in the defense against terrorism—the focus of this book. One is the Office of Intelligence and Analysis (I&A), which provides an intelligence and warning capability to the DHS with a reasonably modest $270 million budget and employing 800 people.[7] The other is the TSA, established in November 2001, which provides security for the American transportation system and has a budget of $7.4 billion with 54,000 employees.

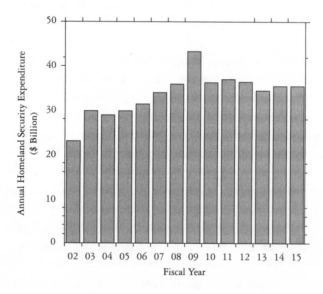

FIGURE 8-1 DHS expenditures related to homeland security (inflation adjusted to 2014 dollars).

Source: 2003–2015: OMB, Analytical Perspectives, Fiscal Years 2005 to 2015. This document includes information about enacted and supplemental/emergency expenditures. The funding level for 2015 is a budget request and does not represent an actual expenditure. Specific budget allocations to "homeland security" are available only after the FY2004 budget. The 2002 estimate is based on the funding level for 2002 in Painter and Lake, "Homeland Security Department: FY2012 Appropriations," 85.

TABLE 8-1   DHS Contributions to Homeland Security

	Expenditures ($ Billion)	Personnel
1. Prevent and Disrupt Terrorist Attacks	26.9	142,800
Office of Intelligence and Analysis	0.3	800
Transportation Security Administration	7.4	54,000
Customs and Border Protection	10.5	52,000
Coast Guard	3.6	18,000
Immigration and Customs Enforcement	4.4	16,000
Others	0.7	2,000
2. Protect the American People, Our Critical Infrastructure, and Key Resources	6.2	-
3. Respond to and Recover from Incidents	2.5	-

Inferred from OMB, Analytical Perspectives FY2015, personnel pro-rata from total personnel for each agency, and budget allocations.

This chapter evaluates these two programs. It does not deal with the other elements arrayed in table 8-1, either because they do not focus much on terrorism or because they do not apply to intelligence and policing.[8]

I&A *and the Fusion Centers*

According to DHS, its Office of Intelligence and Analysis "has a unique role as a central conduit for information sharing" among various federal and local entities in "support [of] the goals of homeland security." Its mission

> includes promoting an understanding of threats to the homeland through intelligence analysis, coordinating the counterintelligence activities of the department, collecting information and intelligence to support homeland security missions, managing intelligence for the homeland security enterprise, and sharing the information necessary for action while protecting the privacy, civil rights, and civil liberties of all Americans.[9]

This mission is carried out through seventy-eight "Fusion Centers," which are located throughout the United States. These are clusters of state and local law enforcement people set up to collect intelligence on terrorist and other criminal activity in their area and then to send reports on their findings to DHS for evaluation. In 2012, DHS Secretary Janet Napolitano declared Fusion Centers to be "one of the centerpieces of our counterterrorism strategy."[10]

For many years, the Department of Homeland Security was unable to determine even for itself how much the Fusion Centers cost.[11] It estimated that it had awarded somewhere between $289 million and $1.4 billion for them between 2003 and 2010—an uncertainty gap of over a billion dollars that is impressive even by Washington standards.[12] However, later data suggest that the funding for Fusion Centers in FY2013 was $308.2 million—rather inexpensive by DHS standards.[13] On average, state and local governments contribute less than $2 million to fund each Fusion Center—enough to pay for ten to sixteen police officers, state troopers, or deputies, or for twenty non-sworn staff.[14]

A total of 390 federal personnel support the Fusion Centers. Of these, DHS contributes 258 employees, at a cost of $40 million. Added to this are 2,396 state, local, tribal, territorial, and private-sector staff members working on either a full-time or a part-time basis. It is not clear if this represents an additional investment in personnel, or redeployment of existing personnel; in the current age of austerity, the latter is more likely. On average, each Fusion Center sports about thirty-six staff members, many of them part-timers.

It is not easy to fathom what Fusion Centers actually do. It seems clear, however, that state and local governments are more concerned about the "all crime and all hazards" role for them, especially in times of tight budgets, whereas the federal government is more focused on countering terrorism.[15] In March 2009, Secretary Napolitano compared Fusion Centers to Joint Terrorism Task Forces (JTTFs)—FBI-led groups that include state and local law enforcement, as well as other federal agencies, whose primary mission is investigating terrorist threats. According to Napolitano, a JTTF "is an FBI-driven group designed to look solely at the issue of terrorism." In contrast, Fusion Centers "are designed to look at many, many more things beyond that," including serial kidnappers, gangs or organized crime syndicates, and serial or pattern murderers. JTTFs, she continued, "have a very defined specific function" while Fusion Centers are "much broader," and have "the capacity for response and recovery."[16] In testimony before the Senate in September 2009, Napolitano was even more direct: "A JTTF is really focused on terrorism and terrorism-related investigations. Fusion Centers are almost everything else."[17]

The justification for the formation and growth of Fusion Centers, however, is often couched in terms that are substantially related to counterterrorism: gathering "national intelligence" and "enhancing understanding of the threat environment across all levels of government." When asked to characterize their broad mission focus, 96 percent of Fusion Centers indicated involvement in counterterrorism, 96 percent reported involvement in "all crimes," and 71 percent indicated involvement in "all hazards."[18] Specific mission areas beyond counterterrorism include corrections, parole, or probation (46 percent); gangs (77 percent); and narcotics (77 percent), as well as seventeen other areas, few of which relate directly to counterterrorism.

Clearly, counterterrorism makes up a small component of Fusion Centers' investigative and analysis tasks. This is tellingly evident in the array of "success stories" promulgated in Fusion Center reports for 2012 and 2013:

- Supports Arrest of Individual Impersonating a Federal Agent
- Collaborate to Support Arrest of Individual Charged with Production of Child Pornography
- Collaborate to Disrupt an Alleged Plot from a Minnesota-based Hate Group
- Supports Multiagency Arrest of Foreign National
- Collaborate to Locate and Apprehend a Wanted Fugitive
- Supports Colorado Wildfire Response Efforts
- Collaborate to Assist in Opening a Homicide Investigation
- Assists in Homicide Investigation
- Collaborate to Support Controlled Drug Seizure
- Collaborate to Solve Murder of Young Child
- Provides Critical Information to International and Federal Partners
- Contributes to Arrest of Armed Suspects
- Contributes to Decrease in Auto Theft
- Supports Apprehension of Armed and Dangerous Fugitives[19]

Apparently, there was not a single counterterrorism "success story" to tell.

In 2013, I&A placed ninety-five intelligence and reports officers in state and major urban area Fusion Centers nationwide. Judging from the listing of "accomplishments" that began with their annual budget-in-brief reports from 2007 onward, Fusion Centers have not accomplished much. Key among the listed achievements is that in 2013 "I&A produced and disseminated 574 original analytic products" and "2,983 Daily Intelligence Highlights articles."[20] Most of the listed "accomplishments" contain words like *improved, coordinated, understanding, integrating, engaged, provided, assisted,* and *deployed.* Words that really matter in counterterrorism—*deterred, foiled, disrupted, prevented, alerted, led to arrest*—do not come up.

Considerable hackles were raised by a 2012 report from the Permanent Subcommittee on Investigations of the Senate Committee on Homeland Security and Governmental Affairs, which concluded that the utility of the terrorism-related reporting from the Fusion Fenters had been at best "questionable."[21] Investigators shuffled through 610 Fusion Center intelligence reports submitted to DHS over a 13-month period. Of the 574 unclassified reports filed, 188 were "cancelled" by DHS reviewers generally because they contained "nothing of value" or because they simply failed to contain "any actual intelligence." While the overall cancellation rate for Fusion Center reports was around 30 percent, nearly half of those that dealt with terrorism were rejected out of hand. That didn't leave many. Of the 386 reports that were accepted, only 94—considerably less than two a week—related "in some way" to potential terrorist activity. Moreover, more than a quarter of these simply duplicated information already known to the FBI, and "some were based on information drawn from publicly available websites or dated public reports." One, in fact, simply relayed information from a Department of Justice press release that had been published months earlier.[22]

Moreover, continues the Senate Committee report, DHS has "struggled" to identify a clear example in which a Fusion Center provided intelligence that helped disrupt a terrorist plot. And, when investigators looked at the four "success stories" touted by DHS, they were "unable to confirm" that the Centers' contributions were "as significant as DHS portrayed them; were unique to the intelligence and analytical work expected of fusion centers; or would not have occurred absent a fusion center."[23]

However, it apparently never occurred to the investigators that the reason intelligence reporting on terrorists is so limited in quantity and so abysmal in overall quality is that there was virtually nothing to report. Absence of evidence, it implies, cannot possibly be evidence of absence. Accordingly, the report recommends that *even more* money should be spent on Fusion Centers. Local intelligence reporting efforts, it suggests, should be reformed to eliminate duplication, the training and numbers of intelligence reporters should be improved, and better efforts should be put into place to evaluate their output.[24]

From the standpoint of counterterrorism, Fusion Centers—those "centerpieces" of DHS's counterterrorism strategy—seem to have been all cost and little or no benefit.

TSA *and the* Air Marshals

Fully $5.8 billion, or 98 percent, of TSA's transport security funding is directed to aviation security—screening airport passengers, baggage, and cargo, and maintaining the Federal Air Marshal Service (FAMS).[25] Only $122 million is allocated to surface transportation security, even though, according to DHS figures, fifteen times more people in the United States use mass transit per year than fly.[26]

The protection of airliners may be particularly important because the downing of an airliner does seem to carry with it the special dangers of a widespread and at least somewhat lingering impact on the airline industry, as well as on related ones such as tourism. By contrast, if a bus or train is blown up, people still need to board them and will do so after a short period of wariness—as was found to be the case after terrorist bombings of trains and buses in Madrid in 2004 and in London in 2005. To a considerable degree, people have a choice about whether to use commercial airliners, and many can turn to other types of transport—or, often, simply not take the trip. Riders of subways, buses, and probably even ferries often do not have the same luxury.

Although an attack on aviation may be the "gold standard" for terrorists, attacks on mass transit are more frequent and almost as deadly. The attacks on trains in Madrid in 2004, on the London Underground and bus system (and the failed ones two weeks later) in 2005, and on the Mumbai railway station in 2008 show that mass transit can be an attractive target.

Much of the concern about airliner terrorism extrapolates from the 9/11 experience, which had a crushing, if temporary, effect on airline passenger traffic. Particularly in the few years after 2001, it was commonly said that if terrorists were able to down two or three more airliners, they would destroy the airline industry. However, contrary to that anticipation, there have been remarkably few terrorist attempts on airplanes since 9/11 anywhere in the world, even though security measures in many places are considerably more lax than in the United States.[27] Terrorists downed two Russian airliners in 2004, plots in Britain and in Yemen to down American-bound planes with on-flight explosives were broken up in 2006 and 2010, and the efforts of terrorists who made it onto flights with (inadequate) bombs in their shoes or underwear were thwarted by crew and passengers in 2001 and 2009. That's not a high rate of frequency. Also relevant is the fact that, of the tens of billions of pieces of checked luggage transported on American carriers in the period after a bomb planted in checked luggage caused a PanAm jet to crash into Lockerbie, Scotland, in 1988, not a single one has exploded to down an aircraft. This, despite the fact that mandatory screening of checked luggage was begun only after the September 11, 2001, attacks—though systems were put into place earlier to match passengers with luggage, thereby requiring that a terrorist trying to duplicate the deed would have to be suicidal.[28]

TSA has arrayed a considerable set of hurdles to deter and disrupt terrorists in what it calls "layers of security." One of these, the FAMS, is essentially policelike. Marshals have police powers and are "riding shotgun." They are armed and are devoted to preventing commercial passenger airliners from being commandeered by small bands of terrorists, kept under control for some time, and then crashed into specific targets—the 9/11 scenario. At the same time, the marshals are unlikely to be important contributors to dealing with other terrorist efforts, such as seeking to down an airliner by exploding bombs in cargo or in carry-on luggage.

Accordingly, we will evaluate the cost-effectiveness of FAMS in the scenario for which it has been constructed. In our earlier book, we found that FAMS failed to be cost-effective.[29] In this extension, we ask the same question but place FAMS in the full context of the array of other layers of airline security. Further extended, the approach we lay out can be used to evaluate the security contribution of each of those layers and in context.

In this analysis, we seek to determine whether FAMS reduces the risk of a successful terrorist hijacking enough to justify its (very considerable) expense. To do so, we estimate the risk reduction using techniques that specifically consider rates of deterrence, detection, and disruption for each layer of security.[30]

Arraying the Layers of Security

We do not include all layers of security in this analysis, only those likely to stop a 9/11–type attack. It should be kept in mind, however, that we do not include an important barrier that costs nothing: the general incompetence and poor tradecraft of terrorists, particularly in complicated plots, a quality assessed at some length in earlier chapters.[31] To a degree, however, at least some of the disruption rates presented in the analysis take this into account, in that a high rate of disruption implies less than perfect terrorist competence.

We focus on those aviation security measures designed to deter or disrupt a terrorist hijacking attempt in four stages.[32]

Stage 1: Terrorists are deterred from attempting an airliner hijacking. All security measures contribute to deterrence. Although a terrorist might be deterred as well by the belief that a hijacking will be counterproductive to the cause, or by an unwillingness to commit suicide, we do not include this consideration in our analysis.

Stage 2: Terrorists attempt a hijacking but are prevented from boarding. The TSA has set up a considerable collection of security measures that are specifically designed to prevent a terrorist from being able to board an airline. These include intelligence, customs and border protection, joint terrorism task forces, the no-fly list, passenger pre-screening, behavioral detection officers, travel document checkers, checkpoint/transportation security officers, transportation security inspectors, crew vetting, and random employee screening.

Stage 3: Terrorists succeed in boarding but are foiled when they attempt to commandeer the flight deck. Six measures are specifically focused on dealing with an on-board effort to commandeer the aircraft, and we particularly want to concentrate on a comparison of the degree to which they reduce the likelihood that such an effort will succeed.

1. As discussed in chapter 4, one key reason for the extent of the losses in 2001 was the lack of *cabin crew and passenger resistance* to the hijackings. The 9/11 attacks radically changed this situation. As demonstrated on the fourth plane, passengers and crew will now fight back, particularly if there is any indication that the terrorists' intent is to enter the cockpit.[33] Beyond hijacking, passenger and cabin crew reactions were also effective in subduing the shoe bomber of 2001 and the underwear bomber of 2009. This important security layer costs essentially nothing.

2. *Law enforcement officers* are on some flights for reasons other than countering terrorism, such as escorting prisoners or protecting VIPs. However, their numbers are small and their impact on security is accordingly likely to be very low.

3. Since 2003, the Federal Aviation Administration has required airlines to install *hardened cockpit doors* to protect cockpits from intrusion and small-arms fire or fragmentation devices. It also requires that the cockpit doors remain locked and that cockpit access be controlled. There is little doubt that hardened cockpit doors will hamper a hijacking attempt. However, if attackers are somehow able to get into the flight deck, the doors become a security device that could protect them.[34]

Then there are, in particular, three additional layers of security that we want to evaluate, one of them quite expensive, the other two much less so.

4. One of them is *flight deck resistance*. With the horrific experience of 9/11 behind them, pilots are likely to put up a fight against any cockpit penetration, whatever their training or armaments. The Federal Flight Deck Officer (FFDO) program enhances their ability to do so by training pilots and other flight deck members and allowing them to transport and carry firearms to defend the flight deck. The program provides the "last line of defense" against a hijacking, and it has dramatically increased in size since its inception in 2003.[35] It is estimated that 10 percent of pilots in the United States were FFDOs in 2008 and that this would grow to 16 to 20 percent by 2012.[36] It is also estimated that trained and armed FFDOs are five times more likely to be

on a flight than are air marshals.[37] It seems reasonable to assume that if FFDOs are present on the flight deck, they are likely to be as effective as any air marshals who happen to be on board. The FY2014 budget for the FFDO program is approximately $25 million.

5. The expensive security measure is the *Federal Air Marshal Service* (FAMS). Currently there are some 2,500 to 4,000 air marshals, up from 33 before 9/11.[38] The FY2014 budget for the service is $819 million, a reduction of $147 million from a high of $966 million in 2012.[39] In addition, airlines are expected to provide free seats to air marshals, and these are generally in first class to allow observation of the cockpit door. The Air Transport Association estimates that this costs the airlines $270 million in 2014 dollars.[40] The total cost of FAMS, then, is close to $1.1 billion a year.

Air marshals ride on no more than 5 percent of flights in the United States.[41] Supposedly, these are often high-risk flights, based on intelligence reports.[42] Exactly how that risk has been determined is difficult to fathom, particularly since air marshals have had almost nothing to do over the years. If an air marshal is spurred into action, it has thus far always been to restrain unruly passengers, such as during a reclined-seat dispute on a 2014 flight from Miami to Paris.[43] Air marshals have made several dozen arrests since 2001, but none of these have been related to terrorism.[44] The potential presence of air marshals may have something of a deterrent effect.[45] However, this is ameliorated somewhat by the low percentage of flights they can cover. It might even be argued that some crew and passengers may be reluctant to be the first to confront a hijacker if they believe an air marshal is on board, a hesitation that could conceivably give attempted hijackers the time they need to execute their plans. On the positive side, air marshals may provide more flexibility than many other security measures because they can be deployed at short notice for emerging threats.

The cost for each air marshal is around $3,300 per flight (and some flights carry more than one). In stark contrast, FFDOs cost approximately $15 per flight, a fact that has inspired the Federal Flight Deck Officers Association to point out that "the same expenditure allows 440 FFDO missions to the single FAM mission."[46] Despite the low cost of the FFDO program, the Obama administration proposed cutting the program by 50 percent in 2012.[47] This was defeated by Congress, but since 2012 TSA has persisted in cutting, or seeking to cut, the FFDO program at every opportunity, an issue to be discussed more fully later in this chapter.

6. On many flights, the cockpit door cannot remain closed for the entire duration of the flight because access is required for rest periods, toilet breaks, and meals. During the time of opening and closing ("door transition"), the

benefit of a hardened cockpit door in protecting the flight deck area is reduced. This has led to a call for Installed Physical Secondary Barriers (IPSB) because, as the Airline Pilots Association (ALPA) has put it, "the reinforced flight deck door, together with supplementary crew procedures, does not provide a complete solution for securing the flight deck."[48]

A report from the Radio Technical Commission for Aeronautics (RTCA) examines a hijacking scenario positing "a team of highly trained, armed, athletic individuals" who might, in a matter of seconds, be able to take over the flight deck during a door transition. Under those circumstances, passengers and crew would scarcely have time to assess the situation, realize the dire threat, communicate with other passengers, and process the information needed for them to summon the courage to fight back. Accordingly, the RTCA report concludes that "passengers are not considered a predictably reliable option for preventing an attempted violent or sudden breach of the flight deck," and it completely excludes "the possibility of passenger intervention as a mitigating measure" from its consideration. Although flight attendants receive little or no training in the use of force, many airlines have instituted procedures during door transition, such as galley trolleys to block access to the flight deck. The report concludes, however, that this did "not produce satisfactory results."[49] To a perhaps somewhat lesser degree, the same may hold for air marshals.

A secondary barrier to the cockpit could deal with this concern, further enhancing security. This is "a lightweight device that is easy to deploy and stow, installed between the passenger cabin or cargo deck and the flight deck door—that blocks access to the flight deck whenever the reinforced door is opened in flight."[50] Further security is provided by the fact that a cabin crew member is generally required to be at the scene when the secondary barrier is put into place, something that adds a complication for would-be hijackers—and at little or no cost.

The barrier weighs about 10 pounds and is normally stowed when the cockpit door is closed and locked. In 2004, United Airlines installed IPSBs on its entire fleet of 500 passenger aircraft.[51] Additionally, Boeing and Airbus have designed them as options on certain models of their next-generation aircraft and have made them standard equipment on their new Boeing 787s.[52] The cost of an IPSB for a single aircraft is less than $10,000.[53] Since there are approximately 6,000 commercial aircraft in the United States, this equates to perhaps no more than $60 million. If we round this up by a quarter, and annualize this cost over the twenty-year design life of an aircraft with a 3 percent discount rate, this equates to a cost of $5 million per year for the entire U.S. commercial airline fleet.[54]

However, beginning in 2012, United Airlines has paid Boeing to remove IPSBs from their new 787s, a move that dismays the Airline Pilots Association, which wrote to United management: "If safety is a top priority, then stop stripping United planes of the one safety measure that guarantees that the cockpit is protected."[55] According to pilots, when United and Continental merged, the company, apparently for consistency, decided to remove the secondary barriers in the United planes—about 1,000 in all—at a cost or some $5,000 to $12,000 each rather than adding them to the Continental planes.[56] This is quite remarkable: paying extra to remove an absurdly cheap countermeasure to a 9/11–type hijacking.

Stage 4. Terrorists succeed in commandeering the airliner but are kept from flying it into their designated target. The final layer of security concerns anti-aircraft measures put into place after 9/11.[57] If a pilot is able to transmit to air controllers that the plane is under a violent hijacking attempt (or passengers or cabin crew members use their phones to warn authorities), anti-aircraft measures might immediately be deployed to shoot down or ground the captured airliner before it can reach an intended target. If this capacity is substantial and terrorists are aware of it, the measure would form a highly effective deterrent to a hijacking attempt. The hijacking efforts might result in the destruction of the airliner, but accomplishing that goal could be done more easily by exploding a bomb on board—something that does not require the complexities of the team effort of a hijacking.

COMPARING REDUCTIONS IN RISK

We are interested in assessing the risk reduction against an airliner hijacking that is supplied by three of the stage 3 security measures—FFDO, FAMS, and IPSB—after taking into consideration the degree to which the risk of a hijacking has been reduced by all the other measures in TSA's layers of security as outlined above.[58] Since we are seeking to explore the cost-effectiveness of TSA's main policing system—FAMS—we will first assess its contribution to risk reduction and then explore the possibility that, by emphasizing risk-reduction measures that are less expensive, the overall risk reduction could be maintained or enhanced. A sensitivity analysis is included to assess changes in risk reduction and cost-effectiveness if some of these rates are changed.[59]

For each security measure, we assign words of estimative probability according to the following pattern: *certain* translates to 100 percent probability, *almost certain* to 93 percent, *highly probable* to 85 percent, *probable* to 75 percent, *chances about even* to 50 percent, *probably not* to 30 percent, *almost certainly not* to 7 percent, and *impossible* to zero percent.[60] These terms are then applied to our best estimates of deterrence and disruption rates in tables 8-2 and 8-3.[61] We tend to err on the low side in estimating these, a process that biases the analysis toward finding FAMS and other levels of security to be cost-effective because it leaves them with a larger share of the residual risk to reduce.

We begin by establishing a base rate for risk reduction for the full array of security measures. As can be seen in table 8-4, which applies the deterrence and disruption rates as given in tables 8-2 and 8-3, these measures combine to reduce the risk of a successful airliner hijacking by 99.8 percent.[62]

The first thing to notice is how high this number is. Under present conditions and applying our estimates, a terrorist hijacking attempt has only one chance in 500 of being successful. Full risk reduction, short of closing down the airline industry entirely, is not possible, but it seems that the array of security measures put into place to prevent another 9/11 hijacking gets pretty close.

TABLE 8-2   Deterrence Rates for Aviation Security Measures (Stage 1)

	Deterrence Rate	Notes
STAGE 1		
All pre-boarding measures	30%	Probably not. Screening technologies are imperfect.
Crew and passenger resistance	30%	Probably not. May not be able to react in time.
Law enforcement officers	1%	Very low probability of being on a flight.
Hardened cockpit doors	30%	Probably not. Flight deck still vulnerable during door transitions for a well-planned and coordinated attack.
Flight deck resistance	30%	Probably not. Probability of FFDOs being on a plane is 15–20%.
FAMS	7%	Almost certainly not. FAMS are on a very small proportion of flights. May not react in time.
IPSB	50%	Chances about even. Ameliorates vulnerability during door transitions and are on every aircraft.
Anti-aircraft measures	30%	Probably not. Particularly when their ability to contact the outside is considered.

TABLE 8-3 Disruption Rates for Aviation Security Measures in Stages 2, 3, and 4

	Disruption Rate	Notes
STAGE 2		
All pre-boarding measures	50%	Chances about even. Metal detectors, X-ray machines, and/or full-body scanners will have high disruption rates. However, adaptive terrorists may develop a scheme that bypasses many layers of security.
STAGE 3		
Passenger resistance	7%	Almost certainly not.
Cabin crew resistance	7%	Almost certainly not. The flight deck is vulnerable during door transition due to lack of training and to the short reaction times needed to defeat an attacker.
Law enforcement officer	1%	Very low probability of being on a flight.
FAMS on flight	20%	FAMS are on no more than 5% of flights, but are placed on "high-risk" flights so assume 20% coverage.
Flight deck resistance with FFDOs	15%	If FFDOs are in every cockpit, they are 80–90% effective in foiling a hijacking. The probability of FFDOs being on a plane is 15–20%. Assumes only trained FFDOs will fight for their lives.
IPSB	75%	Probable. Not 100% due to deployment malfunction or violation of procedures by crew during door transition.
Disrupted by hardened cockpit door when IPSB fails and no FAMS on board	50%	Chances about even. Door is vulnerable during door transitions if IPSB fails and crew unable to react in time.
Disrupted by hardened cockpit door when IPSB fails and FAMS on board	75%	Probable. Requires FAMS to react quickly enough to detain hijacker, or slow hijacker, allowing hardened cockpit door to be closed and locked.
STAGE 4		
Anti-aircraft measures	30%	Probably not. Authorities may not be able to deploy anti-aircraft measures in time.

TABLE 8-4   Risk Reductions

	Risk Reduction	Change in Risk Reduction
Full array of security measures	99.8%	
Remove FAMS	99.7%	−0.1%
Remove IPSB	99.1%	−0.7%
Remove both FAMS and IPSB	98.9%	−0.9%
Policy mix: include IPSB, double the budget for FFDO, reduce FAMS by 75 percent	99.8%	None

Moreover, if anything this is a *low* estimate. In our analysis, we have generally underestimated the likely risk reduction supplied by individual security measures. This can be seen in a perusal of the deterrence and disruption rates applied in tables 8-2 and 8-3. Thus, in table 8-3, the likelihood that cabin crew and passengers will be able to disrupt a hijacking attempt is rated at only 7 percent while flight deck resistance with FFDOs is put at only 15 percent. Yet risk analyst Bruce Schneier concludes that passenger resistance combined with secure cockpit doors is likely to be enough, by itself, to disrupt an attempt, and pilot Patrick Smith argues that crew and passenger resistance alone is likely to do the trick.[63] Another risk analyst, David Banks, argues that "it seems impossible that the United States will ever again experience takeovers of commercial flights that are then turned into weapons—no pilot will relinquish control, and passengers will fight."[64] We also consider the disruption rate for the full array of pre-boarding measures to be 50 percent. This is in line with the suggestions of Susan Martonosi and Arnold Barnett, but Kenneth Fletcher (who is a TSA employee) puts it at 85 percent.[65] And, as noted earlier, we do not include in all this a security barrier that seems likely to be highly effective and comes at no charge whatever: terrorist amateurishness and incompetence.

As seen in table 8-4, we can assess, using the same methods, the individual contribution of a security measure by removing it from the array, and then seeing how that affects overall risk reduction. If we remove FAMS from the array, overall risk reduction declines only slightly from 99.8 percent to 99.7 percent. If we remove IPSB from the array, risk reduction declines to 99.1 percent, and if we remove them both, it declines to 98.9 percent.

The risk reduction supplied to the full array by IPSB is nearly 1 percent, and this can be achieved for an expenditure of about $5 million per year. Including FAMS in the array reduces risk by only 0.1 percent at a cost of over

$1 billion. This observation alone provides strong evidence that the FAMS fails to be cost-effective.

Many policy options and mixes are possible. We assess a plausible one in the bottom line of table 8-4. In this, (1) IPSB is included in the security array; (2) the budget, and therefore the effectiveness, of another inexpensive measure, the FFDO program, is doubled; and (3) funding to FAMS is reduced by 75 percent, leaving roughly 500 to 1,000 air marshals available for deployment, a change that would still enable FAMS to target "high-risk" flights in those instances in which there is a credible threat but would reduce its overall effectiveness in preventing a successful hijacking.

Under this policy mix, total risk reduction is 99.8 percent—the same as for the full array of security measures. That is, risk reduction would remain the same but the yearly cost to the government and to the airlines would be reduced by $800 million: the FAMS budget would go down by $825 million while the FFDO budget would go up by $25 million. The full degree of risk reduction (99.8 percent) could be achieved at a yearly savings of hundreds of millions of dollars both to the taxpayers and to the airlines.

Some Lessons from PreCheck

Although it certainly appears that FAMS does not reduce risk enough to justify its cost, the analysis concedes that FAMS does reduce risk, at least a bit. It might be argued, therefore, that removing FAMS makes us—or seems to make us—less safe, and accordingly that reducing it, however rational, will never be acceptable politically.

However, it is important to note that TSA has recently set something of a precedent by implementing PreCheck, a security measure that lowers the cost while at the same time possibly lowering risk reduction—that is, increasing the risk a bit. This program allows expedited screening for a huge portion of passengers—potentially half of them—selected from frequent flier programs and from Global Entry and other trusted traveler programs. (PreCheck seems to be one of the few TSA programs that is risk-based—or at least it is determined by screening passengers on the basis of risk.) Passengers in the PreCheck line do not need to take off belts, shoes, or jackets, nor do they need to remove liquids and laptops from their carry-on luggage. In addition, they are not required to undergo full-body screening.

In April 2014, TSA Administrator John Pistole testified that 40 percent of passengers were now eligible for PreCheck and that each PreCheck lane provides "the capability for doubling hourly throughput"—an impressive efficiency gain.[66] There are thus strong benefits of PreCheck: it improves the passenger experience, and it reduces screening costs. Indeed, owing to PreCheck efficiencies, TSA expects the number of screeners to decline by nearly 1,500 and screening costs to be reduced by $100 million in FY2015.[67]

The potential problem for PreCheck, however, is that, because it applies screening measures that are, or appear to be, more lax to a substantial portion of passengers, it might increase the likelihood that a terrorist plotting to bring down an airliner would pass through screening undetected. Yet, even though this program might be seen to make us less safe in some sense, it appears to have generated no opposition. Indeed, if it has created any clamor among the public, it has come from those who are anxious to sign up.

As it happens, however, PreCheck might actually *enhance* security overall. In a separate study, we estimate that risk reduction in PreCheck lanes is lowered by 0.7 percent. However, the stated TSA aim of PreCheck is to "focus our resources on those passengers who could pose the greatest risk."[68] This could result in a 0.5 percent increase in risk reduction in regular lanes. That is, if screening disproportionately forces high-risk passengers into the regular lines where they are given more careful scrutiny, PreCheck may actually slightly increase overall risk reduction and therefore increase the benefit supplied by the full array of security measures. Even without that, if one takes into consideration the very substantial co-benefits PreCheck supplies by improving the passenger experience and reducing TSA screening costs—these can easily exceed $1 billion per year—the measure handily passes a cost-benefit assessment.[69]

Further Extensions

In this analysis, we have assessed the full array of security measures designed to protect an airliner from being hijacked, and we have used that to evaluate the risk reduction supplied by various security measures, particularly that of the main policing component, the Federal Air Marshal Service. However, we recognize that the preliminary analysis conducted here will not necessarily give a definitive answer to whether FAMS, FFDO, or IPSB is cost-effective. The analysis provides a snapshot of risk reductions and cost-effectiveness under present conditions. But terrorists may adapt their threats in reaction to new security measures, security measures may lose effectiveness with time, evolving threats may lead to the potential for higher losses, and so forth. Nevertheless, it does not seem that the competence of terrorists and the destruction they inflict are on the rise, even as 9/11 is increasingly standing out as an aberration, not a harbinger.

In general, we have biased the consideration toward leaving FAMS with a perhaps somewhat unrealistically high amount of risk to reduce. However, even with these assumptions in place, it appears that the Federal Air Marshal Service fails to reduce risk enough to justify its very considerable cost. Removing FAMS would lower risk reduction negligibly or not at all while saving a billion dollars a year.

There are likely to be many spending reductions that could be made with little or no consequent reduction in security, and the approach laid out in this chapter may help to suggest how individual security measures can be evaluated in a broader context. In general, it certainly seems likely that far too much is being spent to address the problem of airline hijacking.

One airline security measure that cries out for analysis in the context of the other security measures is the program in which some 3,000 Behavior Detection Officers (BDOs) are employed to roam around 176 airports to detect suspicious passenger behavior.[70] Among the quirks they look for are exaggerated yawning, excessive throat clearing, bobbing Adam's apples, arriving late for the flight, whistling during the screening process, gazing down, repetitive grooming gestures, and wearing improper attire.[71]

The Government Accountability Office has called into question the value of this program. After reviewing more than 400 separate studies about detecting deception, it found that "the ability of human observers to accurately identify deceptive behavior based on behavioral cues or indicators is the same as or slightly better than chance," and it noted that after ten years of implementing and testing, "TSA cannot demonstrate that the agency's behavior detection activities can reliably and effectively identify high-risk passengers who may pose a threat to the U.S. aviation system."[72] Since 9/11, some eight or nine billion passengers have passed through American airports, and although there are no data on how many of these have been gazed at by BDOs, it appears that not a single one has proved to be a terrorist with active designs to do damage on the flight. In an important sense, Behavior Detection Officers are the ultimate ghost-chasers—perhaps even outclassing the National Security Agency. They have had a perfect record of not finding anything. The inspector general of the DHS has concluded that TSA is unable to "show that the program is cost-effective."[73] Perhaps it is time to try to do so. The program currently costs some $200 million a year.[74]

Another program that seems ripe for systematic analysis is the expensive body scanners. In our evaluation, we have found them to be a security measure of highly questionable value.[75]

Risk Assessment and the DHS

That TSA persists with FAMS, a $1.1 billion program with small risk reduction at high cost, flies in the face of the TSA mantra that "TSA focuses its aviation security activities on programs that mitigate the highest amount of risk at the lowest cost."[76] Although we would heartily agree with this sentiment, it seems to have been honored by TSA much more in the breach than in the observance. Especially puzzling in this regard is the testimony in 2012 of DHS Secretary Janet Napolitano before the House Homeland Security Committee, in which she advocated reducing the FFDO budget, a recommendation, she said, that was "predicated on the fact that the program is not risk based."[77] We have seen that the FFDO program supplies a large risk reduction at low cost while FAMS reduces risk at a lower rate at a much higher cost. Where is the evidence TSA is implementing a risk-based approach with respect to cutting FFDOs? And where is the evidence that FFDO is not risk-based, whereas FAMS is?[78]

It happens that the FFDO program has actually been managed by FAMS, a conflict of interest that has been an ongoing concern in aviation security.[79] It has led the Federal Flight Deck Officers Association in 2011 to request that "FAMS and FFDOs should be separate and equal divisions operating under the TSA Office of Law Enforcement."[80] This finally happened in mid-2014, when TSA announced that supervisory responsibilities for the FFDO program would be moved to the TSA's Office of Training and Workforce Engagement.[81]

However, a curious development is that, although the budget for FAMS has always appeared as a separate line item in DHS budgets, this will not continue beyond FY2015, when the FAMS budget will be consolidated into an Aviation Security line budget. The actual cost of FAMS will thus not be revealed in the future. The official justification for this change is intriguingly opaque: "This consolidation of FAMS into Aviation Security better reflects TSA's organization and management structure and will enable the Agency to more rapidly apply its law enforcement and related resources to meet emerging threats."[82] Critics of FAMS may be set to wondering whether this accounting sleight of hand is instead designed to hide the massive cost of the service from prying eyes. Those with a more generous disposition may be inclined to suggest that this may be a device to continue with cuts to the service while preserving the impression that FAMS is still fully in place, thus allowing the service to retain its deterrent impact. While we hope for the latter explanation, we suspect the former may be closer to the mark.

Overall, our results strongly suggest that DHS decision makers are not following robust risk-assessment methodology. If they were, low-cost solutions that are easily deployed and effective would be the first to be implemented. However, it is not simply that the DHS is risk-averse. Its decisions cannot be supported even with the most risk-averse utility functions possible.[83] This issue will be explored more generally in the conclusion of this book.

| Local and Airport Police

M OST LAW ENFORCEMENT in the United States is the preserve of the local and state police arrayed in nearly 18,000 law enforcement jurisdictions. In this chapter, we evaluate the counterterrorism contributions of these forces.

We deal, first, with those of state and local police, with a particular focus on the New York City Police Department. For the most part, these police forces have had little to do in the counterterrorism effort. In the process, while accepting considerable amounts of funding from federal authorities—money that became available mainly because of the 9/11 terror scare—they have spent little of their own funds on the enterprise.

The chapter concludes by evaluating the cost-effectiveness of a specific policing effort: the one designed to deal with the potential for terrorism at airports.

State and Local Police

The latest Department of Justice data show that in 2008, the 17,985 state and local law enforcement agencies in the United States employed about 1,133,000 people on a full-time basis, including 765,000 sworn personnel.[1] There are also 100,000 part-time employees, including 44,062 sworn personnel.[2] In comparison, 120,000 full-time law enforcement officers are employed by seventy-three federal agencies, and 70 percent of these are with Customs and Border Protection, the Federal Bureau of Prisons, the Federal Bureau of Investigation, U.S. Immigration and Customs Enforcement, and the Secret Service.[3]

Many state and local police departments have a counterterrorism or homeland security unit, and over 90 percent of police departments serving a population of 500,000 or more dedicate full-time personnel to the task. Overall, more than 6,300 full-time staff are devoted to counterterrorism tasks, and another 5,241 full-time or part-time personnel are devoted to an antiterrorism task force.[4] Thus, in total, over 11,500 police personnel are assigned to counterterrorism duties, or about 1.2 percent of the total police numbers.[5]

Annual counterterrorism expenditures are $1.4 billion in 2014 dollars, or 1.5 percent of the $85 billion budget for local police and sheriffs' offices.[6] In addition, 50 primary state law enforcement agencies, 1,733 special jurisdiction agencies (including airport and transit police), and 638 other agencies bring total yearly local and state spending on counterterrorism to approximately $1.7 billion in 2014 dollars.[7] Added to this are building construction and major equipment purchases.

Any spending by local and state police of their own money on counterterrorism is thus on the order of $2 billion per year, in 2014 dollars. This is a surprisingly small sum—nationwide, it comprises only about 1 or 2 percent of their combined budgets and comes to $6 per person per year. This represents a rare instance in which funding does not match rhetoric. Assessing the situation, Stephen Morreale and David Lambert note that "while the public perception is that police departments are fully engaged, the reality is much different." In fact, "The Homeland Security role of the state and local officer today is quite limited," and "many police departments' missions are only marginally different than before 9/11." Moreover, "American policing seems to have lost its sense of urgency in relation to the terrorist threat to our public safety."[8] This view is supported as well by analysts at George Mason University:

> [M]ost police agencies in the United States do not appear to prioritize counterterrorism in their daily work and do not specifically dedicate large amounts of resources or personnel to such activities (strategic or tactical). For those that do (usually larger and multi-jurisdiction agencies), their activities tend to fall under the more general categories of planning, interagency cooperation, mutual aid agreements, and information sharing (or at least developing plans to share information). These findings are interesting, especially given the overall increase in the financing of law enforcement activities by the Department of Homeland Security.[9]

Indeed, in the years since 9/11, the Department of Homeland Security has been generously dishing out homeland security grants to state and local governments: they totaled over $21 billion over the fourteen-year period from 2001 to 2014.[10] These grants include the State Homeland Security Grant Program, the Urban Area Security Initiative, and the Law Enforcement Terrorism Prevention Program (LETPP).[11] In 2014, these grants totaled $1.04 billion, of which $250 million was allocated to the LETPP.[12]

Much of this is spent on equipment and training.[13] In addition, DHS has its own "authorized equipment list" for which its grant money can be spent.[14] It lists 592 separate items of equipment that may be purchased from LETPP grants. These include search-and-rescue canines, body armor, fire helmets, respirators, gloves, SCUBA equipment, robotic systems, hand tools, body bags, GPS devices, handheld computing devices, satellite phones, adhesive medical tape, Ibuprofen, batteries, command vehicles, facial recognition software, boats, backpacks, refrigerators, freezers, and a wide assortment of other equipment.

Many of these items, available under a program that specifically says it is devoted to "terrorism prevention," seem to relate little to homeland security, let alone to counterterrorism.

Thus, in a 2012 report, "Safety at Any Price," Tom Coburn, a member of the Senate Homeland Security and Governmental Affairs Committee, pointed out that "[p]reparedness grants were intended to be an initial investment to help state and local governments enhance their emergency response and preparedness capability in the aftermath of the September 11, 2001 attacks." However, ten years later, "the purpose of many DHS grant programs has shifted to provide continuous funding for routine expenses. In this way, states and cities are using their grants to *supplant* the funds they would otherwise spend, rather than *supplementing* them." Coburn lists some examples of what he considers to be questionable DHS grant expenditures:

- Keene, New Hampshire, with a population of just over 23,000 and a police force of 40, purchased a BearCat armored vehicle. Despite reporting only a single homicide in the prior two years, the city of Keene told DHS that the vehicle was needed to patrol events like its annual pumpkin festival.
- Fargo, North Dakota, a town that "has averaged fewer than 2 homicides per year since 2005" bought a "new $256,643 armored truck, complete with a rotating [gun] turret" using homeland security funds. As of December 2011, the vehicle had only been used for "training runs and appearances at the annual Fargo picnic, where it's been displayed near a children's bounce house."
- Indianapolis spent more than $69,000 in 2007 to purchase a new hovercraft for water-based search and rescue operations.

- New Orleans and Baton Rouge urban areas spent nearly $12,000 to pay monthly cellphone bills for emergency management personnel, as well as "$2,400 for a lapel microphone."[15]

Funds for purchases like these exist primarily because of concerns about terrorism. Normally, police departments would apply to purchase such equipment though the Department of Justice.

Although many of the nearly 18,000 local and state police departments in the United States do not have specialized counterterrorism units, some do have "homeland security" or "counterterrorism" divisions.[16] However, these are mostly devoted to other activities.

This can be seen in an examination of the budget of the police department in Columbus, Ohio, the twenty-second largest in the United States with nearly 2,000 police officers. Its "Homeland Security" subdivision contains the Special Services Bureau, the Narcotics Bureau, and the Traffic Bureau. The Special Services Bureau comprises a criminal intelligence unit, a SWAT unit, an emergency management unit, a helicopter unit, an underwater search and recovery unit, and a counterterrorism unit. The main reported achievement in 2012 of the counterterrorism unit was that it "worked 33 protection details with the Secret Service." The word *terrorism* appears nowhere in the department's 2012 and 2013 annual reports, and the counterterrorism unit itself is mentioned only once in each report.[17] The department may well contribute to a Fusion Center or to a Joint Terrorism Task Force, but this would consist only of several officers, and the contribution does not seem to have been important enough to be mentioned in the department's annual reports.

In 2013, the Columbus Police Department's "homeland security" budget more than doubled. However, this was not because counterterrorism had become a new priority. Rather, it was because "homeland security" was now taken to include "regulating traffic." Thus, *homeland security* is defined in this budget as "[t]o provide for the safety of the citizens of Columbus and central Ohio by regulating traffic, gathering intelligence to prevent a terrorist attack, providing specialized policing services such as SWAT and Canine services and managing emergency operations."[18]

When the costs for regulating traffic, handling canines, furnishing SWAT teams, and managing emergency operations are deducted from the department's 2013 "homeland security" budget of $22.5 million, about $1 million remains for the goals of "gathering intelligence to prevent a terrorist attack."[19] This would pay for about ten personnel and constitutes about one-third of 1 percent of the Columbus Police Department's nearly $300 million annual budget.

Overall, note Dana Priest and William Arkin, in most cities and towns, "the reality" is that "there just isn't enough terrorism-related work to keep everyone busy."[20] For the most part, they can't find any ghosts to chase.

The New York City Police Department

Twenty-three New York City police officers were killed in the line of duty on September 11, 2001, and more have since died as a result of illnesses contracted from exposure at Ground Zero.[21] New York City has been a target for terrorism more frequently than any other U.S. city. Even before 9/11, there was a bombing at LaGuardia Airport in 1975 and an attempt on the World Trade Center in 1993. Of the cases listed in appendix A of Islamist terror plots seeking to do damage in the United States since 2001, some thirteen to seventeen, or around 25 percent, had New York City as a specific target.[22] Moreover, the city is also the home of the United Nations and many foreign missions, all of which require special protection.

It is not surprising, then, that the counterterrorism efforts of the NYPD considerably outstrip those of other cities. However, its counterterrorism expenditures are substantially subsidized by the state and federal governments; proportionate to size, New York City taxpayers themselves are not paying a particularly unusual amount to protect themselves from terrorists. And, whatever the source of the funds it expends on the venture, the NYPD's record at counterterrorism is less than fully impressive.

FUNDING THE NYPD COUNTERTERRORISM BUDGET

Estimates of the NYPD budget allocated to counterterrorism vary from $180 million to $330 million.[23] However, there is less variance in estimates of the number of police officers assigned to counterterrorism operations: some 1,000 to 1,200.[24] In 2003, NYPD Commissioner Ray Kelly stated that he had "1,000 cops assigned full-time to his fight against the terrorists."[25]

New York City Council documents reveal that the budget for NYPD counterterrorism activities varied from $190 million to $220 million yearly between FY2013 and FY2015.[26] In 2006, it had been $160 million, and an estimate of the annual budget for intelligence and counterterrorism in 2010 was $195 million, both in 2014 dollars.[27] A reasonable estimate of the NYPD's total yearly expenditure on counterterrorism, then, is approximately $200 million.[28] Thus, less than 4 percent of the total NYPD budget—which was $4.8 billion in 2014—is spent on counterterrorism.

Moreover, the bulk of this substantial budget comes from the state and federal governments. In 2013, 2014, and 2015 (projected), the city of New York spent about $80 million of its own money on counterterrorism and intelligence.[29] For these years, it received grants of $97 million, $142 million, and $134 million, respectively, for those purposes.[30] That means that less than 2 percent of the total NYPD budget for counterterrorism comes from the coffers of the City of New York, and, on average, its counterterrorism bill to New Yorkers is less than $10 per person per year.[31] This is not particularly exceptional: as a percentage of its annual budget, NYPD counterterrorism expenditures are about the same (though possibly a bit higher) than those for the police departments in Los Angeles and Chicago.[32]

THE NYPD'S RECORD AT COUNTERING TERRORIST PLOTS

From time to time, New York officials have made some impressively extravagant claims about the NYPD's prowess in dealing with terrorism. Congressman Peter King declared in 2011 that "at least 14 attacks by Islamic terrorists have been prevented by the NYPD."[33] And in 2012, Mayor Michael Bloomberg proclaimed, "We have the best police department in the world and I think they show that every single day and we have stopped 14 attacks since 9/11 fortunately without anybody dying."[34] When that assertion was challenged later in the year by a reporter, Bloomberg (perhaps) backtracked, contending that "[w]e'll never know."[35]

The NYPD has put out an official list of relevant terror plots that by 2014 had been expanded to sixteen. However, the list is not of terror plots disrupted by NYPD, but of ones that can be said to have targeted New York City.[36] Almost all of these have been subjected to case studies, as arrayed in appendix A. Looked at carefully, the list suggests a somewhat less than impressive performance by the NYPD.[37]

Subway cyanide attack. An embryonic plot apparently dreamed up abroad by al-Qaeda and abandoned. NYPD played no role.[38]

Khan and the Parachas. A young Pakistani sought to smuggle into the country an al-Qaeda operative planning to blow up a set of gas stations. The plot had nothing particular to do with New York City—no specific targets had yet been selected. However, the Pakistani's father may have planned to get materials into the United States through a shipping office in the city. NYPD played no role in the case.

Brooklyn Bridge. An al-Qaeda–linked truck driver considered cutting the Brooklyn Bridge's support cables with a blowtorch. The visible presence of NYPD at the bridge helped dissuade him.

Financial buildings. A group in London tied to al-Qaeda scouted out financial buildings in the United States, including some in New York, with an eye to bombing them. The plot was disrupted abroad long before it even got to the issue of explosives. NYPD played no role.

Herald Square. A loud-mouthed jihadist in New York and a schizophrenic friend, thinking of planting bombs in the city, attracted the attention of an informant from NYPD. NYPD was central to this case, which the FBI thought too trivial to work on.[39]

Hudson River tunnels. Several men based in Lebanon plotted to flood railway tunnels under the Hudson River but were arrested overseas before acquiring bomb materials or setting foot in the United States. NYPD played no role.

Transatlantic airliner bombings. A small group in London plotted to explode liquid bombs on airliners, one of them bound for New York, a plot under scrutiny by police there from the outset. NYPD played no role.

JFK Airport. A small group, with an informant, plotted to blow up fuel lines serving JFK Airport in New York. NYPD was part of the investigation led by the FBI.

Vinas. A New York man plotted with al-Qaeda abroad to plant a bomb in New York but was arrested long before he could return to the United States. NYPD played no role.

Bronx synagogues. Four men, with crucial aid from an FBI informant, plotted to bomb synagogues in the Bronx and shoot down a plane at a military base. NYPD played a supportive role.

Zazi. Muslims from Queens were recruited abroad by al-Qaeda to plant bombs on New York City subways. NYPD played a very limited role.

Times Square. A Pakistani American, trained in Pakistan, tried to set off a car bomb in Times Square. After the failed attempt, NYPD was part of the team that caught up with him before he could leave the country.

Manhattan's pair of lone wolves. A mentally ill New Yorker plotted with an accomplice and an NYPD undercover officer to blow up targets in New York and New Jersey. NYPD was central to this case, which the FBI thought too trivial to work on.

Pimentel. A man plotted with an NYPD informant to make pipe bombs using match heads to attack various targets in New York. NYPD was central to this case, which the FBI thought too trivial to work on.

Bombing the Federal Reserve Bank. A college flunk-out from Bangladesh obtained the help of FBI informants to set off a bomb planted at the Federal Reserve Bank. NYPD cooperated with the FBI on the case.

The brothers. Two brothers were arrested in Florida for planning to bomb popular New York landmarks. NYPD played almost no role.

THE RECORD OF THE NYPD'S DEMOGRAPHICS UNIT

There are also the extensive efforts the NYPD's Demographics Unit, which employs a considerable number of "mosque crawlers" to infiltrate Islamic institutions to pick up helpful information—the goal was to have one infiltrator in every mosque within 250 miles of the city.[40]

However, the program appears to have generated no terrorism cases whatever.[41] It did, however, miss a few that it might have been expected to pick up: the Vinas, Zazi, and Times Square cases in the list above.[42]

THE RECORD OF NYPD'S "IF YOU SEE SOMETHING, SAY SOMETHING" PROGRAM

After 9/11, the entire population made itself into something of a surveillance force, and tips have frequently played an important role in police terrorism investigations. Thus, a specific tip was crucial in the Lackawanna case of 2002; a tip from a Yemeni grocer eventually led to terrorism arrests in Miami in 2006 of a tiny band that was perhaps plotting to topple the Sears Tower in Chicago; a tip from a clerk in a video-duplicating establishment set an investigation going into a potential plot to raid Ft. Dix in New Jersey in 2007; and a tip from a storeowner in Tampa helped focus on a customer who came in seeking to buy an al-Qaeda flag in 2012. Sometimes people have even effectively made themselves into an active policing force: both the shoe bomber of 2001 and the underwear bomber of 2009 were forcibly and effectively interfered with by passengers and crew when they tried to detonate their bombs on airliners. A study conducted by Kevin Strom and colleagues surveyed sixty-eight terrorist plots (both Islamist and non-Islamist) that were foiled in the United States between 1999 and 2009, and they found that in 29 percent of the cases, the "initial clues" were supplied by the public.[43]

This surveillance force certainly (and especially) includes the Muslim community. Although the 9/11 conspirators wisely mostly avoided the Muslim community, homegrown terrorists or would-be terrorists have often foolishly failed to do so. Often they have come out of the community and have been exposed in consequence. In fact, reports Charles Kurzman, for 48 of the 120 instances in which Muslim Americans have been arrested for terrorism, and in which the initial source of information has been disclosed, the initiating tip came from the Muslim community. Indeed, he continues, "in some communities, Muslim-Americans have been so concerned about extremists in their midst that they have turned in people who turned out to be undercover informants."[44]

However, although tips are important in many cases, they also inspire a huge amount of unproductive effort, a phenomenon stressed in chapter 1 and further considered in other chapters. There are very significant attendant costs of sorting through the haystack of tips, all of which need to be processed in one way or another.

A particularly arresting instance of unproductive hay-heaping is the New York Police Department's trademarked and extensively promoted "If You See Something, Say Something™" terrorism hotline. It generates thousands of calls each year—8,999 in 2006 and more than 13,473 in 2007—but not one of these led to a terrorism arrest.[45] This could be taken to suggest that the tipster campaign has been something of a failure. Or perhaps it could be taken to suggest that there isn't all that much out there to be found. Undeterred by repeated failure, however, the NYPD has kept the program going: the number of calls reportedly skyrocketed to 27,127 in 2008, before settling down some in 2009 to 16,191.[46] That comes to 44 each day for the year, more than twice the number of success stories trumpeted in Kevin Strom's survey for an entire decade.

New York has trademarked its snappy slogan, and it has been willing to grant permission for its use by other organizations. However, it has also sometimes refused permission because, according to a spokesman, "The intent of the slogan is to focus on terrorism activity, not crime, and we felt that use in other spheres would water down its effectiveness." (Officials in Los Angeles have sometimes shortened the slogan to "See Something, Say Something," and apparently did not need to get the permission of NYPD to do so—their signs with that slogan do not include the trademark symbol.)

Since it appears that the slogan has been *completely* ineffective at dealing with its supposed focus, terrorism, any watering down of it appears, not to put too fine a point on it, impossible. In consequence, the irreverent may be led to wonder whether the $2 million to $3 million New York pays each year (much of it coming from grants from the federal government) to promote and publicize the hotline is perhaps the wisest investment of taxpayer dollars.[47] However, those grants are likely to keep coming: in one of her early public announcements after becoming secretary of Homeland Security in 2009, Janet Napolitano indicated that she wanted to inspire even *more* participation by the public in the quest to ferret out terrorists.[48]

THE RECORD OF THE NYPD'S INTERNATIONAL
LIAISON PROGRAM

To a degree, the results of the "See Something" campaign have been duplicated by NYPD's International Liaison Program, in which officers are placed in eleven cities abroad (Paris, Lyon, London, Toronto, Montréal, Madrid, Abu Dhabi, Singapore, Santo Domingo, Tel Aviv, and Amman) to snoop around for terrorists who might have New York in their crosshairs. The postings hardly seem to be of the hardship variety, and the program costs $1.5 million per year.[49] Asked in 2013 if these overseas offices had furnished "any actual tips about potential attacks in New York," NYPD Commissioner Ray Kelly said no.[50] However, producing no tips at all is probably quite a bit better than coming up with thousands that never lead anywhere.

Kelly managed to get a private nonprofit group, the well-heeled New York Police Foundation, to fund the program. His concern, understandably, was that, if crime rose in some City Council member's district, Kelly did not want to be questioned about why the city was paying to post cops in Lyon.[51] The foundation covers the expenses for the detectives stationed abroad, but the NYPD still pays their salaries.[52]

On balance, the program seems not to be so much a waste as a net—or perhaps unalloyed—negative. One former federal official says the overseas cops "are ineffective, often angering and confusing the foreign law enforcement officials they are trying to work with, and are usually relegated to the sidelines because they lack national security clearance." Another calls the program "a monster," citing its "lack of security clearances and diplomatic immunity," the "confusion" it causes for the law enforcement and security services of the host countries, and conflicts with U.S. embassies and with agencies such as the CIA and the FBI.[53] The detective posted in Tel Aviv has a "drinking problem" and may have been "used by Israeli intelligence officials to influence thinking in New York and conduct surveillance for them there." Meanwhile, a CIA station chief in France has crisply characterized reports coming out of the NYPD office in Lyon as "shit."[54]

EVALUATING THE COST-EFFECTIVENESS OF NYPD
COUNTERTERRORISM SPENDING

To assess the cost-effectiveness of NYPD counterterrorism measures, we apply a version of the break-even approach as first laid out in chapter 5. The key equation is:

(probability of a successful attack absent the security measure) = (cost of the security measure) / [(losses sustained in the successful attack) × (reduction in risk furnished by the security measure)]

In this case, we calculate how many terrorist attacks would have had to be deterred, averted, or protected against for the NYPD's counterterrorism spending to begin to be justified. To do so, we need as usual to consider the three qualities on the right side of the equation: the cost of the security measure ($200 million per year), the losses sustained in the successful attack, and the reduction in risk furnished by the security measure.

The risk reduction resulting from annual NYPD counterterrorism expenditures—the ability to deter, disrupt, or protect against a terrorist attack—is likely to be modest when compared to the Federal Bureau of Investigation and other lead counterterrorism agencies. In chapter 6 we (rather generously) posited a 90 percent risk reduction for the FBI. The counterterrorism budget of the NYPD at some $200 million per year is one-fifteenth that of the FBI, which is about $3 billion per year.

For our purposes here, we will assess only attacks directed at New York City that have not been deterred, disrupted, or protected against by other policing and security measures. The number of such events is likely to be quite low. Even when New York was (in some sense) the target, the list given earlier suggests that disruption has mostly been the work of the FBI and other policing agencies. We will rather generously assume that there is a 25 percent likelihood that the actions of NYPD counterterrorism units will deter, disrupt, or protect against a terror attack that is directed at New York and that has not been deterred, disrupted, or protected against by other policing and intelligence elements.

The cells in table 9-1 show an array of break-even points: the number of successful attacks in the absence of NYPD counterterrorism measures that are not disrupted by other agencies that would need to take place in New York to begin to justify its counterterrorism budget (mostly paid for by other entities) of $200 million per year. As in tables 5-3 and 6-1, we display results for attacks at various levels of destruction and for various degrees of risk reduction. Barring a lucky lead from the International Liaison Program, these attacks would likely need to be planned in New York for the NYPD to have any role in countering them.

The boxed entries in table 9-1 indicate how many very substantial terrorist attacks in the absence of NYPD counterterrorism measures would need to occur each year in New York if we assume NYPD's efforts to reduce risk—the consequences and/or the likelihood of such an attack—by an impressive 25 percent. Under this condition, the NYPD would have to reduce by 25 percent the

TABLE 9-1 Evaluating Counterterrorism Efforts of the New York City Police Department

Risk Reduction Caused by NYPD Counterterrorism Expenditure	Losses from a Successful Terrorist Attack						
	$100 million Ft Hood shooting	$500 million Boston Marathon bombing	$1 billion Times Square bombing	$5 billion London bombing	$200 billion 9/11	$1 trillion nuclear Port	$5 trillion nuclear Grand Central
5 percent	40	8	4	0.8	0.02	0.0040	0.00080
10 percent	20	4	2	0.4	0.01	0.0020	0.00040
25 percent	8	1.6	0.8	0.16	0.004	0.0008	0.00016
50 percent	4	0.8	0.4	0.08	0.002	0.0004	0.00008
75 percent	2.67	0.53	0.27	0.053	0.001	0.0003	0.00005
90 percent	2.22	0.44	0.22	0.044	0.001	0.0002	0.00004
100 percent	2	0.4	0.2	0.040	0.001	0.0002	0.00004

Cell entries indicate the number of otherwise successful attacks per year directed at New York that have not been disrupted by other policing agencies in the absence of the NYPD's counterterrorism efforts that are required to begin to justify the NYPD's annual budget of $200 million for various levels of loss and risk reduction—that is, for the security benefit of the expenditures to begin to equal their costs.

likelihood or the consequences of one or two Boston Marathon–type attacks each year in New York to begin to justify its $200 million budget. Alternatively, the NYPD's efforts would need to reduce by 25 percent the likelihood or consequences of one or two London-type bombings in New York over the course of a decade. Or, again alternatively, the NYPD budget would justify itself by reducing by 25 percent a huge attack with direct and indirect damage equivalent to that inflicted by 9/11 once every 250 years. Or, looking at the 100 percent line, the NYPD would have to be solely responsible for deterring, disrupting, or protecting against two to four Boston Marathon or Times Square types of attacks per decade for its yearly counterterrorism budget of $200 million to begin to be cost-effective.

The NYPD's very modest record of counterterrorism achievement suggests that its expenditures on counterterrorism pretty much fail a cost-benefit evaluation. Of course, these are also fairly modest—$200 million, or some 4 or 5 percent of the total NYPD budget—and more than half of that is paid for by beguiled or distracted taxpayers in the rest of the country.

Since New York has a track record of terrorist attacks (however exaggerated by its officials), is the center of the universe in the minds of many (including some terrorists as well as most New Yorkers), and is the largest city in the United States, city officials may be able to continue to convince other Americans to fund its substantial, if minimally productive counterterrorism efforts. And there is likely to be little protest from New Yorkers because they foot considerably less than half of the bill.

Airport Policing

Some 3,500 full-time sworn personnel are devoted solely to policing 103 airports in the United States, while another 3,214 police the railroads and mass transit.[55] This constitutes less than 1 percent of all police officers in the country. Moreover, their duties are more related to crime prevention and traffic and parking enforcement than to counterterrorism—a pattern that, in percentage terms, is similar to other law enforcement agencies as we have seen.

Because police at U.S. airports provide a wide variety of services—traffic control, crime prevention, and escorting VIPs, as well as homeland security—it is nearly impossible to separate out the costs of counterterrorism for U.S. airport policing. However, the situation in Australia is more clear-cut, and it can be used to provide a useful benchmark for estimating counterterrorism expenditures associated with airport policing.

The Australian Federal Police (AFP) provides over 600 officers for the policing of the ten largest airports in Australia (Cairns, Brisbane, Gold Coast,

Sydney, Canberra, Melbourne, Hobart, Adelaide, Perth, and Darwin). About half of these perform general policing and crime prevention, targeting serious and organized crime across the aviation network. The other half are devoted to counterterrorism policing, seeking to protect airport terminals and aircraft from terrorist attack. These officers make up the Counter-Terrorism and First Response and the Joint Airport Intelligence Groups.[56] Although most are devoted to the security of the airports themselves, the AFP is a national police agency, and some airport counterterrorism police also have an intelligence role in foiling attacks on aircraft. The cost of AFP policing at ten airports in Australia is approximately $180 million per year.[57] It seems reasonable to suggest, then, that half of this, or $90 million, goes to counterterrorism.

These numbers can be extrapolated to the situation in the United States. Total passenger traffic at Australia's ten largest airports is about 127 million per year.[58] This is about twice the traffic at LAX, at Dallas-Fort Worth, at New York's JFK, and at Chicago's O'Hare airports.[59] Hence, if counterterrorism airport policing duties are similar for Australia and the United States, counterterrorism airport policing at each of these four large American airports (only Atlanta's Hartsfield-Jackson Airport is larger) should total about $45 million per year. Budget and staffing data for Los Angeles Airport Police support this cost estimate. The Los Angeles Airport Police employs 1,100 law enforcement and civilian personnel, with a budget of at least $120 million.[60] It seems reasonable to assume that about a third of these police are engaged in counterterrorism work.

Following the approach we have used throughout this book, a good place to start is with an evaluation of a $45 million yearly expenditure to police large airports like LAX, Dallas-Fort Worth, JFK, and O'Hare. Is such an expenditure cost-effective?

THREATS

We consider four specific threat scenarios to airport terminal buildings and associated facilities:[61]

1. A large truck bomb detonated in front of a crowded terminal
2. A curbside car bomb detonated in front of a crowded terminal
3. A luggage or vest bomb detonated at curbside or inside a crowded terminal
4. A shooting attack in a public area

These threats have been called "major vulnerabilities" or "major" threats that can kill a large number of people.[62] Other threats to airport facilities seem unlikely.[63]

LOSSES SUSTAINED IN A TERRORIST ATTACK

A large truck bomb containing two tons of TNT detonated at Dulles International Airport near Washington, D.C., would wreak "immense destruction," according to a threat and vulnerability analysis conducted by Rudy Weisz, working from studies conducted by the Defense Threat Reduction Agency in the United States. Nearly all windows facing the blast would be destroyed and little of the structure would be left standing, causing the entire roof to collapse and leading to 306 fatalities or severe injuries.[64] This scenario is similar to the 1995 Oklahoma City bombing that killed 165 people, the U.S. Embassy attack in Kenya in 1998 that killed 213 people, and the 2008 truck bombing of the Islamabad Marriott Hotel that resulted in the deaths of 54 people. Assuming an average of 150 fatalities from an on-ground explosion, and assessing the value of a single life at $7.5 million,[65] an economic loss of 150 fatalities comes to $1.1 billion.

These attacks, however, appear to be the exception. One study points out that the average number of fatalities from a truck bomb is thirty-six and that only 0.5 percent of bomb attacks had more than thirty fatalities.[66] Another study concludes that to expect more than fifty fatalities from an airport attack is "unrealistically high."[67] Moreover, the atrium architecture of the ticketing area at Dulles may make it peculiarly vulnerable to a large bomb. However, we will adopt the higher figure to be conservative. Moreover, most losses arise from indirect causes, not from fatalities or injuries, and therefore the results are not very sensitive to assumptions about the average numbers of fatalities. Physical damage might average $100 million. Flight disruptions and diversions, relocation of check-in counters and luggage belts, and so on might total several billion dollars as an upper bound. The additional costs of social and business disruptions, loss of tourism, and the like might total $5 billion to $10 billion. A mean total loss of $10 billion for threat 1 is not unreasonable, though it will be considerably on the high side.[68]

A curbside car bomb containing hundreds of pounds of explosives would result in fewer fatalities and less physical damage, but the indirect losses would still be substantial. The total cost in this case might total $7.5 billion for threat 2, applying a reasonable, but decidedly high estimate.[69]

Weisz found that a smaller 100-pound luggage bomb detonated near a check-in counter would also destroy nearly all the windows at Dulles International Airport but would inflict considerably less structural damage overall and approximately 10 percent of the fatalities caused by a large truck bomb—that would be about thirty fatalities or severe injuries valued at $200 million.[70] The 2011 suicide bombing at the Moscow airport that killed thirty-seven, accomplished with a suitcase bomb reportedly of four to eleven pounds, did cause some flights to be diverted to other airports in Moscow immediately following the attack. However, Domodedovo Airport still remained open, and damage to airport infrastructure was minimal. While fatalities and physical damage would be less than with a large truck bomb, the public averseness to travel could be similar, resulting in social and business disruptions, loss of tourism, and so on. The impact would be larger for a major airport hub like LAX, Dallas-Fort Worth, JFK, or O'Hare, which handle at least twice as many passengers as Moscow's Domodedovo Airport. We will assume a mean loss of $5 billion for threat 3. This is comparable to the full costs inflicted by terrorist bombers in 2005 in London and in 2004 in Madrid that killed 52 and 191 people, respectively.

It should be kept in mind that, since airports sprawl and the buildings are only two or three stories high, damage to a portion is not likely to be nearly as significant as damage to a taller or more compact structure. Moreover, if a bomb does go off at an airport, the consequences would probably be comparatively easier to deal with: passengers could readily be routed around the damaged area, for example, and the impact on the essential function of the airport would be comparatively modest. This suggests, again, that the losses proposed earlier might be high. However, public fears and averseness to air travel could increase these losses.

As part of the terrorist attack in Mumbai in 2008, two shooters targeted a crowded railway station killing over fifty people and injuring a hundred others, and more were killed in nearby hotels and restaurants by other terrorists. As with other threat scenarios, losses resulting from loss of life and physical damage can be minor when compared to indirect losses. The cost in the threat 4 case of a shooting attack in public areas in an airport might total $2 billion.

Our loss assumptions are summarized in table 9-2.

TABLE 9-2   Estimates for Loss and Vulnerability for Each Threat to Airports

Threat	Losses If Attack Attempt Is Successful ($ Billion)	Probability That the Attack Attempt Is Successful
1. Large truck bomb	10	15%
2. Curbside car bomb	7.5	15%
3. Luggage or vest bomb	5	30%
4. Public grounds shooting attack	2	85%

RISK REDUCTION

Risk reduction in this case is the degree to which airport counterterrorism policing will deter, disrupt, or protect against the terrorism threat, either by reducing the likelihood that the terrorists will succeed in the attack or by reducing the consequences of a successful attack. As in the NYPD case, we will assess only attacks that have not been deterred or disrupted by the FBI and other policing and security agencies. For our analysis, we will assume that, should the terrorists, armed with bombs or guns, make it successfully to the airport, the airport policing counterterrorism measures currently in place for the four airports are highly effective against the four kinds of attacks we have been discussing: that they reduce the risk by a full 75 percent in each case.

COST AND CO-BENEFITS

The cost of counterterrorism policing at LAX, Dallas-Fort Worth, JFK, and O'Hare is, as we have estimated above, some $45 million per year for each airport. However, this cost figure should take into account co-benefits. The co-benefits of counterterrorism policing, such as reduction in crime and reassurance to the traveling public, can be substantial. The cost of crime has been estimated to range from $2,000 for theft, to $85,000 for serious assault, and to $9 million for homicide.[71] For example, if each counterterrorism police officer deters or disrupts one assault, theft, or other criminal act once per year at $15,000 per crime averted, then 150 airport counterterrorism police officers supply a co-benefit of approximately $2 million per year.

Data on the effect that visible airport policing has on passengers are scarce. However, it may act to reassure the traveling public—although one study concludes that visible security measures directed at terrorism can have the opposite effect of alarming people.[72] If a visible police presence does prove overall to reassure passengers that air travel is safer, this may lead to higher passenger numbers and more revenue for airport operators and airlines. Operating revenue at LAX was $865.5 million in 2013, including landing fees, building and land rentals, and retail, parking, and other concessions revenue.[73] If airport counterterrorism policing contributed to a very modest passenger growth of one-half of 1 percent in airport revenues, this would add $4 million per year to LAX revenues. Added to this would be increases in airline revenues, and other economic output in hotels, car rentals, and other businesses associated with LAX—Los Angeles World Airports reports that LAX generates a total economic output of more than $39.7 billion each year in Los Angeles and neighboring counties.[74] Irrespective of who benefits from increased passenger numbers at LAX, the co-benefits may be considerable.

The total co-benefit of counterterrorism policing at each of the four major airports under consideration might well come out to be $10 million. Thus, the cost of the security measure is $45 million less $10 million in co-benefits, or $35 million, and we will apply that figure in our analysis.

EXAMINING THE LIKELIHOOD TERRORISTS COULD PULL OFF A SUCCESSFUL AIRPORT ATTACK

We now assess the likelihood that an attempted terrorist attack on an airport—an attempt, undeterred and unthwarted by other security measures, to detonate a bomb or carry out a shooting attack—will succeed for each of the four threat scenarios under consideration.

In principle, a bomb is relatively simple to design and manufacture if done by well-trained personnel, resulting in reliabilities in excess of 90 percent.[75] However, the probability that the bomb will create a damaging effect and inflict casualties reduces to 19 percent for terrorists in Western countries, where there is less opportunity for the relevant operational skills to be acquired.[76] The terrorists' problem is clearly evident in the second attack on the London Underground that was attempted on July 21, 2005, and in the attacks on the Glasgow International Airport in 2007 and in Times Square in 2010—in all these cases the bombs failed to initiate. We assume that for a small (luggage) bomb, where there is less device complexity and fewer placement issues (threat 3), the mean likelihood of successful detonation is 30 percent. This reduces to 15 percent for complex and large bombs (threats 1 and 2), where placement and timing are more crucial to achieve maximum damaging effects and where detonation poses substantial difficulties for terrorists. Since, as noted in earlier chapters, terrorists seem to have great difficulty detonating even simple bombs, these estimates likely quite substantially overestimate the capacities of actual terrorists.

A shooting attack is much easier to accomplish because guns are generally easier to acquire and discharge than bombs. Hence, a well-trained and coordinated shooting has a high chance of doing some damage—terrorists shot and killed more than 100 people in the 2008 attacks in Mumbai. A high-success likelihood of 85 percent for threat 4 seems reasonable.

These assumptions about the likelihood of a successful terrorist attack are summarized in the right column in table 9-2.

The most visible counterterrorism police are those at airports. As discussed previously, aviation seems to be an attractive target for terrorists, or at least security agencies believe this to be so—it is called the "gold standard" in our discussion with police agencies. Accordingly, additional resources are deployed to deal with the problem. The focus of these efforts has mainly been on airplanes, since "any attack guarantees maximum publicity."[77] And a specialist in aviation policy for the U.S. Congressional Research Service contends that an airport has "unique vulnerabilities because it is unsecured."[78] However, it is not clear how airports differ in this quality from myriad other potential terrorist targets.

In a sixteen-year period, 1998–2013, the Global Terrorism Database recorded twenty-two attempted attacks on airports, large and small, in the United States, Canada, Australia, and Europe. Most of these failed to hurt anyone and did no significant damage. In total, these incidents resulted in the deaths of sixty-five people, thirty-seven of them in a single suicide explosion in the baggage-claim section at the Moscow airport in 2011. Notable among the other attacks were an attempted, but failed, bombing of the Glasgow International Airport in 2007, the shooting of two people at the El-Al ticket counter at LAX in 2002, and the shooting of a TSA officer at LAX in 2013 that may or may not be considered to be terrorism.

In total, attacks on airports account for only one-third of 1 percent of all terrorist attacks.[79] This experience led the 2007 U.S. National Strategy for Aviation Security to observe that reported threats to aviation infrastructure, including airports and air navigation facilities, "are relatively few."[80] The several dozen cases listed in appendix A that have come to light since 9/11, in which Islamist terrorists planned, or in many cases just vaguely imagined, doing damage in the United States, finds only three or four in which an airport facility was even on the target list.[81] There have thus been fewer than two attacks per year on airports in the United States, Canada, Australia, and Europe (which contain well over half of the 43,000 airports in the world), and most of these were failures or inflicted minimal damage. In any given year, each of these airports has something like one chance in ten thousand (0.01 percent) of suffering any sort of terrorist attack effort. There are 110 "large" airports in the United States—ones with over five million passengers per year. If we assume terrorists will only target these (which include, of course, the four under examination), the probability of a terrorist attempt increases to something approaching 0.25 percent per airport per year.[82]

This suggests that it may be worthwhile to consider whether airports are actually very attractive targets for terrorists. If the goal of the terrorist is to kill people and inflict physical damage, there are better places to detonate a bomb or undertake a shooting rampage. Moreover, there are thousands of smaller passenger airports, and it is not clear that there is a great deal of comparative advantage to the terrorist in attacking large ones. In addition, enhanced security measures at large airports might have the effect of diverting terrorists to the smaller ones. Even if only the 100 largest of these smaller airports were to be included in the count for each area, the probability an individual airport will be attacked would be greatly reduced.

On the other hand, the low frequency may arise because airports, and particularly aircraft, have been made secure by the expensive and extensive security measures put in place. The target may have become so hardened that terrorists have been deterred from attacking them—though, as discussed in chapter 3, the actual gain to public safety may be somewhat limited because the terrorists may then in principle simply seek out other lucrative, but less secured, targets among the huge array available.

RESULTS

The annual likelihood that a person would be killed at an airport by a terrorist for the period 1998–2013 is approximately one in 1.7 billion for the United States, one in 400 million for Europe, and one in 250 million for the Asia-Pacific region: over that period, there were three airport terrorism fatalities in the United States, thirty-seven in Europe, and twenty-four in the Asia-Pacific area. These are extremely low risks—some 250 to 1,700 times lower than what has generally been deemed "acceptable," as discussed in chapter 5, where an annual fatality risk of less than one in 1 million is generally considered to be "acceptable." However, terrorism is a hazard where risk acceptability is not only a matter of fatalities. There can be direct economic consequences as well as indirect ones, both of which could be significant. This leads us to a fuller evaluation of the costs and benefits of airport policing. We will consider the break-even annual frequency of a terrorist attack attempt (whether successful or unsuccessful) needed for airport counterterrorism policing at a major airport like LAX, JFK, Dallas-Fort Worth, or O'Hare to be deemed cost-effective.[83]

We have concluded that the cost of the security measures for such airports is something like $45 million per year with a co-benefit of $10 million per year that reduces the cost to $35 million. And, as noted, we will assume that the counterterrorism policing measures reduce the likelihood of each of the four kinds of attack attempts and/or its consequences by 75 percent. Finally, we deal only with airport attacks by armed terrorists who have successfully made it to the airport and who have not been thwarted by other security or police agencies or by the public.

TABLE 9-3 Evaluating the Counterterrorism Efforts of Police at Large Airports

Risk Reduction Caused by Airport Counterterrorism Policing	Threats to Airports			
	$10 billion Large truck bomb	$7.5 billion Curbside car bomb	$5 billion Luggage or vest bomb	$2 billion Shooting attack in a public area
5 percent	0.47	0.622	0.47	0.41
10 percent	0.23	0.311	0.23	0.21
25 percent	0.093	0.124	0.093	0.082
50 percent	0.047	0.062	0.047	0.041
75 percent	0.031	0.041	0.031	0.027
90 percent	0.026	0.035	0.026	0.023
100 percent	0.023	0.031	0.023	0.021

Cell entries indicate the number of attack attempts per year (successful or not) by armed terrorists who have not been waylaid by other policing, security, and protection measures in the absence of airport counterterrorism policing measures that are required to begin to justify an annual budget of $45 million (and co-benefit of $10 million) for various threat levels and risk reduction.

Table 9-3 shows the break-even annual frequency of the attempted attack needed for airport counterterrorism policing to begin to be cost-effective as

(probability of attack absent the security measure = [(cost of the security measure) − (co-benefit)] / [(probability that attack is successful) × (losses sustained in the successful attack) × (reduction in risk furnished by the security measure)]

The break-even attack frequency means there is a 50-50 chance of a net benefit.[84] Note that in this case the threat probability is the probability of attack at one large airport in the United States such as LAX, O'Hare, Dallas-Fort Worth, or JFK, absent any airport counterterrorism policing.

As noted, the history-based likelihood that terrorists will attempt to attack one of the four major airports under consideration in any year is extremely low: 0.0025 (0.25 percent). Moreover, most of these attack attempts are likely to fail miserably. And we are assuming that existing airport police measures result in a total risk reduction of 75 percent: three of four terrorist plots that are successfully carried out to the point where the plotters make it to the airport undetected or undeterred will then be deterred, disrupted, or protected against by airport counterterrorism police for each of the four threat scenarios.

We consider, then, very substantial attack attempts on a large airport in the United States. These would be attempts by terrorists who have managed to arm themselves and have been able to get past other security and policing efforts. The question is, in the absence of airport counterterrorism policing, how many of such attempts would need to occur each year for the policing to be cost-effective if we assume the policing efforts reduce risk—the consequences and/or the likelihood of such an attack attempt—by an impressive 75 percent? The number is indicated in the boxed entries in table 9-3.

Under the conditions we have set out, airport counterterrorism policing would only begin to be cost-effective if the frequency of an attempted attack exceeds 0.03 or 0.04 (3 or 4 percent), or one attack every twenty-five or thirty years. Given that there are at least thirty very large airports in the United States—ones about as big as LAX, Dallas-Fort Worth, JFK, and O'Hare—an attack probability per airport of that magnitude equates to more than one attack every year in the United States—absent airport counterterrorism policing—that is not foiled by other policing or intelligence agencies.

To say the least, such a high incidence of attacks in the United States is not being observed; as noted earlier, the likelihood of an attempted attack (whether successful or not) is more like .00025 than like 0.03 or 0.04—ten times lower. And it should be kept in mind that many threats against the aviation industry would be deterred, foiled, or protected against by other (nonairport) police and security measures, as well as by public awareness and response, and so on.

Table 9-3 also suggests that if the annual frequency of a terrorist attack attempt on a large airport in the United States is less than 0.02 or 0.03 (2 to 3 percent), there is no net benefit for airport counterterrorism policing, even if that policing reduces risk by a perfect 100 percent.

The history-based annual threat probability of 0.0025 (0.25 percent), or one attempted attack per airport every 400 years, yields the largest net loss of $32.9 million for a car bombing and the smallest net loss of $31.8 million for a shooting threat.[85] And even if every plot is foiled by airport police—a 100 percent risk reduction—the net benefit is still a net loss of around $31 million for all threats. That is, even if airport policing effectiveness were perfect, airport counterterrorism policing would not be cost-effective, and $1 of cost would buy only 12 cents in benefits.

Because of the uncertainties inherent in such an analysis, a sensitivity analysis is recommended. Doubling the cost of physical damages or loss of life has a negligible effect on net benefit or break-even attack probabilities, which illustrates that in this situation the expected losses are dominated by indirect losses. Many of the assessed security measures would begin to be cost-effective only if the current rate of attack at airports in the United States increases by a factor of ten to twenty. Thus, even if input parameters are doubled or halved, the fundamental findings would not change. In all cases, airport counterterrorism policing as it presently exists fails a cost-benefit assessment.

CONCLUSION

Current airport counterterrorism policing measures costing $45 million per year at major airports are not cost-effective under many combinations of risk reduction and threat probability. In fact, spending $45 million (or $35 million when co-benefits are factored in) at a major airport to achieve such a risk reduction would not be cost-effective even if the risk reduction were a perfect 100 percent.

However, it does not follow that zero spending on airport counterterrorism policing is cost-effective, nor should it be the preferred policy option. Security measures that are at once effective and relatively inexpensive are generally the first to be implemented, and any visible police presence tends to have an immediate deterrent effect. The first dollars spent on counterterrorism measures are likely to be worthwhile, even if the last are not. On the other hand, reduced spending, even if it reduces the risk reduction, may sometimes increase the marginal level of cost-effectiveness.[86]

Moreover, the co-benefit of counterterrorism airport policing may well exceed $10 million per year for a large airport in the United States. For example, counterterrorism airport policing might be able productively to apply such devices as license plate recognition capability and photo ID of passengers to apprehend people with outstanding criminal issues. Also, if the security measure enhances the passenger experience more than we have assumed, there would be an additional co-benefit. If co-benefits reached $42.5 billion (95 percent of the cost of the security measures), the measures would be deemed to be cost-effective following our approach.

In general, however, we find that the likelihood an airport will undergo a terrorist attack needs to be vastly higher than it is now to justify the counterterrorism policing measures currently in place. This was the result even though the analysis was substantially biased toward coming to the opposite conclusion. Thus, we assumed a terrorist attack would inflict very considerable direct and indirect damage, and we were quite generous in our estimates about how much the security measures in place would reduce risk. We also underestimated the costs of the security measures by ignoring any costs entailed in inconveniencing travelers or deterring them from flying.

It may, thus, be time not only to refrain from enhancing the policing at airports but also to consider if some of the security arrangements already in place are excessive.

CONCLUSION | Horrible Imaginings and
Painted Devils

"PRESENT FEARS ARE less than horrible imaginings," notes Macbeth in
Shakespeare's dark and famous play about ghosts and witches. That
play, as it happens, is filled with observations that often suit the themes of
this book.

Under the sway of the horrible imaginings that have emerged from living with a Threat Matrix mentality, assiduous ghost-chasers can testify that
"wicked dreams abuse the curtain'd sleep," that they have "supp'd full with
horrors," and that they often "eat our meal in fear and sleep in the affliction of
these terrible dreams that shake us nightly." They also may observe that they
are "troubled with thick coming fancies" and that they often "hold rumor
from what we fear, yet know not what we fear, but float upon a wild and violent sea." Yet, in the words in Macbeth's most famous soliloquy, the millions
of leads they follow are overwhelmingly "full of sound and fury, signifying
nothing," and on those exceedingly rare occasions when the ghost-quest actually turns up someone who might be, or might become, a terrorist, he generally proves to be "a poor player that struts and frets his hour upon the stage
and then is heard no more."

From time to time the ghost-chasers may even be tempted to ask, "Have we
eaten on the insane root that takes the reason prisoner?" Or, in *New York Times*
reporter James Risen's somewhat less resonant update, "Crazy became the new
normal in the war on terror."[1]

Assessing the Importance of Terrorism

In contrast, it might be useful to evaluate the proposition that, overall, terrorism actually isn't really a terribly important phenomenon and that the heroic and very lonely handful at the bottom of figure 2-15 (p. 88) has it about right. As Fawaz Gerges puts it, "[T]here is a substantial disconnect between the dominant terrorism narrative based on perception—which portrays al-Qaeda and others who subscribe to its ideology as a strategic, existential threat—and the reality of the threat, which is significantly smaller and primarily tactical."[2] Accordingly, it might be argued, terrorism scarcely deserves the reaction it has inspired from ghost-chasers and others.

SEPTEMBER 11, 2001

To evaluate, one must begin with the events of 9/11. Had that tragedy become typical—had 9/11 proved to be a harbinger—it would be reasonable to conclude, as was commonly held in the aftermath of that terrible day, that "everything has changed." But 9/11 has proved to be an aberration, and its success owes a great deal to luck on the part of the perpetrators. It is certainly *possible*, at least, that terrorists could get lucky again, but it seems clear that any such events are scarcely likely to become anything that could be called routine.

The most commonly embraced method by which it has been suggested that terrorists would be able to repeat, or even top, the destruction of 9/11 would be by becoming capable of setting off an atomic explosion. It was in 2004, in his influential book, *Nuclear Terrorism*—a work Nicholas Kristof of the *New York Times* found to be "terrifying"—that Harvard's Graham Allison relayed his "considered judgment" that "on the current path, a nuclear terrorist attack on America in the decade ahead is more likely than not." As discussed in chapter 1, Allison has had a great deal of company in his alarming pronouncements. For example, in 2007, the distinguished physicist Richard Garwin put the likelihood of a nuclear explosion on an American or European city by terrorist or other means at 20 percent per year, which would work out to 89 percent over a ten-year period.[3]

Allison's time is up, and so, pretty much, is Garwin's. And it is important to point out that not only have terrorists failed to go nuclear, but in the words of William Langewiesche who has assessed the process in detail, "The best information is that no one has gotten anywhere near this. I mean, if you look carefully and practically at this process, you see that it is an enormous undertaking full of risks for the would-be terrorists."[4]

DEFINITIONS: TERRORISM AND INSURGENCY

If one removes 9/11 from the consideration (which does *not* mean ignoring either the event or its consequences), the number of fatalities committed by terrorists of all stripes outside war zones, has been, with very few exceptions, remarkably low both before and after 9/11.[5] This is evident in table 5-2 (p. 138) for the terrorism fatality rates in places like the United States (outside of 2001, of course), Great Britain, Canada, and Australia. The exceptions are instances of fairly sustained terrorism, as in Northern Ireland during the "troubles" and in Israel during the intifadas.

The vast majority of what is now commonly being tallied as terrorist destruction has occurred in war zones. This is especially true for fatalities.[6] But to a considerable degree, this is the result of a more expansive application since 9/11 of standard definitions of terrorism, to the point where virtually any violence perpetrated by rebels in civil wars is now being taken to be terrorism. Gary LaFree and colleagues note that, although there are a great many definitions of terrorism,

> most commentators and experts agree on several key elements, captured in the definition we use here: "the threatened or actual use of illegal force and violence by non-state actors to attain a political, economic, religious, or social goal through fear, coercion, or intimidation."[7]

But the whole effort in war is to attain a goal by means of coercion and by inflicting fear and intimidation: it is called "breaking the will of the enemy." In battle, stresses Carl von Clausewitz, "the loss of morale" is the "major decisive factor."[8]

Terrorism differs from warfare not in its essential method or goal, but in its frequency and persistence. When terroristic violence by substate actors (or elements) became really extensive in an area in the past, the activity was no longer called terrorism but, rather, war or insurgency.

The Irish Republican Army, which inflicted only sporadic damage, was generally taken to be a terrorist enterprise. But rebel fighters in places like Sri Lanka in the 1990s were considered at the time to be combatants who were employing guerrilla techniques in a civil war. The same held when the communists systematically assassinated thousands of civilian leaders and officials in South Vietnam in the early 1960s, or when massacres of civilians became a common feature of the civil war in Algeria in the 1990s, in which perhaps a hundred thousand people perished.[9]

The U.S. military saw the distinction in the war in Iraq. In the early days when violence was sporadic, those opposing the American presence were called "terrorists." When the violence became more continuous, they became "insurgents."

Without this distinction, much civil warfare would have to be included in the terrorist category. And so would most "primitive warfare," which, like irregular warfare more generally, relies mostly on raids rather than on set-piece battles.[10] This is particularly the case when, as in the widely accepted LaFree definition, violence by substate elements against military targets is not differentiated from their violence against civilians.[11]

The confusion can be seen currently when ISIS is commonly labeled a band of terrorists, even though it occupies territory, runs social services, and regularly confronts armed soldiers in direct combat. In any armed conflict before the current century, that would be called an insurgency.[12] In the civil war in Syria, the United States brands those fighting the government of Bashar Al-Assad to its own convenience. ISIS fighters are "terrorists" while insurgents approved by the United States are labeled the "moderate opposition." Assad himself is more consistent, if equally self-serving: any violent opposition to a sitting government, he says, is "terrorism."[13] That perspective, one that has become increasingly popular since 9/11, would allow us to retire the concept of "civil war" just about entirely.

This can be taken a step further. Some people argue that terrorism is very frequently committed by states, as well as by "non-state actors." If that element of the definition is adjusted, the category of "war," including those of the international variety, could substantially vanish. Almost all purposeful violence would become terrorism.

While it is not true, then, that 9/11 "changed everything," it did have a strong impact on language. By the standards of an earlier age, terrorism is, by definition, a limited phenomenon. That could have changed if terrorists became capable of routinely launching sporadic destruction on a vast scale—of repeatedly replicating 9/11. However, that hasn't happened and, fortunately, it does not seem to be in the cards.

THE LIMITED IMPACT OF TERRORISM

If terrorism, properly regarded, is a quite limited phenomenon in human affairs, it has also had a limited impact on history.[14] There are two classes of events in which terrorism, by itself, does at times seem to have had a direct historical impact: assassination, and in situations where the terrorized have both a low evaluation of the stakes at risk and a low tolerance for casualties.

If political assassination is considered to be terrorism, there do seem to be instances when it has had a notable historical effect. Thus, the murder of John F. Kennedy in 1963 violently removed from office a man who, some people argue, was less likely than his successor, Lyndon B. Johnson, to enter and to sustain the Vietnam War. There are historians skeptical of this speculation, but it is a plausible one. On the other side, one might also note that the assassination proved consequential because the political skills of Johnson, combined with the emotional reaction to the Kennedy assassination, were vital ingredients in getting historic civil rights legislation passed in 1964. The assassination of Yitzhak Rabin in 1994 in Israel may have had some notable negative effect on the peace process (one of the goals of the assassin), because the leader who replaced him had less prestige and was less politically skillful.

If the terrorized entity has a low tolerance for casualties and a low evaluation of the stakes at hand, relatively small acts of terrorism can be important in changing its policy. U.S. forces sent to Lebanon in 1982 and to Somalia in 1992 were engaging in peacekeeping, a venture few Americans considered to be worth many American lives. Therefore, when terrorist bombs in the first case, or a wild firefight in the second (possibly something that could be labeled terrorism), took the lives of a significant number of those forces, American policy shifted and the troops were withdrawn. The phenomenon seems to be general. By 1997, Spanish troops had suffered seventeen deaths in Bosnia policing the deeply troubled situation in postwar Mostar, and the government indicated that this was enough for them.[15] Similarly, in 1994, Belgium abruptly withdrew from Rwanda, and to save face urged others to do so as well, when ten of its policing troops were massacred and mutilated early in the genocide.[16] Zionist terrorism may have been influential in impelling the British to leave Palestine in 1947.[17] However, to the degree that it did so, an important element in the process was the British government's low tolerance for casualties in its onerous protectorate duties.

Beyond these kinds of cases, any significant historical impact that terrorism may have had seems to have derived much more from the reaction or overreaction it inspired or facilitated, than from anything the terrorists accomplished on their own.

In some instances, a terrorist act has had significant historical consequences because it was opportunistically used as an excuse for—or seized upon to carry out—a policy desired for other reasons. The terrorist act did not trigger or cause these historically significant ventures; rather, it facilitated them by shifting the emotional or political situation, making possible a policy desired for other reasons by political actors. Yet the policy was no more necessary after the terrorist act than it was before it took place.

An important case in point is the reaction of Austria and Germany to the assassination in Sarajevo in June 1914. It is frequently suggested that the terrorist act triggered, or even caused, the cataclysm of World War I. It seems clear, however, that rather than causing the massive (and in the end, spectacularly counterproductive) Austrian and German overreaction, the violence in Sarajevo more nearly gave some Austrian leaders an excuse to impose Serbia-punishing policies they were seeking to carry out anyway.[18]

Similarly, people in the George W. Bush administration who had been yearning for a war to depose Saddam Hussein in Iraq immediately moved into operation after 9/11 in the belief that the attacks by al-Qaeda might have cleared the air sufficiently to allow them to carry out the policy they had been longing for. In like manner, in 2004, Vladimir Putin seized the political opportunity afforded by some Chechen terrorist acts (and by some incompetent policing measures taken by the Russian police) to enhance his control over the Russian political system—something that had absolutely nothing to do with the acts themselves. To say that the acts of terrorism caused this power grab would be absurd; they simply facilitated it.

Sometimes states react, or overreact, to terrorist events not so much to carry out a preexisting agenda as simply out of rage, fear, or a desire to exact revenge. In 1999, for example, responding to several vicious acts of terrorism apparently perpetrated by Chechens, the Russian government reinstituted a war against the breakaway republic that resulted in far more destruction of Russian (and, of course, Chechen) lives and property than the terrorists ever brought about. When two American embassies in Africa were bombed in 1998, killing over 200 (including a few Americans), President Bill Clinton retaliated by bombing some of Osama bin Laden's terrorist training camps in Afghanistan, which caused the Taliban-led Afghan government to renege on pledges to extradite the troublesome and egoistic bin Laden to Saudi Arabia, made him into an international celebrity, turned his al-Qaeda organization into a magnet for more funds and recruits, and converted the Taliban from reluctant hosts to allies and partners.[19] Eager to "do something" about terrorism in 1986, Ronald Reagan bombed Libya after terrorists linked to Libya had blown up a Berlin discotheque, killing two people, one of them American. The bombing raid, notes Ray Takeyh, "only enhanced Qaddafi's domestic power and led to his lionization in the developing world."[20] Outraged by a series of terrorist attacks and shellings perpetrated by Palestinian forces based in bordering Lebanon, the Israelis moved in with massive force in 1982, and, by the time the forces were withdrawn in 2000, vastly more Israeli soldiers had been killed by harassing Arab attacks than had been killed by terrorists before 1982. Similarly, the Indian government massively overreacted to Sikh terrorism in 1984 by attacking the Sikhs' holiest place, the Golden Temple, and by engaging in other excessive behavior. The result was a huge escalation in the conflict.[21] And, of course, there was the reaction to 9/11: the number of Americans (and, of course, Iraqis and Afghans) who have perished thus far in the wars triggered by that event now far exceeds the number killed on September 11.

Excessive reactions to terrorism have often led to massive and unjustified persecution, some of it of considerable historic consequence. The Jewish pogroms in Russia at the end of the nineteenth century, for instance, were activated in major part because Jews were perceived by the Russians to be key contributors to terrorist movements at the time.[22]

In addition, regimes have frequently allowed their participation in peace talks to be importantly affected by terrorists. By stating that they will not negotiate as long as terrorist attacks continue, both the Israeli government and the British government (over Northern Ireland) effectively permitted individual terrorists to set their agendas. If those governments didn't want to negotiate anyway, the terrorist acts simply supplied a convenient excuse for taking that position.

Not only have governments often overreacted counterproductively and sometimes self-destructively to acts of terrorism, but so have electorates.[23] In Israel, Arab terrorists have apparently had the goal of sabotaging Israeli-Palestinian peace talks. In both 1996 and 2001, Israeli voters responded to Arab terrorism at the time by obligingly electing to office parties and prime ministers (Benjamin Netanyahu and Ariel Sharon) who were, like the terrorists, hostile to the negotiations.

Public Opinion

By itself, then, substate terrorism rarely, if ever, has had significant direct historical consequences, except perhaps in a few cases of political assassination or where both the stakes and the tolerance for casualties of the terrorized are very low. Beyond this, any historically significant developments that emerge from terrorism primarily derive not from the act itself but from the reactions, or overreactions, of states and electorates to that act. Sometimes these reactions are self-defeating or even self-destructive, and very often they play into the hands of the terrorists.

It is probably best to see public opinion as the primary driver in the excessive and somewhat bizarre counterterrorism process that took place after 9/11. As discussed in chapter 2, the impact of 9/11 on the collective American consciousness was enormous, and it appears that the fears and anxieties about terrorism established in 2001 have scarcely faded. This, even though there has been nothing remotely like 9/11 anywhere in the world and no major attacks (ones inflicting at least twenty-five deaths) in the United States at all, and even though official alarmism has generally dampened some.

Opinion elites did not create the fears. Although they have been quite willing to exacerbate those fears and to see advantage in doing so, it seems fair to conclude that, overall, they have been "baited with the rabble's curse," as Macbeth rather irreverently puts it. Elites have been substantially united in expressing horrible imaginings about terrorism, but public concerns have not been caused or manipulated by this unity. Rather, the elites are unified on the terrorism issue because they fear that to appear to be dismissive of the threat terrorism presents is exceedingly bad politics. People simply have not come to agree with Bruce Schneier's straightforward dictum: "there isn't much of a threat of terrorism to defend against."[24] And even officials and other members of the opinion elite who agree with Schneier have generally been unwilling to counter the unchanging popular consensus in any important way. President Obama's suggestion that terrorists just might not have the capacity to totally annihilate the country, discussed in chapter 1, was rather tentative, absurdly overdue, and appears to have been short-lived.

As Daniel Byman points out about a popular concern in the months before 9/11, "There was no 'shark attack' industry in the summer of 2001." Indeed, "officials desperately tried to calm Americans down." Yet "panic ensued none-theless."[25] Eventually, officials did sternly forbid the feeding of sharks.[26] But the absurd ban arose from the popular fear; it did not cause it. The essential momentum, then, is substantially bottom-up.

Elite consensus has frequently preceded shifts of opinion.[27] But, as officials found when they tried to dampen fears of sharks, the public has at least as frequently failed to follow.[28] Risen is certainly correct to observe that "fear sells."[29] However, not all fearmongering finds a receptive audience. As they sort through products on the shelf, people pick and choose which threats to be scared of. Americans, unlike many Europeans, have been generally unwilling to accept arguments made by those who wish them to fear genetically modified food, and a great many have remained substantially unmoved by concerns about global warming—even though they have been barraged by continual warnings from authorities that sometimes are of apocalyptic proportions.

Thus, people who downplay the threat presented by global warming have found (but not created) a responsive, and therefore encouraging, audience. On the other hand, people who downplay the threat presented by terrorism (or, as we would prefer to put it, people who seek responsibly to put that threat in a sensible and rational context) have generally not found one.[30] And accordingly, many of those so tempted have been dissuaded by that fact from coming out of their closet—particularly those who deem their office or position to be at stake.

Responsible Counterterrorism Policy

In an important sense, then, policy makers have been democratic when they craft counterterrorism policy. As Robert Jervis points out, "[P]olicy never strays too far and too long from what is desirable, or at least acceptable, to the public."[31] In this case, policy makers are responding as best they can to the fears, anxieties, and irrationalities of public opinion with fears, anxieties, and irrationalities of their own that are quite complementary (or even identical). And in the process, they are dutifully, perhaps even willfully, exacerbating those emotional qualities. Counterterrorism policy, suggests Jeremy Shapiro, is "born of public fear and political cowardice," and there have been almost no official efforts to help Americans understand "that terrorism really isn't much of a threat."[32]

However, as declared in the first sentence of the United States Constitution (and throughout the work of Thomas Hobbes), a key reason for founding governments is to "insure domestic Tranquility." Accordingly, officials serving the public are tasked at the most fundamental level to spend funds in a manner that most effectively and efficiently keeps people safe.

Doing so is neither easy nor precise, and the funds available for that purpose are, of course, limited. Moreover, distortions inevitably stem from public and personal emotions and from political pressures. But, to the degree possible, the task should be carried out systematically and professionally. To do otherwise is irresponsible and costs lives.[33]

As suggested in chapter 5, terrorism is a hazard to human life, and it should be dealt with in a manner similar to that applied to other such hazards—albeit with an appreciation for the fact that terrorism often evokes extraordinary fear and anxiety. However, although allowing emotion to overwhelm sensible analysis is both understandable and common among ordinary people, it is simply not appropriate—however democratically generated—for officials charged with, and responsible for, keeping them safe. As Cass Sunstein puts it, "If people's values lead them to show special concern with certain risks, government should take that concern into account." But "any official response should be based on a realistic understanding of the facts," not on "factual mistakes."[34]

The important distinction in all this, as risk analyst David Banks has suggested, is "between realistic reactions to plausible threats and hyperbolic overreaction to improbable contingencies."[35] To be irrational with your own money may be to be foolhardy, to give in to guilty pleasure, or to wallow in caprice. But to be irrational with other people's money, particularly where public safety is concerned, is to be irresponsible, to betray an essential trust. In the end, it becomes a dereliction of duty that cannot be justified by political pressure, bureaucratic constraints, or emotional drives.

People who join the army or become firefighters accept the possibility that at some point they may be shot at or required to enter a burning building. People who become decision makers should in equal measure acknowledge that in order to carry out their job properly and responsibly, they may be required on occasion to make some difficult, even career-threatening decisions.

Actually, it is possible that politicians and bureaucrats are overly fearful of the political consequences of reacting moderately to terrorism. Sometimes, leaders have been able to restrain their instinct to overreact, and this has often proved to be entirely acceptable politically. For example, the United States did not massively overreact to terrorist bombings against its soldiers and citizens in Lebanon in 1983 or over Lockerbie, Scotland, in 1988.[36]

This issue is particularly important because it certainly appears that avoiding overreaction is by far the most cost-effective counterterrorism measure. Thus, 9/11 not only led to considerable indirect costs as people avoided flying and traveling for a time, but the attacks were also used to propel the United States and its allies into costly overseas wars. To the extent that extreme reactions like multitrillion-dollar wars are considered to be a (self-inflicted) part of the cost of the terrorist attack, they do far more damage to the attacked than is accomplished by the terrorists themselves.

One might, in that respect, compare the reaction to 9/11 with that to the worst terrorist event in the developed world before then, the downing of an Air India airliner departing Canada in 1985, in which 329 people, 280 of them Canadian citizens, perished. Journalist Gwynne Dyer points out that, proportionate to population, the losses were almost exactly the same in the two cases. But, continues Dyer, "[H]ere's what Canada didn't do: it didn't send troops into India to 'stamp out the roots of the terrorism' and it didn't declare a 'global war on terror.' Partly because it lacked the resources for that sort of adventure, of course, but also because it would have been stupid."[37] A similar conclusion was presumably reached by the Indian government after the dramatic and costly mass-shooting terrorist attacks in Mumbai in 2008.

Moreover, although political pressures may force actions and expenditures that are unwise, they usually do not precisely dictate the level or direction of expenditure. Thus, although there are public demands to "do something" about terrorism, nothing in those demands specifically requires American officials to mandate removing shoes in airport security lines, to require passports to enter Canada, to spread bollards like dandelions, to gather vast quantities of private data, or to make a huge number of buildings into forbidding fortresses. The United Kingdom, which faces an internal threat from terrorism that may well be greater than that for the United States, nonetheless spends proportionately much less than half as much on homeland security, and the same holds for Canada and Australia.[38] Yet politicians and bureaucrats in those countries do not seem to suffer threats to their positions or other political problems because of it.

RISK COMMUNICATION

To begin with, there is a fundamental responsibility to inform the public honestly and accurately about the risk that terrorism presents. This may well be especially difficult for the terrorism risk because of the emotions involved.[39] Yet, as a matter of fundamental responsibility, officials should at least *try*. Americans may well remain mired in fear even when they are repeatedly informed that under present circumstances their chance of being killed by a terrorist is one in 4 million per year. But they should know the number.

Instead, as noted frequently in this book, the emphasis has been on exacerbating fears and neglecting probabilities.[40] Indeed, for more than a decade after 9/11, just about the *only* official in the United States who ever openly put the threat presented by terrorism into some sort of context is New York's former mayor, Michael Bloomberg, who in 2007 pointed out that people should "get a life" and that they have a greater chance of being hit by lightning than of being struck by terrorism.[41] It might be noted that his unconventional outburst did not have negative consequences for him; although he had some difficulties in his reelection two years later, his blunt and essentially accurate comments about terrorism were not the cause. Nor, officials might be interesting in noting, did it generate the response they may fear: "If the danger is that low, why are we spending so much money trying to deal with it?"

Similarly, as far as we can see, only once has DHS actually, if accidentally, engaged in a public assessment of acceptable risk. It involves concerns that body scanners using X-ray technology will cause cancer. Asked about it, the DHS official in charge, John Pistole, essentially said that, although the cancer risk was not zero, it was acceptable. A set of studies, he pointed out, "have all come back to say that the exposure is very, very minimal" and "well, well within all the safety standards that have been set."[42] Since the radiation exposure delivered to each passenger is known, one can calculate the risk of getting cancer from a single exposure using a standard approach that, although controversial, is officially accepted by nuclear regulators in the United States and elsewhere. On the basis of a 2012 review of scanner safety, that cancer risk per scan is about 1 in 60 million.[43] As it happens, the chance that an individual airline passenger will be killed by terrorists on an individual flight is much lower—1 in 90 million.[44] Therefore, unless one believes that terrorists will in the near future become far more capable of downing airliners with body-borne bombs than they have been in the past, the risk of being killed by a terrorist on an airliner is already fully acceptable by the standards applied to the cancer risk from body scanners using X-ray technology. But no official has drawn that comparison.

Things are no better in the media. As noted in chapter 1, when the anchor on the *PBS NewsHour* happened to observe that, even with 9/11 included in the count, there had been but one terrorist incident on American airliners over the previous decade for every 16.5 million flights, no one in the ensuing discussion thought it useful to reflect a bit on that impressive statistic.[45]

It was concluded in chapter 2 that the many expensive, ad hoc, and hasty post-9/11 measures that have been adopted to deal with (or that have been fabricated and then thrown at) the terrorism problem have not allayed concerns about personal security. Accordingly, public officials, in some sense, are free to do it right—they are unlikely to scare people even more than they are scared now. It is true that few voters spend much time following the ins and outs of policy issues, and even fewer are certifiable policy wonks, but they *are* grownups, and it is just possible they would respond reasonably to an adult conversation about terrorism.[46]

It took until 2015, nearly a decade and a half after 9/11, before a president was willing to suggest that terrorism did not, as it happens, present a threat to the country that was "existential" in nature. That this utterance of what might seem a banality of cosmic proportions should come off as an apparent act of political courage suggests the depth of the problem—and, essentially, of the ongoing irresponsibility of officials. Five years after 9/11, journalist James Fallows suggested that Americans have "lacked leaders to help keep the danger in perspective."[47] Despite Obama's almost embarrassingly modest effort, Fallows's observation remains valid today.

EVALUATING COUNTERTERRORISM PROGRAMS

More generally, the government should responsibly respond to the urgent plea to "develop a comprehensive methodology for assessing the efficacy and relative value of counterterrorism programs." That was a key recommendation of a 2014 report of the Privacy and Civil Liberties Oversight Board after it had evaluated surveillance programs designed to pursue terrorists. In making this recommendation, the board stressed that "determining the efficacy and value of particular counterterrorism programs is critical" because, without doing so, "policymakers and courts cannot effectively weigh" the benefits that derive from such programs against their costs. Accordingly, "the government should develop a methodology to gauge and assign value to its counterterrorism programs, and use that methodology to determine if particular programs are meeting their stated goals." Such "important work" would help policy makers come up with "informed, data-driven decisions."[48] Similar sentiments have been expressed by the Government Accountability Office.[49]

And also by the presidential review group constituted to explore the value and appropriateness of intelligence technologies in 2013. It argues that the issue is not whether a surveillance program "makes us incrementally safer, but whether the additional safety is worth the sacrifice in terms of individual privacy, personal liberty, and public trust."[50] It is that (rather elemental) balancing process that should be—but very often is not—central to responsible security policy making.

We have attempted to do exactly that in this book and in our earlier one, *Terror, Security, and Money.* For the most part, we have concluded that the costs of many programs as presently carried out generally outweigh their benefits—though this doesn't necessarily mean the programs should be abandoned entirely. We also recognize that risk and cost-benefit considerations should not be the sole criteria for public decision making. Nonetheless, they provide important insights into how security measures may (or may not) perform, their effect on risk reduction, and their cost-effectiveness. In the process, they can reveal wasteful expenditures and allow limited funds to be directed to where the most benefit can be attained.

Moreover, it seems to us that, if risk and cost-benefit advice is to be ignored, the onus is on public officials to explain why this is so and to detail the tradeoffs and cuts to other programs that will inevitably ensue. As far as we can see, this work, deemed "important" and "critical" by the board, is simply not being done.

Interestingly, and perhaps uniquely within the Department of Homeland Security, the Coast Guard has actually set out to develop risk-based performance measures that are quantitative in nature. Specifically, it estimates "threat, vulnerability, and consequence levels" for a variety of scenarios, generating an index value of "raw risk."[51] According to the Government Accountability Office, the Coast Guard first estimates "the total amount of terrorism risk that exists in the maritime domain, in the absence of any Coast Guard activities." It then has subject-matter experts estimate how much its various security measures have reduced the risk to U.S. ports and waterways for sixteen potential maritime terrorist-attack scenarios. The

GAO has concluded that "[t]he Coast Guard's efforts to develop an outcome measure to quantify the impact its actions have had on risk is [*sic*] a positive step."

The metric used for quantifying risk reduction is less than perfect—an index is not as useful as the absolute risks that we calculate in this book. However, as the GAO stresses, it is clearly a step in the right direction, and this laudable approach should be repeated across the DHS. In stark contrast, however, DHS has decided to do the opposite. The GAO has noted that because "DHS leadership did not feel the risk reduction measure and its methodology would be easily understandable by the public," it should not be used as a "strategic measure." Accordingly, DHS will not include the risk-reduction measure in its annual performance plan.[52]

RISK AVERSION

Although we understand that people are often risk averse when considering issues like terrorism, extreme risk aversion severely distorts sensible analysis and can even make it impossible. With this in mind, the U.S. Office of Management and Budget actually *requires* that government agencies expending tax money be neutral when assessing risks, something that entails focusing primarily on mean estimates in risk and cost-benefit calculations, not primarily on worst-case or pessimistic ones.[53]

As far as we can see, however, the level of risk averseness needed to justify current expenditures for homeland security is considerable. Indeed, it appears that agencies dealing with terrorism exhibit far more risk aversion than do other government agencies, even ones like the U.S. Nuclear Regulatory Commission or Environmental Protection Agency that often deal with issues that are emotionally or politically charged.[54]

"Policy-making is a risky business," one group of analysts has acknowledged. But, they continue, "regardless of the varied desires and political pressures, we believe that it is the responsibility of analysts forcefully to advocate rational decision methods in public policy-making, especially for those with high risk."[55] Or as Elisabeth Paté-Cornell observes, if rational approaches to public policy making are not applied, a politically driven process "may lead to raising unnecessary fears, wasting scarce resources, or ignoring important problems."[56] And, one might add, when public safety is the issue at hand, that process may cost lives.

Terrorists do, of course, exist—as they have throughout history. They may even get lucky again sometime. Thus, concern and watchfulness about terrorism are certainly justified. But counterterrorism expenditures that are wildly disproportionate to the limited hazard terrorism presents are neither wise nor responsible.

Consequences of the Ghost Chase

Lady Macbeth's doctor observes that "unnatural deeds do breed unnatural troubles." It appears that a number of undesirable consequences, or troubles, have rather naturally evolved from the unnatural (or supernatural) process of chasing ghosts.

HIDING BEHIND SECRECY

Macbeth characterizes his witches as "imperfect speakers," and, finding that what they are telling him "stands not within the prospect of belief," he implores them to "say from whence you owe this strange intelligence." At this point, according to a stage direction, the witches vanish.

Many have found echoes of this experience when ghost-chasers say, "If you'd have seen the intelligence I've seen, you'd be scared as hell," and then, when asked to explain, disappear with: "I can't tell you. It's classified." We have explored this conundrum at some length in this book, especially in chapters 1 and 7. Our imperfect speakers do seem genuinely to be terrified by what they are seeing. However, it also appears, particularly in retrospect, that they have very often vastly exaggerated the significance and reality of what they are seeing. Overwhelmingly, the alarming information, or "strange intelligence," before them proves to be "a false creation, proceeding from the heat-oppressed brain"—one in which "what seem'd corporal melted as breath into the wind" and in which "function is smother'd in surmise, and nothing is but what is not."

Glenn Carle is a twenty-three-year veteran of the Central Intelligence Agency where he was deputy national intelligence officer for transnational threats. Americans, he argues, have become "victims of delusion," a quality he defines as "a persistent false belief in the face of strong contradictory evidence."[57] Intelligence assessments, he continues, have been "spinning in self-referential circles" in which "premises were flawed" and "facts used to fit our premises," while fears "justified our operational actions, in a self-contained process that arrived at a conclusion dramatically at odds with the facts." The process has "projected evil actions where there was, more often, muddled indirect and unavoidable complicity, or not much at all." These "delusional ratiocinations," he further observes, "were all sincerely, ardently held to have constituted a rigorous, rational process to identify terrorist threats" in which "the avalanche of reporting confirms its validity by its quantity," in which there is a tendency to "reject incongruous or contradictory facts as erroneous, because they do not conform to accepted reality," and in which potential dissenters are not so subtly reminded of career dangers:. "Say what you want at meetings. It's your decision. But you are doing yourself no favors."[58] There may well be resonance in a short colloquy in *Macbeth*:

You see, her eyes are open.
Ay, but their sense is shut.

The ability to cloak this process can have considerable deleterious effects. As Ron Wyden and John Dickas have pointed out, it has allowed intelligence agencies to make "greatly exaggerated claims about the usefulness of mass surveillance and torture" even in secret presentations to Congress. Such mischaracterizations, "allowed to fester for years under a veil of secrecy," then "crumbled quickly when they were publicly exposed."[59]

The penchant for secrecy (and the ability to hide behind it) is especially problematic for evaluating the cost-effectiveness of security measures. As can be seen in the various analyses in this book, it is necessary for analysts repeatedly to make estimates and assumptions about costs, risks, and consequences; and it is incumbent on them to explain and justify each estimate and each assumption. Others, then, are free to re-evaluate and critique. This has underpinned scientific methods at least since the age of the enlightenment.

Sometimes the process leads to considerable disagreement, but it can also sometimes lead to a fair amount of agreement. For example, several studies have attempted to estimate the direct and indirect costs inflicted by the 9/11 attacks, and most estimates congeal around roughly the same figure.[60] But in all cases, transparency is at the very heart of the exercise.

One example may help illuminate the problem with secrecy. Over a number of years, the Boeing Corporation developed a risk-analysis tool for the Department of Homeland Security. Finally, in 2012, a team of analysts from the RAND Corporation was invited to evaluate the tool. Their report was highly critical. It noted that the tool has "thousands of input variables," many of which cannot be estimated with much precision, and it could generate results that are "completely wrong." Moreover, it takes so long to run that it was not possible "to conduct even a superficial sensitivity analysis" of its "many thousands of assumptions and parameter estimates." In addition, it only deals with relative risk, not absolute risk, and its estimates of these "are subject to strong, probably untenable, assumptions." The tool is also insensitive to changes in the magnitude of risk and "assumes no attack can be deterred."[61]

It seems likely that many of these defects would have been uncovered far earlier if the tool had been fully open for evaluation by other researchers. On the other hand, other analysts might conclude that the RAND study itself is flawed and that there is merit to the tool after all, perhaps after some judicious adjustments are made to it. But we'll never know. Neither the full RAND report nor full information on the workings of the analysis tool (or even of its costs) is available to be assessed. In this case, DHS did call in outsiders to evaluate a risk model—albeit one created and paid for by an independent company. We have not been able to determine whether DHS calls in outsiders to evaluate its own risk models.

To a degree, our own experience may be relevant to this issue. In the last years, we have published some two dozen articles in peer-reviewed journals applying risk and cost-benefit analysis to the terrorism phenomenon. We have openly and critically discussed threat likelihoods as well as the vulnerabilities of aviation, bridges, buildings, and other critical infrastructure in order to determine how cost-effective various counterterrorism measures are at reducing risk. At no point have editors or reviewers questioned the appropriateness of publishing this material out of concerns about national security, secrecy, or aiding the enemy. As we would expect, what was important to them were the scientific method and the robustness of the results.

TAKING UNJUSTIFIED CREDIT FOR THE ABSENCE OF MAJOR ATTACKS

In December 2014, the Senate Intelligence Committee issued what became known, rather cheerlessly, as "the Torture Report." It concluded that, in the months or years after 9/11, those questing after terrorists, particularly those in the CIA, frequently used torture to interrogate people they thought could supply information.

In a spirited defense of the program, Bill Harlow, a spokesman for the CIA from 1997 to 2004, sought to put the program in context. His statement, with some bracketed insertions, was,

> We [thought we] didn't have time to wait around and see if we might eventually find out this information. This was a period when we [thought we] were under great threat for a second [9/11-type] attack on the United States. We had a handful of people who we knew were [at least somewhat] responsible for the first attack and [we thought they] would very likely be able to tell us how to stop the next one. We [thought we] couldn't afford to wait. We didn't. And we were successful.[62]

Without the bracketed information, Harlow's bold assertions about conditions after 9/11 are essentially an exercise in dissembling, though some might want to apply a stronger word. His final extrapolation is essentially that, and no evidence is given to support it. As usual, his interviewer did not deem it necessary to ask for details or further explanation—though if she had done so, he would always be able to hide behind secrecy where convenient.

At about the same time, a column by Charles Krauthammer in the *Washington Post* is more sophisticated—and correct—about the post-9/11 world:

> In the aftermath of 9/11, there was nothing irrational about believing that a second attack was a serious possibility and therefore everything should be done to prevent it. Indeed, this was the considered opinion of the CIA, the administration, the congressional leadership and the American people.

But Krauthammer then abruptly concludes with an evidence-free assertion that is as out-of-joint as Harlow's:

> Under the direction of the Bush administration and with the acquiescence of congressional leadership, the CIA conducted an uncontrolled experiment. It did everything it could, sometimes clumsily, sometimes cruelly, indeed, sometimes wrongly. But successfully. It kept us safe.[63]

Similarly, when New York City Police Department Commissioner David Cohen is asked how he knows whether his extensive counterterrorism programs have been successful, he curtly responds, "They haven't attacked us." Reporting this comment, Matt Apuzzo and Adam Goldman note that "the absence of a terrorist attack has been the silver-bullet argument for national security professionals." Although it is a "flawed argument" logically, they continue, it has been "nearly irrefutable" politically.[64]

The ghost-chasers' dodge, at once "flawed" and "nearly irrefutable," beneficially derives from an often-stupendous exaggeration of the determination and capacities of the terrorist enemy. Since our adversaries are at once very capable and hugely dedicated, and yet haven't done much of anything, it is held, it must be that their schemes have been disrupted or deterred by our costly and extensive counterterrorism measures. That is, (1) we are trying to keep them from attacking; (2) they haven't attacked; and therefore (3) it must be our efforts that have kept them from doing so.

But there are at least four objections.

First, as discussed earlier, it is not to be expected that there would normally be very many attacks, especially large ones. Although counterterrorism measures vary considerably in their scope and adequacy around the world, terrorism is, and always has been, a rare phenomenon. Even as 9/11 has proved to be an aberration, "terrorism" of late has overwhelmingly taken place in civil war situations, particularly in the Middle East, where one or more sides apply terrorist tactics as an instrument of warfare. However, this has long been a feature of civil warfare. What has changed is not the destructiveness or the effectiveness of such tactics, but that after 9/11 they have commonly been labeled "terrorism." Although counterterrorism measures around the world have certainly undercut and hampered some terrorist groups, it is not at all clear that they needed to be ramped up so very considerably after 2001. As discussed in chapter 4, al-Qaeda's record for violence is scarcely less impressive since 9/11 than it was before that tragedy. The costly maintenance of a no-fly list has doubtless made it more difficult for terrorists to enter the United States, but getting operatives into the country was already a primary problem for them before 9/11. Moreover, there has not been a great amount of terrorism in Europe even though its Muslim population is large and even though entry and exit are much easier. And outside war zones, counterterrorism has primarily been accomplished using old-fashioned police work.

Second, as has been demonstrated repeatedly in this book, the actual terrorist "adversaries" we face in the West scarcely deserve accolades for either dedication or prowess. For the most part, they are a confused, inadequate, incompetent, blundering, and gullible bunch, rarely able to get their act together. To a considerable degree, as chapter 4 suggests, that conclusion holds even for those international terrorist operators who are routinely labeled "masterminds." All seem to be far better at frenetic and often self-deluded scheming than at actual execution. It is true, of course, that sometimes even incompetents can get lucky, but such instances, however tragic, are rare. Moreover, for the most part, the consequences of individual successful attacks have been quite limited—scarcely any really do enough damage to be considered "major," and except perhaps in the occasional fantasies, there has been nothing again like 9/11.

Third, as discussed in chapter 3, the deterrence argument suffers from a special defect. It may well be that certain sets of targets, like airplanes and rural military bases, are so well protected that terrorists have been successfully deterred from attacking them. However, of necessity the world remains full of lucrative terrorist targets that are substantially unprotected. It simply cannot be that competent and dedicated terrorists have been deterred from attacking all such targets by protective or policing measures.

And, fourth, as we have shown both in this book and in *Terror, Security, and Money*, counterterrorism security measures generally do not survive a standard cost-effectiveness analysis in which the question is: How many terrorist attacks would have had to occur without the measure in place to justify its cost? Even assuming the counterterrorism measures greatly reduce the risk (the consequences and/or the likelihood) of terrorist attack, and even assuming any terrorist acts successfully consummated would be highly destructive, the cost of most (though certainly not all) security measures has proven to be excessive.

In its deterrence form, the self-serving thinking process of the ghost-chasers has a long pedigree. It reached perhaps its greatest height during the cold war, when the American nuclear force (a.k.a. its "deterrent") was deemed to be successful because the horror it was designed to deter, a major Soviet military attack, never took place. Left unconsidered was the obvious alternative explanation suggested by diplomat George Kennan: "I have never believed that they have seen it as in their interests to overrun Western Europe militarily, or that they would have launched an attack on that region generally even if the so-called nuclear deterrent had not existed."[65]

President Dwight Eisenhower does seem to have grasped the fundamental reality that the Soviets had no interest whatever in a direct military confrontation and therefore that an ever-enlarged military was scarcely required to deter them.[66] However, he never summoned the political courage to say this openly, presumably because, like officials today who worry about appearing to downplay the threat terrorism is deemed to present, he feared a public opinion backlash. Thus, he chose to flail at the "military-industrial complex" rather than at the faulty and underexamined premise that gave that complex its political potency.

The grand mistake of the cold war was to infer desperate intent from apparent capacity. For the war on terrorism, it is to infer desperate capacity from apparent intent.

FAILING TO HOLD CLASSIFIERS ACCOUNTABLE

Macbeth is notably hostile to fearmongering and to lying, suggesting rather unpleasantly of the former that we "hang those that talk of fear" and warning a messenger about his zero-tolerance policy toward the latter: "if thou speak'st false, upon the next tree shalt thou hang alive, till famine cling thee." Although we wish to distance ourselves from such extreme remedies, they do express a sentiment about lying and fearmongering that should be considered, if not perhaps quite so colorfully embraced.

In particular, it seems pertinent to wonder why officials aren't held to account when they violate the relevant executive orders by classifying as secret information that, by any reasonable standard, would not damage national security if disclosed. Often, note Wyden and Dickas, "the main reason for keeping important information secret is to avoid public criticism or to prevent embarrassment to agencies or individuals."[67]

The degree to which classification has been overdone is suggested by the case of Bradley Manning, who downloaded hundreds of thousands of classified documents that were subsequently made public by WikiLeaks in 2010. As it turned out, these documents, while embarrassing to some officials, contained no really significant new disclosures. According to Bill Keller, the *New York Times* editor in charge when the newspaper reported the material, just about all the information was already essentially public, though in many cases it was less textured, detailed, and nuanced.[68]

Although prosecutors forcefully argued in Manning's military trial that he was guilty of "aiding the enemy"—surely the key issue in determining whether something should be classified—the judge failed to find him guilty on that charge.[69] If Manning's disclosures failed to "aid the enemy," it would be difficult to argue that Edward Snowden's 2013 revelations, which are primarily about methods of data collection that were already known and/or easy to surmise, would be of much aid either.

TMI: BEING SWEPT AWAY BY BIG DATA AND IGNORING ITS PERILS

As stressed particularly in the chapter on NSA, there has been a tendency to collect everything in part because it has become technologically possible to do so. The mentality emerged out of a program whose title is an exquisite exercise in self-parody: Total Information Awareness, or TIA.[70] Combined with the "9/11 Commission Syndrome," which dictates that all leads must be followed up because the one you skip might be the next 9/11, the result has been a costly, even absurd surfeit of information commonly rendered (with slightly different nuance) as TMI, or "too much information." For Marc Sageman it is an "ocean," while Carle calls it an "avalanche"—one that "confirms its validity by its quantity."[71]

Nevertheless, there is also a tendency to believe—very attractive to data-gathering geeks—that, with enough data to sort through, one can come up with algorithms disclosing patterns that will point to the solution, even without knowing very much substantively about the actual phenomenon of interest, in this case terrorism. However, under the sway of the 9/11 Commission Syndrome, the geeks are wary of casting the identifying algorithm too tightly, and consequently they tend to pass on potential leads in great number.

As suggested in chapter 7, the results have not been very impressive. Old-fashioned police work seems to have been far more reliable for catching terrorists. Mattathias Schwartz quotes a former CIA case officer who argues that mass surveillance "gives a false sense of security. It sounds great when you say you're monitoring every phone call in the United States. You can put that in a PowerPoint. But, actually, you have no idea what's going on." Schwartz observes that "by flooding the system with false positives, big-data approaches to counterterrorism might actually make it harder to identify real terrorists before they act."[72] Or concludes Shane Harris, the huge amounts of information overwhelmed analysts who found that compressing information into more and more manageable forms "actually diluted nuance."[73] Perhaps the common metaphor should be advanced: with enough hay, you won't even be able to find the haystack.

Big data are likely to have value in establishing, or nailing down, correlations that may lurk within vast data collections—although there is a danger in this in that the common problem of confusing statistical significance with substantive significance will be embellished: the larger the data set, the more likely a relationship will be deemed to be statistically significant.[74]

However, the key problem with big data in the terrorist quest arises from the fact that analysts are not looking simply for correlations or connections.

When Amazon.com routinely culls through its huge customer database, it is not concerned that there may be a considerable error rate when correlating the buying or surfing habits of one customer with another one. But there are, in fact, very few likely terrorists in the information haystack, and few of those, as this book seeks to stress at various points, are actually capable or dedicated enough to justify concerted and therefore costly policing efforts. Thus, it is important to be precise, not just co-relative, when searching for them. A high error rate wastes time and effort, has considerable civil liberties complications, and may dim the senses of the chasers, making the quest less likely to succeed. Adding huge amounts of hay only exacerbates the problem. The issue is put in more general form by Sageman: "Throwing more analysts at the problem compounds the issue as it creates more false leads for analysts who err on the side of security."[75]

Relevant here is a study finding that, as more information becomes readily available to scientists, they can "more easily find prevailing opinion" and are "more likely to follow it." This leads to "more citations referencing fewer articles" even as "findings and ideas that do not become consensus" are "forgotten quickly."[76]

Another concern arises from the fact that big data sets are often literally unfathomable—that is, essentially bottomless. Thus, the fact that none of the leads dredged up from a data set have yet led anywhere is not necessarily deflating to the quest. There is still a great amount of unplumbed information out there, and rather than giving up, there is a consequent temptation to re-jigger the algorithm in an increasingly straw-grasping hope for success. The larger the haystack, the less likely it will ever be deemed to be free of needles.

Chasing—and Believing in—Ghosts

If you believe in ghosts (like 49 percent of the American public) but have never seen one (like half of these), two plausible explanations are likely to spring to mind. One, you're not looking hard enough. Or, two, the ghosts are diabolically clever. Our counterterrorists have routinely applied both explanations in their frantic quest to make us safe at taxpayers' expense.

In addition, the process of chasing ghosts makes the chasers more likely to believe they exist. As Richard Heuer puts it in *Psychology of Intelligence Analysis,* a book published by the CIA, one of the factors that influences the "imaginability of scenarios" is "the act of analysis itself," because "constructing a detailed scenario for a possible future event makes that event more readily imaginable and, therefore, increases its perceived probability."[77] If the general notion is that analysts should focus very disproportionately on worst-case scenarios, those scenarios will come to seem to be more likely in the process.

The experience with the Threat Matrix and its various derivatives certainly suggests the validity of Heuer's observation. It is exemplified nicely by the assertions in congressional testimony by FBI Director Robert Mueller, an avid consumer of the Threat Matrix: "the greatest threat is from al-Qaeda cells in the U.S. that we have not yet identified" and "I remain very concerned about what we are not seeing."

In neither instance did he flesh out the picture a bit by acknowledging, at least for purposes of discussion, that there might be a plausible alternative—that the massive homeland security apparatus in the United States has persecuted some, spied on many, inconvenienced most, and taxed all to defend against a domestic enemy that scarcely exists. Throughout the costly post-9/11 counterterrorism saga, that continues to be the hypothesis that dare not speak its name.[78]

The fundamentally absurd result of all this is suggested in a scene at the end of the 2014 Oscar-winning documentary *Citizenfour,* in which Edward Snowden and journalist Glenn Greenwald are shown "conversing" in a room. Presumably out of concern that the room is bugged, the conversation is conducted in a strange, rather Orwellian manner: Greenwald constantly writes notes, shoves them at Snowden, and then Snowden reads them and responds orally, but tersely and without revealing their content. A few of these notes are shown to the viewer. One says, "There are 1.2m people on various stages of their watch list."[79] One might think that Snowden would, at this point, no longer be capable of being surprised by the vastness of the American counterterrorism enterprise. But he is, nonetheless. He smiles in disbelief, snorts derisively, and says, "That's fucking ridiculous."

As Lady Macbeth puts it sardonically (and a bit more poetically), "'tis the eye of childhood that fears a painted devil."

Appendix A The Cases: Terrorism in the United States Since 9/11

T HE FOLLOWING IS a list of the sixty-two cases that have come to light of Islamist extremist terrorism since September 11, 2001, whether based in the United States or abroad, in which the United States itself has been, or apparently has been, targeted. They are listed by case number ordered by date of arrest. The case number is followed by the case title, case type, year, and a brief description of the case. Information on the case types follows this list. In addition, there are two cases, numbered 98 and 99, in which the culprits sought to go abroad to join the fight against American interests there. Detailed studies for the great majority of the cases are available in a webbook edited by John Mueller: *Terrorism Since 9/11: The American Cases*. It can be accessed through politicalscience.osu.edu/faculty/jmueller/since.html. This webbook is expanded and updated yearly.

1. *The shoe bomber* (4), 2001: British man tries to blow up a U.S.-bound airliner with explosives in his shoes but is subdued by passengers and crew.
2. *Padilla* (1), 2002: American connected to al-Qaeda who had discussed a dirty bomb attack returns to United States and is arrested.
3. *Mt. Rushmore* (3), 2002: Prior to 9/11, two men in Florida, one of them possibly connected to an al-Qaeda operative, and crucially aided by an informant, plot to bomb local targets and Mt. Rushmore and are arrested and tried the year after.

4. *El-Al at LAX* (4), 2002: In an act later deemed to be one of terrorism, a depressed anti-Israel Egyptian national shoots and kills two people at the El-Al ticket counter at LAX before being killed himself.

5. *Lackawanna* (1), 2002: Seven Americans in Lackawanna, New York, are induced to travel to an al-Qaeda training camp, but six return disillusioned (all before 9/11) and are arrested the next year.

6. *Khan and the Parachas* (2), 2003: A young Pakistani seeks to help an al-Qaeda operative enter the country to attack underground storage tanks at gas stations.

7. *Abu Ali in Saudi Arabia* (2), 2003: A U.S. citizen joins a terrorist cell in Saudi Arabia and plots to hijack a plane in the United States, and to assassinate President Bush; he is arrested by the Saudis and extradited to the United States for trial.

8. *Columbus and the Brooklyn Bridge* (2), 2003: American connected to al-Qaeda discusses shooting up a shopping mall in Columbus, Ohio, with two friends, then scouts taking down the Brooklyn Bridge for al-Qaeda, but decides it's too difficult.

9. *Barot and the financial buildings* (2), 2004: Group in London tied to al-Qaeda scouts out financial buildings in the United States, with an eye to bombing them, but never gets to the issue of explosives.

10. *Albany* (3), 2004: Two men in Albany, New York, effectively help fund an informant's terror plot.

11. *Nettles* (3), 2004: An American with a long history of criminal and mental problems plots, using the nickname "Ben Laden," to blow up a federal courthouse in Chicago and reaches out for help to a Middle Eastern terrorist group, but gets the FBI instead.

12. *Herald Square* (3), 2004: Loud-mouthed jihadist in New York City and a schizophrenic friend attract an informant, who helps them lay plans to bomb the Herald Square subway station.

13. *Grecula* (3), 2005: An American with visions of being a modern-day Spartacus agrees to build a bomb to be exploded in the United States for undercover agents claiming to be al-Qaeda.

14. *Lodi* (1), 2005: An American in Lodi, California, who may have attended a training camp in Pakistan, but who has no apparent plan to commit violence, is arrested with the aid of an informant.

15. *JIS* (2), 2005: An American in jail masterminds a plot with three others to shoot up military recruitment centers, synagogues, and a nonexistent military base in the Los Angeles area but, although they are close to

their first attack, the plot is disrupted when they leave a cellphone behind at a robbery to obtain funds.

16. *Pipelines and the terrorist hunter* (3), 2005: An American offers on the Internet to blow up pipelines in Canada as an aid to al-Qaeda, and attracts the attention of a freelance informant.

17. *University of North Carolina* (4), 2006: To punish the U.S. government for its actions around the world, a former student, after failing to go abroad to fight or to join the Air Force so he could drop a nuclear bomb on Washington, D.C., drives a rented SUV onto campus to run over as many Americans as possible and manages to injure nine people.

18. *Hudson River tunnels* (2), 2006: Angered by the U.S. invasion of Iraq, several men based in Lebanon plot to flood railway tunnels under the Hudson River but are arrested overseas before acquiring bomb materials or setting foot in the United States.

19. *Sears Tower* (3), 2006: Seven men in Miami plot with an informant, who they claim they were trying to con, to take down the Sears Tower in Chicago, then focus on closer buildings.

20. *Transatlantic airliner bombings* (2), 2006: A small group in London, under intense police surveillance from the beginning, plots to explode liquid bombs on U.S.-bound airliners.

21. *Rockford* (3), 2006: A loud-mouthed jihadist attracts the attention of an informant, and together they plot to explode grenades at a shopping mall in Rockford, Illinois.

22. *Fort Dix* (3), 2007: A small group target-practices and at least one of them plots to attack Fort Dix, in New Jersey, while working with an informant, who joins the group when the FBI is told about a jihadist video they took into a shop to be duplicated.

23. *JFK Airport* (3), 2007: A small group, working with an informant, plots to blow up the fuel lines serving JFK in New York City.

24. *Vinas* (2), 2008: A New York man travels to Pakistan, is accepted into al-Qaeda, and plots to plant a bomb in the United States, but he is watched and talks after being arrested.

25. *Bronx synagogues* (3), 2009: Four men, with crucial aid from an informant, plot to bomb synagogues in the Bronx, New York City, and to shoot down a plane at a military base.

26. *Little Rock* (4), 2009: An American man travels to the Middle East to get training, but fails, and upon return works as a lone wolf, eventually shooting and killing one soldier at a military recruitment center in Little Rock, Arkansas.

27. *Boyd and Quantico* (2), 2009: A complicated conspiracy in North Carolina, which includes an informant, to gather weapons, possibly with Quantico Marine Corps Base as its target.

28. *Zazi* (2), 2009: An Afghan American and two friends travel to Pakistan to join the Taliban but are recruited by al-Qaeda to plant bombs on the New York City subways instead, and they fall under police surveillance.

29. *Springfield* (3), 2009: A jihadist plots, along with informants, to set off a bomb in Springfield, Illinois.

30. *Dallas skyscraper* (3), 2009: A Jordanian on a student visa arouses interest from the FBI in his Internet postings, and, together with three agents, tries to detonate a fake bomb in the basement of a Dallas skyscraper.

31. *Mehanna* (2), 2009: A well-educated Muslim jihadist may have plotted briefly to shoot up a shopping center in the Boston area, and he tries to join the insurgency in the Middle East but is arrested for spreading jihadist propaganda.

32. *Fort Hood* (4), 2009: A military psychiatrist, acting as a lone wolf, shoots up a military deployment center in Fort Hood, Texas, killing twelve soldiers and one civilian, shortly before he is supposed to be deployed to Afghanistan.

33. *The underwear bomber* (4), 2009: A Nigerian man tries to blow up a U.S.-bound airliner with explosives hidden in his underwear, but he is subdued by passengers and crew.

34. *Times Square* (4), 2010: A Pakistani American gets training in Pakistan and on his own tries, but fails, to set off a car bomb in Times Square, New York City.

35. *Alaska* (3), 2010: A Muslim convert in a remote Alaska town plots the assassination of twenty people with the aid of an informant.

36. *Parcel bombs on cargo planes* (2), 2010: An effort by al-Qaeda in the Arabian Peninsula to set off parcel bombs that have been implanted in printer cartridges on cargo planes bound for the United States is disrupted by an insider.

37. *DC Metro bomb plot* (3), 2010: A Pakistani American aids FBI operatives posing as al-Qaeda, in a plot to bomb the Washington, DC, Metro.

38. *Oregon* (3), 2010: A teenage Somali American jihadist, unable to go abroad to fight, works with FBI operatives, apparently alerted by his father, to set off a van bomb at a Christmas-tree lighting ceremony in Portland, Oregon.

39. *DC Metro Facebook* (2), 2010: A Virginia man brags without substance to a female Facebook correspondent that he will bomb the Washington Metro soon but is quickly arrested for making interstate threats.

40. *Baltimore* (3), 2010: A Baltimore man seeks allies on Facebook for violent jihad, and the FBI supplies him with an informant and with a fake SUV bomb, with which he tries to blow up a military recruitment center.

41. *Texas* (2), 2011: A Saudi student in Texas, flunking out and displaying intense discontent on his blog and Facebook profile, is arrested after buying bomb-making materials and considering potential targets, including crowded streets in distant New York City and a local residence of former president George W. Bush.

42. *Manhattan's pair of lone wolves* (3), 2011: A mentally ill U.S. citizen, with an accomplice and undercover officer, upset with how the United States treats Muslims around the world, purchases weapons as the first step in a plot to blow up synagogues, the Empire State Building, and other targets in New York and New Jersey.

43. *Pentagon shooter* (2), 2011: A U.S. marine reservist with jihadist literature shoots at military buildings in the Washington, D.C., area and is arrested as he seeks to desecrate the graves of veterans of the Iraq and Afghanistan wars.

44. *Seattle* (3), 2011: Two financially destitute men, alarmed over U.S. foreign policy, are arrested in Seattle after they purchase an FBI-supplied machine gun that they plan to use in attacking a military recruiting center, after they save up enough money to purchase bullets and other materials.

45. *Abdo* (2), 2011: A U.S. Army private, unwilling to wage war on Muslims, is arrested after he buys ammunition and materials to explode a bomb in a restaurant popular with soldiers.

46. *Model planes* (3), 2011: Seeking to "decapitate" the U.S. "military center," a mentally ill hobbyist plots with police operatives to attack the Pentagon and Capitol with remote-controlled model planes bearing explosives, and then to shoot at people fleeing the buildings.

47. *Iran and Scarface* (3), 2011: An Iranian American used-car salesman from Texas, nicknamed "Scarface" for the results of an earlier street brawl, is engaged for a promised $1.5 million by members of the Iranian government to arrange for a Mexican drug cartel to blow up Saudi Arabia's ambassador in a Washington restaurant, but he is foiled by an undercover Drug Enforcement Agency operative who was wired $100,000 as a down payment for the job.

48. *Pimentel* (3), 2011: A naturalized U.S. citizen and Muslim convert, hostile to U.S. military ventures in the Middle East, seeks to make pipe bombs using matchstick heads to attack various targets.

49. *Tampa* (3), 2012: Under suspicion after he walked into a store seeking to purchase an al-Qaeda flag, an Albanian American loner plots in Tampa with a police operative to detonate a car bomb, fire an assault rifle, wear an explosive belt, take hostages, and bomb nightclubs, a police center, a bridge, and a Starbucks coffee shop to avenge wrongs against Muslims and to bring terror to his "victims' hearts."

50. *Capitol bomber* (3), 2012: A Moroccan man who overstays his visa for years, and is thrown out of his apartment for nonpayment of rent, concludes that the war on terror is a war on Muslims, so he plots with FBI operatives and is arrested as he seeks to carry out a suicide bombing at the Capitol Building.

51. *Chicago bar* (3), 2012: An unemployed and apparently retarded eighteen-year-old Egyptian American issues some violent jihadist emails and Internet postings contending that the United States is at war with Islam, and he attracts the attention of the FBI, which sends agents who gain his confidence and, supply him with a fake bomb that he parks outside a Chicago bar (which he said was filled with "the evilest people"). He is then is arrested when he attempts to detonate the bomb from a nearby alley.

52. *Bombing the Federal Reserve Bank* (3), 2012: A college flunkout from Bangladesh uses his parents' life savings to study in the United States, and while working as a busboy in Manhattan, reaches out on Facebook, obtains the help of the FBI to do something that will "shake the whole country," and is arrested when he tries to remotely set off an FBI-supplied bomb planted at the Federal Reserve Bank.

53. *The brothers* (2), 2012: Two brothers in Florida plot to set off a bomb in New York in revenge for U.S. drone attacks in Afghanistan but are arrested before getting far beyond bicycling around Manhattan, looking for targets.

54. *Boston Marathon* (4), 2013: Two Chechen American brothers, working alone, detonate two homemade bombs in a crowd of bystanders at the Boston Marathon, killing three, and then are killed or captured a few days later after an exhaustive and dramatic manhunt.

55. *Wichita airport* (3), 2013: A worker at the Wichita, Kansas, airport plots with FBI agents to detonate a car bomb at the airport.

56. *Rochester* (3), 2014: A local man, in sympathy with Islamic State militants, plots with FBI operatives to shoot and kill members of the U.S. military.

57. *Cincinnati* (3), 2015: A young local loner, in sympathy with ISIS, plots with FBI operatives to set off a bomb at the Capitol Building in Washington, D.C.

58. *Aurora* (3), 2015: Unable to travel abroad to fight because of a felony conviction for robbing a McDonalds, an Illinois man plots with FBI operatives to "unleash the lion" by attacking a local National Guard Armory.

59. *Two women in Queens* (3), 2015: Protesting that "It's war" and "Protests don't work" and "Why can't we be some real bad bitches?" two women, one in communication with al-Qaeda in Yemen, try to fabricate bombs with the aid of an undercover officer.

60. *Fort Riley* (3), 2015: A young man declaring on Facebook about being killed in jihad plots with FBI operatives to explode a 1,000-pound bomb at a nearby military base.

61, *Ohio returnee from Syria* (2), 2015: A Somali American, actively communicating about his plans on social media, travels to the Middle East, stays about a month, receives some training, returns, and may have planned to commit violence

62. *Shooting at a Muhammad cartoon exhibit* (4), 2015: Two men drive from Arizona and open fire at a Prophet Muhammad cartoon exhibit and contest in Garland, Texas, and are killed by police.

Case Types

1. An Islamist extremist conspiracy or connection that, in the view of the authorities, might eventually develop into a plot to commit violence in the United States.

2. An Islamist extremist terrorist plot to commit violence in the United States, no matter how embryonic, that is disrupted, but not by infiltration of a police operative.

3. An Islamist extremist plot to commit violence in the United States that is essentially created or facilitated in a major way by the authorities via infiltration of a police operative, followed by arrest of the plotters when enough evidence is accumulated.

4. An Islamist extremist terrorist or terrorist group that reaches the stage of committing, or trying to commit, violence in the United States.

Cases of Efforts to Go Abroad

98. *New York Stock Exchange,* 2010: Three men seek to join the fight against
    the United States in the Middle East and find a couple of operatives
    in Yemen who agree to help them (and after being arrested, identify
    them), but only after the men send tens of thousands of dollars and case
    the New York Stock Exchange for a possible attack.
99. *Toledo,* 2006: Three men in Toledo, Ohio, seek to join the fight against
    the United States in the Middle East but fail to get there while
    attracting the attention of an informant who trains them.

Appendix B   Assessing the Costs Inflicted by Terrorism

To view the spectrum of damage caused by terrorism from all sources (not just Islamist ones), we make use of two widely used terrorism databases—the University of Maryland's Global Terrorism Database (GTD) and the RAND Database of Worldwide Terrorism Incidents. We focus, in particular, on terrorism damage in the United States and the United Kingdom.

The Global Terrorism Database (GTD) is collated by the National Consortium for the Study of Terrorism and Responses to Terrorism (START) at the University of Maryland. It is an open-source database that includes information on terrorist events around the world, from 1970 through 2013. For each of the more than 140,000 GTD incidents, information is available on the date and location of the incident, on the weapons used and nature of the target, on the number of casualties, and on any known groups or individuals responsible.[1]

Our analysis of the GTD applies the following criteria for a terrorist attack: (1) it must be aimed at attaining a political, economic, religious, or social goal, (2) there must be evidence of an intention to coerce, intimidate, or convey some other message to a larger audience (or audiences) than the immediate victims, (3) the action is outside the context of legitimate warfare activities in that it targets noncombatants, and (4) there is essentially no doubt as to whether the incident was intended to be an act of terrorism. We then define an attack as being a success if it causes loss of life or property damage.

The RAND Database of Worldwide Terrorism Incidents covers over 40,000 attacks worldwide for the period 1968 to 2009.[2] There is no definition of terrorism that all can agree on, and the RAND database definition differs from that of the GTD: violence or the threat of violence calculated to create fear and alarm, intended to coerce certain actions, motived by a political objective, and generally directed against civilian targets. It can be perpetrated either by a group or by an individual.

Applying the GTD, table B-1 shows that few terrorist attacks within the United States over the 1970–2013 period killed anyone and that very few killed more than two people. And only seven of these attacks (three excluding the 9/11 attacks) resulted in the death of more than ten people. Terrorism statistics for the United Kingdom find a slightly higher frequency of terrorist attacks that inflict multiple fatalities, but the overall patterns are similar.[3]

The fatalities per terrorist attack for the 1968–2009 period and for various regions around the world from the RAND Database are shown in figure B-1. The number of attacks that have killed more than one or two people in North America and Europe is low, while the threat environment is more dire in other regions. Yet, although Southeast Asia and Oceania suffer more frequent attacks, few of these kill more than three people. As we would expect, attacks in the Middle East and Persian Gulf are the most deadly, with 511 attacks killing 10 to 50 people, and 65 attacks killing 50 to 500 people. The worst attack, the second largest in history, killed nearly 800 people in a poor rural area in Iraq in 2007, when four truck bombs were detonated in two towns in Yazidi.

Terrorism inflicts not only casualties and human suffering but economic loss as well. In addition to direct physical damage, economic costs can arise from drops in tourism, business, or other economic activity, and these losses can be considerable.

The GTD provides estimates of property damage that have been inflation-adjusted to 2014 dollars. We then add to this Robinson's value of life of $7.5 million for each fatality, and estimate other indirect losses, such as loss of tourism and loss of GDP, to arrive at a total loss for each large terrorist attack in the GTD for the United States and the United Kingdom. A summary of total losses for such attacks is shown in table B-2.

Figure B-2 shows that the total loss is generally less than $1 million for the average terrorist attack in the United States, while catastrophic damage in excess of $1 billion is limited to a few isolated instances. And while any death is tragic, the most likely outcome from a deadly terrorist attack is one

TABLE B-1 Frequency of Fatalities per Terrorist Attack That Causes Loss of Life or Property Damage in the United States and the United Kingdom, 1970–2013

Number of Fatalities from a Single Terrorist Attack	Frequency			
	United States	Great Britain	Northern Ireland	United Kingdom
0	923	336	851	1187
1	126	45	1165	1210
2	21	9	119	128
3		4	37	41
4	3		18	18
5	1	2	8	10
6	2	2	6	8
7	1	2	1	3
8			1	1
9			1	1
10			1	1
11	1		1	1
12				
13	1	1		1
14			1	1
15			1	1
16			1	1
17				
18				
19				
20				
21		1		1
22				
23				
24				
25				
26		1		1
27				
28			1	1
29				
30				
40	1			
168	1			
184	1			
270		1		1
1,376	2			

Source: START, Global Terrorism Database.

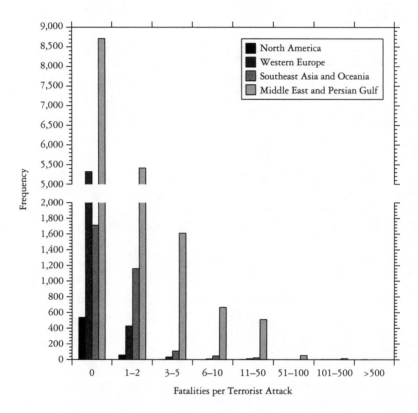

FIGURE B-1 Frequency of Fatalities per Terrorist Attack, 1968–2009
Source: RAND Database of Worldwide Terrorism Incidents

TABLE B-2 Total Economic Loss, Including Loss of Life, for Large Terrorist
Attacks in the United States and the United Kingdom

Country	Location	Year	Fatalities	Total Economic Loss
UNITED STATES				
LaGuardia Airport Bombing	New York	1975	11	$250 million
World Trade Center	New York	1993	6	$1 billion
Murrah Federal Building	Oklahoma City	1995	168	$3 billion
9/11: World Trade Center	New York	2001	2,751	$180 billion
9/11: Pentagon	Washington	2001	184	$10 billion
9/11: UA Flight 93	Pennsylvania	2001	40	$5 billion
Anthrax Postal Attacks	—	2001	5	$6 billion
Fort Hood Shooting	Texas	2009	13	$100 million
Boston Marathon Bombing	Boston	2013	4	$500 million
UNITED KINGDOM				
Pub Bombings	Birmingham	1974	21	$200 million
Omagh Bombing	Omagh	1998	28	$250 million
Pan Am Flight 103	Lockerbie	1988	270	$3 billion
Baltic Exchange Bombing	London	1992	3	$4 billion
Manchester City Bombing	Manchester	1996	0	$1.5 billion
Bishopgate Bombing	London	1993	1	$3 billion
Shankill Road Bombing	Belfast	1993	9	$150 million
Kings Cross Station	London	2005	27	$1 billion
Tavistock Square	London	2005	14	$1 billion
Liverpool Street Station	London	2005	8	$1 billion
Edgeware Road Station	London	2005	7	$1 billion

Source: START, Global Terrorism Database.

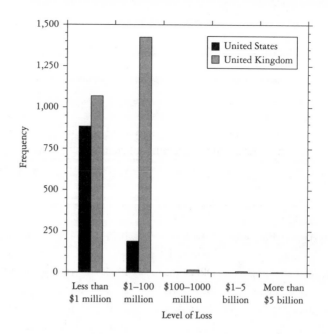

FIGURE B-2 Total Losses, 1970–2013, for the United States and the United Kingdom

or perhaps two fatalities. The average loss per successful attack in the United States is skewed to a high $400 million, owing to the large influence of the 9/11 attacks on the average, but it is only $10 million if we omit the 9/11 attacks. For the United Kingdom, the mean loss is around $20 million per attack, which increases to $50 million if we exclude Northern Ireland from the calculations.[4]

Appendix C   Marginal Costs and Benefits of FBI Counterterrorism Expenditures

THE COUNTERTERRORISM BUDGET for the FBI in 2001 was approximately $600 million in 2014 dollars. We will assume that this expenditure reduced the terrorism risk by 50 percent and that doubling the expenditure to $1.2 billion by 2003 reduced the remaining (residual) risk by 50 percent, for a total risk reduction of 75 percent. And we will assume that each additional $600 million increment in counterterrorism expenditure reduces the residual risk by another 50 percent. Thus, the total risk reduction for expenditures of $1.2, $1.8, $2.4, and $3 billion is 75 percent, 87.5 percent, 93.8 percent, and 96.9 percent, respectively.[1] Hence, we posit that by its efforts the bureau with a counterterrorism budget of $3 billion in 2014 reduced risk—the consequences and/or the probability of an otherwise successful attack—by nearly 97 percent.

These estimates are likely to err on the generous side because additional increments in expenditure are unlikely to generate the same return as the initial (2001) expenditure. As noted in chapter 5, security measures that are at once effective and relatively inexpensive are generally the first to be implemented, and thus the first dollars spent on counterterrorism measures are more likely to be worthwhile—that is, to be cost-effective—than the last are.

In this book, as in tables 5-3, 6-1, 7-1, and 9-1, we have mostly assessed major attacks, ones that inflict losses from $100 million to $5 trillion. However, as figure B-2 in the previous appendix shows, almost all terrorist attacks cause considerably less damage than $100 million and attacks inflicting higher losses are very unlikely—less than 1 percent of terrorist attacks in the United States or the United Kingdom are of this magnitude, according to GTD figures.

Although large terrorist attacks are rare, they are understandably of the greatest concern both to homeland security officials and to the general public. From the terrorist's perspective, then, it makes sense to attempt attacks that are large and devastating. Terrorist attacks inflicting more than $100 million in damage in the United States have occurred on only ten occasions in the forty-five years from 1970 through 2014. They are arrayed in table C-1. The table supplies a rough estimate of the total costs of the damage each inflicted.

We will assume that, if a large attack were to occur, there is a 10 percent likelihood that it would inflict damage equivalent to one of these ten attacks. And we will further assume that the benefit of a security measure is directly proportional to the damage that would have been inflicted by the terrorist attack it deters, disrupts, or protects against: if the damage doubles, the benefit of a risk-reducing measure, we assume, also doubles.

Under those assumptions, we can calculate the probability that the benefit of a security measure will exceed its cost over the set of equally likely scenarios. Consider, for example, a situation in which a $600 million security measure is solely responsible for preventing each year a large terrorist attack that would otherwise have inflicted $1 billion in damage—that is, it reduces the risk of such an event by 100 percent. Under that condition, table C-1 shows that the probability that the benefit of the security measure will exceed its cost is 70 percent over the ten attack scenarios. This is because, if the security measure is cost-effective when it disrupts on its own an attack that would otherwise inflict $1 billion in damage each year, it will also be cost-effective if the benefit it provides rises proportionately so that it can solely disrupt any of the six, equally likely terrorist attack scenarios on the list that inflict even greater damage.

TABLE C-1   Probability of Exceeding a Loss for Large Terrorist Attacks

Terrorist Attack	Total Loss Inflicted	Probability of Higher Loss
Fort Hood Shooting	$100 million	100%
LaGuardia Airport Bombing	$250 million	90%
Boston Marathon Bombing	$500 million	80%
World Trade Center Bombing	$1 billion	70%
Oklahoma City Bombing	$3 billion	60%
9/11: UA Flight 93	$5 billion	50%
Anthrax Postal Attacks	$6 billion	40%
9/11: Pentagon	$10 billion	30%
9/11: World Trade Center, North	$90 billion	20%
9/11: World Trade Center, South	$90 billion	20%

Following this approach, table C-2 shows the probability that an expenditure will generate enough benefit to justify its cost for large attacks—ones that inflict $100 million or more in damage. This is calculated for various levels of counterterrorism expenditures (with assumed increases in risk reduction as expenditures rise) and for a range of attack probabilities—the annual probability that a successful large-scale attack will occur in the absence of the FBI's counterterrorism efforts.

As can be seen, the 2001 expenditure of $600 million has the highest chance of being cost-effective. Clearly, no level of expenditure generates enough benefit to justify its cost when the attack probability is less than 50 percent. However, at higher attack probabilities there is a more than 50 percent chance that a 2001 expenditure of $600 million is cost-effective.

If, without any FBI counterterrorism measures in place and where there would be five otherwise successful large-size terrorist attacks each year (the 500 percent line in table C-2), the spending of $600 million per year on FBI counterterrorism measures would deter, disrupt, or protect against half of those attacks, and there is consequently a 90 percent likelihood that security

TABLE C-2 Probability That Benefit Exceeds the Cost for FBI Counterterrorism Expenditures

Annual Probability of a Successful Large-scale Attack in the Absence of the FBI's Counterterrorism Efforts	Annual FBI Counterterrorism Expenditure and Total Risk Reduction				
	$600 million 2001	$1.2 billion 2003	$1.8 billion	$2.4 billion	$3 billion 2014
	50% risk reduction	75% risk reduction	87.5% risk reduction	93.8% risk reduction	96.9% risk reduction
1 percent	0%	0%	0%	0%	0%
5 percent	20%	20%	20%	20%	20%
10 percent	20%	20%	20%	20%	20%
50 percent	60%	50%	50%	40%	30%
100 percent	60%	60%	60%	60%	50%
200 percent	70%	70%	60%	60%	60%
500 percent	90%	80%	80%	70%	70%
1,000 percent	90%	90%	90%	80%	80%

The table deals with large terrorist attacks, ones inflicting more than $100 million in damage. It is assumed that as expenditures rise, they reduce risks from 50 percent in 2001 to 96.9 percent in 2014. An annual attack probability of 100 percent denotes one attack per year; one of 500 percent denotes five attacks per year.

measures would be worth their cost. For counterterrorism expenditures above 2001 levels (assuming that corresponding increase in risk reduction), the probability that the expenditure will be cost-effective declines to 70 or 80 percent.

If the attack probability is only one attack per year (the 100 percent line), the chance that FBI counterterrorism expenditures will be cost-effective is 60 percent for an expenditure of $600 million, but only 50 percent for current expenditures of $3 billion.

Thus, we begin to see diminishing returns: even when we assume that higher counterterrorism expenditures increase the risk reduction markedly, this increase is not enough to outweigh the additional costs of providing for this reduction in risk. FBI counterterrorism expenditures of up to $1.2 billion—the 2001 or 2003 levels of expenditure—seem to be optimal. Expenditures above this level are less likely to be worthwhile.

We can look at this in another way. According to table C-1, the median loss from a "large" terrorist attack is $4 billion: half of such attacks will cause losses lower than that figure, and half will result in higher losses. The net benefit as a function of the level of counterterrorism expenditure and of the attack probability is arrayed in table C-3. If there is one large attack once every two years (the 50 percent line), the 2001 FBI expenditure has the highest net benefit. However, if there is expected to be one terrorist attack in the absence of the FBI's counterterrorism measures each year (the 100 percent line), the bureau's costs and efforts in 2003 are optimal, and spending above that level results in a reduction in net benefit. Only when there would have been at least five attacks per year without the FBI expenditures (the 500 percent line) would current FBI counterterrorism expenditures be justified, assuming, of course, that these efforts reduce risk by an impressive 96.9 percent.

At the bottom of table C-3 we extrapolate to determine that the likelihood of a large attack needs to be higher than 30 percent (suggesting one large $4 billion attack every three years) for 2001 levels of counterterrorism expenditure to be cost-effective. For current expenditures of $3 billion per year, that probability needs to be 78 percent, or nearly one every year. A relevant consideration here, of course, is that there has been no such attack—or anything remotely close to it—in the United States since 2001. Nor has there been an attack that destructive anywhere in the developed world since 2005.

TABLE C-3 Net Benefit in Billions of Dollars for FBI Counterterrorism Expenditures

Annual Probability of a Successful $4 Billion Attack in the Absence of the FBI's Counterterrorism Efforts	Annual FBI Counterterrorism Expenditure and Total Risk Reduction				
	$600 million *2001*	$1.2 billion *2003*	$1.8 billion	$2.4 billion	$3 billion *2014*
	50% risk reduction	75% risk reduction	87.5% risk reduction	93.8% risk reduction	96.9% risk reduction
1 percent	−0.6	−1.2	−1.8	−2.4	−3.0
5 percent	−0.5	−1.1	−1.6	−2.2	−2.8
10 percent	−0.4	−0.9	−1.5	−2.0	−2.6
50 percent	**0.4**	0.3	−0.1	−0.5	−1.1
100 percent	1.4	**1.8**	1.7	1.4	0.9
200 percent	3.4	4.8	**5.2**	5.1	4.8
500 percent	9.4	13.8	15.7	16.3	**16.4**
1,000 percent	19.4	28.8	33.2	35.1	**35.8**

Break-even Analysis

The annual probability of otherwise successful attacks required for FBI counterterrorism expenditures to be cost-effective for a large-scale attack causing $4 billion in losses

30%	40%	52%	64%	78%

This table assumes that FBI counterterrorism expenditures reduce risks from 50 percent in 2001 to 96.9 percent in 2014, and it is concerned with successful attacks inflicting $4 billion in losses. The boxed value indicates optimal expenditure for each attack probability. (There is no box in column 4 because $2.4 billion is not optimal for any attack probability.) After a successful terrorist attack, a co-benefit can be derived from the prompt identification and arrest of the terrorists and their supporters. Hence, co-benefit = probability of a successful attack absent security measures × probability that attack is not thwarted by security measures × proportion of attacks where FBI efforts lead to prompt identification or apprehension of suspects × percentage reduction in losses × losses sustained in the successful attack. We assume that the FBI is the lead agency that identifies, locates, and/or apprehends the suspects quickly in 50 percent of successful attacks, and this reduces the follow-on consequences of terrorism by a modest 25 percent. For an annual probability of a successful attack in the absence of security measures of 500 percent (5 attacks per year), 96.9 percent risk reduction, and losses from a successful attack of $4 billion, the co-benefit is 5 × 1 − 0.969 × 0.5 × 0.25 × $4 billion, or $77.5 million. Adding these co-benefits to the net benefits in table C-3 has a minor effect on the results and is accordingly ignored in our calculations. An annual attack probability of 100 percent denotes one attack per year; a negative value denotes a net loss.

NOTES

Introduction Counting Ghosts

1. Bush, *Decision Points,* 153–54.
2. Sale, "US al Qaida Cells Attacked"; Gertz, "5,000 in U.S. Suspected of Ties to al Qaeda."
3. Sale, "US al Qaida Cells Attacked."
4. Priest and Arkin, *Top Secret America,* 86 (organizations), 25–26 (listing), 12 (covert).
5. Priest and Arkin, *Top Secret America,* 86.
6. Graff, *The Threat Matrix,* 398. Mudd, *Takedown,* 69.
7. Graff, *The Threat Matrix,* 399.
8. Leinwand, "Psst—Leads from Public to FBI Rise."
9. Mueller and Stewart, *Terror, Security, and Money,* 160.
10. Pinker, *The Better Angels,* 137–38.
11. Trevor-Roper, *The European Witch-Craze,* 154 (stakes), 156 (intercourse), 120-21 (torture), 97 (numerous).
12. Trevor-Roper, *The European Witch-Craze,* 162n2.
13. Trevor-Roper, *The European Witch-Craze,* 172.
14. Pinker, *The Better Angels,* 138.
15. Trevor-Roper, *The European Witch-Craze,* 182 (substitute), 172 (centre).
16. Trevor-Roper, *The European Witch-Craze,* 182.
17. Thurston, *The Witch Hunts.*
18. *FOX News*/Opinion Dynamics Poll, conducted September 23–24, 2003.
19. For the argument that the information supplied was unnecessary for the main Soviet nuclear effort, see Mueller, *Atomic Obsession,* 49–50.
20. Hoover, *Masters of Deceit,* 81. See also McCarthy, "Enemies from Within."
21. Trevor-Roper, *The European Witch-Craze,* 190. See also Thurston, *The Witch Hunts,* 270.

22. O'Connor, *Crisis, Pursued by Disaster,* 278–79.

23. Stephan, *"Communazis,"* xii. See also Mueller, "Extrapolations from a Book about Nothing,"

24. Trevor-Roper, *The European Witch-Craze,* 148–49.

25. Mueller, "What Was the Cold War About?"; Mueller, *War and Ideas,* chap. 5.

26. *FOX News*/Opinion Dynamics Poll, conducted September 23–24, 2003.

27. *CBS News* Poll press release, October 30, 2005.

28. Hoffman, *Inside Terrorism;* Sageman, *The Turn to Political Violence;* Rapoport, "The Four Waves of Modern Terror."

29. Mueller and Stewart, *Terror, Security, and Money,* introduction.

30. For one rather tentative effort, see Miller, "Cheney Assertions of Lives Saved Hard to Support."

31. On these issues, see also Mueller and Stewart, "Witches, Communists, and Terrorists"; Diab, *The Harbinger Theory.*

Chapter 1   Official Perceptions: The Threat Matrix

1. Rudy Giuliani, interview by Miles O'Brien and Carol Costello, "Giuliani: 'Have to Be Relentlessly Prepared,'" *CNN,* July 22, 2005; Mayer, *The Dark Side,* 3; Bush, *Decision Points,* 140, 159; McLaughlin: Baker, *Days of Fire,* 162; McGrath: Baker, *Days of Fire,* 163; Mudd, *Takedown,* 3; Poindexter: Harris, *The Watchers,* 144.

2. Morell, *The Great War of Our Time,* 266–67. On reports about an imminent atomic attack on New York, see Allison, *Nuclear Terrorism,* 2004, 1-6.

3. Baker, *Days of Fire,* 162.

4. Mueller, "Harbinger or Aberration," 45–50; Mueller, "False Alarms"; Mueller, "Blip or Step Function?"; Seitz, "Weaker Than We Think."

5. Tenet and Harlow, *At the Center of the Storm,* 239.

6. Ross, "Secret FBI Report." Architect: McDermott and Meyer, *The Hunt for KSM,* 141.

7. Gaddis, *George F. Kennan,* 403. For the unpleasant suggestion that, if *no one* anticipated this distinct possibility in 1950, the United States might have been better served if those running foreign policy had been replaced by coin-flipping chimpanzees who would at least occasionally get it right from time to time out of sheer luck, see Mueller, "History and Nuclear Rationality."

8. On this issue, see Mueller, "The Bomb's Pretense as Peacemaker"; Mueller, "The Essential Irrelevance of Nuclear Weapons"; Mueller, *Retreat from Doomsday*; Mueller, *Quiet Cataclysm,* ch. 5; Mueller, Atomic Obsession, ch. 3.

9. Gertz, "5,000 in U.S. Suspected of Ties to al Qaeda"; Sale, "U.S. al-Qaida Cells Attacked."

10. Lines, "War on Terror."

11. Mayer, *The Dark Side,* 179–80.

12. Morell, *The Great War of Our Time,* 267.

13. "The Enemy Within," *Frontline,* PBS, October 10, 2006.

14. Clarke, "Ten Years Later."
15. "The Terrorism Index," *Foreign Policy*, July/August 2006. See also Mueller, "New Year Brings Good News."
16. Morell, *The Great War of Our Time*, 130. On the 2007 NIE, see also Sageman, *Leaderless Jihad*, 127–33.
17. Graff, *The Threat Matrix*, 524.
18. Mueller, *Overblown*, 7.
19. *Lehrer NewsHour*, PBS, October 16, 2009.
20. Serrano, "U.S. Faces 'Heightened' Threat Level." For commentary, see MacDonald, "The Ever-Renewing Terror Threat"; Brooks, "Muslim 'Homegrown' Terrorism," 43–44; Mueller, "Why al Qaeda May Never Die."
21. Ignatius, "The bin Laden Plot." See also Silber, "The Mutating al Qaeda Threat."
22. Office of the Press Secretary, White House, remarks by the president at the National Defense University, May 23, 2013.
23. Rather inconsistently, however, Obama ended his speech with what might be taken to be a glimmer of hope. While realistically acknowledging early in the speech that he could not "promise the total defeat of terror," he ended it by positing that we can still somehow achieve victory against it and that we'll know that moment has come when (1) parents take their kids to school, (2) immigrants come to American shores, (3) fans take in a ballgame, (4) a veteran starts a business, (5) city streets bustle, and (6) a citizen shouts at a president. Actually, those things happen now, can easily happen in the future, and have happened repeatedly not only during the decade before the speech but also for all of American history before that.
24. Graff, *The Threat Matrix*, 339.
25. Mudd, *Takedown*, 53. According to CIA Director George Tenet, the menu on the Threat Matrix is refreshed each day. Tenet and Harlow, *At the Center of the Storm*, 232.
26. FBI: Mudd, *Takedown*, 44; CIA: Graff, *The Threat Matrix*, 339.
27. "Between 9/11 and mid-2003," relates George W. Bush, "the CIA reported to me on an average of 400 specific threats each month. The CIA tracked more than twenty separate alleged large-scale attack plots, ranging from possible chemical attack and biological weapons operations in Europe to potential homeland attacks involved [*sic*] sleeper operatives." Bush, *Decision Points*, 153. See also Mudd, *Takedown*, 49.
28. Graff, *The Threat Matrix*, 345.
29. Baker, *Days of Fire*, 157.
30. Graff, *The Threat Matrix*, 400.
31. Graff, *The Threat Matrix*, 344.
32. Mudd, *Takedown*, 43, 55. Also: "Every time the CIA picked up a squib of information, it tossed it into the Threat Matrix." Graff, *The Threat Matrix*, 405.
33. Graff, *The Threat Matrix*, 398.

34. Leinwand, "Psst—Leads from Public to FBI Rise."
35. Graff, *The Threat Matrix,* 399.
36. Greenberg, *Terrorism Trial Report Card;* Theoharis, *The Quest for Absolute Security,* 248, 255–56.
37. Hawley and Means, *Permanent Emergency,* 232.
38. Graff, *The Threat Matrix,* 579. See also Harris, *The Watchers,* 291.
39. Mudd, *Takedown,* 53.
40. Hawley and Means, *Permanent Emergency,* 221–26.
41. Hoffman, Meese, and Roemer, "The FBI," 16–17, 56–58, 116, 118. Although the commission considered the problem to be becoming both worse and more dangerous, it did not appear to suggest the bureau's budget should be appropriately boosted so that all the secondary and tertiary ghosts could be chased in full and increasingly urgent ardor.
42. Mudd, *Takedown,* 55.
43. Baker, *Days of Fire,* 157.
44. Quoted in Jervis, *Why Intelligence Fails,* 166.
45. Graff, *The Threat Matrix,* 345, 19, 489, 345.
46. Goldsmith, *The Terror Presidency,* 72; Tenet: "Virtually every day you would hear something about a possible impending threat that would scare you to death." Tenet and Harlow, *At the Center of the Storm,* 230.
47. Bush, *Decision Points,* 153; Wife: Baker, *Days of Fire,* 157.
48. Mudd, *Takedown,* 33.
49. Graff, *The Threat Matrix,* 400.
50. Goldsmith, *The Terror Presidency,* 72.
51. Graff, *The Threat Matrix,* 411.
52. Goldsmith, *The Terror Presidency,* 72.
53. Adam Garfinkle, conversation with John Mueller, August 28, 2014. See also Garfinkle, "Comte's Caveat," 403–21.
54. Goldsmith, *The Terror Presidency,* 73.
55. Hawley and Means, *Permanent Emergency,* 226.
56. Mudd, *Takedown,* 69.
57. Congressional testimony by Director Mueller can be found through www.fbi.gov/news/testimony.
58. Department of Homeland Security, news release, December 21, 2003.
59. Myers, "Terror Threat Source Called into Question." See also Mueller, *Overblown,* 162. For an array of such predictions, see Mueller and Schricker, "Terror Predictions." See also Nacos, Block-Elkon, and Shapiro, *Selling Fear.*
60. Ross, "Secret FBI Report."
61. Priest and White, "War Helps Recruit Terrorists."
62. "FBI Can't Find Sleeper Cells," *Fox News,* March 10, 2005.
63. George Tenet, on *60 Minutes,* CBS, May 1, 2007.
64. Tenet and Harlow, *At the Center of the Storm,* 247.
65. Hawley and Means, *Permanent Emergency,* 236.

66. However, see Diab, *The Harbinger Theory*; Mueller, *Overblown*, 45–46; Mueller and Stewart, "Hardly Existential"; Mueller and Stewart, *Terror, Security, and Money*, 20; Healy, "Al Qaeda: Never an 'Existential Threat.'"

67. Harris and Taylor, "Homeland Security Chief Looks Back."

68. Scheuer, *Imperial Hubris*, 160, 177, 226, 241, 242, 250, 252, 263.

69. "All the Time He Needs," *New York Times*, April 16, 2008. For McCain, see, for example, "In Florida, Rivals Focus on Economy and Security," *New York Times*, January 28, 2008, and "Obama Leads McCain in Four Key Battleground States," *Washington Post*, June 26, 2008.

70. Hawley and Means, *Permanent Emergency*, 237. On this issue, see also Carle, *The Interrogator*, 293; Mueller and Stewart, "Hardly Existential."

71. McMahon, "Truth or Gaffe?"

72. Office of the Press Secretary, White House, remarks by President Obama and Prime Minister Cameron, January 16, 2015; Barack Obama, interview by Fareed Zakaria, *CNN*, February 1, 2015.

73. Office of the Press Secretary, White House, remarks by National Security Adviser Susan Rice on the 2015 National Security Strategy, February 6, 2015.

74. Schneier, "Obama Says Terrorism Is Not an Existential Threat."

75. Dozier, "Spy General Unloads."

76. Bush, *Decision Points*, 155.

77. Something similar happened during the cold war with the development of what Robert Johnson calls "nuclear metaphysics." For a discussion, see Mueller, *Atomic Obsession*, 63–67; Johnson, *Improbable Dangers*, 78.

78. Goldsmith, *The Terror Presidency*, 74, emphasis added.

79. *60 Minutes*, CBS, May 1, 2007.

80. Tenet and Harlow, *At the Center of the Storm*, 257; Schneier, "Why Are We Spending $7 Billion on TSA?" The process is hardly new. Two months after Pearl Harbor, columnist Walter Lippmann informed his readers that "the fact that since the outbreak of the Japanese war there has been no important sabotage on the Pacific Coast is a sign that the blow is well-organized and that it is held back until it can be struck with maximum effect." Lippmann, "Fifth Column on the Coast."

81. Sageman, "The Stagnation in Terrorism Research," 573–74. Relevant is Mudd's observation that "the first debriefings might inevitably result in overdramatic, embellished threat reporting that we felt obligated to disseminate." Mudd, *Takedown*, 61.

82. Jervis, "Why Intelligence Fails," 34–35, 161.

83. On this issue, see also Mueller and Stewart, *Terror, Security, and Money*, 13–20.

84. Mueller and Stewart, *Terror, Security, and Money*, 135.

85. On this issue more extensively, see Mueller and Stewart, *Terror, Security, and Money*, 13–20; Sunstein, "Terrorism and Probability Neglect."

86. Tenet and Harlow, *At the Center of the Storm*, 232.

87. Sageman, "The Stagnation in Terrorism Research," 574.

88. Bush, *Decision Points,* 161–62.

89. Department of Homeland Security, *National Infrastructure Protection Plan,* 11.

90. Hawley and Means, *Permanent Emergency,* 61.

91. Jenkins, *Will Terrorists Go Nuclear?,* 250–51.

92. Quoted in Graham, *World at Risk,* 43. For a discussion of the connection between nuclear weapons and sleep disorders, see Mueller, *Atomic Obsession,* ix–xi, 239.

93. Stenersen, *Al-Qaida's Quest for Weapons of Mass Destruction,* 35–36.

94. For the extended argument that the likelihood of atomic terrorism is vanishingly small, see Mueller, *Atomic Obsession,* chs. 12–15. See also Diab, *The Harbinger Theory*; Jenkins, *Will Terrorists Go Nuclear?*; Mueller, "The Truth About al Qaeda"; Lieber and Press, "Why States Won't Give Nuclear Weapons to Terrorists."

95. See www.globalsecurity.org/security/library/report/2003/n0335167.pdf. For similar expressions of alarm, see Allison, *Nuclear Terrorism,* 15; Michael Scheuer, on *60 Minutes,* CBS, November 14, 2004: "probably a near thing." For earlier concerns, see Allison, "Must We Wait for the Nuclear Morning After?," which held that "[i]n the absence of a determined program of action, we have every reason to anticipate acts of nuclear terrorism against American targets before this decade is out."

96. Graff, *The Threat Matrix,* 366. See also Rapoport, "Terrorists and Weapons of the Apocalypse," 49–67; Bergen, "WMD Terrorism Fears Are Overblown."

97. Richard Clarke, the counterterrorism coordinator from the Clinton administration who alarmingly predicted that plague of terrorism after 2006 ("Ten Years After"), has now become an energetic figure in the escalating, and lucrative, concern about cyberterrorism: Clarke and Knake, *Cyber War.*

98. On this issue, see Mueller, *Atomic Obsession,* 11–15. On the history of "WMD" and for data on the use of the term, see Carus, *Defining "Weapons of Mass Destruction."* See also Mueller and Mueller, "The Rockets' Red Glare."

99. Actually, however, the "weapons of mass destruction" supplied to would-be terrorists by the FBI in several cases were essentially "redesigned" to be something other than a weapon—i.e., a fake. This might make them non-WMDs because the law specifically excludes from the category "any device, although originally designed for use as a weapon, which is redesigned for use as a signaling, pyrotechnic, line throwing, safety, or similar device." If defense lawyers have tried to exploit this potential loophole, it doesn't seem to have worked.

100. See also Brooks, "Muslim 'Homegrown' Terrorism," 18–20; Schneier, "Portrait of the Modern Terrorist as an Idiot"; Aaronson, "The Informants"; Aaronson, *The Terror Factory*; Greenwald and Fishman, "Latest FBI Claim."

101. In particular, cases 21, 22, 25, 29, 30, 38, 40, 42, 44, 49, 50, 51, 52, 55, 56.

102. Brooks, "Muslim 'Homegrown' Terrorism," 17; Savage, "F.B.I. Casts Wide Net Under Relaxed Rules for Terror Inquiries."

103. See also Aaronson, *The Terror Factory*, 234.

104. Cases 12, 19, 22, 23, 25, and perhaps 3, 16, and 22. See also Aaronson, *The Terror Factory*, 84, 144.

105. Aaronson, *The Terror Factory*, 44.

106. On this process in a different context, see Sageman, *Leaderless Jihad*, 79.

107. Aaronson, *The Terror Factory*, 151–52.

108. As in cases 3, 10, 11, 12, 14, 16, 19, 21, 22, 23, 25, 29, 30, 35, 37, 38, 40, 41, 42, 44, 46, 48, 49, 50, 51, 52, 55, 56, 57, 59, 60.

109. Jenkins, *Stray Dogs*, 19, 23.

110. Weiser, "3 Men Draw 25-Year Terms in Synagogue Bomb Plot."

111. Finn, "Documents Provide Rare Insight into FBI's Terrorism Stings." See also Greenwald and Fishman, "Latest FBI Claim."

112. Jenkins, *Would-Be Warriors*, 10.

113. Johnston and Shane, "Terror Case Is Called One of the Most Serious."

114. Graff, *The Threat Matrix*, 368. See also Dahl, "The Plots That Failed," 624; Aaronson, *The Terror Factory*, 202–206, 215–16.

115. Cases 42 and 48.

116. Yoo, "Conclusion"; Sofan, "Enemies Domestic."

117. Loy, "Al-Qaeda's Undimmed Threat."

118. Quoted in Lohmann, "Jihad on Main Street," 38–39. Although Lohmann considers the plot to be a "serious" one, she also finds it "unclear" whether the plotters "received top-notch training" (77).

119. Hoffman, "Radicalization and Subversion," 1107.

120. Harris, *The Watchers*, 311.

121. See Mueller and Stewart, *Terror, Security, and Money*, ch. 7.

122. Puhl, "Case 20: Bombing Transatlantic Airliners."

123. "Justice Department Oversight—Part 1—Newsflash," Associated Press release, April 14, 2010.

124. Hays, "Feds: Terror Suspects' Mingling Fed NYC Threat."

125. *PBS NewsHour*, February 18, 2015.

126. See, for example, White House, Office of the Press Secretary, "Fact Sheet: The White House Summit on Countering Violent Extremism," February 18, 2015.

127. Ignatius, "The Internet Isn't to Blame for Radicalization."

128. Cases 5, 10, and 19.

129. See also Gerges, *The Rise and Fall of Al-Qaeda*, 153-67; Pape and Feldman, *Cutting the Fuse*, 76–79; Walt, "Why They Hate Us"; Bergen, "Five Myths About Osama bin Laden"; Fallows, *Blind into Baghdad*, 142; Sageman, *Leaderless Jihad*, 72–82; Mearsheimer, "Imperial by Design." Marc Sageman has provided an arresting comparison with Jewish youths who felt called upon to go abroad to fight for besieged Israel in wars in 1948, 1967, and 1973: *Leaderless Jihad*, 74–75. On the religion issue, see also Patel, *Rethinking Radicalization*, 10, 13, 29.

130. See also Brooks, "Muslim 'Homegrown' Terrorism," 12–14; Patel, *Rethinking Radicalization*; Sedgwick, "The Concept of Radicalization."

131. *60 Minutes* (CBS), November 2, 2014.

132. For sources and context, see "Case 44: Seattle," in Mueller, *Terrorism Since 9/11*.

133. Silber and Bhatt, *Radicalization in the West*.

134. Rashbaum, "S.I. Man Describes Shattered Life."

135. Chang, "Bloomberg in Times Square."

136. Tan, "Case 34: Times Square." For other examples, see Gerges, *The Rise and Fall of Al-Qaeda*, 153-57, 160.

137. See, in particular, Jacobson, *A Divider, Not a Uniter*.

138. See also Sageman, *Leaderless Jihad*; Brooks, "Muslim 'Homegrown' Terrorism," 13–14; Horgan, "Discussion Point"; Jenkins, *Stray Dogs*, 17; Patel, *Rethinking Radicalization*, 12; Horgan, "Can Science Solve Terrorism?"

139. R. Mueller: Isikoff and Hosenball, "The Flip Side of the NIE"; Officer: Gertz, "Al Qaeda Seen in Search of Nukes."

140. Napolitano: Hsu, "Homeland Security Chief Warns of Threat"; Holder: Gerges, *The Rise and Fall of Al-Qaeda*, 7. See also Brooks, "Muslim 'Homegrown' Terrorism."

141. Serrano, "U.S. Faces 'Heightened' Threat Level."

142. Bergen and Hoffman, "Assessing the Terrorist Threat," 4 (mass-casualty), 32 (less sophisticated operations, worrisome trend). See also Mudd, "Evaluating the Al-Qa'ida Threat," 1–4. For additional argument on the unlikelihood of a major attack on the United States, see "Biden: Major Terror Attack on U.S. Unlikely."

143. See cases 2, 5, and 8.

144. Cases 1, 9, 20, 24, 33, and 36.

145. For an extended analysis, see Brooks, "Muslim 'Homegrown' Terrorism." See also Dratel, "Nothing New About Homegrown Terrorism."

146. "Suspect in Seattle Terror Plot Intent on Attacking a Recruiting Station to 'Wake the Muslims Up,'" Associated Press release, June 23, 2011; available at www.oregonlive.com.

147. McClam, "Attorney General Eric Holder Revives Domestic Terror Task Force." For a broader assessment, see Simon, *Lone Wolf Terrorism*.

148. Cases 4, 26, 32, and 53.

149. Abrahms, "Fear of 'Lone Wolf' Misplaced."

150. See also Brooks, "Muslim 'Homegrown' Terrorism," 35–36.

151. Wilson, "From Smiling Coffee Vendor."

152. Apuzzo and Goldman, *Enemies Within*, 109–14.

153. Frieden, "Top U.S. Security Officials Share Afghan-Pakistan Border Concerns."

154. Moreno and Banda, "Prosecutor: Terror Plot Focus was 9/11 Anniversary." Zazi also foolishly attracted attention by racing at more than 90 miles per hour across the country in his bomb-material–laden car. Apuzzo and Goldman, *Enemies Within*, 10.

155. Johnson, "Weakened al-Qaeda Is Still a Threat"; Temple-Raston, "Terrorism Case Shows Range of Investigators' Tools."

156. Gerges, *The Rise and Fall of Al-Qaeda*, 195.

157. Welsh-Huggins, *Hatred at Home*, 65–66.

158. Byman and Shapiro, "Homeward Bound?"; Byman and Shapiro, "Be Afraid." Byman and Shapiro, "We Shouldn't Stop Terrorists from Tweeting." See also Kenner, "Mr. Bean to Jihadi John"; Witt, "Westerners Fighting in Syria Disillusioned."

159. Hoffman, "Scarier Than Bin Laden"; Bergen, "Where You Bin?"

160. Miller, "Al-Qaeda Is Weaker"; Jones, "Think Again: al-Qaeda"; Jones, "Al Qaeda Is Far from Defeated."

161. For example, Hawley and Means, *Permanent Emergency*, 61.

162. Miller, "Al-Qaeda Is Weaker"; Dozier, "Weaker al-Qaida Still Plots."

163. "Boeing 747 Survives Simulation Bomb Blast," *BBC News*, March 4, 2010; Hawley and Means, *Permanent Emergency*, 234.

164. Both discussed in McClure, "Case 36: Parcel Bombs on Cargo Planes."

165. Institute for Economics and Peace, *Global Terrorism Index*, 75.

166. *Fox News Sunday*, June 29, 2014.

167. McCain: Buchanan, "ISIS Poses No Existential Threat"; Graham: Buchanan, "Is ISIS 'an Existential Threat'?"

168. Froomkin, "The Congressional Hyperbole Caucus," emphasis added.

169. Zenko, "Exaggeration Nation."

170. Logiurato, "Defence Secretary: ISIS An 'Imminent' Threat."

171. *PBS NewsHour*, February 13, 2015.

172. Byman, "Five Myths About the Islamic State"; Byman and Williams, "Jihadism's Global Civil War," 13–14. In contrast, see Morell, *The Great War of Our Time*, 305. For similar disputes between al-Qaeda Central and a previous group in Iraq from which ISIS emerged, see Sageman, *Leaderless Jihad*, 53–64; Gerges, *The Rise and Fall of Al-Qaeda*, 108–112.

173. Institute for Economics and Peace, *Global Terrorism Index*, 78. See also Giraldi, "How to Understand the ISIS Threat."

174. For example, see Ignatius, "A Nightmare Group in Syria."

175. Mardini, "The Islamic State Threat Is Overstated."

176. Shatz, "To Defeat the Islamic State"; Sly, "The 'Islamic State' Is Failing"; Sly, "Islamic State Appears to Be Fraying." See also Mueller, "The Islamic State"; Shapiro, *The Terrorist's Dilemma*.

177. Mazzetti, Schmitt, and Landler, "Struggling to Gauge ISIS Threat."

178. "Iraq Crisis: ISIS Militants Threaten UK, Says Cameron," *BBC News*, June 18, 2014.

179. Naylor, "Islamic State Leader Purportedly Urges Muslims to Launch Attacks."

180. Sheehan, *Crush the Cell*, 14; Dickey, *Securing the City*, 118–19. On this phenomenon, see also Mueller, *Overblown*, ch. 2.

181. Schwartz, "We're at Greater Risk."

182. Mueller, *Overblown,* ch. 2. See also Lustick, *Trapped in the War on Terror;* Friedman, Harper, and Preble, *Terrorizing Ourselves;* Schneier, *Beyond Fear;* Furedi, *Culture of Fear;* Fallows, "Declaring Victory."

183. Risen, *Pay Any Price,* xiii.

184. Risen, *Pay Any Price,* 224–25.

185. Risen, *Pay Any Price,* 203.

186. Richardson, "In Security," 11.

187. "All the Time He Needs," *New York Times,* April 16, 2008.

188. Gardner, *Future Babble;* Zenko, "Exaggeration Nation"; Mueller and Schricker, "Terror Predictions"; Nacos, Block-Elkon, and Shapiro, *Selling Fear.*

189. This is discussed more fully on p. 94 in chapter 3.

190. Mueller, *Overblown,* 216n50.

191. "Juval Aviv Interviewed About Possible Thanksgiving Terrorist Attack," December 8, 2008, youtu.be/lfKMOsL084Y. For more on Aviv, see Mueller, *Overblown,* 42.

192. Dozier, "Weaker al-Qaida," 2012.

193. Jenkins, *Would-Be Warriors,* 13.

194. Blalock, Kadiyali, and Simon, "The Impact of Post-9/11 Airport Security Measures"; Blalock, Kadiyali, and Simon, "Driving Fatalities After 9/11"; Kenny, "Airport Security Is Killing Us."

195. Cooper and Block, *Disaster.*

196. Sheridan, "U.S. May Ease Anti-Terror Rules."

197. Priest and Arkin, *Top Secret America,* xviii–xix, 103.

Chapter 2 Public Perceptions: Perpetual Anxiety and War Wariness

1. Atran, *Talking to the Enemy,* xiv.

2. On this issue, see Stouffer, *Communism, Conformity, and Civil Liberties,* ch. 3.

3. See Mueller and Stewart, "Trends in Public Opinion on Terrorism." The data derive from materials deposited at the extensive iPoll collection of the Roper Center for Public Opinion Research at the University of Connecticut, supplemented at times by press releases and reports by the polling agencies and by information posted at www.pollingreport.com.

4. On the behavior of this question over time more broadly, see Mueller, *War and Ideas,* ch. 8.

5. On this issue, see Betts, "Maybe I'll Stop Driving"; Mueller, "Six Rather Unusual Propositions"; Lewis, "The Terror That Failed."

6. See also Nacos, Block-Elkon, and Shapiro, *Selling Fear,* ch. 3; Brooks and Manza, *Whose Rights?,* ch. 3.

7. On this phenomenon, see Mueller, *War, Presidents, and Public Opinion;* Mueller, "Police Work or War?"

8. See also Mueller, "Will Obama's Libya 'Victory' Aid Re-Election Bid?"

9. On this issue, see also Greenwald, *No Place to Hide,* 197–99.

10. On this issue, see also Mueller, *War and Ideas,* 215–17.

11. In contrast, some scholars have argued that support for war is determined by the prospects for success rather than by casualties—that Americans are "defeat phobic" rather than "casualty phobic," and therefore that "persuading the public that a military operation will be successful" is "the linchpin of public support." Gelpi, Feaver, and Reifler, *Paying the Human Costs of War*, 236–37. Essentially, the argument seems to hold that Americans, or at least a substantial portion of them, don't really care how many casualties they suffer so long as their side comes out the winner. This perspective led, in part, to an effort by President George W. Bush to push the idea of "victory" in a set of speeches at the end of 2005. Shane, "Bush's Speech on Iraq Echoes Analyst's Voice." As it happened, after 2007 things actually *did* improve in Iraq for various reasons, to the point where, by 2009 or 2010, some could claim that victory had been achieved. The public clearly got the message: by late 2008, the percentage of people who thought U.S. efforts were making things better had risen from 30 to 46 percent, while those believing they were having no impact had dropped from 51 to 32 percent. And the percentage holding that the United States was making significant progress rose from 36 to 46 percent, while the percentage concluding that it was winning the war rose from 21 to 37 percent. Despite this change, as figure 2-13 suggests, support for the war did not increase during its 4th or 5th year—nor did it do so on measures tapping those who favored the war, those who felt it had been worth the effort or the right decision, or those who favored staying as long as it takes. Successful prosecution of a war, it appears, is unlikely to convert people who have already decided it was not worth the costs. American casualty rates also declined after 2007, but this, too, had no effect on support for the war, thereby confounding predictions that decreasing casualty rates would cause an increase of support, as in Gartner, "The Multiple Effects of Casualties," 105. On this issue, see also Mueller, *War and Ideas*, ch. 9.

12. The data are posed at Mueller and Stewart, "Trends in Public Opinion on Terrorism." See also Smeltz and Daadler, "Foreign Policy in the Age of Retrenchment," 13–14. As was found in earlier wars, asking whether the decision was a "mistake" or whether it was the "right decision" does not seem to make much difference. Mueller, *War, Presidents, and Public Opinion*, 44.

13. Bacevich, *The New American Militarism;* Kagan, *Of Paradise and Power;* Mearsheimer, "Imperial by Design"; Maddow, *Drift;* Putin, "A Plea for Caution from Russia."

14. However, there had been a rise of support for getting more involved in the war in Europe after the fall of France in May 1940. Berinsky, *In Time of War*, 45–52. Unfortunately, no relevant question seems to have been asked by polling agencies both before and after Pearl Harbor to gauge its specific effect.

15. There is another variant: "Since the United States is the most powerful nation in the world, we should go our own way in international matters, not worrying too much about whether other countries agree with us or not." Responses to this formulation follow much the same trajectory as the "stay out" question, but

it has been asked much less frequently. It is excluded from the figure to reduce clutter and to enhance readability.

16. George Bush, "Remarks to the American Legislative Exchange Council," March 1, 1991, www.presidency.ucsb.edu/ws/?pid=19351. On the personal importance of Bush in the drive for war, see Mueller, *Policy and Opinion in the Gulf War,* 49–53.

17. See also Smeltz and Daadler, "Foreign Policy in the Age of Retrenchment," 154.

18. Respectively, Keller, "Our New Isolationism"; Cohen, "An Anchorless World"; Rubin, "Rubio and Others Run from Internationalism."

19. For data, see Mueller and Stewart, "Trends in Public Opinion on Terrorism."

20. On this process, see Mueller, *The Remnants of War,* chs. 7–8; Zenko, "Exaggeration Nation."

21. Mueller, *War and Ideas,* 177.

22. Smeltz, "United in Goals, Divided in Means."

23. Holsti, *Public Opinion and American Foreign Policy,* 266–82. See also Smeltz and Daadler, "Foreign Policy in the Age of Retrenchment," 7–9, 11–12, 28, but also 31.

24. Mueller, "The Iraq Syndrome"; Mueller, "The Iraq Syndrome Revisited"; Mueller, "Iraq Syndrome Redux"; Mueller, *War and Ideas,* 207–10.

25. Reagan, *Public Papers,* 1096.

26. Kearns, *Lyndon Johnson,* 252–53. Johnson's assumption, a popular one, that McCarthyism was impelled by the "loss" of China in 1949 is highly questionable. Much more important in this development would be the Korean War, which came later.

27. Kraus, *The Great Debates,* 538–39.

28. Kearns, *Lyndon Johnson,* 253.

29. Mueller, *War and Ideas,* ch. 8.

30. Over most of the course of the genocide, the three major networks, responding as always to the preferences of their viewers, devoted a total of 29 minutes of their newscasts to a cataclysm in which millions perished in the wake of the American war there. In July 1975, the *New York Times* ringingly editorialized that the silence about the genocide in Cambodia "must be broken" and then ignored the issue in its editorial column for over three years. And when a proposal to intervene was made in 1978 by former peace candidate George McGovern, his plea generated a total of 20 seconds of coverage. Adams and Joblove, "The Unnewsworthy Holocaust," 217–25.

31. Mueller, "Questing for Monsters to Destroy." Indeed, one of Kennan's favorite quotes came from Gibbon: "[T]here is nothing more contrary to nature than the attempt to hold in obedience distant provinces." Gaddis, *Strategies of Containment,* 47.

32. Breslauer, "Ideology and Learning in Soviet Third World Policy"; Jervis, "Was the Cold War a Security Dilemma?," 50.

33. On the rising costs of the Soviet overseas empire at the time, see Wolf et al., *The Costs of Soviet Empire*; Kotkin, "The Kiss of Debt." On Soviet policy, also see Zubok, *A Failed Empire*; Andrew, *The World Was Going Our Way*.

34. On this process, see Mueller, "What Was the Cold War About?" (also in Mueller, *War and Ideas,* ch. 5); Mueller, "Questing for Monsters to Destroy." See also Gould-Davies, "Rethinking the Role of Ideology"; Jervis, "Was the Cold War a Security Dilemma?," 60.

35. Landler and Gladstone, "Chemicals Would Be 'Game Changer.'"

36. Harris, "John Kerry: U.S. Attack."

37. Reilly, "Poll Shows Alabamians Still Support President."

38. *CBS News* Poll Release, June 20–22, 2014.

39. ABC/*Washington Post* Poll Release, June 22, 2014.

40. Ignatius, "A Nightmare Group."

41. See Mueller and Stewart, "Terrorism Poses No Existential Threat."

42. On this issue, see Friedman, Harper, and Preble, *Terrorizing Ourselves*; Thrall and Cramer, *American Foreign Policy*; Lustick, *Trapped in the War on Terror*; Diab, *The Harbinger Theory*; Preble and Mueller, *A Dangerous World?*; Mueller, *Overblown*; Johnson, *Improbable Dangers*.

43. Politico poll: Likely Voters in Competitive U.S. House and Senate Races, July 3–13, 2014.

44. *CBS News* Poll Release, June 20–22, 2014.

45. *CBS News* Poll Release, March 26, 2015. See John Mueller, "Why the ISIS Threat Is Totally Overblown," *theweek.com*, July 23, 2015.

46. In addition, as the United States works its way out of—or away from—the costly 9/11-induced wars with an increasing wariness about using ground troops, the need for having a very large military force-in-being may come under question. See Mueller, "Embracing Threatlessness."

47. Compare Berinsky, *In Time of War*.

48. Western, *Selling Intervention and War*, especially 5, 20–21, 179, 229; Mueller, *War and Ideas*, 216–17. Another way to express this is to suggest that the message has "activated latent beliefs and dispostions." Brooks and Manza, *Whose Rights?*, 157n3.

49. Kean and Hamilton, "Today's Rising Terrorist Threat," 8, 13, 37.

50. As the figure shows, concern about international terrorism was already high in 1998 at the time of the bombings of two U.S. embassies in Africa. Figure 2-15 is developed from responses to the question as deposited at the Roper Public Opinion Research Center. For a somewhat different array, see Smeltz and Daalder, "Foreign Policy in the Age of Retrenchment," 20.

51. "The New Threats from 'Bin Laden,'" *BBC News*, October 6, 2002.

52. Cases 4, 26, 32, and 53, in appendix A.

53. It might be added that the number of homicides committed by Muslim extremists within the United States represents one-fiftieth of 1 percent of the total. Schanzer, Kurzman, and Mooza, "Anti-Terror Lessons of Muslim-Americans."

54. The same was true about domestic communist violence during the cold war. FBI informant Herbert Philbrick's confessional book *I Led Three Lives* at no point documents a single instance of communist violence or planned violence. Nevertheless, violence became a central focus when his story was transmuted into a popular television series.

55. For a fuller discussion, see note 4 in chapter 4, this volume. See also Mueller and Stewart, *Terror, Security and Money,* 42.

56. See also Mueller, *Overblown*; Nacos, Block-Elkon, and Shapiro, *Selling Fear.* For an array of such predictions, see Mueller and Schricker, "Terror Predictions."

57. On this issue, see also Brooks and Manza *Whose Rights?*, 154. On the terrorism industry, see Mueller, *Overblown*, ch. 2. On more recent media hype, see Mueller, "America's Terrorism Fear Factory Rolls On"; Greenwald and Fishman, "NPR Is Laundering CIA Talking Points."

58. Harris, *The Watchers*, 137.

59. Mueller, *Overblown,* 159.

60. Gerges, *The Rise and Fall of Al-Qaeda*, 194.

61. On the important impact the anthrax attacks had in the White House, see Baker, *Days of Fire,* 162–63, 170.

62. On the impact of the shoe bomber episode on President Bush, see Bush, *Decision Points,* 164–65.

63. On the special and persistent fear that has traditionally been evoked by nuclear and other "weapons of mass destruction," see Mueller, *Atomic Obsession.*

64. This is suggested as well by some of the experiments conducted by Brooks and Manza. "Getting people to think about the specter of terrorism," they conclude, "tends to bolster anew their willingness to support coercive new measures." *Whose Rights?*, 104.

65. See Schneier, "Portrait of the Modern Terrrorist"; Gerges, *The Rise and Fall of Al-Qaeda*, 192 Conceivably, the visibility of Muslim women in headscarves contributes as a continuing semiconscious reminder.

66. On this issue, see also Brooks and Manza, *Whose Rights?*, 147; Brooks, "Muslim 'Homegrown' Terrorism," 44, 45–46; German, *Thinking Like a Terrorist,* ix.

67. Jenkins, *Would-Be Warriors,* 8–9. See also LaFree, Dugan, and Miller, *Putting Terrorism in Context.*

68. Jenkins, *Would-Be Warriors,* 8.

69. Slovic, Fischhoff, and Lichtenstein, "Facts and Fears"; Stewart and Melchers, *Probabilistic Risk Assessment,* 208–16.

70. Gilbert, "If Only Gay Sex Caused Global Warming."

71. For some earlier reflections, see Mueller, "Police Work or War?"

72. This issue is discussed more fully in chapter 4 in this volume for the 9/11 planners. Historian Samuel Eliot Morison's conclusion is that the Pearl Harbor attack, "far from being a 'strategic necessity,' as the Japanese claimed even after the war, was a strategic imbecility." Morison, *The Rising Sun in the Pacific,* 132.

73. For exaggerations of the destruction at Pearl Harbor: Mueller, "Pearl Harbor," 187-88; Mueller, *Quiet Cataclysm*, 97–98. The reported death toll for 9/11 was initially much higher than it turned out to be: Lipton, "The Toll."

74. For the conclusion that Japan entered the war "on a shoestring," see Barnhart, *Japan Prepares for Total War.*

75. As H. P. Wilmott notes, "not a single operation planned after the start of the war [by the Japanese] met with success." Wilmott, *Empires in the Balance*, 91. See also Mueller, "Pearl Harbor"; Mueller, *Quiet Cataclysm*, ch. 7.

76. Before Pearl Harbor, President Franklin Roosevelt's approval rating was quite high—72 percent—but when next tapped, a month after Pearl Harbor, it had risen to 84 percent. Cantril and Strunk, *Public Opinion*, 756. The impact of September 11 on President George W. Bush's ratings was similar—except that he had further to go. Only about 53 percent expressed approval of the job he was doing before the attacks, but this abruptly soared into the 80s, even into the 90s in some polls, after the attacks—the greatest uptick in approval ever recorded. Mueller, "Police Work or War?" Most rally effects tend to be spike-like. Mueller, *War, Presidents, and Public Opinion*; Mueller, *Policy and Opinion in the Gulf War*. However, in these cases, the decline in presidential approval from stratospheric highs was very gradual. Two years after December 7, when the polls last sought to tap Roosevelt's approval rating, it still stood at 66 percent. And two years after September 11, Bush's rating had declined only into the 60s, a particularly impressive achievement in light of his tepid pre–September 11 approval ratings. Mueller, *War and Ideas,* 193.

77. On these issues, see Mueller, "Pearl Harbor"; Mueller, *Quiet Cataclysm,* ch. 7.

78. Russett, *No Clear and Present Danger,* 58–60.

79. Mueller, "Pearl Harbor"; Mueller, *Quiet Cataclysm,* ch. 7; Mueller, *Overblown,* ch. 3.

80. Simon, *The Terrorist Trap,* 233–34.

81. Zenko, "Mission Improbable." See also Van Linschoten, Van Linschoten, and Kuehn, *An Enemy We Created;* Wright, *The Looming Tower.*

82. Mueller, *Policy and Opinion in the Gulf War,* 160, 214.

83. Mueller, "The Perfect Enemy."

84. Mueller, *Policy and Opinion in the Gulf War,* 90.

85. Mueller, *Policy and Opinion in the Gulf War,* 103–4. Expectations: see Toner, "Democrats Don't Need a Sacrificial Lamb"; Quindlen, "The Microwave War." A comparison might be made with the Iranian hostage crisis of 1979–81, in which a few dozen Americans were held hostage by people representing an often rather formless new regime. Like the Gulf War, it very much engaged the emotions for months on end. Mueller, *Overblown* 105–9. However, whereas the Gulf War substantially receded from recall, the hostage experience—the less important of the two events—continues to be vividly remembered.

86. Mueller, "Questing for Monsters to Destroy," 124.

87. See also Mueller and Stewart, "The Curse of the Black Swan."

88. Linderman, *Embattled Courage.*

89. Mueller, *War, Presidents, and Public Opinion,* 234.

90. Hickey, *The War of 1812: A Forgotten Conflict*; Blair, *The Forgotten War.*

91. Mueller, *Policy and Opinion in the Gulf War,* 161–63.

92. Scherlen, "The Never-Ending Drug War."

93. Sherrill, "The Political Power of Lesbians, Gays, and Bisexuals"; Yang, "Trends: Attitudes Toward Homosexuality."

94. However, one likely public opinion difference is in the response to the poll question asking respondents to name the most important problem facing the country today. As seen in figure 2-1, terrorism was soon topped by other problems—though the war in Iraq, which soon came to dominate the poll response, was hardly unrelated to terrorism concerns. The "most important problem" question had been asked before Pearl Harbor, but it was posed only two times during the war, both times introduced by the phrase, "Aside from winning the war. . . ." Obviously, pollsters expected people overwhelmingly to mention the war if the question was put in its standard form while the war was still being waged. Mueller, *War and Ideas,* 166–67.

95. Brooks and Manza, *Whose Rights?,* 146.

Chapter 3 *Terrorism and the United States*

1. William Manchester's characterization—what he calls his "odd metaphor"—is classic and evocative: "If you put six million dead Jews on one side of a scale and on the other side put the Nazi regime—the great gang of criminals ever to seize control of a modern state—you have a rough balance: greatest crime, greatest criminals. But if you put the murdered President of the United States on one side of a scale and that wretched waif Oswald on the other side, it doesn't balance. You want to add something weightier to Oswald." Manchester, "No Evidence of a Conspiracy to Kill Kennedy."

2. On al-Qaeda as a fringe group, see especially Gerges, *The Far Enemy,* and Gerges, *The Rise and Fall of Al-Qaeda.*

3. Gendar and Kennedy, "U.S. Commandos Find 'Mother Lode.'"

4. Hoffman, "Bin Laden's Death Shatters Conventional Wisdom"; Arquilla, "The New Seeds of Terror"; Lieberman: Chapman, "We Worry Too Much About Terrorism."

5. Miller, "Bin Laden Documents Reveal Strain"; Shane, "Pornography Is Found in Bin Laden Compound Files." See also Ignatius, "The bin Laden Plot to Kill President Obama."

6. Jenkins, *Stray Dogs,* 26.

7. Michael Morell says that, at the time of the raid, he "felt closure for the first time since 9/11." The feeling clearly didn't last, however: he soon came to believe that "the war against Islamic extremism was far from over" and will have to be fought by "multiple generations." *The Great War of Our Time,* 174, 302.

8. Lustick, *Trapped in the War on Terror,* 124, 171–72.

9. Department of Homeland Security, *National Infrastructure Protection Plan*, 11; Hawley and Means, *Permanent Emergency*, 61.

10. See also Schneier, "Portrait of the Modern Terrrorist"; Byman and Fair, "The Case for Calling Them Nitwits"; Klarevas, "The Idiot Jihadist Next Door."

11. Jenkins, *Stray Dogs*, 1.

12. Weiser, "3 Men Draw 25-Year Terms." See also Greenwald and Fishman, "Latest FBI Claim."

13. Dalmia, "What Islamist Terrorist Threat?"

14. See, in particular, cases 21, 22, 25, 29, 30, 38, 40, 42, 44, 46, 49, 50, 51, 52, 55, 56, and 57.

15. Cases 1, 20, 28, 33, and 34.

16. For the suggestion that case 4, the El-Al case, should not be considered terrorism, see Jenkins, *Stray Dogs*, 20. See also Feldman, "Federal Investigators: L.A. Airport Shooting."

17. Some compilations come up with somewhat different numbers. For example, some include the policeman killed by the Boston Marathon terrorists as they were attempting to escape, or add those killed by snipers in 2002 in the Washington, D.C., area. Others do not consider the El-Al case of 2002 to be an act of terrorism.

18. Grant and Stewart, "A Systems Model."

19. Grant and Stewart, "A Systems Model."

20. Hawley and Means, *Permanent Emergency*, 168.

21. Department of Homeland Security, *National Infrastructure Protection Plan*, 11.

22. Office of Management and Budget, Analytical Perspectives—Fiscal Year 2011, 381.

23. Department of Homeland Security, *National Infrastructure Protection Plan*, 15n.

24. The very phrase "homeland security" contains aspects of a similar inflation in its suggestion that the essential security of the entire country is at stake. In Canada, the comparable department is labeled with the more accurate and less dramatic "public safety." Given the actual magnitude of the terrorist hazard, the "homeland" is, as it happens, really quite secure, though there may be justifiable concerns about the public's safety under some conditions.

25. However, the practical import of this conclusion is certainly far from clear, as when the report rather opaquely says there is a consequent "necessity for a balanced, comparative approach that focuses on managing risk commensurately across all sectors and scenarios of concern." Department of Homeland Security, *National Infrastructure Protection Plan*, 11.

26. As in cases 2, 9, 12, 19, 23, 30, 42, and 49.

27. One compilation concludes that terrorists lived near to the target in 77 percent of the cases. Shurong Feng and Yue Li, personal communication, February 2013.

28. Military targets, including members of the military, were explicitly considered in cases 15, 22, 25, 26, 27, 32, 35, 40, 43, 44, 45, 46, 48, 55, 56, 58, 60, and 61. See also Sageman, *Leaderless Jihad*, 142.

29. Cases 26 in Little Rock and 32 at Fort Hood. See also Brooks, "Muslim 'Homegrown' Terrorism," 38.

30. See also Jenkins, *Stray Dogs*, 22; Bjelopera, 2013, 33–34.

31. Bjelopera 2013, 22. For a similar conclusion, see Gartenstein-Ross and Grossman, *Homegrown Terrorists*, 58–59.

32. Ukman, "Are Muslim Americans Being Radicalized?"

33. Sageman, *Leaderless Jihad*, 78–79. See also Graff, *The Threat Matrix*, 570.

34. Variously, for example, in cases 12, 14, 21, 22, 25, 38, 40, 48, 52, and 60. See also the letter by the would-be terrorist at the end of case 52.

35. "Text: Bin-Laden Tape," *BBC News*, January 19, 2006. For a catalog of such explicitly threatening, and thus far empty, threats that have been promulgated by al-Qaeda over the years, see Mueller and Stewart, *Terror, Security, and Money*, 36.

36. On this issue more generally, see German, *Thinking Like a Terrorist*.

37. Wilber, "Inside an FBI Anti-Terrorist Sting Operation." Interesting as well is the 2015 documentary film *(T)error*, which deals with the life and lifestyle of an informant.

38. See also Barkun, *Chasing Phantoms*, 45.

39. See Sageman, *Leaderless Jihad*, 71, 91, 138–39, 152, 157, 182. See also Morell, *The Great War of Our Time*, 107.

40. Weimann, *Terror on the Internet*; Jenkins, *Stray Dogs*, 15–17.

41. Sageman, *Leaderless Jihad*, 114.

42. As in cases 16, 30, 39, 40, 41, 48, 49, 55, 56, 57, and 60.

43. Kenney, "Beyond the Internet."

44. Stenersen, "Al-Qaeda's Thinking on CBRN," 56. See also Stenersen, "The Internet: A Virtual Training Camp?"; Eilstrup-Sangiovanni and Jones, "Assessing the Dangers," 32; Brooks, "Muslim 'Homegrown' Terrorism," 30–34; Benson, "Why the Internet Is Not Increasing Terrorism." By contrast, see Weimann, *Terror on the Internet*.

45. Benson, "Why the Internet Is Not Increasing Terrorism," 306–7.

46. Klarevas, "The Idiot Jihadist Next Door."

47. The link is in Klarevas, "The Idiot Jihadist Next Door."

48. Available at www.youtube.com/watch?v=poV6lc2b070.

49. Jenkins, *Stray Dogs*, 17.

50. For critiques of the notion that cyberterrorism presents a severe problem, see the sources arrayed at www.cato.org/research/cyberskeptics. Criminals may be adept at exploiting some vulnerabilities. However, it is extremely difficult to carry out an attack that has far-reaching security consequences. For a discussion, see Preble and Mueller, *A Dangerous World?*, particularly the contributions by Martin Libicki. See also Diab, *The Harbinger Theory*, 232–35.

51. See also Jenkins, *Stray Dogs,* 21. The Council on American-Islamic Relations (CAIR) is viewed very suspiciously in some quarters—in particular, Gaubatz and Sperry, *Muslim Mafia.* In the cases, however, the organization played almost no role except in a few instances to comment on the cases after arrests were made.

52. Cases 8 and 26.

53. Cases 6 and 8. See McDermott and Meyer, *The Hunt for KSM,* 260.

54. Informant: Cases 10 and 25. Al-Awlaki: Cases 32 and 33.

55. Sageman, *Leaderless Jihad,* 69–70.

56. See Risen, *Pay Any Price,* 202–10.

57. Sageman, *Leaderless Jihad,* 107.

58. Lustick, *Trapped in the War on Terror,* 172n32. See also the bizarre case described in Risen, *Pay Any Price,* ch. 2.

59. Cases 2, 5, 6, and 8.

60. For a similar conclusion by Israelis about foreign Jews who came to join the fight, see Sageman, *Leaderless Jihad,* 74.

61. Hsu and Wright, "Plot to Attack N.Y. Foiled."

62. Block, "Al-Qaida Magazine Details Parcel Bomb Attempt."

63. Dickens: "Yemen-based al Qaeda Group Claims Responsibility for Parcel Bomb Plot," CNN News, November 6, 2010. Thousand cuts: Gerges, *The Rise and Fall of Al-Qaeda,* 28.

64. *Talk of the Nation,* NPR broadcast, July 19, 2010.

65. Marc Sageman, email to John Mueller, July 11, 2014.

66. Glenn Carle, interview with John Mueller, May 1, 2014, Washington, DC.

67. Bjelopera, *The Federal Bureau of Investigation,* 20–21.

68. Graff, *The Threat Matrix,* 420-21n. See also Bjelopera, *The Federal Bureau of Investigation,* 20.

69. Graff, *The Threat Matrix,* 420–21, 557.

70. See Nakashima, "Audit: Justice Department Office Overstated Terrorism Conviction Statistics." See also Theoharis, *The Quest for Absolute Security,* 248, 255–56. In the three years after 9/11, some twenty-one terrorism arrests were made in San Diego County. Although several of these led to deportation and seven to prosecutions for "offenses related to terrorism," none ended up in the kind of full-blown trials as happened in most of the cases listed in appendix A. Schwartz, "The Whole Haystack."

71. Brooks, "Muslim 'Homegrown' Terrorism," 18.

72. "Disappearing Act: Rendition by the Numbers: Piecing Together a Picture of the CIA's Secret Rendition Program," *motherjones.com,* March 3, 2008.

73. Greenberg, *Terrorism Trial Report Card,* 13–14; see also 59.

74. Wilber, "Inside an FBI Anti-Terrorist Sting Operation."

75. For various versions of this story, including one maintaining that the bridge had been blocked to truck traffic, see Welsh-Huggins, *Hatred at Home,* 57, 63, 86.

76. See also Mueller and Stewart, *Terror, Security, and Money,* 98–99.
77. Horgan, "Discussion Point"; Horgan, "Can Science Solve Terrorism?"
78. See also Aaronson, *The Terror Factory,* 70.
79. There is also the danger, from the perspective of the terrorist group, that any implants will go native over time and lose their will to commit terrorism. For a satirical consideration, see "After 5 Years in U.S., Terrorist Cell to Complacent to Carry Out Attack," *theonion.com,* June 18, 2007. Also: "FBI Uncovers Al-Qaeda Plot to Just Sit Back and Enjoy Collapse of United States," *theonion.com,* April 15, 2014.
80. On this issue more broadly, see Abrahms, "Does Terrorism Really Work?"
81. On the suggestion of a Pennsylvania dentist during World War II, the U.S. Air Force tested outfitting bats with tiny time-delayed incendiary devices to see if they would fly into the eaves of Japanese houses and set them afire. When released from airplanes, however, the bomb-laden bats simply crashed to the earth. Waller, *Wild Bill Donovan,* 104.
82. Cases 16, 30, 39, 40, 41, 48, 49, 55, 56, and 60.
83. Faiola and Mufson, "N.Y. Airport Target of Plot."
84. Harris, *The Watchers,* 312.
85. Miller, "FBI Response to *Rolling Stone* Magazine Article."

Chapter 4 The Foreign Adversary and the Myth of the Mastermind

1. Kenney, "'Dumb' Yet Deadly." See also Brooks, "Muslim 'Homegrown' Terrorism"; Sageman, *Leaderless Jihad,* 141; Burton, "Beware of 'Kramer.'"
2. Horgan, *Walking Away from Terrorism,* 44.
3. Eilstrup-Sangiovanni and Jones, "Assessing the Dangers of Illicit Networks."
4. Three publications from think tanks have independently provided lists or tallies of such violence committed in the several years after the 9/11 attacks. Anthony H. Cordesman tallies "major attacks by Islamists" outside of Iraq: 830 fatalities for the period April 2002 through July 2005, in *The Challenge of Biological Weapons,* 29–31. We have corrected the total for the 2005 London bombings, given as 100 in this source, to 52. Brian Michael Jenkins tallies "major terrorist attacks worldwide" by "jihadist extremists" outside Afghanistan, Iraq, Israel, Palestine, Algeria, Russia, and Kashmir: 1,129 fatalities for the period October 2001 through April 2006, in *Unconquerable Nation,* 179–84. And IntelCenter tallies the "most significant attacks executed by core al-Qaeda, regional arms and affiliate groups excluding operations in insurgency theaters": 1,632 fatalities for the period January 2002 through July 2007, in "Jihadi Attack Kill Statistics," www.intelcenter.com, August 17, 2007, 11. For additional details, see Mueller and Stewart, *Terror, Security, and Money,* 42. For later years, the results would likely be comparable although "war zones" or "insurgency theaters" in, say, 2015 would include Afghanistan, Pakistan, Iraq, Syria, Yemen, Libya, and Nigeria. The distinction between terrorism and insurgency is discussed more fully in this book's conclusion.

5. Seitz, "Weaker Than We Think." See also Diab, *The Harbinger Theory*; Mueller, "Harbinger or Aberration?"; Mueller, "False Alarms"; Mueller, "Blip or Step Function?"

6. Smith, "The Airport Security Follies."

7. Koerner, *The Skies Belong to Us*, 46–48.

8. Koerner, *The Skies Belong To Us*, 203–12, 216–19, 261–63; Mueller, *Overblown*, 152.

9. McDermott and Meyer, *The Hunt for KSM*, 154, 311; *U.S. v. Moussaoui*, para. 76–89.

10. Smith, "The Airport Security Follies."

11. *U.S. v. Moussaoui*, para. 89.

12. McDermott and Meyer, *The Hunt for KSM*, 160, 328n2.

13. Kenney, "'Dumb' Yet Deadly," 916–17.

14. Wright, *The Looming Tower*, 174, 200; Byman and Williams, "Jihadism's Global Civil War," 15; Gerges, *The Rise and Fall of Al-Qaeda*, 85, 90.

15. Gerges, *The Rise and Fall of Al-Qaeda*, 92.

16. McDermott and Meyer, *The Hunt for KSM*, 183; *U.S. v. Moussaoui*, para. See also German, *Thinking Like a Terrorist*, 180.

17. Full transcript of bin Laden's speech, October 30, 2004, www.aljazeera.net.

18. On this issue, see Porter, *The Global Village Myth*, 109; Mueller, *War and Ideas*, ch. 7.

19. Hirsh, "Bin Laden Journal." On this belief in 2001, see Gerges, *The Rise and Fall of Al-Qaeda*, 90–91.

20. Ignatius, "Bin Laden's Ambitious Final Plans." Ignatius says that in his letters bin Laden "ominously presses for news about 'a big operation inside America.'" However, the document actually says bin Laden was pressing for news about his "nomination of a qualified brother to be in charge of a big operation inside America."

21. The documents are posted at Will McCants, New Abbottabad Documents, March 15, 2015, jihadica.com/new-abbottabad-documents/. Bin Laden says that, although 57,000 deaths were not enough to inspire "public outrage and internal opposition" to end the war in Vietnam, that point was reached when President Richard Nixon "made the mistake of ordering the draft so as to continue the war." But, of course, the draft was in place when Nixon took office and it was he who eventually ended it. For other evidence of bin Laden's delusional ramblings, see Ignatius, "The bin Laden Plot"; Ignatius, "A Lion in Winter."

22. Graff, *The Threat Matrix*, 218.

23. Graff, *The Threat Matrix*, 252.

24. Graff, *The Threat Matrix*, 263.

25. For sources of these threats and for additional threats, see Mueller and Stewart, *Terror, Security, and Money*, 36.

26. See Sageman, *Leaderless Jihad*. See also Ignatius, "The Fading Jihadists."

27. Silber, *The Al Qaeda Factor*. See also Sageman, *Leaderless Jihad*, 139.

28. Apuzzo and Goldman, *Enemies Within*, 9.

29. Carle, "Overstating Our Fears."

30. Porter, "Long Wars and Long Telegrams," 300.

31. Warrick, "U.S. Cites Big Gains Against Al-Qaeda." See also Gerges, *The Far Enemy,* ch. 5; Sageman, *Leaderless Jihad,* 149.

32. Bergen and Cruickshank, "The Unraveling"; Wright, "The Rebellion Within"; Gerges, *The Rise and Fall of Al-Qaeda.*

33. Gerges, *The Far Enemy,* 232, and, for a tally of policing activity, 318–19. See also Pillar, *Terrorism and U.S. Foreign Policy,* xxviii–xxix; Lynch, "Al-Qaeda's Media Strategies," 54–55; Sageman, *Leaderless Jihad,* 149; Cole, *Engaging the Muslim World,* 163; Abrahms, "Does Terrorism Really Work?"

34. For Indonesia: Sageman, *Understanding Terror Networks,* 53, 142, 173. For Saudi Arabia: Gerges, *The Far Enemy,* 249; Sageman, *Understanding Terror Networks,* 53, 144. Jordan polls: Pew Global Attitudes Project, "The Great Divide: How Westerners and Muslims View Each Other," June 22, 2006, www.pewglobal. org; see also Lynch, "Al-Qaeda's Media Strategies," 54–55. See also Gerges, "Word on the Street," 75; Pillar, *Terrorism and U.S. Foreign Policy,* xxiv; Zakaria, "Post-9/11, We're Safer."

35. Woodward, "Why Did Violence Plummet?"; Wehrey, "The Iraq War"; Mansoor, *Surge,* ch. 10.

36. Mack, "Dying to Lose," 15–17.

37. Quoted in Warrick, "U.S. Cites Big Gains Against Al-Qaeda." See also Bergen and Cruickshank, "Self-Fulfilling Prophecy"; Jenkins, *Will Terrorists Go Nuclear?,* 191; Gerges, *The Rise and Fall of Al-Qaeda,* 204.

38. Ignatius, "The bin Laden Plot." See also Ignatius, "A Lion in Winter."

39. Wood, "What ISIS Really Wants."

40. Lustick, *Trapped in the War on Terror,* 171–72.

41. Miniter, *Mastermind,* 2.

42. McDermott and Meyer, *The Hunt for KSM,* 310–13.

43. Miniter, *Mastermind,* 157; McDermott, and Meyer, *The Hunt for KSM,* 240.

44. McDermott and Meyer, *The Hunt for KSM,* 47.

45. McDermott and Meyer, *The Hunt for KSM,* 241–42, 268.

46. Reeve, *The New Jackals,* 45, 46, 55, 98, 254.

47. Reeve, *The New Jackals,* 25, 138, 75, 132, 249.

48. Reeve, *The New Jackals,* 131.

49. Reeve, *The New Jackals,* 77; Graff, *The Threat Matrix,* 181.

50. Kenney, "'Dumb' Yet Deadly," 915.

51. A structural damage assessment of the 1993 attacks reveals that the World Trade Center towers "were structurally sound" and "suffered no serious damage to their integrity," owing to the "tubular design of the tower and its ability to re-distribute loads to alternate load paths." Ramabhushanam and Lynch, "Structural Assessment of Bomb Damage to World Trade Centre," 233, 235.

52. Reeve, *The New Jackals,* 50, 53.

53. Reeve, *The New Jackals,* 54.

54. Reeve, *The New Jackals*, 64–65.

55. Reeve, *The New Jackals*, 66.

56. Reeve, *The New Jackals*, 70n73.

57. Reeve, *The New Jackals*, 76–77, 89.

58. Reeve, *The New Jackals*, 76–79.

59. Reeve, *The New Jackals* 78, 86.

60. Reeve, *The New Jackals*, 87; Graff, *The Threat Matrix*, 182.

61. Graff, *The Threat Matrix*, 182.

62. Reeve, *The New Jackals*, 87–91, 95–96.

63. Reeve, *The New Jackals*, 97–99.

64. Reeve, *The New Jackals*, 99–106.

65. Schuster, "Producer's Notebook."

66. Morell, *The Great War of Our Time*, 309–10.

67. Hawley and Means, *Permanent Emergency*, 234.

68. Friedman, "*Washington Post* Defines Worst Fears Down"; Benson, "Why the Internet Is Not Increasing Terrorism," 320–21.

69. Sageman, *Leaderless Jihad*, 153–54.

Chapter 5 Evaluating the Counterterrorism Enterprise

1. Bush, *Decision Points*, 267.

2. On the 9/11 costs, see Mueller and Stewart, *Terror, Security, and Money*, 59–61. On the costs of the wars, see Stiglitz and Bilmes, *The Three Trillion Dollar War*; Londoño, "Iraq, Afghan Wars Will Cost $4 Trillion to $6 Trillion." Writing in 2010, Bush concludes, "America is safer without a homicidal dictator pursuing WMD and supporting terror at the heart of the Middle East. The region is more hopeful with a young democracy setting an example for others to follow. And the Iraqi people are better off with a government that answers to them instead of torturing and murdering them." Bush, *Decision Points*, 267. On this issue, see Walt, "Being a Neocon Means Never Having to Say You're Sorry."

3. For a discussion, see Mueller and Stewart, *Terror, Security, and Money*, 1–9; Mueller and Stewart, "Evaluating Counterterrorism Spending."

4. National Research Council of the National Academies, *Review of the Department of Homeland Security's Approach to Risk Analysis*, emphasis added. See also Mueller and Stewart, *Terror, Security, and Money*, introduction.

5. Kunreuther, "Risk Analysis and Risk Management," 662–63. See also Mueller, "Some Reflections on What, If Anything"; Brooks, "Muslim 'Homegrown' Terrorism," 43.

6. Mueller and Stewart, *Terror, Security, and Money*, 1–3.

7. See, for example, International Organization for Standardization, *Risk Management*; Bernstein, *Against the Gods*. For a more extensive discussion, see Mueller and Stewart, *Terror, Security, and Money*.

8. We here summarize and update material in Mueller and Stewart, *Terror, Security, and Money*. See also Mueller and Stewart, "Evaluating Counterterrorism Spending."

9. For additional discussion of this issue, see Mueller and Stewart, *Terror, Security, and Money*, 56–59.

10. Robinson et al. "Valuing the Risk of Death."

11. Stewart and Mueller, *Terror, Security, and Money*, 1–3. The cost figures in that book have been updated here to include the FY2014 federal budget and are given in 2014 dollars.

12. Islamist extremist terrorists have killed fewer than four people per year in the UK, and two each in the last decade in Canada and Australia. Proportionate to size, the spending of these countries on homeland security is 25 to 50 percent that of the United States.

13. Los Angeles, "Fiscal Year 2014–15," 43–47. The FY2014–15 proposed budget is similar to FY2013–14 expenditures (397).

14. Dougherty, "U.S. Cities with Bigger Economies."

15. Travis et al., "Cancer Risk Management."

16. For additional discussion of this issue, see Mueller and Stewart, *Terror, Security, and Money*, 45–53.

17. See also Bogen and Jones, "Risks of Mortality and Morbidity," 56; Gardner, *The Science of Fear*, 250–51.

18. Mueller and Stewart, *Terror, Security, and Money*, 182–85; Mueller and Stewart, "Evaluating Counterterrorism Spending."

19. Analysts of the Global Terrorism Database define a "mass fatality attack" as one that inflicts twenty-five or more deaths. LaFree, Duggan, and Miller, *Putting Terrorism in Context*, 132.

20. See the discussion in chapter 1 as well as in Mueller, *Atomic Obsession*, and Diab, *The Harbinger Theory*.

21. The Department of Homeland Security defines Risk as (Threat) × (Vulnerability) × (Consequence). In this formulation, Threat is the annual probability of a terrorist attempt, Vulnerability is the probability of loss (that the explosive will be successfully detonated or the gun will fire, leading to damage and loss of life) given the attempt, and Consequence is the loss (economic costs, number of people harmed) if the attack is successful in causing damage. Since there is no particular reason to expend funds to deal with terrorist attempts that are unsuccessful (that is, that cause no damage), this can be simplified to deal with successful attacks—ones that actually do damage. That approach is the one applied here.

22. For a fuller assessment, see Mueller and Stewart, *Terror, Security, and Money*, 81–82.

23. Mueller and Stewart, "Hapless, Disorganized, and Irrational."

24. In evaluating indirect costs, a concern is whether they should include those imposed in the efforts to catch the terrorists—efforts that included in this

case a costly lockdown of the Boston area for a day. From the beginning, the police were after a person or a group that was willing to kill innocent people in a crowd. It was reasonable to suspect that the culprits were terrorists, though the act could have been committed by a deranged individual, with or without accomplices, who like a serial killer was simply bent on destruction. Once the police sent out pictures of the two men they thought had set off the explosions, the culprits moved into action, killing a campus police officer in the process. They then became not only armed serial (or mass) killers but also cop-killers, something that police take very seriously, as had been demonstrated earlier in the year with a widespread police dragnet in Los Angeles focused on Christopher Dorner, a cop-killer there. It could be argued, then, that the police forces would have done exactly the same thing whether the people they sought were terrorists or not.

25. Department of Commerce, Economic Growth Widespread.
26. For a more detailed assessment, see Mueller and Stewart, *Terror, Security, and Money*, 61–62.
27. On these studies, see Mueller and Stewart, *Terror, Security, and Money*, 59–61.
28. Meade and Molander, *Considering the Effects of a Catastrophic Terrorist Attack*. On this study, see also Mueller, *Atomic Obsession*, 270n30.
29. Bunn, Weir, and Holdren, "Controlling Nuclear Warheads and Materials."
30. For an extensive discussion of this issue, see Mueller, *Atomic Obsession*, chs. 11–12. See also Gardner, *The Science of Fear*, 253–259; Diab, *The Harbinger Theory*; Jenkins, *Will Terrorists Go Nuclear?*
31. This issue is discussed more fully in the conclusion to this book and in Mueller, "Action and Reaction."
32. Sheehan, *Crush the Cell*, 263.
33. LaTourrette et al., "Reducing Terrorism Risk at Shopping Centers."
34. Rice, "USA Saw Fewest Lightning Deaths."
35. Mueller and Stewart, *Terror, Security, and Money*, ch. 6.

Chapter 6 The Federal Bureau of Investigation

1. FBI, *The FBI: A Centennial History*, 4, 17.
2. FBI, *The FBI: A Centennial History*, 38.
3. Kean, *The 9/11 Commission Report*, 77, 423.
4. FBI, *Project Megiddo*, 6, 32.
5. Kean, *The 9/11 Commission Report*, 359.
6. Kean, *The 9/11 Commission Report*, 77–78.
7. Department of Justice, *Report to the National Commission*, 12. See also German, *Thinking Like a Terrorist*, 67.
8. Kean, *The 9/11 Commission Report*, 78.
9. Department of Justice, *Report to the National Commission*, 12.
10. Theoharis, *The Quest for Absolute Security*, 248.

11. Transactional Records Access Clearinghouse, *Terrorism/National Internal Security Prosecutions for February 2013*, TRAC Report 316, TRAC Report 231. Its priorities, in order, are to "prevent, disrupt, and defeat terrorist operations before they occur," to protect the United States against foreign intelligence operations and espionage, and to protect the United States against cyber-based attacks and high-technology crimes. Other goals are fighting corruption, protecting civil rights, and combating criminal organizations and white-collar and violent crime. Department of Justice, *FY2015—Authorization and Budget Request to Congress;* Department of Justice, *Today's FBI Facts & Figures*, 7. There is nothing unusual in having a centralized or federal agency devoted to the task of counterterrorism. The bureau's domestic counterterrorism operations and responsibilities are similar to those of the British Security Service (MI5), whose role is defined as "the protection of national security and, in particular, its protection against threats from espionage, terrorism and sabotage, from the activities of agents of foreign powers and from actions intended to overthrow or undermine parliamentary democracy by political, industrial or violent means"; see www.mi5.gov.uk/home/about-us/what-we-do/objectives-and-values.html. This role is augmented considerably by London's Metropolitan Police Service Counter-Terrorism Command. Most of the resources of the Australian Security Intelligence Organisation (ASIO) are "aimed at preventing a terrorist attack in Australia, countering terrorist-related activity, warning of security threats and countering espionage and foreign interference against Australia"; see www.asio. gov.au/About-ASIO/What-we-do.html. Their role is augmented considerably by the Australian Federal Police. The role of the Canadian Security Intelligence Service (CSIS) is to "investigate threats, analyze information and produce intelligence. Key threats include terrorism, the proliferation of weapons of mass destruction, espionage, foreign interference and cyber-tampering affecting critical infrastructure"; see www.csis-scrs.gc.ca/bts/role-en.php. This role is augmented considerably by the Royal Canadian Mounted Police.

12. Department of Justice, *Report to the National Commission on Terrorist Attacks,* 10.

13. Department of Justice, *FY2015—Authorization and Budget Request to Congress.*

14. The budget for the Australian Security Intelligence Organisation has increased more than sixfold (in real terms) since 2000–2001, and the British intelligence and Canadian Security Intelligence Service budgets have more than doubled since 2000. The 2000–2001 budget for ASIO was A$69.5 million (A$100 million inflation adjusted), which increased to A$635 million in 2013–14. (See Report to Parliament 2000–2001, Australian Security Intelligence Organisation, Commonwealth of Australia, December 2001, 13; and Portfolio Budget Statements 2014-15 Budget Related Paper No. 1.2, Attorney-General's Portfolio, Commonwealth of Australia 2014, 259.) This excludes equity injections of over $600 million to fund a new ASIO headquarters in Canberra. The new ASIO headquarters is the largest and most expensive construction project in Canberra since the new Parliament House was completed in 1988. Geoff

Kitney and John Kerin, *State of Security*, Financial Review, July 30, 2010; Tobias Feakin, "The Post-Olympic Challenge: Staying Secure," *UK Terrorism Analysis,* Royal United Services Institute, No. 1, February 2012, 11.

British expenditures include Security Service (MI5), the Secret Intelligence Service (MI6), and the Government Communications Headquarters (GCHQ).

In Canada, the 2000 budget for CSIS was C$157 million (C$210 million inflation adjusted), which increased to C$535 million in 2013–14. (Supplementary Estimates [B], 2013–14, Treasury Board of Canada Secretariat, Ottawa; Collins, "Spies Like Them,"506.)

15. MI5: "Terrorism is the biggest national security threat that the UK currently faces. Our highest priority is the threat of international terrorism from groups such as Al Qaida. Terrorist organisations based in Northern Ireland also continue to pose a serious threat"; www.mi5.gov.uk/home/about-us/faqs-about-mi5/what-are-the-biggest-current-threats-to-national-security.html.

CSIS: "Terrorism is still our greatest preoccupation" and "countering terrorist violence is the top priority for CSIS"; www.csis-scrs.gc.ca/index-en.php.

ASIO: "Terrorism remains the most immediate threat to the security of Australians and Australian interests." (ASIO Report to Parliament, 2012–13, Australian Security Intelligence Organisation, Commonwealth of Australia, 2013, vii.) The Australian Federal Police has seen their budget increase by more than three and a half times (in real terms) from 1998 to 1999, and the British intelligence budget has increased 60 percent since 2000. Donkin and Bronitt, "Critical Perspectives on the Evaluation of Counter-Terrorism Strategies," 186. Australian Federal Police expenditures increased due to the expanded role for the AFP in both counterterrorism and peacekeeping operations. (Intelligence and Security Committee of Parliament Annual Report 2012–2013, House of Commons, July 10, 2013; Intelligence and Security Committee Annual Report 2001–2002, Presented to Parliament by the Prime Minister by Command of Her Majesty, June 2002.)

16. Department of Justice, *Today's FBI Facts & Figures*, 9, 57.

17. Transactional Records Access Clearinghouse. *Terrorism/National Internal Security Prosecutions for February 2013*, TRAC Report 316, TRAC Report 231.

18. FBI budget data prior to 2006 do not distinguish between counterterrorism and counterintelligence expenditures. The 2001 expenditures for these activities are $1.4 billion (inflation adjusted to 2013 dollars). We assume that counterterrorism accounted for 40 to 50 percent of these expenditures in 2001, compared with 65 percent in 2013. This amounts to approximately $500–$600 million. FBI counterterrorism expenditures thus increase from 2001 levels by $3 billion (2013) minus this amount, or approximately $2.5 billion.

19. Department of Justice, *FY2015—Authorization and Budget Request to Congress.* See also Graff, *The Threat Matrix*, 522; Aaronson, *The Terror Factory*, 16, 201.

20. Department of Justice, *FY2015—Authorization and Budget Request to Congress.*

21. Aaronson, *The Terror Factory*, 201.

22. Graff, *The Threat Matrix*, 579.

23. Savage, "F.B.I. Casts Wide Net."

24. Aaronson, *The Terror Factory*, 208–10, 233.

25. Swarts, "Director Warns Shutdown Would Harm FBI."

26. Graff, *The Threat Matrix*, 521–22, 630–31.

27. Chayes, "Blinded by the War on Terrorism."

28. Mueller and Stewart, *Terror, Security, and Money*, 43, 46.

29. Cloutier, "Incidents Like S.C. Shootings on the Rise."

30. However, as suggested elsewhere, it is not clear that other 9/11-like attacks would trigger the extreme economic reaction engendered by the original intensely shocking event—that is, the full costs of another terrorist event like 9/11 might not reach those sustained in the original event.

31. The ratio of benefit to cost is equal to: { (attack probability) × (losses) × (risk reduction) } / (security cost).

32. See table 6-1 for 100 percent risk reduction by the FBI.

33. Stossel, *Give Me a Break,* 77.

34. Blalock, Kadiyali, and Simon, "The Impact of Post-9/11 Airport Security Measures"; Blalock, Kadiyali, and Simon, "Driving Fatalities After 9/11."

35. Analysts of the Global Terrorism Database define a "mass fatality attack" as one that inflicts twenty-five or more deaths. LaFree, Duggan, and Miller, *Putting Terrorism in Context*, 132.

36. Marshall, "MI5 Boss Warns of Growing UK Terror Threat."

37. Cases 1, 2, 7, 9, 18, 20, 24, 33, and 36.

38. On this issue, see also Mueller and Stewart, *Terror, Security, and Money*, 83–89.

39. The only case in the set in which it could even remotely be maintained that 9/11 destruction could have been approached was based abroad—in the 2006 transatlantic airline bombing case.

40. Cases 1, 9, 20, and 33 overseas, and 28 and 34 in the United States.

41. As in Cases 2, 8, 12, 19, 23, 30, and 42.

42. Such as Cases 3, 10, 11, 12, 14, 16, 19, 21, 22, 23, 25, 29, 30, 35, 37, 38, 39, 40, 41, 42, 44, 46, 48, 49, 50, 51, 52, 55, 56, 57, 58, 59, and 60.

43. Aaronson, *The Terror Factory,* 206–7; also 29–30, 55.

44. In addition, with the terminology set out earlier, it should be kept in mind that there have been notable follow-on costs to the FBI's counterterrorism enterprise as a considerable number of aspiring terrorists who were unlikely ever to do much damage have been sentenced to long terms in taxpayer-funded prisons.

45. For more detail, see Brady, "Case 39: DC Metro—Facebook."

46. For more detail, see Brady, "Case 19: Sears Tower."

47. Author discussions with Michael German, Marc Sageman, and Secret Service agents.

48. See also Mueller and Stewart, "Can Terrorists Be Scared Straight?"

49. And, in general, it is not a very good way to do so. See Mueller, "Crime Is Caused by the Young and Reckless."

50. Actually, it appears that most people, like Lee Harvey Oswald, contemplating presidential assassination have not commonly raved about their violent desires in public, but have behaved essentially as "lone wolves."

51. See also Aaronson, *The Terror Factory*, 23, 55.

52. Horgan, "Discussion Point." See also Horgan, *Walking Away from Terrorism*.

53. However, those who were deported obviously became limited in their ability to commit terrorism in the United States.

54. Rizzo, "Terror Charges Filed Against Topeka Man"; *U.S. v. John T. Booker Jr.*

55. Koerner, "The Garland, Texas, Shooters' Quiet Plan"; Bever and Murphy, "Gunmen Shot Dead in Texas."

56. See Bernstein, "Case 38: Oregon."

Chapter 7 *The National Security Agency*

1. Office of the Director of National Intelligence, "FY2013 Congressional Budget Justification," 132. See also Andrews and Lindeman, "The 'Black Budget'"; Schwartz, "The Whole Haystack."

2. Priest and Arkin, *Top Secret America*, 74.

3. Priest and Arkin, *Top Secret America*, 74.

4. Priest and Arkin, *Top Secret America*, 77. See also Schwartz, "The Whole Haystack."

5. Andrews and Lindeman, "The 'Black Budget.'"

6. Office of the Press Secretary, Statement by the President.

7. Clarke et al., *Liberty and Security,* 114.

8. Office of the Press Secretary, Statement by the President.

9. Greenwald, *No Place to Hide,* 207.

10. For example, there is no discussion of the antiterror value of NSA, or lack thereof, in the PBS *Frontline* programs on the issue. Nor is there any in *Citizenfour,* the Oscar-winning 2014 documentary on the Snowden affair.

11. Leon, "Memorandum Opinion," 61–62, emphasis in the original.

12. Pauley, "Memorandum & Order," 1, 48–49.

13. A useful discussion of the two programs is Pincus, "NSA Should Be Debated on the Facts." See also Sanchez, "Decoding the Summer of Snowden"; Bergen et al., "Do NSA's Bulk Surveillance Programs?"

14. On "known or unknown," see Eagan, Docket BR 13-109.

15. Bergen et al., "Do NSA's Bulk Surveillance Programs?," 7.

16. It is possible as well that the cost figure for the program remains undisclosed in part because no one actually knows how much the program costs. On this issue, see p. 52.

17. "So What's the Big Deal?" *iiNet*, July 2014, www.blog.iinet.net.au/wp-content/uploads/2014/07/Mandatory-Data-Retention-Infographic-v41.png.

18. Assuming a 2 percent telephone market share for iiNet with U.S. telephone demands scaled up based on population size. Edward W. Felten, professor of computer science and public affairs at Princeton University, estimates 50 terabytes of data per year. U.S. Senate, Judiciary Hearing on Continued Oversight, testimony of Edward W. Felten, 3.

19. Telecommunications (Interception and Access) Amendment (Data Retention) Bill 2014, Submission by the Australian Communications Consumer Action Network to the Parliamentary Joint Committee on Intelligence and Security, January 2015.

20. Nakashima, "If Not the NSA?"

21. Savage, "N.S.A. Calls Violations of Privacy."

22. Graff, *The Threat Matrix,* 527.

23. Schwartz, "Three Big Questions."

24. Walt, "The Real Threat." See also Sanchez, "Decoding the Summer of Snowden."

25. "57% Fear Government Will Use NSA Data to Harass Political Opponents," *Rassmussen Reports,* June 13, 2013. See also Robinson, "We Can Handle the Truth"; Greenwald, *No Place to Hide,* 197–200.

26. Cauley, "NSA Has Massive Database." See also Burdick, "Does Nobody Read *USA Today?*"

27. Bamford, "The NSA Is Building the Country's Biggest Spy Center."

28. Bamford, "They Know Much More."

29. Gellman, "NSA Broke Privacy Rules."

30. Nakashima and Warrick, "For NSA Chief, Terrorist Threat Drives Passion."

31. Robinson, "We Can Handle the Truth." See also Bamford, "They Know Much More"; Lake, "Spy Chief."

32. Nakashima, "NSA Gathered Thousands." See also Savage and Shane, "Secret Court Rebuked."

33. Gellman, "NSA Broke Privacy Rules."

34. Nakashima, "NSA Gathered Thousands."

35. Shane, "Court Upbraided NSA."

36. Savage, "NSA Calls Violations of Privacy."

37. Gellman, "NSA Broke Privacy Rules."

38. Shane, "Court Upbraided N.S.A."; Sanchez, "Decoding the Summer of Snowden."

39. Quoted in Bamford, "They Know Much More."

40. Greenwald, "Congress Is Irrelevant."

41. Nakashima, "NSA Bills Set Up a Choice in Congress." See also Leahy, Statement.

42. "Senate Investigates NSA Leak," *CNN Newsroom,* June 12, 2013.

43. Compare Young, "National Insecurity," 380.

44. Nakashima, "NSA Cites Case."

45. Bergen et al., "Do NSA's Bulk Surveillance Programs?," 1.

46. On this issue, see also Bergen et al., "Do NSA's Bulk Surveillance Programs?," 1.

47. Pincus, "NSA Should Be Debated."

48. Priest, "NSA Growth."

49. Graff, *The Threat Matrix*, 527.

50. Harris, "The Cowboy of the NSA." See also Harris, *The Watchers*, ch. 16.

51. Harris, "The Cowboy of the NSA."

52. Pincus, "NSA Should Be Debated."

53. Finn, "NSA Chief Says Surveillance Programs."

54. Muñoz, "NSA Chief Cites 50."

55. German, "No NSA Poster Child." See also Leahy, Statement; Greenwald, *No Place to Hide*, 202–5.

56. German, "No NSA Poster Child"; Vitka, "The Dragnet's Day in Court."

57. On this issue, see Schwartz, "The Whole Haystack." Schwartz points out that the terrorist group became progressively extreme and then lost all support among American Somalis in late 2009 when it bombed a university commencement in Somalia. The cab driver's contributions had stopped by then.

58. Dilanian, "NSA Faces Backlash."

59. Schwartz, "The Whole Haystack."

60. U.S. House of Representatives, Permanent Select Committee hearing.

61. Nakashima, "NSA Cites Case."

62. PCLOB, Report on the Telephone Records Program, 152. See also Schwartz, "The Whole Haystack."

63. Muñoz, "NSA Chief Cites 50."

64. Communication data: Bergen et al., "Do NSA's Bulk Surveillance Programs," 17.

65. Morris, "Al-Qaeda Bunco Artist"; $93,000, prove seriousness: Douglas, "Case 98: New York Stock Exchange." See also Morris, "KC Terrorist Supported Plan."

66. U.S. House of Representatives, Permanent Select Committee hearing; McCarthy, "NSA Chief Says Exposure."

67. Ross et al., "NSA Claim of Thwarted Plot."

68. Bump, "After an Easy Hearing." See also Harris, "FBI Concocted Bomb Plot."

69. PCLOB, Report on the Telephone Records Program, 151.

70. Rotella, "Did NSA Surveillance Help?" See also Gillespie, "Do the Zazi and Headley Arrests?"; Bergen et al., "Do NSA's Bulk Surveillance Programs?," 18–19. Joyce testified that the terrorist operative was uncovered "through 702 coverage of an al-Qaeda-affiliated terrorist." U.S. House of Representatives, Permanent Select Committee hearing.

71. U.S. House of Representatives, Permanent Select Committee hearing.

72. Heilman, "Case 28: Zazi"; More recent: Smith, "Public Documents Contradict"; Bergen et al., "Do NSA's Bulk Surveillance Programs?," 20–21; British tip: "British Spies Help Prevent Attack," *Telegraph*, November 9, 2009. It is conceivable that the 702 program played a role in this process, but is not at all clear that this is so or that, if so, its role was necessary. For a discussion, see Amira, "Did Controversial NSA Spy Programs Really Help?" Alexander has said that 702 was "critical" but that 215 was not essential to the case: McCarthy, "NSA Chief Says Exposure." See also Finn and Miller, "How an E-mail Address";

Molotch, *Against Security*, 56, 58; Apuzzo and Goldman, *Enemies Within*, 53–55; Gillespie, "Do the Zazi and Headley Arrests?"; Dilanian, "NSA Faces Backlash."

73. Nakashima, "NSA Cites Case." See also Finn and Miller, "How an E-mail Address."

74. PCLOB, Report on the Telephone Records Program, 149.

75. Schwartz, "We're at Greater Risk."

76. See also Mueller, "Mueller on the Zazi Case."

77. German, "No NSA Poster Child"; Elliott, "Judge on NSA Case."

78. PCLOB, Report on the Telephone Records Program, 154. See also Bergen et al., "Do NSA's Bulk Surveillance Programs?," 12–14.

79. U.S. House of Representatives, House Permanent Select Committee hearing.

80. Bergen et al., "Do NSA's Bulk Surveillance Programs."

81. Schwartz, "The Whole Haystack."

82. Senator Ron Wyden, keynote speech at the Cato Institute program, "NSA Surveillance: What We Know; What to Do About It," Washington, DC, October 9, 2013, www.cato.org/events/nsa-surveillance-what-we-know-what-do-about-it. As he observes, "just because it is said a program catches terrorists doesn't mean it does." See also Elliott, "Claim on 'Attacks Thwarted.' "

83. PCLOB, Report on the Telephone Records Program, 153.

84. Dilanian, "AP Exclusive."

85. Leahy, Statement.

86. Priest, "NSA Growth." However, Leiter has also said he considers 215 to be useful, but not essential. Schwartz, "The Whole Haystack."

87. U.S. House of Representatives, Permanent Select Committee hearing.

88. Schwartz, "We're at Greater Risk."

89. Nakashima, "NSA Cites Case."

90. Finn and Miller, "How an E-mail Address."

91. Dilanian, "AP Exclusive."

92. Clarke et al., *Liberty and Security,* 104, 119n119. However, Robert Jervis (and the CIA) argue in a somewhat different context that this is not a completely adequate test of the program's value. There may be value, for example, if the program contributed importantly to a more general understanding of the terrorist problem or if it generated information that aided interrogators in another investigation. Jervis, "The Torture Blame Game," 124.

93. PCLOB, Report on the Telephone Records Program, 145–46, emphasis in the original.

94. Center on Law and Security, "Terrorist Trial Report Card," 2, 27–28.

95. Greenwald, "Congress Is Irrelevant."

96. Hirsh, "Why the Surveillance State Lives On."

97. Bamford, "They Know Much More." See also Clarke et al., *Liberty and Security,* 97.

98. "Wyden, Udall Statement on the Disclosure of Bulk Email Records Collection Program," press release, July 2, 2013, www.wyden.senate.gov.

99. Dilanian, "AP Exclusive."

100. Kunreuther,"Risk Analysis and Risk Management," 662–63. See also Mueller, "Some Reflections on What."

101. Clarke et al., *Liberty and Security*, 25.

102. PCLOB, Report on the Telephone Records Program, 168.

103. Fact Sheet: Office of the Press Secretary, White House, Administration's Proposal for Ending Bulk Telephone Metadata Program.

104. For example: Office of the Director of National Intelligence, Joint Statement from the ODNI and the U.S. DOJ on the Declassification.

105. For varying assessments, see Greenwald, "Congress Is Irrelevant," and Hirsh, "Why the Surveillance State Lives On."

106. "U.S. Phone Companies Escape New Data Storage Mandate in Surveillance Bill," *reuters.com*, June 2, 2015.

107. Clarke et al., *Liberty and Security*, 144–45.

108. PCLOB, Report on the Surveillance Program, 111–12 (favorably impressed), 104 (proven valuable).

109. PCLOB, Report on the Surveillance Program, 110.

110. PCLOB, Report on the Surveillance Program, 112 (content), 113 (targeted), 108 (reports).

111. PCLOB, Report on the Surveillance Program, 108–9.

112. PCLOB, Report on the Surveillance Program, 109.

113. PCLOB, Report on the Surveillance Program, 109–10.

114. Harper, Mueller, and Stewart, "Comments on Notice of Proposed Rulemaking," 13.

115. Priest and Arkin, *Top Secret America*, 10n6.

116. Kenber, "Outgoing Director Robert S. Mueller, III Tells How."

117. Harris, "The Cowboy of the NSA." Mike Morell, former deputy director of the FBI, dramatically contends that the Snowden leaks constitute "the most serious compromise of classified information in the history of the U.S. intelligence community." However, his chief concern was not about communications data, but about the leak of a top secret document the CIA calls its "Black Budget," contending that it allows adversaries to "focus their counterintelligence efforts on those places where we're being successful, and not have to worry as much about those places where we're not being successful." *60 Minutes*, CBS, October 27, 2013.

118. Young, "National Insecurity," 282–86.

119. Carnevale, "Tracking Use of Bin Laden's Satellite Phone."

120. Movie and TV viewers have reason to suspect this as well, with programs that frequently include American satellite surveillance of phones and computers. The 2010 British spoof *Four Lions* contains an opening scene in which a group of would-be homegrown terrorists are instructed by their leader, "Look, the way to stop the Feds tracking you is very simple. You eat your SIM card." And published twenty-five years ago, the Tom Clancy novel *Clear and Present Danger* has the CIA intercepting cell phone communications of drug cartels in Colombia.

121. Greenwald and Fishman, "NPR Is Laundering CIA."

122. Arkin, "What the 9/11 Plotter Tells Us."

123. As in Cases 16, 30, 39, 40, 41, 48, 49, 51, 52, 57, and 60.

124. *Meet the Press* (NBC), June 16, 2013. Asked on CBS's *Face the Nation* on June 30, 2013, about what harm had been done, Hayden said, "Three things. Number one: Operational things have been disclosed. I mean you're a newsman, you know about protecting sources and methods and here now our sources and methods have been made public, so that's one. Second: Look, we cooperate with a lot of governments around the world. They expect us to be discreet about that cooperation. I can't imagine a government anywhere on the planet who now believes we can keep a secret." He was never given an opportunity to divulge the third as his impatient interviewer rushed to move on. Although the second "harm" is a relevant concern for programs that are secret, it is scarcely relevant to the issue of why the program was made secret in the first place. Updating his opinion on *Face the Nation* on December 28, 2013, Hayden extravagantly declared without further explanation that the NSA had become "infinitely weaker" because of the disclosures.

125. For example, when former NSA agent William Binney was asked if he believed that the government was only collecting metadata, he responded, "Well, I don't believe that for a minute. OK? I mean, that's why they had to build Bluffdale, that facility in Utah with that massive amount of storage that could store all these recordings and all the data being passed along the fiberoptic networks of the world. I mean, you could store 100 years of the world's communications here. That's for content storage. That's not for metadata. Metadata, if you were doing it and putting it into the systems we built, you could do it in a 12-by-20-foot room for the world. That's all the space you need. You don't need 100,000 square feet of space that they have at Bluffdale to do that." *PBS NewsHour*, August 1, 2013. There is also a suspicion that the 215 program sucks up Internet metadata as well: "The PRISM presentation seems to imply that Section 215 applies not only to phone metadata but also to email, chats, photos, video, logins, and other online user data." Roller, "This Is What Section 215 of the Patriot Act Does."

126. Lake, "Spy Chief."

127. Young, "National Insecurity," 386–87, 395. See also note 124 above.

128. Young, "National Insecurity," 402–5.

129. Young, "National Insecurity," 399–402.

130. See, however, Greenwald, "Congress Is Irrelevant."

131. Shalal-Esa and Menn, "U.S. Domestic Spying Controversy."

132. Office of the Press Secretary, White House, Remarks by the President on Review of Signals Intelligence.

133. Young, "National Insecurity," 406.

134. For example, Kinkaid, "NSA Leaker 'Outed.'" For a related perspective, see Morell, *The Great War of Our Time*, 285.

Chapter 8 The Department of Homeland Security

1. Executive Order 13228, "Establishing the Office of Homeland Security and the Homeland Security Council," White House, Washington, DC, October 8, 2001.

2. Office of Homeland Security, "National Strategy for Homeland Security," July 2002, vii. For a critique of this development, see Rittgers, "Abolish the Department of Homeland Security." While nomenclature may vary, many governments have similar agencies, although often without the responsibility for emergency management that DHS has. Morag, "Does Homeland Security Exist?," 1–5. The UK Home Office has oversight and funding authority over regional and national police forces, as well as over MI5, Serious and Organized Crime Agency (SOCA), UK Border Agency, and immigration. A newly elected Australian government in 2007 toyed with the idea of a new homeland security department, but the advice it received was telling: because "big departments risk becoming less accountable, less agile, less adaptable and more inward-looking," what was needed was "not a new agency but a new level of leadership, direction and co-ordination among the existing agencies." Nicholson, "Rudd Scraps Plan."

3. Department of Homeland Security, Budget in Brief—Fiscal Year 2015.

4. Kraft and Marks, *U.S. Government Counterterrorism*, 196.

5. See www.dhs.gov/our-mission.

6. Office of Management and Budget, Analytical Perspectives: Fiscal Years 2005 to 2015. Includes enacted and supplemental/emergency expenditures.

7. Inferred from an analysis of Office of Management and Budget, Analytical Perspectives: Fiscal Year 2015.

8. Table 8-1 includes several other elements. Customs and Border Protection (CBP) "is responsible for securing America's borders to protect the United States against terrorist threats and prevent the illegal entry of inadmissible persons and contraband, while facilitating lawful travel, trade, and immigration." Department of Homeland Security, Budget in Brief—Fiscal Year 2015, 41. Protecting borders is a crucial task for any country, and most activity is related to vetting new arrivals, stemming illegal immigration, and detecting the importation or trade of narcotics and other illicit goods. A primary CBP priority is securing the land borders of the United States, particularly that with Mexico. Counterterrorism does not feature prominently in this, and terrorism policing and intelligence even less so.

   The U.S. Coast Guard designates ports, waterways, and coastal security to be its primary focus alongside search and rescue. This mission entails "the protection of the U.S. Maritime Domain and the U.S. Marine Transportation System and those who live, work or recreate near them; the prevention and disruption of terrorist attacks, sabotage, espionage, or subversive acts; and response to and recovery from those that do occur." See www.uscg.mil/hq/cg5/cg532/pwcs.asp. Clearly, the Coast Guard's main counterterrorism role is to protect ports and harbors, and this costs $1.8 billion or 21 percent of its total budget of around $10 billion. U.S. Coast Guard, "Always Ready," table 2.

The Immigration and Customs Enforcement (ICE) is considered by DHS to be its principal investigative arm, and it is the second largest investigative agency in the federal covernment after the FBI. Kraft and Marks, *U.S. Government Counterterrorism*, 221. ICE "disrupts and dismantles transnational criminal organizations that exploit our borders by preventing terrorism and enhancing security, and enforcing and administering our immigration laws. It also identifies, apprehends, and removes criminal and other removable aliens from the United States." It carries out this mission through three principal components: Homeland Security Investigations (HSI), Enforcement and Removal Operations (ERO), and Management and Administration (M&A). Department of Homeland Security, Budget in Brief—Fiscal Year 2015, 57. HSI employs 6,400 special agents throughout the United States and abroad (93). However, it is not focused on terrorism but overwhelmingly on immigration and customs violations, including "export enforcement, human rights violations, narcotics, weapons and contraband smuggling, financial crimes, cybercrimes, human trafficking and smuggling, child exploitation, intellectual property violations, transnational gangs, and immigration benefit fraud." Immigration authorities may detect terrorists entering the United States—mostly from tip-offs from foreign and domestic intelligence and policing agencies and from terrorism watch lists, rather than from ICE-derived intelligence. A more important role might be the processing of visa applications, and the HIS did submit fifteen new subjects for terrorist watch lists in FY2013 (60). Added to this are the 300 HSI special agents assigned to joint terrorism task forces (JTTFs) nationwide (59). In 2013, HSI arrested 47,052 individuals, making 32,401 criminal arrests and 14,651 administrative arrests. However, few, if any, of these were directly related to terrorism. The most notable terrorism-related achievement listed in its annual budget statement in 2013 noted that "ICE played a critical role in the April 15, 2013 Boston Marathon bombing response and investigation" (59). How its role was "critical" is unstated—and for good reason. The FBI was the lead investigative agency in that case with hundreds of agents assigned to the task, and it was a witness interviewed by the FBI who identified one of the bombers while their names only became apparent after they shot an MIT police officer. McElroy, "Boston Marathon Victim Jeff Bauman."

Much the same reasoning holds for elements from the remaining two broad categories of homeland security measures listed in table 8-1: those designed to protect the American people, critical infrastructure, and key resources, and those designed to respond to, and recover from, incidents. Neither the U.S. budget nor the DHS budget provides detailed breakdowns of homeland security spending in these categories. However, they consist mainly of the National Protection and Programs Directorate ($2.8 billion), the Federal Emergency Management Agency ($2.7 billion), and possibly a decent chunk of the U.S.

Secret Service ($1.5 billion). These expenditures are not directly related to counterterrorism policing or intelligence, although the U.S. Secret Service does provide an intelligence role.

9. Department of Homeland Security, Budget in Brief—Fiscal Year 2015, 31.

10. Smith, "Senate Report Says."

11. Priest and Arkin, "Monitoring America." See also Mueller, "Confusion"; Rollins, "Fusion Centers," 41–44.

12. U.S. Senate, Permanent Subcommittee on Investigations, *Federal Support*, 61.

13. Department of Homeland Security, 2013 National Network of Fusion Centers: Final Report, 5. Some $134.9 million of this came from direct federal expenditures and grants to state, local, tribal, and territorial (SLTT) entities; $900,000 from tribal, territorial, and private sectors; $70.3 million from state governments; and $102.1 million from local governments.

14. The most recent census data from the Department of Justice are for 2007. Local police operating costs (inflation adjusted to 2014 dollars) of $135,000 per sworn officer and $100,000 per employee (Reaves, "Census," 6). Sheriffs' offices operating costs are $195,000 per sworn deputy and $97,000 per employee (Burch, "Sheriffs' Offices," 7).

15. Kraft and Marks, *U.S. Government Counterterrorism,* 209.

16. Department of Homeland Security, Remarks by Homeland Security Secretary Janet Napolitano.

17. U.S. Senate, Testimony of DHS Secretary Janet Napolitano.

18. Department of Homeland Security, 2013 National Network of Fusion Centers: Final Report, 14.

19. Department of Homeland Security, 2012 National Network of Fusion Centers: Final Report, 89–91; Department of Homeland Security, 2013 National Network of Fusion Centers: Final Report, 71. See also Schwartz, "The Whole Haystack."

20. Department of Homeland Security, Budget in Brief—Fiscal Year 2015, 33.

21. U.S. Senate, Permanent Subcommittee on Investigations. On hackles, see Smith, "Senate Report Says."

22. U.S. Senate, Permanent Subcommittee on Investigations, 32.

23. U.S. Senate, Permanent Subcommittee on Investigations, 83.

24. U.S. Senate, Permanent Subcommittee on Investigations, 106. On this issue, see also Mueller, "Confusion."

25. The remaining TSA budget allocates $1.2 billion to Transportation Security Support, and Intelligence and Vetting (formerly Transportation Threat Assessment and Credentialing).

26. Department of Homeland Security, Budget in Brief—Fiscal Year 2015, 67.

27. Nelson and Walker, *International Standardization of Air Passenger and Cargo Screening.*

28. Elias, *Airport and Aviation Security*, 196, 25.

29. Mueller and Stewart, *Terror, Security, and Money,* 137–45.

30. For a literature review of probabilistic terrorism risk assessment, see Stewart and Mueller, "Terrorism Risks," 893–94.

31. Kenney, " 'Dumb' Yet Deadly"; Mueller and Stewart, "The Terrorism Delusion"; Mueller, *Terrorism Since 9/11*; Aaronson, *The Terror Factory*; Schneier, "Portrait of the Modern Terrorist"; Byman and Fair, "The Case for Calling Them Nitwits"; Brooks, "Muslim 'Homegrown' Terrorists."

32. For more details of costs and characteristics of security measures, see Stewart and Mueller, "Terrorism Risks," 897–902.

33. Smith, "The Airport Security Follies."

34. As happened on a Germanwings Flight in 2015, as 150 perished when the co-pilot deliberately crashed the airliner while the flight captain was locked out of the flight deck. The only other such case since 9/11 seems to be on a LAM Mozambique Airlines Flight in 2013. Hardened cockpit doors do contribute considerably to reducing the risk of a successful airline hijacking. On the other hand, as the analysis that follows suggests, the other counter-hijacking security measures already combine to reduce that risk very substantially. Thus, taking the Germanwings case into account, the doors may actually have been the cause of more loss of life than they have saved. U.S. airline (FAA) policy is for a cabin crew member to replace the pilot if he leaves the cockpit so that the remaining pilot is never alone in the cockpit. After the Germanwings crash, many other countries instituted a similar policy.

35. Lee Moak, president of Airline Pilots Association International, letter to U.S. House of Representatives, Subcommittee on Transportation Security, July 12, 2011.

36. Frank, "More Than 10% of Pilots"; Elias, *Airport and Aviation Security*, 247. More recent data on the number of FFDOs are classified.

37. U.S. Senate, Committee on Homeland Security and Governmental Affairs, statement by Marcus W. Flagg, president of the Federal Flight Deck Officers Association, November 1, 2011.

38. Meckler and Carey, "Sky Patrol"; Seidenstat, "Federal Air Marshals."

39. Department of Homeland Security, Budgets in Brief FY2012–2013. According to the TSA, this reduction reflects efficiencies and program changes that leverage other aviation security system enhancements, allowing for more efficient mission deployments focused on high-risk flights. A hiring freeze on air marshals was begun in 2012. U.S. House of Representatives, Committee on Homeland Security, Subcommittee on Oversight and Management Efficiency, "The Impact of Sequestration."

40. U.S. House of Representatives, Department of Homeland Security Appropriations Act 2006, Amendment No. 10.

41. Elias, *Airport and Aviation Security*; Hudson, "Air Marshals Cover Only a Few Flights"; Seidenstat, "Federal Air Marshals"; Griffin, "Sources."

42. Seidenstat, "Federal Air Marshals"; Kearney, "Air Marshal's Role Now VIP Security."

43. Blessing, "Seat Spat Diverts Paris-bound Flight." On the killing by air marshals of an apparently deranged passenger in 2005 when the plane was still on the ground, see Mueller, *Overblown*, 160–61.

44. Meckler and Carey, "Sky Patrol"; Griffin, "Four Arrests for $800M."

45. Kiekintveld et al., "Computing Optimal Randomized Resource Allocations," 689–96.

46. U.S. Senate, Committee on Homeland Security and Government Affairs, statement by Marcus Flagg. Assumes two air marshals per flight.

47. Office of Management and Budget, Fiscal Year 2013, 45.

48. ALPA, "Secondary Flight Deck Barriers," 3.

49. RTCA, "Aircraft Secondary Barriers, Final Report."

50. ALPA, "Secondary Flight Deck Barriers," 4; RTCA, "Airplane Secondary Barriers, Terms of Reference."

51. ALPA, "Secondary Flight Deck Barriers," 4; "United Airlines Installing Secondary Security Barrier for Cockpit Protection," *Aviation Today*, September 27, 2004.

52. RTCA, "Airplane Secondary Barriers, Terms of Reference"; Wells, "Has United Made Its 787 Less Safe?"

53. Elias, *Airport and Aviation Security,* 237.

54. A higher figure of $30,000 per IPSB was assumed in our earlier study (Stewart and Mueller, "Terrorism Risks," 898), but recent advice places the cost at between $5,000 and $7,000. An estimate of $10,000 each is therefore on the high side.

55. Wells, "Has United Made Its 787 Less Safe?"

56. Nixon, "Widow of Sept. 11 Pilot."

57. Elias, *Airport and Aviation Security*, 392.

58. This soon becomes a multidimensional decision problem with many possible interactions among security measures, threat scenarios, threat probabilities, risk reduction, and losses. Fault trees and logic diagrams, together with systems engineering and reliability approaches, can aid in assessing these and other complex interactions involving threats, vulnerabilities, and consequences. Stewart and Melchers, *Probabilistic Risk Assessment*. Information about risk reductions can also be inferred from expert opinions, scenario analysis, and statistical analysis of prior performance data, as well as from system and reliability modeling.

59. Additional sensitivity analyses can be found in Stewart and Mueller, "Aviation Security," 630.

60. Fletcher, "Aviation Security".

61. For details of the calculation of probabilities in the four stages, see Stewart and Mueller, "Aviation Security." We recognize that there are uncertainties with predicting deterrent and disruption rates. An analysis can describe these rates probabilistically with low, mid, and upper values that, when incorporated with Monte Carlo simulation methods, allows for the 10th, mean, and 90th percentiles of risk and risk reduction to be calculated. We apply only the mean values in the present analysis.

62. Risk reduction is

$$R = 1 - \left\{ \begin{array}{l} \left[1 - \Pr\left(\text{deterred} \right) \right] \\ \times \left[1 - \Pr\left(\text{disrupted pre-boarding} \right) \right] \\ \times \left[1 - \Pr\left(\text{fail to commandeer aircraft} \right) \right] \\ \times \left[1 - \Pr\left(\text{anti-aircraft measures} \right) \right] \end{array} \right\}$$

This equation shows the collected benefits of the multiple layers of security. For example, in a process that looks rather cluttered, but is essentially straightforward, the overall deterrence risk reduction rate when one combines the eight elements in table 8-2 would be 1 − [(1−0.3) × (1−0.3) × (1−0.01) × (1−0.3) × (1−0.3) × (1−0.07) × (1−0.5) × (1−0.3)] = 92.3 percent. Any additional layer of security will add to this risk reduction, but such additional risk reductions will tend to be small because there is less risk remaining to be reduced. We recognize that security measures may not be perfectly substitutional (i.e., independent of each other). For example, passengers might be less willing to try to stop a hijacking if they know the flight deck officers are specially trained to do so. Therefore, we assume a series system where many event probabilities for all layers of security are treated as conditional probabilities.

63. Schneier, *Beyond Fear*, 247–48; Smith, "The Airport Security Follies."

64. Banks, "Statistics for Homeland Defense," 10. See also Mueller, *Overblown*, 152–53; Mueller and Stewart, *Terror, Security, and Money*, 153–54.

65. Martonosi and Barnett, "How Effective Is Security Screening"; Fletcher, "Aviation Security." However, a recent internal investigation by DHS suggests that this may be a generous estimate: it found a 5 percent detection rate for weapons and fake explosives. Costello, "TSA Failed 95% of Fake Weapons Tests."

66. U.S. Senate, Committee on Commerce, Science, and Transportation, testimony of TSA Administrator John Pistole. Related developments in the United States are found elsewhere. The International Air Transport Association (IATA) is developing its "Checkpoint of the Future," whose main concepts are "(1) strengthened security by focusing resources where risk is greatest, (2) supporting this risk-based approach by integrating passenger information into the checkpoint process, and (3) maximizing throughput for the vast majority of travelers who are deemed to be low risk with no compromise on security levels." IATA, "IATA Reveals Checkpoint of the Future." According to IATA's Global Passenger Survey, queuing time is the most frequent complaint with security. In late 2013, the "Checkpoint of the Future" morphed into "Smart Security"—a collaborative venture between IATA and Airports Council International. IATA, "ACI and IATA Collaborate to Deliver Smart Security." The "Smart Security" concept goes well beyond PreCheck and will involve redesign of screening lanes to include new and emerging screening technologies.

67. Department of Homeland Security, Budget in Brief—Fiscal Year 2015, 73.

68. Pistole, "Counterterrorism, Risk-Based Security and TSA's Vision."

69. For further discussion, see Stewart and Mueller, "Responsible Policy Analysis."

70. Government Accountability Office, Aviation Security, 2.

71. Winter and Currier, "TSA's Secret Behavior."

72. Government Accountability Office, Aviation Security: TSA, 16, 47. See also Government Accountability Office, Aviation Security: Efforts.

73. Winter and Currier, "TSA's Secret Behavior."

74. Government Accountability Office, Aviation Security: TSA, 2

75. Stewart and Mueller, "Cost-Benefit Analysis of Advanced Imaging Technology."

76. Department of Homeland Security, Budget in Brief—Fiscal Year 2013.

77. U.S. House of Representatives, Homeland Security Committee, hearing on fiscal year 2013 budget proposal.

78. Lee Moak, president of the Airline Pilots Association International, argues that the "FFDO program has been acknowledged by industry and government to be an extremely successful and cost-effective layer of aviation security." Lee Moak, letter to House Subcommittee on Transportation Security, July 12, 2011. The Coalition of Airline Pilots Associations (CAPA) recommends doubling the FFDO budget over five years. CAPA, "Federal Flight Deck Officer (FFDO) Program," 2011, www.capapilots.org/Websites/capa/images/Documents/Legislative/CAPA_FFDO_Program.pdf. And Paul Seidenstat ("Federal Air Marshals") argues that "[a]rming pilots and training crew members to deal with hijackers appear to serve as substitutes for placing marshals on flights and seem to be effective and far less costly."

79. Elias, *Airport and Aviation Security,* 247.

80. U.S. Senate, Committee on Homeland Security and Government Affairs, statement by Marcus Flagg.

81. CAPA, statement on TSA's FFDO Program, Coalition of Airline Pilots Associations, Washington, DC, August 7, 2014, www.capapilots.org/capa-statement-on-tsas-ffdo-program.

82. Department of Homeland Security, Budget in Brief—Fiscal Year 2015, 73.

83. For further development of this point, see Stewart, Ellingwood, and Mueller, "Homeland Security"; Stewart and Mueller, "Aviation Security."

Chapter 9 Local and Airport Police

1. A law enforcement agency is defined as one that employs at least one full-time officer.

2. Reaves, "Census," 2. More than 800,000 police officers come from 12,501 local police departments, over 3,000 sheriffs' offices, 50 primary state law enforcement agencies, 1,733 special jurisdiction agencies (e.g., campus police, parks police, airport police, etc.), and 638 other agencies, primarily county constable offices in Texas.

3. Reaves, "Federal Law Enforcement Officers, 2008," 1–2.

4. Reaves, "Local Police Departments, 2007," 30, 40; Burch, "Sheriffs' Offices, 2007," 20.

5. The total number of full-time and part-time employees in local police and sheriffs' offices was 946,000 in 2007. Reaves, "Census," 2.

6. The latest census data from the Department of Justice are for 2007. Local police operating costs are $116,500 per sworn officer and $88,200 per employee. Reaves, "Local Police Departments, 2007," 6. Sheriffs' offices' operating costs are $169,800 per sworn deputy and $83,900 per employee. Burch, "Sheriffs' Offices, 2007," 7. This excludes budgets for 50 primary state law enforcement agencies, 1,733 special jurisdiction agencies, and 638 other agencies—or 20 percent of the total number of state and local police.

7. The $1.7 billion per year spent on counterterrorism policing is an operating cost. This total is based on adding 20 percent to the $1.4 billion budget for local police and sheriffs' offices' counterterrorism tasks. It includes local police and sheriffs' staffing contributions to fusion centers and to joint terrorism task forces.

8. Morreale and Lambert, "Homeland Security,"

9. Lum et al., "Police Activities to Counter Terrorism," 108.

10. Reese, "Department of Homeland Security Assistance to States and Localities," 21; Department of Homeland Security, DHS Announces Grant Guidance for Fiscal Year (FY)2011. See also similar DHS press announcements for fiscal years 2012–2015.

11. The State Homeland Security Grant Program (SHSP) addresses state-identified planning, equipment, training, and exercise needs to improve response capabilities to acts of terrorism. It also supports the implementation of the National Preparedness Goal, the National Incident Management System, and the National Response Plan. The Urban Area Security Initiative (UASI) designates urban areas that may use its funds to purchase specialized homeland security equipment, to plan and execute exercises, to pay first responder overtime costs associated with heightened alert threat levels, and to train first responders. LETPP provides funding to law enforcement and public safety entities to support terrorism prevention activities. This includes establishing and enhancing information fusion centers and collaborating with non-law enforcement partners, other government agencies, and the private sector. LETPP merged with the SHSP in 2008.

12. Department of Homeland Security, DHS Announces Grant Guidance for Fiscal Year (FY)2014. The 9/11 Act requires states to dedicate 25 percent of their total allocation under the SHSP and UASI programs to law enforcement terrorism prevention activities.

13. Marion and Cronin, "Law Enforcement Responses."

14. Department of Homeland Security, DHS Authorized Equipment List.

15. Coburn, "Safety at Any Price," 4, 23, 26, 30, 37, emphasis in the original.

16. Bayley and Weisburd, "Cops and Spooks," 81–99. See also U.S. Senate, Committee on Homeland Security and Governmental Affairs, written testimony by Michael O'Hanlon, Brookings Institution, July 14, 2005.

17. Columbus Police Department, 2012 Annual Report, 16; Columbus Police Department, 2013 Annual Report, 1.

18. City of Columbus, 2013 Budget, Department of Public Safety, Department of Finance and Management.

19. The 2013 Homeland Security budget for Columbus was $22.5 million. The latest available budget for regulating traffic ("To reduce vehicular accidents resulting in injury and/or property damage through enforcement of traffic-related laws") was $9.2 million in 2010. In 2011, a new budget category, "Police—Homeland Security" ("To provide for the safety of the citizens of Columbus and central Ohio by regulating traffic, gathering intelligence to prevent terrorist attack, and managing emergency operations"), had a budget of $10.2 million. If the 2010 police traffic cost of $9.2 million is deducted from the 2011 $10.2 million budget for "regulating traffic, gathering intelligence to prevent terrorist attack, and managing emergency operations," approximately $1 million was devoted to "gathering intelligence to prevent terrorist attack" and "managing emergency operations."

20. Priest and Arkin, *Top Secret America*, 137.

21. See www.nyc.gov/html/nypd/html/memorial/memorial_wtc.shtml.

22. Cases 8, 9, 12, 18, 23, 24, 25, 28, 34, 42, 48, 52, 53, and perhaps 41, 54, 59, and 98.

23. Miller, "How the NYPD Foiled the Post-9/11 Terror Plots", Garcia, "In the Name of National Security."

24. Miller, "How the NYPD Foiled the Post-9/11 Terror Plots"; Celona and Doyle, "NYPD High-Profile Patrols Take Big Hit"; MacIsaac, "NYPD Trims Budget"; "Fighting Terrorism in New York City," *60 Minutes* (CBS), September 25, 2011.

25. Horowitz, "The NYPD's War on Terror."

26. New York City Council, Hearing on the Fiscal Year 2015 Preliminary Budget & the Fiscal 2014 Preliminary Mayor's Management Report: Police Department, Finance Division Briefing Paper, March 21, 2014.

27. 2006: New York City, Independent Budget Office, IBO's Programmatic Review of the 2007 Preliminary Budget: New York City Police Department, March 2006. 2010: Stein, "NYPD Intelligence Detectives Go Their Own Way."

28. It is unclear whether the NYC budget includes the NYPD staffing cost of the Joint Terrorism Task Force. This is likely to be a few dozen officers and staff at most, costing no more than $1–2 million. The NYPD receives federal government reimbursement to help protect foreign missions and United Nations gatherings and events. Hennelly, "NYPD Plays Key Role." Since this task is not really related very much to counterterrorism, we do not include it and its costs in our analysis.

29. New York City Council, Hearing on the Fiscal Year 2015 Preliminary Budget & the Fiscal 2014 Preliminary Mayor's Management Report: Police Department, Finance Division Briefing Paper, March 21, 2014. The NYPD's counterterrorism program includes sections devoted to terrorism threat analysis, training, critical infrastructure protection, transportation security, chemical, biological, radiological, nuclear, and explosives policy and planning, special projects, and emergency response and planning, as well as a "shield unit." The intelligence program handles all of the intelligence-gathering activities of the NYPD, including counterterrorist functions. In our estimate, we assume that half of the program's efforts are devoted to counterterrorism.

30. Includes federal security/counterterrorism grants. These grants include the Urban Areas Security Initiative (UASI), State Homeland Security Block Grant (SHSG), Law Enforcement Terrorism Prevention Program (LETPP), COPS Homeland Security Overtime Program, COPS Interoperable Communications Program and the Citizens Corp, and MMRS grants. Also included is reimbursable overtime whereby private, state, and federal grants reimburse the NYPD for overtime expenses mostly related to counterterrorism and homeland security programs, such as the federally funded UASI Grant.

31. Eighty million dollars divided by the population served by NYPD of 8.2 million in 2006.

32. The NYPD is nearly three times larger than the police departments in Chicago and Los Angeles, the next largest in the United States. Reaves, "Census," 4. In 2012, the Chicago Police Department employed 327 counterterrorism officers with a combined budget of $25 million, but in 2013, that budget reportedly was cut to $8 million and the number of officers was reduced to 100 after Chicago moved its counterterrorism intelligence operations under the command of a new Office of Crime Control Strategies. Price, "National Security and Local Police," 9–10. This amounts to 1 to 2 percent of the Chicago Police Department's budget of $1.25 billion for 2013. City of Chicago, Mayor's Budget Recommendations for Year 2014, 155–57. The police department of Los Angeles has a budget of $1.2 billion and spends roughly 2 percent, or $24 million, on counterterrorism. Miller, "On the Front Line."

33. Apuzzo, Goldman, and Sullivan, "NYPD's Spying Programs."

34. Elliott, "Fact-Check"; Apuzzo and Goldman, Enemies Within, 280.

35. Elliott, "Bloomberg on NYPD."

36. New York Police Department, "Terrorist Plots." The listing also includes several New York or New York–related people who were trying to go overseas to fight there. The URL for the 2012 listing of fourteen plots (now taken down from the web) includes this: www. nypt_foils_plots_targeting_nyc.

37. See also Apuzzo, Goldman, and Sullivan, "NYPD's Spying Programs"; Elliott, "Fact-Check."

38. See Mueller, Overblown, 40–41. There is no case study of this episode because it is not clear that it ever existed.

39. Apuzzo and Goldman, *Enemies Within*, 151–52. See also Horowitz, "Anatomy of a Foiled Plot"; Dickey, *Securing the City*, 187–98.

40. Apuzzo and Goldman, *Enemies Within*, 129.

41. Apuzzo and Goldman, *Enemies Within*, 142.

42. On this issue, see Apuzzo and Goldman, *Enemies Within*.

43. Strom et al., "Building on Clues," 12.

44. Kurzman, "Muslim-American Terrorists Since 9/11."

45. Neuman, "In Response to M.T.A.'s 'Say Something' Ads." See also Mueller, "Terror Tipsters"; Mueller and Stewart, *Terror, Security, and Money*, 162; Molotch, *Against Security*, 54–55.

46. Fernandez, "A Phrase for Safety."

47. Fernandez, "A Phrase for Safety."

48. Hsu, "Security Chief Urges 'Collective Fight.'"

49. Okochi, "Anti-Terrorism Measures," 77–86. See also Apuzzo and Goldman, *Enemies Within*, 82.

50. Levitt, "Kelly and AP."

51. Apuzzo and Goldman, *Enemies Within*, 82.

52. Weiss, "Posting NYPD Detectives Overseas."

53. Weiss, "Posting NYPD Detectives Overseas."

54. Apuzzo and Goldman, *Enemies Within*, 83.

55. Reaves, "Census." Law enforcement services for some large airport and transit systems are provided by a local police department or sheriff's office. For example, the Chicago Police provides law enforcement services for O'Hare and Midway airports.

56. Stewart and Mueller, "Risk and Cost-Benefit Analysis." Based on 2013 deployments.

57. U.S. and Australian dollars are roughly equivalent over the five-year period 2010–2014. Passenger checkpoint and luggage screening is conducted by private-sector security personnel contracted by the airports for these tasks. Immigration and customs duties are undertaken by the Australian Customs and Border Protection Service.

58. Airport traffic data, 1985–86 to 2013–14, Department of Infrastructure and Regional Development, Australian Government, www.bitre.gov.au/publications/ongoing/airport_traffic_data.aspx, accessed September 14, 2014.

59. Passenger traffic for 2013: O'Hare was 66.9 million, LAX was 66.7 million, Dallas-Fort Worth was 60.4 million, and JFK was 50 million, while Atlanta was 94.4 million. "Passenger Traffic in 2013," *Airport World*, February 14, 2014.

60. See www.lawa.org/airportpolice/.

61. See also Stewart and Mueller, "Cost-Benefit Analysis."

62. Elias, *Airport and Aviation Security*, 82–83; Stevens et al., "Near-Term Options," 35.

63. Stevens et al., "Near-Term Options."

64. Weisz, "America's Lack of Airport Security." In another study, blast pressure modeling from a 900-pound vehicle-borne bomb detonated in the passenger drop-off area of a generic airport predicted approximately 250 fatalities. See Lord et al., "Airport Front-of-House Vulnerabilities."

65. Robinson et al., "Valuing the Risk of Death."

66. LaTourrette et al., "Reducing Terrorism Risk," 13.

67. Morral et al., *Modeling Terrorism*, 53.

68. IATA revenue projections to 2020 show approximately 5 percent annual increases in passengers and revenues, with worldwide revenues of $598 billion in 2011 (IATA, "2012 Annual Review"). An attack at a major airport might result in a more wary traveling public and no global growth in revenue/passengers for one year, equivalent to a 5 percent revenue or passenger decrease for one year. This would entail a loss of at least $30 billion.

69. Morral et al., *Modeling Terrorism*. Note that the TSA's RMAT estimates indirect losses of only $11.1 billion for an attack on aircraft, and less for threats to airports.

70. Weisz, "America's Lack of Airport Security." Another study predicted approximately 100 fatalities from a 36-kg (80-pound) bomb detonated in the check-in area of a generic airport: Lord et al., "Airport Front-of-House Vulnerabilities."

71. Heaton, *Hidden in Plain Sight*.

72. Grosskopf, "Evaluating the Societal Response."

73. Los Angeles, Department of Airports, Comprehensive Annual Financial Report: Fiscal Year Ended June 30, 2013, Los Angeles World Airports, 70.

74. Los Angeles, Department of Airports, Comprehensive Annual Financial Report: Fiscal Year Ended June 30, 2013, iii.

75. Grant and Stewart, "A Systems Model."

76. Grant and Stewart, "A Systems Model," 86.

77. George and Whatford, "Regulation of Transport Security Post 9/11."

78. Elias, *Airport and Aviation Security*.

79. The Global Terrorism Database tallies 126 attacks on airports out of 35,700 terrorist attacks in total.

80. Department of Homeland Security, "National Strategy for Aviation Security," 11.

81. Cases 4, 23, 25, and 55.

82. The threat probability is equal to 3 threats divided by 13 years divided by 110 airports.

83. Expert opinions, fault trees, and logic diagrams, together with systems engineering and reliability approaches, will aid in assessing complex interactions involving threats, vulnerabilities, and consequences. See Stewart and Mueller, "Cost-Benefit Analysis of Advanced Imaging"; Stewart and Mueller, "Terrorism Risks"; Stewart and Mueller, "Aviation Security" for details of airliner security techniques. A more detailed and comprehensive study is required to properly model the complex interactions and interdependencies in airport passenger terminal security.

84. As in previous chapters, we take costs and benefits as mean—that is, as single-point or deterministic—values. Since we use mean values, there is a 50-50 or break-even chance that net benefit may be higher or lower than in our mean calculations. An advantage of this is that the calculations are straightforward and can, in the main, be done using a simple hand calculator. They can also be readily replicated and checked by others. However, this simplified approach ignores the uncertainties and variabilities in the parameter estimates—and uncertainties in the realm of terrorist intentions and predictions are large. Some of our recent papers use Monte Carlo simulation methods to propagate vulnerability, risk reduction, and loss uncertainties in the calculation of net benefits (Stewart and Mueller, "Cost-Benefit Analysis of Advanced Imaging"; Stewart and Mueller, "Cost-Benefit Analysis of Airport Security"). This allows us to calculate the probability that the benefit exceeds the cost. In principle, risk averseness has no role in public decision making (Mueller and Stewart, *Responsible Counterterrorism Policy*). Reality is different of course, and modest risk aversion is tolerable when there is considerable doubt about costs and benefits. A risk-averse decision maker will prefer a small likelihood of a net loss. For example, this may mean that information about the minimum attack probability to ensure that there is 90 percent surety that benefits exceed the cost is more useful as a deciding factor than knowing the 50–50 or break-even attack probabilities that feature so often in this book.

85. Net benefit = (co-benefits) + [(probability of attack absent the security measure) × (probability that the attack is successful) × (losses sustained in the successful attack) × (reduction in risk)] − (cost of the security measure).

86. For more detail on this issue, see Stewart and Mueller, "Risk and Cost-Benefit Analysis," and appendix C.

Conclusion *Horrible Imaginings and Painted Devils*

1. Risen, *Pay Any Price*, 74.

2. Gerges, *The Rise and Fall of Al-Quada*, 192.

3. Allison, *Nuclear Terrorism*, 15; Kristof, "An American Hiroshima." Allison repeated his judgment in an article published two years later, albeit without reducing the terminal interval to compensate. Allison, "The Ongoing Failure of Imagination," 39. He had presumably relied on the same inspirational mechanism in 1995 to predict (as noted earlier): "In the absence of a determined program of action, we have every reason to anticipate acts of nuclear terrorism against American targets before this decade is out." "Must We Wait for the Nuclear Morning After?" Garwin: Allison, "How Likely Is a Nuclear Terrorist Attack?" For more on alarmism about the atomic terrorist, see Mueller, *Overblown*, 45–46; Mueller, *Atomic Obsession*, 181–83; Diab, *The Harbinger Theory*.

4. *Morning Edition,* National Public Radio, May 15, 2007. See also Langewiesche, *The Atomic Bazaar*; Mueller, *Atomic Obsession*, chs. 12–15; Mueller, "The Truth About al Qaeda"; Diab, *The Harbinger Theory*.

5. For a broad-scaled examination, see LaFree, Dugan, and Miller, *Putting Terrorism in Context*. See also appendix B.

6. See especially LaFree, Dugan, and Miller, *Putting Terrorism in Context,* ch. 4.

7. LaFree, Dugan, and Miller, *Putting Terrorism in Context*, 13.

8. Clausewitz, *On War*, 231.

9. Karnow, *Vietnam: A History,* 254–55.

10. See Keeley, *War Before Civilization.* For more on the distinction between terrorism and civil war, see Mueller, *The Remnants of War,* 18–20.

11. On the importance of this distinction, see Abrahms, "Why Terrorism Does Not Work."

12. On this issue, see also Cronin, "ISIS Is Not a Terrorist Group."

13. "An Hour with Syrian President Bashar Al-Assad," *charlierose.com,* March 29, 2015.

14. On this issue, see also Mueller, "Action and Reaction."

15. Hedges, "On Bosnia's Ethnic Fault Lines."

16. Des Forges, *"Leave None to Tell the Story"* 618–20.

17. Simon, *The Terrorist Trap,* 43–46.

18. Concerning the episode, Richard Ned Lebow argues that "the Sarajevo assassinations changed the political and psychological environment in Vienna and Berlin in six important ways, all of which may have been necessary for the decisions that led to war. First, they constituted a political challenge to which Austrian leaders believed they had to respond forcefully; anything less was expected to encourage further challenges by domestic and foreign enemies. Second, they shocked and offended Franz Josef and Kaiser Wilhelm and made both emperors more receptive to calls for decisive measures to preserve Austria's honor and its standing as a great power. Third, they changed the policy-making context in Vienna by removing the principal spokesman for peace. Fourth, they may have been the catalyst for [German Chancellor] Bethmann Hollweg's gestalt shift. Fifth, they made it possible for Bethmann Hollweg to win the support of the socialists, without which he never would have risked war. Sixth, they created a psychological environment in which Wilhelm and Bethmann Hollweg could proceed in incremental steps toward war, convincing themselves at the outset that their actions were unlikely to provoke a European war, and at the end of the crisis, that others were responsible for war." Lebow, *Forbidden Fruit,* 85. Except for the third way in this catalogue, all these apparently necessary consequences deal with emotional or calculated reactions, none of which was a necessary result of the event itself. Because a terrorist gets lucky with a couple of shots in a distant province does not mean that key decision makers are required to shift beliefs or to give in to emotions to embrace policies they had previously rejected.

19. Burke, *Al-Qaeda: Casting a Shadow of Terror,* 167–68; Byman, *Deadly Connections,* 201–203; Wright, *The Looming Tower,* 267–68, 287–89, 354. On this process more generally, see Lake, "Rational Extremism," 15–29.

20. Takeyh, "The Rogue Who Came in from the Cold."

21. Pape, *Dying to Win,* 156–60; Simon, *The Terrorist Trap,* 186.

22. Rapoport, "Modern Terror: The Four Waves," 68. On the often deadly and indiscriminate overreaction to anarchist terrorism in the United States and elsewhere, see Jensen, "The United States, International Policing, and the War."

23. Despite the fact that the 9/11 experience caused Americans to pull together, some commentators confidently predict that the government and people would respond by going on a rampage of self-destruction in the event of further major attacks. For example, Michael Ignatieff argues that, although Americans did allow their leaders one fatal mistake in September 2001, they simply "will not forgive another one." If there are several large-scale attacks, he confidently predicts, the trust that binds the people to its leadership and to each other will crumble, and the "cowed populace" will demand that tyranny be imposed upon it, and quite possibly fragment itself into a collection of rampaging lynch mobs devoted to killing "former neighbors" and "onetime friends." For a discussion, see Mueller, *Overblown,* 46.

24. Schneier, "Why Are We Spending $7 Billion on TSA?"

25. Byman, "A Corrective That Goes Too Far?," 521.

26. Rosen, *The Naked Crowd,* 79.

27. Berinsky, *In Time of War,* 217.

28. On this issue, see Mueller, "Public Opinion, the Media, and War"; Mueller, *War and Ideas,* chs. 8, 9.

29. Risen, *Pay Any Price,* 203.

30. However, see Mueller, *Overblown,* 197–98. Some debunking efforts: Friedman, Harper, and Preble, *Terrorizing Ourselves*; Thrall and Cramer, *American Foreign Policy*; Schneier, *Beyond Fear*; Furedi, *Culture of Fear*; Rosen, *The Naked Crowd*; Lustick, *Trapped in the War on Terror*; Fallows, "Declaring Victory"; Mueller, *Overblown.* See also Johnson, *Improbable Dangers.*

31. Jervis, "Do Leaders Matter?" For a different perspective, see Glennon, *National Security and Double Government.*

32. Shapiro, "Countering Violent Extremism."

33. See also Mueller and Stewart, "Responsible Counterterrorism Policy."

34. Sunstein, "Misfearing," 15, 18.

35. Banks, "Statistics for Homeland Defense," 10.

36. On this issue, see also Mueller and Stewart, *Terror, Security, and Money,* 179–82.

37. Dyer, "The International Terrorist Conspiracy."

38. Mueller and Stewart, *Terror, Security, and Money,* ch. 4.

39. See Sunstein, "Terrorism and Probability Neglect."

40. A recent case in point is Kean and Hamilton, "Today's Rising Terrorist Threat."

41. Chan, "Buzz over Mayor's 'Get a Life' Remark." For another (potential) instance, see Mueller, *Overblown,* 151–52.

42. *PBS NewsHour,* November 16, 2010.

43. SCENIHR, "Health Effects of Security Scanners." Passenger exposure to backscatter scanners is 0.4 microsieverts per scan. A dose of 1 microsievert, according

to standard models, increases the risk of fatal cancers by 0.004 percent. The increase in fatal cancer risk per scan is thus $0.4 \times 0.001 \times 0.00004 = 1$ in 60 million.

44. During the 15-year period, 1999–2013, 363 airline passengers were killed by terrorists (mainly, of course, on 9/11). The total number of global airline passengers over the same period was approximately 32 billion.

45. The media has also repeatedly let alarmed and irresponsible comment from officials go unchallenged. Thus, in December 2014, Mike Rogers, chair of the House Intelligence Committee, dramatically warned on CNN that the release of a Senate Intelligence report on the CIA's use of torture would result in "violence and death." He based this prediction, he said, on information supplied by "foreign leaders" and by "our own intelligence community." "State of the Union," CNN, December 7, 2014. As it happened, no "violence and death" did greet the report's release (nor has it since), perhaps because it did not come as news to jihadists around the world that the CIA had used "enhanced interrogation techniques" against them in the past. When asked about this curious development later in the month on CBS, Rogers replied that he had come to his conclusion because of what those "foreign leaders" had told him and because "our own intelligence services issued an analytic report" that "believed" release of the torture report "would cause and lead to violence and likely death." Rather than suggest that perhaps Rogers and other officials had completely misjudged the situation or that their dire predictions were essentially self-serving, Rogers's interrogator simply said, "Well so far, so good. And obviously you and I hope that doesn't happen." Replied Rogers: "Sure." "Face the Nation," CBS, December 14, 2014.

46. For some reflections on this, see Mueller, Stewart, and Friedman, "Finally Talking Terror Sensibly."

47. Fallows, "Declaring Victory," 73.

48. PCLOB, Report on the Surveillance Program, 148.

49. Mueller and Stewart, *Terror, Security, and Money*, 6.

50. Clarke et al., *Liberty and Security*, 114. See also Schneier, "The Efficacy of Post-9/11 Counterterrorism."

51. Department of Homeland Security, Office of Inspector General, Annual Review of U.S. Coast Guard's Mission Performance, 24.

52. Government Accountability Office, Report to Congressional Requesters: Coast Guard, 41–42, 45–46.

53. The OMB states that "the standard criterion for deciding whether a government program can be justified on economic principles is *net present value*—the discounted monetized value of expected net benefits (i.e., benefits minus costs)" and "the expected value (an unbiased estimate) is the appropriate estimate for use." Office of Management and Budget, "Guidelines and Discount Rates for Benefit-Cost Analysis." Although over twenty years old, this circular is still the most current. See also Faber and Stewart, "Risk Assessment for Civil Engineering Facilities"; Ellingwood, "Mitigating Risk from Abnormal Loads"; Sunstein, *The Cost-Benefit*

State. As considered at various points in this book, terrorism is a frightening threat that influences our willingness to accept risk, a willingness that is influenced by psychological, social, cultural, and institutional processes. Moreover, events involving high consequences can cause losses to individuals that they cannot bear, such as bankruptcy or loss of life. On the other hand, governments, large corporations, and other self-insured institutions can absorb such losses more readily. The follow-on consequences from a terrorist attack—such as loss of consumer confidence, economic decline, reduced tourism, and lowered tax revenue—can and should be included in the estimation of losses in a risk-neutral analysis as we have repeatedly shown in this book and in *Terror, Security, and Money*. Utility theory can be used if the decision maker wishes to explicitly factor risk aversion into the decision process.

54. Stewart, Ellingwood, and Mueller, "Homeland Security"; Ball and Floyd, "Societal Risks."
55. Hardaker, Fleming, and Lien, "How Should Governments Make Risky Policy Decisions?"
56. Paté-Cornell, "Risk and Uncertainty Analysis," 644.
57. Carle, *The Interrogator*, 269, 293n1.
58. Carle, *The Interrogator,*, 249, 274, 275, 288. See also Sageman, "The Stagnation in Terrorism Research"; Jervis, *Why Intelligence Fails*, 23–24, 49, 51–52, 191–92.
59. Wyden and Dickas, "Too Many Secrets."
60. Blomberg and Rose, "Editor's Introduction to the Economic Impacts."
61. Morral et al., *Modeling Terrorism Risk*.
62. *PBS NewsHour*, December 10, 2014.
63. Krauthammer, "A Travesty of a Report." In 2004 Krauthammer characterized the post-9/11 period as one in which, "contrary to every expectation and prediction," the second shoe never dropped. Krauthammer, "Blixful Amnesia."
64. Apuzzo and Goldman, *Enemies Within*, 154–55.
65. For a discussion, see Mueller, *Atomic Obsession*, especially 35–36.
66. See Preble, *John F. Kennedy and the Missile Gap*. See also Mueller, "Questing for Monsters to Destroy."
67. Wyden and Dickas, "Too Many Secrets," 116.
68. Bill Keller, conversation with John Mueller, April 9, 2011, Berkeley, CA.
69. Savage, "Manning Is Acquitted."
70. For an extended discussion, see Harris, *The Watchers*.
71. Sageman, *Understanding Terror Networks*, 573; Carle, *The Interrogator*, 249. On this issue in intelligence more broadly, assessing the problem of separating out the signals from the noise, see Wohlstetter, *Pearl Harbor*. For the arresting argument that sometimes there are really no valid signals at all—only noise—see Kahn, "The Intelligence Failure of Pearl Harbor," 136–52. See also Silver, *The Signals and the Noise*.
72. Schwartz, "The Whole Haystack."

73. Harris, *The Watchers*, 209.

74. On this issue, see Ziliak and McCloskey, *The Cult of Statistical Significance*.

75. Sageman, "The Stagnation in Terrorism Research," 573.

76. Evans, "Electronic Publication." See also Benson, "Why the Internet Is Not Increasing Terrorism," 306.

77. Heuer, *Psychology of Intelligence Analysis*, 149. See also Carle, *The Interrogator*, 295.

78. On these issues, see also Mueller, *Overblown*, 7, 179–82.

79. On this number, see also Schwartz, "The Whole Haystack."

Appendix B   Assessing the Costs Inflicted by Terrorism

1. START, Global Terrorism Database. The GTD has been updated since 2007 to include more terrorist incidents for the period 1970–2007 than were included in earlier editions of the compilation. For an extended analysis of this database, see LaFree, Dugan, and Miller, *Putting Terrorism in Context*.

2. RAND Database of Worldwide Terrorism Incidents.

3. The GTD defines a single terrorist attack as one occurring in the same geographic area and at the same point in time. Hence, the 9/11 attacks and those on the London transit system in 2005 are each included in the count as four separate incidents.

4. Of the 3,000 terrorist incidents in the United Kingdom, only two inflicted damage that the GTD considered "catastrophic"—a bombing in London that killed three people in 1992 and the London financial area bombing of 1993, each causing damage of 1 to 2 billion dollars. Only nine attacks resulted in the death of more than ten people, the worst being the 1988 bombing of PanAm Flight 103 over Lockerbie (270 deaths), followed by the 28 killed in the 1998 bombing in Omagh, Northern Ireland. In some instances, Republican terrorists warned authorities of the impending attack; they did so in Omagh, but the warnings were unclear, and the wrong areas were evacuated.

Appendix C   Marginal Costs and Benefits of FBI Counterterrorism Expenditures

1. Total risk reduction is given by the equation $\Delta R = 1 - (1-R)^N$, where $R = 50\%$ and N is equal to 1 for the first \$600 million of expenditure, and increases to $N = 5$ for the final \$3 billion of expenditure.

REFERENCES

Aaronson, Trevor. "The Informants." *Mother Jones*, October 2011, 30–43.

Aaronson, Trevor. *The Terror Factory*. Brooklyn, NY: Ig Publishing, 2013.

Abrahms, Max. "Does Terrorism Really Work? Evolution in the Conventional Wisdom Since 9/11." *Defence and Peace Economics* 22, no. 6 (2011): 583–94.

Abrahms, Max. "Fear of 'Lone Wolf' Misplaced." *Baltimore Sun*, January 5, 2011.

Abrahms, Max. "Why Terrorism Does Not Work." *International Security* 31, no. 2 (2006): 42–78.

Adams, William C., and Michael Joblove. "The Unnewsworthy Holocaust: TV News and Terror in Cambodia." In William C. Adams, ed., *Television Coverage of International Affairs*. Norwood, NJ: Ablex, 1982, 217–25.

Airline Pilots Association International (ALPA). "Secondary Flight Deck Barriers and Flight Deck Access Procedures: A Call for Action." White paper, Washington, DC, July 2013.

Allison, Graham T. (in debate with Michael A. Levi). "How Likely Is a Nuclear Terrorist Attack on the United States?" New York: Council on Foreign Relations, 2007. Available at www.cfr.org/publication/13097/how_likely_is_a_nuclear_attack_on_the_united_states.html.

Allison, Graham T. "Must We Wait for the Nuclear Morning After?" *Washington Post*, April 30, 1995.

Allison, Graham T. *Nuclear Terrorism: The Ultimate Preventable Catastrophe*. New York: Times Books, 2004.

Allison, Graham T. "The Ongoing Failure of Imagination." *Bulletin of the Atomic Scientists*, September/October 2006.

Amira, Dan. "Did Controversial NSA Spy Programs Really Help Prevent an Attack on the Subway?" *nymag.com*, June 10, 2013.

Andrew, Christopher M. *The World Was Going Our Way*. New York: Basic Books, 2005.

Andrews, Wilson, and Todd Lindeman. "The 'Black Budget': How Intelligence Agencies Spend $52 Billion." *Washington Post*, August 29, 2013. Available at http://www.washingtonpost.com/wp-srv/special/national/black-budget/.

Apuzzo, Matt, and Adam Goldman. *Enemies Within: Inside the NYPD's Secret Spying and Bin Laden's Final Plot Against America*. New York: Simon and Schuster, 2013.

Apuzzo, Matt, Adam Goldman, and Eileen Sullivan. "NYPD's Spying Programs Yielded Only Mixed Results." Associated Press, December 23, 2011.

Arkin, William M. "What the 9/11 Plotter Tells Us." *washingtonpost.com*, March 30, 2006.

Arquilla, John. "The New Seeds of Terror." *foreignpolicy.com*, May 10, 2011.

Atran, Scott. *Talking to the Enemy: Faith, Brotherhood, and the (Un)making of Terrorists*. New York: Ecco, 2010.

Bacevich, Andrew J. *The New American Militarism: How Americans Are Seduced by War*. New York: Oxford University Press, 2005.

Baker, Peter. *Days of Fire: Bush and Cheney in the White House*. New York: Doubleday, 2013.

Ball, David J., and P. J. Floyd. "Societal Risks." Final report, commissioned by the Health and Safety Executive, UK, 1998.

Bamford, James. "The NSA Is Building the Country's Biggest Spy Center (Watch What You Say)." *Wired*, March 15, 2012.

Bamford, James. "They Know Much More Than You Think." *New York Review of Books*, August 15, 2013.

Banks, David L. "Statistics for Homeland Defense." *Chance* 15, no. 1 (2002): 8–10.

Barkun, Michael. *Chasing Phantoms: Reality, Imagination, and Homeland Security Since 9/11*. Chapel Hill: University of North Carolina Press, 2014.

Barnhart, Michael A. *Japan Prepares for Total War: The Search for Economic Security, 1919–1941*. Ithaca, NY: Cornell University Press, 1987.

Bayley, David H., and David Weisburd. "Cops and Spooks: The Role of the Police in Counterterrorism." In *To Protect and to Serve: Policing in an Age of Terrorism*, edited by David Weisburd et al., 81–99. New York: Springer, 2009.

Benson, David C. "Why the Internet Is Not Increasing Terrorism." *Security Studies*, 23, no. 2 (2014): 293–328.

Bergen, Peter. "Five Myths About Osama bin Laden." *washingtonpost.com*, May 6, 2011.

Bergen, Peter. "Where You Bin? The Return of Al Qaeda." *New Republic*, January 29, 2007, 16–19.

Bergen, Peter. "WMD Terrorism Fears Are Overblown." *cnn.com*, December 5, 2008.

Bergen, Peter, and Paul Cruickshank. "Self-Fulfilling Prophecy." *Mother Jones*, November–December 2007.

Bergen, Peter, and Paul Cruickshank. "The Unraveling: The Jihadist Revolt Against bin Laden." *New Republic*, June 11, 2008.

Bergen, Peter, and Bruce Hoffman. "Assessing the Terrorist Threat." Report of the Bipartisan Policy Center's National Security Preparedness Group. Bipartisan Policy Center, September 10, 2010.

Bergen, Peter, David Sterman, Emily Schneider, and Bailey Cahall. "Do NSA's Bulk Surveillance Programs Stop Terrorists?" New America Foundation, January 2014.

Berinsky, Adam. *In Time of War: Understanding Public Opinion, from World War II to Iraq*. Chicago: University of Chicago Press, 2009.

Bernstein, David. "Case 38: Oregon." In *Terrorism Since 9/11: The American Cases*, edited by John Mueller. Columbus: Mershon Center, Ohio State University, 2015.

Bernstein, Peter L. *Against the Gods: The Remarkable Story of Risk*. New York: John Wiley, 1996.

Betts, Richard. "Maybe I'll Stop Driving." *Terrorism and Political Violence* 17, no. 4 (Autumn 2005): 487–505.

Bever, Lindsey, and Brian Murphy, "Gunmen Shot Dead in Texas After Opening Fire Outside Prophet Muhammad Cartoon Show." *washingtonpost.com*, May 3, 2015.

Bjelopera, Jerome P. *American Jihadist Terrorism: Combating a Complex Threat*. Washington, DC: Congressional Reference Service, January 23, 2013.

Bjelopera, Jerome P. *The Federal Bureau of Investigation and Terrorism Investigations*. Washington, DC: Congressional Research Service, January 14, 2013.

Blair, Clay, *The Forgotten War: America in Korea, 1950–1953*. New York: Times Books, 1987.

Blalock, Garrick, Vrinda Kadiyali, and Daniel H. Simon. "Driving Fatalities After 9/11: A Hidden Cost of Terrorism." *Applied Economics* 41, no. 14 (2009): 1717–1729.

Blalock, Garrick, Vrinda Kadiyali, and Daniel H. Simon. "The Impact of Post-9/11 Airport Security Measures on the Demand for Air Travel." *Journal of Law and Economics* 50, no. 4 (November 2007): 731–755.

Blessing, Kiera. "Seat Spat Diverts Paris-bound Flight to Logan Airport." *Boston Globe*, August 29, 2014.

Block, Melissa. "Al-Qaida Magazine Details Parcel Bomb Attempt." *npr.org*, November 22, 2010.

Blomberg, S. Brock, and Adam Z. Rose. "Editor's Introduction to the Economic Impacts of the September 11, 2001, Terrorist Attacks." *Peace Economics, Peace Science, and Public Policy* 15, no. 2 (2009): 1–14.

Bogan, Kenneth T., and Edwin D. Jones. "Risks of Mortality and Morbidity from Worldwide Terrorism: 1968–2004." *Risk Analysis* 26, no. 1 (2006): 56.

Brady, Lauren. "Case 19: Sears Tower." In *Terrorism Since 9/11: The American Cases*, edited by John Mueller. Columbus: Mershon Center, Ohio State University, 2015.

Brady, Lauren. "Case 39: DC Metro—Facebook." In *Terrorism Since 9/11: The American Cases*, edited by John Mueller. Columbus: Mershon Center, Ohio State University, 2015.

Breslauer, George W. "Ideology and Learning in Soviet Third World Policy." *World Politics* 39, no. 3 (April 1987): 436–437.

Brooks, Clem, and Jeff Manza. *Whose Rights? Counterterrorism and the Dark Side of American Public Opinion.* New York: Russell Sage, 2013.

Brooks, Risa A. "Muslim 'Homegrown' Terrorism in the United States: How Serious Is the Threat?" *International Security* 36, no. 2 (Fall 2011): 7–47.

Buchanan, Patrick J. "Is ISIS 'an Existential Threat'?" *townhall.com*, August 12, 2014.

Buchanan, Patrick J. "ISIS Poses No Existential Threat to America." *theamericanconservative.com*, June 17, 2014.

Bump, Philip. "After an Easy Hearing, the NSA and FBI Are Ready for a Drink." *The Wire*, June 18, 2013.

Bunn, Matthew, Anthony Weir, and J. P. Holdren. "Controlling Nuclear Warheads and Materials: A Report Card and Action Plan." Cambridge, MA: Nuclear Threat Initiative and Project on Managing the Atom, Harvard University, 2003.

Burch, Andrea M. "Sheriffs' Offices, 2007—Statistical Tables." Washington, DC: U.S. Department of Justice, Office of Justice Programs, Bureau of Justice Statistics, 2012.

Burdick, Kelly. "Does Nobody Read *USA Today*? The Surprising Furor over NSA Spying." *mhpbooks.com*, June 13, 2013.

Burke, Jason. *Al-Qaeda: Casting a Shadow of Terror.* New York: Tauris, 2003.

Burton, Fred. "Beware of 'Kramer': Tradecraft and the New Jihadists." *Stratfor Weekly*, January 18, 2006.

Bush, George W. *Decision Points.* New York: Crown, 2010.

Byman, Daniel L. "A Corrective That Goes Too Far?" *Terrorism and Political Violence* 17, no. 4 (Autumn 2005): 511–516.

Byman, Daniel. *Deadly Connections: States that Sponsor Terrorism.* New York: Cambridge University Press, 2005.

Byman, Daniel. "Five Myths About the Islamic State." *washingtonpost.com*, July 3, 2014.

Byman, Daniel, and Christine Fair. "The Case for Calling Them Nitwits." *Atlantic*, July–August 2010.

Byman, Daniel, and Jeremy Shapiro. "Be Afraid. Be a Little Afraid. The Threat of Terrorism from Foreign Fighters in Syria and Iraq." Washington, DC: Brookings Institution, Policy Paper 34, November 2014.

Byman, Daniel, and Jeremy Shapiro. "Homeward Bound? Don't Hype the Threat of Returning Jihadists." *foreignaffairs.com*, September 30, 2014.

Byman, Daniel, and Jeremy Shapiro. "We Shouldn't Stop Terrorists from Tweeting." *washingtonpost.com*, October 9, 2014.

Byman, Daniel, and Jennifer Williams. "Jihadism's Global Civil War." *National Interest*, March/April 10–18, 2015.

Cantril, Hadley, and Mildred Strunk, *Public Opinion 1935–1946.* Princeton, NJ: Princeton University Press, 1951.

Carle, Glenn L. *The Interrogator: An Education.* New York: Nation, 2011.

Carle, Glenn L. "Overstating Our Fears." *Washington Post*, July 13, 2008.

Carnevale, Mary Lu. "Tracking Use of Bin Laden's Satellite Phone." *blogs.wsj.com*, May 28, 2008.

Carus, W. Seth. *Defining "Weapons of Mass Destruction."* Washington, DC: National Defense University Press, 2006.

Cauley, Leslie. "NSA Has Massive Database of America's Phone Calls." *USA Today*, May 11, 2006.

Celona, Larry, and John Doyle. "NYPD High-Profile Patrols Take Big Hit." *New York Post*, October 6, 2010.

Center on Law and Security. "Terrorist Trial Report Card: September 11, 2001–September 11, 2009." New York University School of Law, January 2010.

Chan, Sewell. "Buzz over Mayor's 'Get a Life' Remark." *New York Times*, June 6, 2007.

Chang, Ailsa. "Bloomberg in Times Square: 'We're Not Going to Let Them Win'." *wnyc.org*, May 2, 2010.

Chapman, Steve. "We Worry Too Much About Terrorism." *Chicago Tribune*, January 15, 2015.

Chayes, Sarah. "Blinded by the War on Terrorism." *Los Angeles Times*, July 28, 2013.

Clarke, Richard A. "Ten Years Later." *Atlantic*, January/February 2005, 61–77.

Clarke, Richard A., and Robert K. Knake. *Cyber War: The Next Threat to National Security and What to Do About It*. New York: Ecco, 2010.

Clarke, Richard A., Michael J. Morell, Geoffrey R. Stone, Cass R. Sunstein, and Peter Swire. *Liberty and Security in a Changing World*. Report and Recommendations of the President's Review Group on Intelligence and Communications Technologies, Washington, DC, 2013.

Clausewitz, Carl von. *On War*. Princeton, NJ: Princeton University Press, 1976.

Cloutier, Catherine. "Incidents Like S.C. Shootings on the Rise, Study Says." *bostonglobe.com*, June 19, 2015.

Coburn, Tom. "Safety at Any Price: Assessing the Impact of Homeland Security Spending in U.S. Cities." Report, Office of Senator Tom Coburn, December 2012.

Cohen, Roger. "An Anchorless World." *New York Times*, September 13, 2013.

Cole, Juan. *Engaging the Muslim World*. New York: Palgrave Macmillan, 2009.

Collins, David. "Spies Like Them: The Canadian Security Intelligence Service and Its Place in World Intelligence." *Sydney Law Review* 24, no. 4 (December 2002): 506.

Cooper, Christopher, and Robert Block. *Disaster: Hurricane Katrina and the Failure of Homeland Security*. New York: Times Books, 2006.

Cordesman, Anthony H. *The Challenge of Biological Weapons*. Washington, DC: Center for Strategic and International Studies, 2005.

Costello, Tom. "TSA Failed 95% of Fake Weapons Tests, Investigation Finds." *time.com*, June 1, 2015.

Cronin, Audrey. "ISIS Is Not a Terrorist Group." *Foreign Affairs*, March/April 2015.

Dahl, Erik J. "The Plots That Failed: Intelligence Lessons Learned from Unsuccessful Terrorist Attacks Against the United States." *Studies in Conflict and Terrorism* 34, no. 8 (August 2011): 621–648.

Dalmia, Shikha. "What Islamist Terrorist Threat?" *reason.com*, February 15, 2011.

Department of Commerce, Bureau of Economic Analysis. Economic Growth Widespread Across Metropolitan Areas in 2012. News release, September 17, 2013.

Department of Homeland Security. Budgets in Brief—Fiscal Years 2012–2013. Washington, DC.

Department of Homeland Security. Budget in Brief—Fiscal Year 2013. Washington, DC.

Department of Homeland Security. Budget in Brief—Fiscal Year 2015. Washington, DC.

Department of Homeland Security. DHS Announces Grant Guidance for Fiscal Year (FY) 2011 Preparedness Grants. New release, Office of the Press Secretary, May 19, 2011.

Department of Homeland Security. DHS Announces Grant Guidance for Fiscal Year (FY) 2014 Preparedness Grants. News release, Office of the Press Secretary, July 25, 2014.

Department of Homeland Security. DHS Authorized Equipment List. Washington, DC, August 26, 2013.

Department of Homeland Security. *National Infrastructure Protection Plan: Partnering to Enhance Protection and Resiliency.* Washington, DC: Department of Homeland Security, 2009.

Department of Homeland Security. "National Strategy for Aviation Security." Washington, DC, 2007.

Department of Homeland Security. Remarks by Homeland Security Secretary Janet Napolitano to the National Fusion Center Conference, Kansas City, MO, March 11, 2009. Available at www.dhs.gov/news/2009/03/13/napolitanos-remarks-national-fusion-center-conference.

Department of Homeland Security. 2012 National Network of Fusion Centers: Final Report. Washington, DC, 2013.

Department of Homeland Security. 2013 National Network of Fusion Centers: Final Report. Washington, DC, June 2014.

Department of Homeland Security, Office of Inspector General. Annual Review of the United States Coast Guard's Mission Performance (FY2012). Washington, DC, September 17, 2013.

Department of Justice. *FY2015—Authorization and Budget Request to Congress.* Washington, DC: Federal Bureau of Investigation, 2014.

Department of Justice. *Report to the National Commission on Terrorist Attacks upon the United States: The FBI's Counterterrorism Program Since September 2001.* Washington, DC: Federal Bureau of Investigation, 2004.

Department of Justice. *Today's FBI Facts & Figures.* Washington, DC: Federal Bureau of Investigation, Office of Public Affairs, 2013.

Des Forges, Alison. *"Leave None to Tell the Story": Genocide in Rwanda.* New York: Human Rights Watch, 1999.

Diab, Robert. *The Harbinger Theory: How the Post-9/11 Emergency Became Permanent and the Case for Reform.* New York: Oxford University Press, 2015.

Dickey, Christopher. *Securing the City: Inside America's Best Counterterror Force—the NYPD.* New York: Simon and Schuster, 2009.

Dilanian, Ken. "AP Exclusive: NSA Weighed Ending Phone Program Before Leak." *washingtonpost.com,* March 30, 2015.

Dilanian, Ken. "NSA Faces Backlash over Collecting Phone Data." *latimes.com,* July 27, 2013.

Donkin, Susan, and Simon Bronitt. "Critical Perspectives on the Evaluation of Counter-Terrorism Strategies: Counting the Costs of the 'War on Terror' in Australia." In *Counter-Terrorism, Human Rights and the Rule of Law: Crossing Legal Boundaries in Defence of the State,* edited by Aniceto Masferrer and Clive Walker, 169–188. Cheltenham, UK: Edward Elgar Publishing, 2013.

Dougherty, Conor. "U.S. Cities with Bigger Economies than Entire Countries." *Wall Street Journal,* July 20, 2012.

Douglas, Jake A. "Case 98: New York Stock Exchange." In *Terrorism Since 9/11: The American Cases,* edited by John Mueller. Columbus: Mershon Center, Ohio State University, 2015.

Dozier, Kimberly. "Spy General Unloads on Obama's ISIS War Plan." *thedailybeast. com,* January 27, 2015.

Dozier, Kimberly. "Weaker al-Qaida Still Plots Payback for U.S. Raid." Associated Press, April 30, 2012.

Dratel, Joshua L. "Nothing New About Homegrown Terrorism." *centerlineblog.org,* July 27, 2010.

Dyer, Gwynne. "The International Terrorist Conspiracy." *gwynneDyer.com,* June 3, 2006. Available at gwynnedyer.com/2006/the-international-terrorist-conspiracy/.

Eagan, Judge Claire V. U.S. Foreign Surveillance Court, Washington, DC, Docket BR 13-109, 2013.

Eilstrup-Sangiovanni, Mette, and Calvert Jones. "Assessing the Dangers of Illicit Networks." *International Security* 33, no. 2 (Fall 2008): 7–44.

Elias, Bartholomew. *Airport and Aviation Security: U.S. Policy and Strategy in the Age of Global Terrorism.* Boca Raton, FA: CRC Press, 2010.

Ellingwood, Bruce R. "Mitigating Risk from Abnormal Loads and Progressive Collapse." *Journal of Performance of Constructed Facilities* 20, no. 4 (2006): 315–323.

Elliott, Justin. "Bloomberg on NYPD Counter-Terrorism: 'We'll Never Know.'" *propublica.org,* July 10, 2012.

Elliott, Justin. "Claim on 'Attacks Thwarted' by NSA Spreads Despite Lack of Evidence." *propublica.org,* October 23, 2013.

Elliott, Justin. "Fact-Check: How the NYPD Overstated Its Counterterrorism Record." *propublica.org,* July 10, 2012.

Elliott, Justin. "Judge on NSA Case Cites 9/11 Report, But It Doesn't Actually Support His Ruling." *propublica.org*, December 28, 2013.

Evans, James A. "Electronic Publication and the Narrowing of Science and Scholarship." *Science* 321 (2008): 395-99.

Faber, Michael, and Mark G. Stewart. "Risk Assessment for Civil Engineering Facilities: Critical Overview and Discussion." *Reliability Engineering and System Safety* 80, no. 2 (2003): 173–84.

Faiola, Anthony, and Steven Mufson. "N.Y. Airport Target of Plot, Officials Say." *Washington Post*, June 3, 2010.

Fallows, James. *Blind into Baghdad: America's War in Iraq.* New York: Vintage, 2006.

Fallows, James. "Declaring Victory." *Atlantic*, September 2006, 60–73.

Federal Bureau of Investigation (FBI). *The FBI: A Centennial History, 1908–2008.* Washington, DC: Office of Public Affairs, 2008.

Federal Bureau of Investigation (FBI). *Project Megiddo, an FBI Strategic Assessment of the Potential for Domestic Terrorism in the United States Undertaken in Anticipation of or Response to the Arrival of the New Millennium.* Washington, DC: Federal Bureau of Investigation, 1999.

Federal Bureau of Investigation (FBI). *Today's FBI Facts & Figures 2013–2014.* Washington, DC: Office of Public Affairs, 2013.

Feldman, Charles. "Federal Investigators: L.A. Airport Shooting a Terrorist Act." *cnn.com*, September 4, 2002.

Fernandez, Manny. "A Phrase for Safety After 9/11 Goes Global." *New York Times*, May 10, 2010.

Finn, Peter. "Documents Provide Rare Insight into FBI's Terrorism Stings." *Washington Post*, April 13, 2012.

Finn, Peter. "NSA Chief Says Surveillance Programs Helped Thwart Dozens of Plots." *Washington Post*, June 27, 2013.

Finn, Peter, and Greg Miller. "How an E-mail Address Disrupted Plots in Britain and U.S." *Washington Post*, June 18, 2013.

Fletcher, Kenneth C. "Aviation Security: Case for Risk-Based Passenger Screening." Master's thesis, Naval Postgraduate School, Monterey, CA, 2011.

Frank, Thomas. "More Than 10% of Pilots Allowed to Fly Armed." *USA Today*, April 1, 2008.

Frieden, Terry. "Top U.S. Security Officials Share Afghan-Pakistan Border Concerns." *cnn.com*, September 30, 2009.

Friedman, Benjamin H. "*Washington Post* Defines Worst Fears Down." *nationalinterest. org*, May 10, 2012.

Friedman, Benjamin H., Jim Harper, and Christopher A. Preble, eds. *Terrorizing Ourselves.* Washington, DC: Cato Institute, 2010.

Froomkin, Dan. "The Congressional Hyperbole Caucus," *firstlook.org/theintercept*, September 10, 2014.

Furedi, Frank. *Culture of Fear: Risk-Taking and the Morality of Low Expectations.* Revised ed. London: Continuum, 2002.

Gaddis, John Lewis. *George F. Kennan*. New York: Penguin, 2012.

Gaddis, John Lewis. *Strategies of Containment*. New York: Oxford University Press, 1982.

Garcia, Michelle. "In the Name of National Security." *El Diaro*, September 7, 2011.

Gardner, Dan. *Future Babble: Why Expert Predictions Fail—and Why We Believe Them Anyway*. Toronto: McClelland & Stewart, 2010.

Gardner, Daniel. *The Science of Fear: Why We Fear the Things We Shouldn't—and Put Ourselves in Greater Danger*. New York: Dutton, 2008.

Garfinkle, Adam. "Comte's Caveat: How We Misunderstand Terrorism." *Orbis*, Summer 2008, 403–21.

Gartenstein-Ross, Daveed, and Laura Grossman. *Homegrown Terrorists in the U.S. and U.K: An Empirical Examination of the Radicalization Process*. Washington, DC: Center for Terrorism Research, Foundation for the Defense of Democracies, 2009.

Gartner, Scott Sigmund. "The Multiple Effects of Casualties on Public Support for War: An Experimental Approach." *American Political Science Review* 102, no. 1 (February 2008): 95–106.

Gaubatz, P. David, and Paul Sperry. *Muslim Mafia: Inside the Secret Underworld That's Conspiring to Islamize America*. Los Angeles: WND, 2009.

Gellman, Barton. "NSA Broke Privacy Rules Thousands of Times per Year, Audit Finds." *Washington Post*, August 15, 2013.

Gelpi, Christopher, Peter D. Feaver, and Jason Reifler. *Paying the Human Costs of War: American Public Opinion and Casualties in Military Conflicts*. Princeton, NJ: Princeton University Press, 2009.

Gendar, Alison, and Helen Kennedy. "U.S. Commandos Find 'Mother Lode' of Material on Al Qaeda inside Osama Bin Laden's Compound." *New York Daily News*, May 4, 2011.

George, Bruce, and Natalie Whatford. "Regulation of Transport Security Post 9/11." *Security Journal* 20, no. 3 (2007): 158–70.

Gerges, Fawaz A. *The Far Enemy: Why Jihad Went Global*. New York: Cambridge University Press, 2005.

Gerges, Fawaz A. *The Rise and Fall of Al-Qaeda*. New York: Oxford University Press, 2011.

Gerges, Fawaz A. "Word on the Street." *democracyjournal.org*, Summer 2008.

German, Michael. "No NSA Poster Child: The Real Story of 9/11 Hijacker Khalid al-Mihdnar." *defenseone.com*, October 16, 2013.

German, Michael. *Thinking Like a Terrorist: Insights of a Former FBI Undercover Agent*. Washington, DC: Potomac Books, 2007.

Gertz, Bill. "Al Qaeda Seen in Search of Nukes: Defense Official Warns U.S. Still Group's Target." *Washington Times*, July 26, 2007.

Gertz, Bill. "5,000 in U.S. Suspected of Ties to al Qaeda; Groups Nationwide Under Surveillance." *Washington Times*, July 11, 2002.

Gilbert, Daniel. "If Only Gay Sex Caused Global Warming." *Los Angeles Times*, March 21, 2007.

Gillespie, Nick. "Do the Zazi and Headley Arrests Prove the Power of NSA Total Surveillance?" *reason.com*, June 13, 2013.

Giraldi, Philip. "How to Understand the ISIS Threat: Talk Show Rhetoric Doesn't Equal Good Intelligence on the Domestic Danger Posed by Iraq's Terrorists." *American Conservative*, July 1, 2014.

Glennon, Michael J. *National Security and Double Government.* New York: Oxford University Press, 2015.

Goldsmith, Jack. *The Terror Presidency: Law and Judgment Inside the Bush Administration.* New York: Norton, 2007.

Gould-Davies, Nigel. "Rethinking the Role of Ideology in International Politics During the Cold War." *Journal of Cold War Studies* 1 (Winter 1999): 90–109.

Government Accountability Office. Aviation Security: Efforts to Validate TSA's Screening Behavior Detection Program Underway, but Opportunities Exist to Strengthen Validation and Address Operational Challenges, GAO-10-763, May 2010.

Government Accountability Office. Aviation Security: TSA Should Limit Future Funding for Behavior Detection Activities, GAO-14-159, November 2013.

Government Accountability Office. Report to Congressional Requesters: Coast Guard—Security Risk Model Meets DHS Criteria, but More Training Could Enhance Its Use for Managing Programs and Operations, GAO-12-14, November 2011.

Graff, Garrett. *The Threat Matrix: The FBI in the Age of Terror.* New York: Little, Brown, 2011.

Graham, Bob. *World at Risk: The Report of the Commission on the Prevention of WMD Proliferation and Terrorism.* New York: Vintage, 2008.

Grant, Matthew, and Mark G. Stewart. "A Systems Model for Probabilistic Risk Assessment of Improvised Explosive Device Attack." *International Journal of Intelligent Defence Support Systems* 5, no. 1 (2012): 75–93.

Greenberg, Karen J., ed. *Terrorism Trial Report Card: September 11, 2001–September 11, 2009.* New York: New York University School of Law, Center on Law and Security, 2010.

Greenwald, Glenn. "Congress Is Irrelevant on Mass Surveillance. Here's What Matters Instead." *firstlook.org/theintercept*, November 19, 2014.

Greenwald, Glenn. *No Place to Hide: Edward Snowden, the NSA, and the U.S. Surveillance State.* New York: Metropolitan Books, 2014.

Greenwald, Glenn, and Andrew Fishman. "Latest FBI Claim of Disrupted Terror Plot Deserves Much Scrutiny and Skepticism." *firstlook.org/theintercept*, January 16, 2015.

Greenwald, Glenn, and Andrew Fishman. "NPR Is Laundering CIA Talking Points to Make You Scared of NSA Reporting." *firstlook.org/theintercept*, August 12, 2014.

Griffin, Drew. "Four Arrests for $800M." *cnn.com*, February 4, 2010.

Griffin, Drew. "Sources: Air Marshals Missing from Almost All Flights." *cnn.com*, March 25, 2008.

Grosskopf, Kevin R. "Evaluating the Societal Response to Antiterrorism Measures." *Journal of Homeland Security and Emergency Management* 3, no. 2 (2006).

Hardaker, J. Brian, Euan Fleming, and Gudbrand Lien. "How Should Governments Make Risky Policy Decisions?" *Australian Journal of Public Administration* 68, no. 3 (2009): 256–271.

Harper, Jim, John Mueller, and Mark G. Stewart. "Comments on Notice of Proposed Rulemaking: Passenger Screening Using Advanced Imaging Technology," TSA-2013-0004 (RIN 1652-AA67), Cato Institute, June 21, 2013.

Harris, John R. "FBI Concocted Bomb Plot Against NYSE to Mute NSA Surveillance Criticism." *john.harris.io*, June 25, 2013.

Harris, Katie. "John Kerry: U.S. Attack on Syria Would Be 'Unbelievably Small.'" *world.time.com*, September 9, 2013.

Harris, Shane. "The Cowboy of the NSA." *foreignpolicy.com*, September 9, 2013.

Harris, Shane. *The Watchers: The Rise of America's Surveillance State*. New York: Penguin, 2010.

Harris, Shane, and Stuart Taylor Jr. "Homeland Security Chief Looks Back, and Forward." *governmentExecutive.com*, March 17, 2008.

Hawley, Kip, and Nathan Means. *Permanent Emergency: Inside the TSA and the Fight for the Future of American Security*. New York: Palgrave Macmillan, 2012.

Hays, Tom. "Feds: Terror Suspects' Mingling Fed NYC Threat," *KIDK.com*, September 26, 2009.

Healy, Gene. "Al Qaeda: Never an 'Existential Threat.'" *cato-at-liberty*, September 13, 2011.

Heaton, Paul. *Hidden in Plain Sight: What Cost-of-Crime Research Can Tell Us About Investing in Police*. Santa Monica, CA: RAND, 2010.

Hedges, Chris. "On Bosnia's Ethnic Fault Lines, It's Still Tense, but World Is Silent." *New York Times*, February 28, 1997.

Heilman, Justin. "Case 28: Zazi." In *Terrorism Since 9/11: The American Cases*, edited by John Mueller. Columbus: Mershon Center, Ohio State University, 2015.

Hennelly, Bob. "NYPD Plays Key Role in Securing UN for General Assembly." *WNYC News*, September 20, 2011.

Heuer, Richard J., Jr. *Psychology of Intelligence Analysis*. Washington, DC: Center for the Study of Intelligence, Central Intelligence Agency, 1999.

Hickey, Donald R. *The War of 1812: A Forgotten Conflict*. Urbana: University of Illinois Press, 1989.

Hirsh, Michael. "Bin Laden Journal Reveals Future Planning, Possible Targets." *National Journal*, May 11, 2011.

Hirsh, Michael. "Why the Surveillance State Lives On: The Snowden Revelations Have Fizzled Politically, and Reform Isn't Coming Any Time Soon." *politico.com*, November 20, 2014.

Hoffman, Bruce. "Bin Laden's Death Shatters Conventional Wisdom." *nationalinterest.com*, May 2, 2011.

Hoffman, Bruce. *Inside Terrorism*. New York: Columbia University Press, 2006.

Hoffman, Bruce. "Radicalization and Subversion: Al Qaeda and the 7 July 2005 Bombings and the 2006 Airline Bombing Plot." *Studies in Conflict & Terrorism* 32, no. 12 (September 2009): 1100–1116.

Hoffman, Bruce. "Scarier Than Bin Laden." *washingtonpost.com*, September 9, 2007.

Hoffman, Bruce, Edwin Meese III, and Timothy J. Roemer. "The FBI: Protecting the Homeland in the 21st Century." Report of the Congressionally Directed 9/11 Review Commission to the Director of the Federal Bureau of Investigation, March 2015.

Holsti, Ole R. *Public Opinion and American Foreign Policy*. Ann Arbor: University of Michigan Press, 2004,

Hoover, J. Edgar. *Masters of Deceit: The Story of Communism in America and How to Fight It*. New York: Holt, Rinehart, and Winston, 1958.

Horgan, John. "Can Science Solve Terrorism? Q&A with Psychologist John Horgan." *blogs.scientificamerican.com/cross-check*, March 2, 2015.

Horgan, John. "Discussion Point: The End of Radicalization?" National Consortium for the Study of Terrorism and Responses to Terrorism, College Park, MD, September 28, 2012.

Horgan, John. *Walking Away from Terrorism: Accounts of Disengagement from Radical and Extremist Movements* New York: Routledge, 2009.

Horowitz, Craig. "Anatomy of a Foiled Plot." *New York*, May 21, 2005.

Horowitz, Craig. "The NYPD's War on Terror." *New York*, February 3, 2003.

Hsu, Spencer S. "Homeland Security Chief Warns of Threat from al-Qaeda Sympathizers in U.S." *Washington Post*, December 3, 2009.

Hsu, Spencer S. "Security Chief Urges 'Collective Fight' Against Terrorism." *Washington Post*, July 29, 2009.

Hsu, Spencer S., and Robin Wright. "Plot to Attack N.Y. Foiled: Transit Tunnels to N.J. Called Targets." *Washington Post*, July 8, 2006.

Hudson, Audrey. "Air Marshals Cover Only a Few Flights." *Washington Times*, August 16, 2004.

Ignatius, David. "Bin Laden's Ambitious Final Plans." *washingtonpost.com*, May 5, 2015.

Ignatius, David. "The bin Laden Plot to Kill President Obama." *Washington Post*, March 16, 2012.

Ignatius, David. "The Fading Jihadists." *Washington Post*, February 28, 2008.

Ignatius, David. "The Internet Isn't to Blame for Radicalization." *washingtonpost.com*, January 15, 2015.

Ignatius, David. "A Lion in Winter." *Washington Post*, March 18, 2012.

Ignatius, David. "A Nightmare Group in Syria Could Target the United States." *Washington Post*, May 13, 2014.

Institute for Economics and Peace. *Global Terrorism Index 2014: Measuring and Understanding the Impact of Terrorism*. Washington, DC: Institute for Economics and Peace, 2014.

International Air Transport Association (IATA). "ACI and IATA Collaborate to Deliver Smart Security." Press Release No. 70, December 12, 2013.

International Air Transport Association (IATA). "2012 Annual Review," Geneva, Switzerland.

International Air Transport Association (IATA). "IATA Reveals Checkpoint of the Future." Press Release No. 35, June 7, 2011.

International Organization for Standardization (ISO). *ISO 31000–2009: Risk Management—Principles and Guidelines.* Geneva, Switzerland: ISO, 2009.

Isikoff, Michael, and Mark Hosenball. "The Flip Side of the NIE." *newsweek.com*, August 15, 2007.

Jacobson, Gary C. *A Divider, Not a Uniter.* New York: Pearson, 2006.

Jenkins, Brian Michael. *Stray Dogs and Virtual Armies: Radicalization and Recruitment to Jihadist Terrorism in the United States Since 9/11.* Santa Monica, CA: RAND, 2011.

Jenkins, Brian Michael. *Unconquerable Nation: Knowing Our Enemy and Strengthening Ourselves.* Santa Monica, CA: RAND, 2006.

Jenkins, Brian Michael. *Will Terrorists Go Nuclear?* Amherst, NY: Prometheus, 2008.

Jenkins, Brian Michael. *Would-Be Warriors: Incidents of Jihadist Terrorist Radicalization in the United States Since September 11, 2001.* Santa Monica, CA: RAND, 2010.

Jensen, Richard Bach. "The United States, International Policing and the War Against Anarchist Terrorism, 1900–1914." *Terrorism and Political Violence* 15, no. 1 (2002): 15–46.

Jervis, Robert. "Do Leaders Matter and How Would We Know?" *Security Studies*, 22 (2013): 153-79.

Jervis, Robert. "The Torture Blame Game: The Botched Senate Report on the CIA's Misdeeds." *Foreign Affairs*, May/June 2015, 120-27.

Jervis, Robert. "Was the Cold War a Security Dilemma?" *Journal of Cold War Studies* 3 (Winter 2001): 36–60.

Jervis, Robert. *Why Intelligence Fails: Lessons from the Iranian Revolution and the Iraq War.* Ithaca, NY: Cornell University Press, 2010.

Johnson, Kevin. "Weakened al-Qaeda Is Still a Threat." *USA Today*, September 8, 2009.

Johnson, Robert H. *Improbable Dangers: U.S. Conceptions of Threat in the Cold War and After.* New York: St. Martin's, 1997.

Johnston, David, and Scott Shane. "Terror Case Is Called One of the Most Serious in Years." *New York Times*, September 25, 2009.

Jones, Seth G. "Al Qaeda Is Far from Defeated." *wsj.com*, April 28, 2012.

Jones, Seth G. "Think Again: al-Qaeda." *foreignpolicy.com*, April 23, 2012.

Kagan, Robert. *Of Paradise and Power: America and Europe and the New World Order.* New York: Knopf, 2003.

Kahn, David. "The Intelligence Failure of Pearl Harbor." *Foreign Affairs*, Winter 1991/92, 136–52.

Karnow, Stanley. *Vietnam: A History.* New York, Penguin, 1991.

Kean, Thomas H. *The 9/11 Commission Report: Final Report of the National Commission on Terrorist Attacks upon the United States.* Washington, DC: U.S. Government Printing Office, 2004.

Kean, Thomas H., and Lee H. Hamilton. "Today's Rising Terrorist Threat and the Danger to the United States: Reflections on the Tenth Anniversary of the 9/11 Commission Report." Washington, DC: Bipartisan Policy Center, July 2014.

Kearney, Simon. "Air Marshal's Role Now VIP Security." *The Australian*, December 9, 2005.

Kearns, Doris. *Lyndon Johnson and the American Dream*. New York: Harper & Row, 1976.

Keeley, Lawrence H. *War Before Civilization: The Myth of the Peaceful Savage*. New York: Oxford University Press, 1996.

Keller, Bill. "Our New Isolationism." *New York Times*, September 9, 2013.

Kenber, Billy. "Outgoing Director Robert S. Mueller, III Tells How 9/11 Reshaped FBI Mission." *Washington Post*, August 22, 2013.

Kenner, David. "Mr. Bean to Jihad John." *foreignpolicy.com*, September 12, 2014.

Kenney, Michael. "Beyond the Internet: *Mētis, Techne*, and the Limitations of Online Artifacts for Islamist Terrorists." *Terrorism and Political Violence* 22, no. 2 (April 2010): 177–97.

Kenney, Michael. " 'Dumb' Yet Deadly: Local Knowledge and Poor Tradecraft Among Islamist Militants in Britain and Spain." *Studies in Conflict & Terrorism* 33, no. 10 (October 2010): 911–922.

Kenny, Charles. "Airport Security Is Killing Us." *Bloomberg Businessweek*, November 18, 2012.

Kiekinveld, Christopher, Manish Jain, Jason Tsai, James Pita, Fernando Ordonez, and Milind Tambe. "Computing Optimal Randomized Resource Allocations for Massive Security Games." In *Proceedings of 8th International Conference on Autonomous Agents and Multiagent Systems*, edited by Keith S. Decker, Jamie Sichman, Carles Sierra, and Cristiano Castelfranchi, 680–696. Budapest, 2009.

Kinkaid, Cliff. "NSA Leaker 'Outed' as Russian Agent." *Accuracy in Media*, August 27, 2013.

Klarevas, Louis. "The Idiot Jihadist Next Door." *foreignpolicy.com*, December 1, 2011.

Koerner, Brendan I. *The Skies Belong to Us: Love and Terror in the Golden Age of Hijacking*. New York: Crown, 2013.

Koerner, Claudia. "The Garland, Texas, Shooters' Quiet Plan to Violent Jihad." *buzzfeed.com*, May 14, 2015.

Kotkin, Stephen. "The Kiss of Debt: The East Goes Borrowing." In *The Shock of the Global: The 1970s in Perspective*, edited by Niall Ferguson, Charles Maier, Erez Manela, and Daniel Sargent, 80–93. Cambridge, MA: Harvard University Press, 2010.

Kraft, Michael B., and Edward Marks. *U.S. Government Counterterrorism: A Guide to Who Does What*. Roca Baton, FL: CRC Press, 2012.

Kraus, Sidney, ed., *The Great Debates: Carter vs. Ford, 1976*. Bloomington: Indiana University Press, 1979.

Krauthammer, Charles. "Blixful Amnesia." *Washington Post*, July 9, 2004.

Krauthammer, Charles. "A Travesty of a Report." *washingtonpost.com*, December 12, 2014.

Kristof, Nicholas. "An American Hiroshima." *New York Times*, August 11, 2004.

Kunreuther, Howard. "Risk Analysis and Risk Management in an Uncertain World." *Risk Analysis* 22, no. 4 (August 2002): 655–64.

Kurzman, Charles. "Muslim-American Terrorists Since 9/11: An Accounting." Triangle Center on Terrorism and Homeland Security, February 2, 2011.

LaFree, Gary, Laura Dugan, and Erin Miller. *Putting Terrorism in Context: Lessons from the Global Terrorism Database*. London: Routledge, 2015.

Lake, David A. "Rational Extremism: Understanding Terrorism in the Twenty-first Century," *Dialog-IO*, Spring 2002, 15–29.

Lake, Eli. "Spy Chief: We Should've Told You We Track Your Calls." *The Daily Beast*, February 17, 2014.

Landler, Mark, and Rick Gladstone. "Chemicals Would Be 'Game Changer' in Syria, Obama Says." *nytimes.com*, March 20, 2013.

Langewiesche, William. *The Atomic Bazaar: The Rise of the Nuclear Poor*. New York: Farrar, Straus and Giroux, 2007.

LaTourrette, Tom, David R. Howell, David E. Mosher, and John MacDonald. "Reducing Terrorism Risk at Shopping Centers: An Analysis of Potential Security Options." Santa Monica, CA: RAND, 2006.

Leahy, Patrick. Hearing on the report of the Privacy and Civil Liberties Oversight Board on Reforms to the Section 215 Telephone Records Program and the Foreign Intelligence Surveillance Court. Statement, February 12, 2014. Available at www.judiciary.senate.gov/imo/media/doc/02-12-14LeahyStatement.pdf.

Lebow, Richard Ned. *Forbidden Fruit: Counterfactuals and International Relations*. Princeton, NJ: Princeton University Press, 2009.

Leinwand, Donna. "Psst—Leads from Public to FBI Rise." *USA Today*, August 15, 2008.

Leon, Judge Richard J. "Memorandum Opinion." U.S. District Court for the District of Columbia, December 16, 2013.

Levitt, Len. "Kelly and AP: Ray's Pants Are on Fire." *nypdconfidential.com*, January 14, 2014.

Lewis, Carol W. "The Terror That Failed: Public Opinion in the Aftermath of the Bombing in Oklahoma City." *Public Administration Review* 60, no. 3 (May/June 2000): 201–10.

Lieber, Keir A., and Daryl G. Press. "Why States Won't Give Nuclear Weapons to Terrorists." *International Security* 38, no. 1 (Summer 2013): 80–104.

Linderman, Gerald F. *Embattled Courage: The Experience of Combat in the Civil War*. New York: Free Press, 1987.

Lines, Andy. "War on Terror: Bin Laden Army: 11,000 Terror Agents Set to Strike." *Mirror* (London), September 24, 2001.

Lippmann, Walter. "Fifth Column on the Coast." *Washington Post*, February 12, 1942.

Lipton, Eric. "The Toll: Numbers Vary in Tally of the Victims." *New York Times*, October 25, 2001.

Logiurato, Brett. "Defence Secretary: ISIS An Imminent Threat to Every Interest We Have." *businessinsider.com*, August 1, 2014.

Lohmann, Ashley. "Jihad on Main Street: Explaining the Threat of Jihadist Terrorism to the American Homeland Since 9/11." Honors program for International Security Studies, Center for International Security and Cooperation, Stanford University, CA, May 18, 2010.

Londoño, Ernesto. "Iraq, Afghan Wars Will Cost $4 Trillion to $6 Trillion, Harvard Study Says." *Washington Post*, March 29, 2013.

Lord, Steven, Rick Nunes-Vaz, Alexei Filinkov, and Glenis Crane. "Airport Front-of-House Vulnerabilities and Mitigation Options." *Journal of Transportation Security* 3, no. 3 (2010): 149–77.

Los Angeles, City of. "Los Angeles Fiscal Year 2014–15." Detail of *Department Programs: Volume II*, April 2014.

Loy, James. "Al-Qaeda's Undimmed Threat." *Washington Post*, November 7, 2010.

Lum, Cynthia, Maria Haberfeld, George Fachner, and Charles Lieberman. "Police Activities to Counter Terrorism: What We Know and What We Need to Know." In *To Protect and to Serve: Policing in an Age of Terrorism*, edited by David Weisburd et al., 101–141. New York: Springer, 2009.

Lustick, Ian S. *Trapped in the War on Terror*. Philadelphia: University of Pennsylvania Press, 2006.

Lynch, Marc. "Al-Qaeda's Media Strategies." *National Interest*, Spring 2006, 50–56.

MacDonald, Heather. "The Ever-Renewing Terror Threat." *secularright.org*, February 13, 2011.

MacIsaac, Tara. "NYPD Trims Budget." *The Epoch Times*, March 17, 2011.

Mack, Andrew. "Dying to Lose: Explaining the Decline in Global Terrorism." In *Human Security Brief 2007*, edited by Andrew Mack, 8–21. Vancouver, British Columbia: Human Security Report Project, School for International Studies, Simon Fraser University, 2008.

Maddow, Rachel. *Drift: The Unmooring of American Military Power*. New York: Crown, 2012.

Manchester, William. "No Evidence of a Conspiracy to Kill Kennedy." *New York Times*, February 5, 1992.

Mansoor, Peter R. *Surge: My Journey with General David Petraeus and the Remaking of the Iraq War*. New Haven, CT: Yale University Press, 2013.

Mardini, Ramzy. "The Islamic State Threat Is Overstated." *washingtonpost.com*, September 12, 2014.

Marion, Nancy, and Kelley Cronin. "Law Enforcement Responses to Homeland Security Initiatives: The Case of Ohio." *Southwest Journal of Criminal Justice* 6, no. 1 (2009): 4–24.

Marshall, Tim. "MI5 Boss Warns of Growing UK Terror Threat." *SkyNews*, October 9, 2013.

Martonosi, Susan E., and Arnold Barnett. "How Effective Is Security Screening of Airline Passengers?" *Interfaces* 36, no. 6 (2006): 545–52.

Mayer, Jane. *The Dark Side: The Inside Story on How the War on Terror Turned into a War on American Ideals*. New York: Doubleday, 2008.

Mazzetti, Mark, Eric Schmitt, and Mark Landler. "Struggling to Gauge ISIS Threat, Even as U.S. Prepares to Act." *New York Times*, September 10, 2014.

McCarthy, Joseph. "Enemies from Within." Speech to the Women's Club, Wheeling, WV, February 9, 1950.

McCarthy, Ken. "NSA Chief Says Exposure of Surveillance Programs Has 'Irreversible' Impact." *theguardian.com*, June 18, 2013.

McClam, Erin. "Attorney General Eric Holder Revives Domestic Terror Task Force." *nbcnews.com*, June 3, 2014.

McClure, Ruxton. "Case 36: Parcel Bombs on Cargo Planes." In *Terrorism Since 9/11: The American Cases*, edited by John Mueller. Columbus: Mershon Center, Ohio State University, 2015.

McDermott, Terry, and Josh Meyer. *The Hunt for KSM: Inside the Pursuit and Takedown of the Real 9/11 Mastermind, Khalid Sheikh Mohammed*. New York: Little, Brown, 2012.

McElroy, Damien. "Boston Marathon Victim Jeff Bauman Helped Identify Bombers." *Telegraph*, April 19, 2013.

McMahon, Lucian. "Truth or Gaffe? Biden Admits U.S. Faces No Existential Threat from Terrorism." *reason.com*, October 3, 2014.

Meade, Charles, and Roger C. Molander. *Considering the Effects of a Catastrophic Terrorist Attack*. Santa Monica, CA: RAND, 2006.

Mearsheimer, John J. "Imperial by Design," *National Interest*, January/February 2011, 16–34.

Mearsheimer, John J. *Why Leaders Lie: The Truth About Lying in International Politics*. New York: Oxford University Press, 2011.

Meckler, Laura, and, Susan Carey. "Sky Patrol: U.S. Air Marshal Service Navigates Turbulent Times." *Wall Street Journal*, February 9, 2007.

Miller, Greg. "Al-Qaeda Is Weaker Without bin Laden, but Its Franchise Persists." *washingtonpost.com*, April 28, 2012.

Miller, Greg. "Bin Laden Documents Reveal Strain, Struggle in al-Qaida." *Washington Post*, July 1, 2011.

Miller, Greg. "Cheney Assertions of Lives Saved Hard to Support." *latimes.com*, May 23, 2009.

Miller, John J. "FBI Response to *Rolling Stone* Magazine Article." *Rolling Stone*, February 22, 2008.

Miller, Judith. "How the NYPD Foiled the Post-9/11 Terror Plots." *Wall Street Journal*, September 10, 2011.

Miller, Judith. "On the Front Line in the War on Terrorism." *City Journal*, Summer 2007.

Miniter, Richard. *Mastermind: The Many Faces of the 9/11 Architect, Khalid Shaikh Mohammed.* New York: Sentinel, 2011.

Molotch, Harvey. *Against Security: How We Go Wrong at Airports, Subways, and Other Sites of Ambiguous Danger.* Princeton, NJ: Princeton University Press, 2012.

Morag, Nadav. "Does Homeland Security Exist Outside the United States?" *Homeland Security Affairs* 7 (September 2011): 1–5.

Morell, Michael. *The Great War of Our Time: The CIA's Fight Against Terrorism from al Qa'ida to ISIS.* New York: Twelve, 2015.

Moreno, Ivan, and P. Solomon Banda. "Prosecutor: Terror Plot Focus Was 9/11 Anniversary." Associated Press, September 26, 2009.

Morison, Samuel Eliot. *The Rising Sun in the Pacific: 1931–April 1942.* Boston: Little, Brown, 1948.

Morral, Andrew R., Carter C. Price, David S. Oritz, Bradley Wilson, Tom LaTourrette, Blake W. Mobley, Shawn McKay, and Henry H. Willis. *Modeling Terrorism Risk to the Air Transportation System.* Santa Monica, CA: RAND, 2012.

Morreale, Stephen A., and David E. Lambert. "Homeland Security and the Police Mission." *Journal of Homeland Security and Emergency Management* 6, no. 1 (2009): Article 68.

Morris, Mark. "Al-Qaeda Bunco Artist Rolls Terrorist from KC." *Kansas City Star,* June 29, 2013.

Morris, Mark. "KC Terrorist Supported Plan to Bomb New York Stock Exchange, FBI Tells Congress." *Kansas City Star,* June 18, 2013.

Mudd, Philip. "Evaluating the Al-Qa'ida Threat to the Homeland." *CTC Sentinel,* August 2010, 1–4.

Mudd, Philip. *Takedown: Inside the Hunt for Al Qaeda.* Philadelphia: University of Pennsylvania Press, 2013.

Mueller, John. "Action and Reaction: Assessing the Historic Impact of Terrorism." In *Terrorism, Identity, and Legitimacy: The Four Waves Theory and Political Violence,* edited by Jean E. Rosenfeld, 112–122. New York: Routledge, 2011.

Mueller, John. "America's Terrorism Fear Factory Rolls On." *nationalinterest.org,* January 17, 2015.

Mueller, John. *Atomic Obsession: Nuclear Alarmism from Hiroshima to Al Qaeda.* New York: Oxford University Press, 2010.

Mueller, John. "Blip or Step Function?" Paper presented at the Annual Convention of the International Studies Association, Portland, OR, February 27, 2003, available at politicalscience.osu.edu/faculty/jmueller/ISA2003.PDF.

Mueller, John. "The Bomb's Pretense as Peacemaker." *Wall Street Journal,* June 4, 1985.

Mueller, John. "Confusion." *foreignpolicy.com,* October 8, 2012.

Mueller, John. "Crime Is Caused by the Young and Reckless." *Wall Street Journal,* March 6, 1985, available at politicalscience.osu.edu/faculty/jmueller/WSJcrime.pdf.

Mueller, John. "Embracing Threatlessness." *national interest.org,* January 31, 2012.

Mueller, John. "The Essential Irrelevance of Nuclear Weapons: Stability in the Postwar World." *International Security* 13, no. 2 (Fall 1988): 55–79.

Mueller, John. "Extrapolations from a Book about Nothing." In *Cultural Politics and the Politics of Culture: Essays to Honor Alexander Stephan*, edited by Helen Fehervary and Bernd Fischer, 39–45. Bern: Peter Lang, 2007.

Mueller, John. "False Alarms." *Washington Post*, September 29, 2002.

Mueller, John. "Harbinger or Aberration? A 9/11 Provocation." *National Interest*, Fall 2002, 45–50.

Mueller, John. "History and Nuclear Rationality." *nationalinterest.org*, November 19, 2012.

Mueller, John. "The Iraq Syndrome." *Foreign Affairs*, November–December 2005, 44–54.

Mueller, John. "Iraq Syndrome Redux: Behind the Tough Talk." *foreignaffairs.com*, June 18, 2014.

Mueller, John. "The Iraq Syndrome Revisited: U.S. Intervention, from Kosovo to Libya." *foreignaffairs.com*, March 28, 2011.

Mueller, John. "The Islamic State Will Probably Be Defeated, but It's Not Thanks to President Obama." *washingtonpost.com*, September 16, 2014.

Mueller, John. "Mueller on the Zazi Case: 'This Is It?' " *juancole.com*, November 4, 2009.

Mueller, John. "New Year Brings Good News on Terrorism: Experts Wrong Again," *nationalinterest.org*, January 3, 2012.

Mueller, John. *Overblown: How Politicians and the Terrorism Industry Inflate National Security Threats, and Why We Believe Them*. New York: Free Press, 2006.

Mueller, John. "Pearl Harbor: Military Inconvenience, Political Disaster." *International Security* 16, no. 3 (Winter 1991/92): 172–203.

Mueller, John. "The Perfect Enemy: Assessing the Gulf War." *Security Studies* 5, no. 1 (Autumn 1995): 77–117.

Mueller, John. "Police Work or War? Public Reactions to Dates of Infamy." *Public Perspective*, March/April 2003, available at politicalscience.osu.faculty/jmueller/PubPers2003fin.pdf.

Mueller, John. *Policy and Opinion in the Gulf War*. Chicago: University of Chicago Press, 1994.

Mueller, John. "Public Opinion, the Media, and War." In *Oxford Handbook on American Public Opinion and the Media*. edited by Robert Y. Shapiro and Lawrence R. Jacobs, 675–89, Oxford: Oxford University Press, 2011.

Mueller, John. "Questing for Monsters to Destroy." In *In Uncertain Times: American Foreign Policy After the Berlin Wall and 9/11*, edited by Melvyn Leffler and Jeffrey W. Legro, 117–130. Ithaca, NY: Cornell University Press, 2011.

Mueller, John. *Quiet Cataclysm: Reflections on the Recent Transformation of World Politics*. New York: HarperCollins, 1995.

Mueller, John. *The Remnants of War*. Ithaca, NY: Cornell University Press, 2004.

Mueller, John. *Retreat from Doomsday: The Obsolescence of Major War.* New York: Basic Books, 1989.

Mueller, John. "Six Rather Unusual Propositions About Terrorism." *Terrorism and Political Violence* 71 no. 4 (Autumn 2005): 487–505.

Mueller, John. "Some Reflections on What, If Anything, 'Are We Safer?' Might Mean." *cato-unbound,* September 11, 2006.

Mueller, John, ed. *Terrorism Since 9/11: The American Cases.* Columbus: Mershon Center, Ohio State University, 2015. Available at politicalscience.osu.edu/faculty/jmueller/since.html.

Mueller. John. "Terror Tipsters." *nationalinterest.org,* January 24, 2012.

Mueller, John. "The Truth About al Qaeda: Bin Laden's Files Revealed the Terrorists in Dramatic Decline." *foreignaffairs.com,* August 2, 2011.

Mueller, John. *War and Ideas: Selected Essays.* New York: Routledge, 2011.

Mueller, John. *War, Presidents and Public Opinion.* New York: Wiley, 1973.

Mueller, John. "What Was the Cold War About?" *Political Science Quarterly* 119, no. 4 (Winter 2004–2005): 609–631.

Mueller, John. "Why al Qaeda May Never Die." *nationalinterest.org,* May 1, 2012.

Mueller, John. "Will Obama's Libya 'Victory' Aid Re-Election Bid?" *nationalinterest.org,* December 1, 2011.

Mueller, John, and Karl Mueller. "The Rockets' Red Glare: Just What Are 'Weapons of Mass Destruction,' Anyway?" *foreignpolicy.com,* July 7, 2009.

Mueller John, with Ezra Schricker. "Terror Predictions." May 2, 2012. Posted at politicalscience.osu.edu/faculty/jmueller/predict.pdf.

Mueller, John, and Mark G. Stewart. "Can Terrorists Be Scared Straight?" *lawfare.com,* May 3, 2015.

Mueller, John, and Mark G. Stewart. "The Curse of the Black Swan." *Journal of Risk Research,* forthcoming.

Mueller, John, and Mark G. Stewart. "Evaluating Counterterrorism Spending." *Journal of Economic Perspectives* 28, no. 3 (Summer 2014): 237–248.

Mueller, John, and Mark G. Stewart. "Hapless, Disorganized, and Irrational." *slate.com,* April 22, 2013.

Mueller, John, and Mark G. Stewart. "Hardly Existential: Thinking Rationally About Terrorism." *foreignaffairs.com,* April 2, 2010.

Mueller, John, and Mark G. Stewart. *Responsible Counterterrorism Policy.* Washington, DC: Cato Institute, Policy Analysis No. 755, 2014.

Mueller, John, and Mark G. Stewart. "The Terrorism Delusion: America's Overwrought Response to September 11." *International Security* 37, no. 1 (Summer 2012): 81–110.

Mueller, John, and Mark G. Stewart. "Terrorism Poses No Existential Threat to America. We Must Stop Pretending Otherwise." *Guardian,* February 24, 2015.

Mueller, John, and Mark G. Stewart. *Terror, Security, and Money: Balancing the Benefits, Risks, and Costs of Homeland Security.* New York: Oxford University Press, 2011.

Mueller, John, and Mark G. Stewart. "Trends in Public Opinion on Terrorism." Posted at politicalscience.osu.edu/faculty/jmueller/terrorpolls.pdf.

Mueller, John, and Mark G. Stewart. "Witches, Communists, and Terrorists: Evaluating the Risks and Tallying the Costs," *ABA Human Rights* 38, no. 1 (Winter 2011): 18–20.

Mueller, John, Mark G. Stewart, and Benjamin H. Friedman. "Finally Talking Terror Sensibly." *nationalinterest.com*, May 24, 2013.

Muñoz, Carlo. "NSA Chief Cites 50 Foiled Plots in Defense of Spying Program." *The Hill*, June 18, 2013.

Myers, Lisa. "Terror Threat Source Called into Question," *NBC News*, May 28, 2004.

Nacos, Brigette L., Yaeli Block-Elkon, and Robert Y. Shapiro. *Selling Fear: Counterterrorism, the Media, and Public Opinion*. Chicago: University of Chicago Press, 2011.

Nakashima, Ellen. "Audit: Justice Department Office Overstated Terrorism Conviction Statistics." *Washington Post*, September 17, 2013.

Nakashima, Ellen. "If Not the NSA, Who Should Store the Phone Data?" *Washington Post*, December 25, 2013.

Nakashima, Ellen. "NSA Bills Set Up a Choice in Congress: End Bulk Collection of Phone Records or Endorse It." *Washington Post*, October 28, 2013.

Nakashima, Ellen. "NSA Cites Case as Success of Phone Data-Collection Program." *Washington Post*, August 8, 2013.

Nakashima, Ellen. "NSA Gathered Thousands of Americans' E-mails Before Court Struck Down Program." *washingtonpost.com*, August 21, 2013.

Nakashima, Ellen, and Joby Warrick. "For NSA Chief, Terrorist Threat Drives Passion to 'Collect it All,' Observers Say." *Washington Post*, July 14, 2013.

National Consortium for the Study of Terrorism and Responses to Terrorism (START). Global Terrorism Database, University of Maryland. See www.start.umd.edu/gtd/.

National Research Council of the National Academies. *Review of the Department of Homeland Security's Approach to Risk Analysis*. Washington, DC: National Academies Press, 2010.

Naylor, Hugh. "Islamic State Leader Purportedly Urges Muslims to Launch Attacks." *washingtonpost.com*, May 14, 2015.

Nelson, Rick, and Kimberly Walker. *International Standardization of Air Passenger and Cargo Screening*. Washington, DC: Center for Strategic and International Studies, 2011.

Neuman, William. "In Response to M.T.A.'s 'Say Something' Ads, a Glimpse of Modern Fears." *New York Times*, January 7, 2008.

New York Police Department. "Terrorist Plots Targeting New York City." Available at www.nyc.gov/html/nypd/html/pr/plots_targeting_nyc.shtml, accessed December 14, 2014.

Nicholson, Brendan. "Rudd Scraps Plan for New Department, Coast Guard." *The Age*, December 5, 2008.

Nixon, Ron. "Widow of Sept. 11 Pilot Seeks More Cockpit Security." *New York Times,* July 16, 2013.

O'Connor, Mike. *Crisis, Pursued by Disaster, Followed Closely by Catastrophe: A Memoir of Life on the Run.* New York: Random House, 2007.

Office of Management and Budget (OMB). Analytical Perspectives: Budget of the United States Government, Fiscal Year 2005. Washington, DC.

Office of Management and Budget (OMB). Analytical Perspectives: Budget of the United States Government, Fiscal Years 2005 to 2015. Washington, DC.

Office of Management and Budget (OMB). Analytical Perspectives, Budget of the United States Government, Fiscal Year 2011. Washington, DC.

Office of Management and Budget (OMB). Annual Report to Congress on Combating Terrorism, Fiscal Years 2001 to 2003. Washington, DC.

Office of Management and Budget (OMB). Fiscal Year 2013, Cuts, Consolidations, and Savings, Budget of the U.S. Government. Washington, DC.

Office of Management and Budget (OMB). "Guidelines and Discount Rates for Benefit-Cost Analysis of Federal Programs (Revised)." Circular No. A-94, Washington, DC, October 29, 1992.

Office of the Director of National Intelligence. "FY2013 Congressional Budget Justification, Volume I: National Intelligence Program Summary." Washington, DC, February 2012.

Office of the Director of National Intelligence. "Joint Statement from the ODNI and the U.S. DOJ on the Declassification of Renewal of Collection Under Section 501 of the FISA, Director of National Intelligence." Press release, Washington, DC, September 12, 2014.

Office of the Press Secretary, White House. "The Administration's Proposal for Ending the Section 215 Bulk Telephony Metadata Program." Washington, DC, March 27, 2014.

Office of the Press Secretary, White House. Remarks by the President at the National Defense University, May 23, 2013.

Office of the Press Secretary, White House. Remarks by President Obama and Prime Minister Cameron of the United Kingdom in Joint Press Conference, January 16, 2015.

Office of the Press Secretary, White House. Statement by the President, Fairmont Hotel, San Jose, CA, June 7, 2013.

Office of the Press Secretary, White House. Remarks by National Security Advisor Susan Rice on the 2015 National Security Strategy, February 6, 2015.

Office of the Press Secretary, White House. Remarks by the President on Review of Signals Intelligence, Department of Justice, January 17, 2014. Available at www.whitehouse.gov/the-press-office/2014/01/17/remarks-president-review-signals-intelligence.

Okochi, Mika. "Anti-Terrorism Measures Implemented by the New York City Police Department—Extraterritorial Law Enforcement Activities by Local Police

Department." *Journal of the Tokyo University of Marine Science and Technology* 8 (2012): 77–86.

Painter, William L., and Jennifer E. Lake. "Homeland Security Department: FY2012 Appropriations." Congressional Research Service, Washington, DC, November 2, 2011.

Pape, Robert A. *Dying to Win: The Strategic Logic of Suicide Terrorism.* New York: Random House, 2005.

Pape, Robert A., and James K. Feldman. *Cutting the Fuse: The Explosion of Global Suicide Terrorism and How to Stop It.* Chicago: University of Chicago Press, 2010.

Paté-Cornell, Elisabeth. "Risk and Uncertainty Analysis in Government Safety Decisions." *Risk Analysis* 22, no. 3 (2002): 633–46.

Patel, Faiza. *Rethinking Radicalization.* New York: New York University Law School, Brennan Center for Justice, 2011.

Pauley, Judge William. "Memorandum & Order." U.S. District Court Southern District of New York, December 27, 2013.

Philbrick, Herbert. *I Led Three Lives.* New York: Grosset & Dunlap, 1952.

Pillar, Paul R. *Terrorism and U.S. Foreign Policy.* Washington, DC: Brookings Institution Press, 2003.

Pincus, Walter. "NSA Should Be Debated on the Facts." *washingtonpost.com,* July 29, 2013.

Pinker, Steven. *The Better Angels of Our Nature: Why Violence Has Declined.* New York: Viking, 2011.

Pistole, John S. "Counterterrorism, Risk-Based Security and TSA's Vision for the Future of Aviation Security." Remarks at National Press Club, March 5, 2012. Available at www.tsa.gov/press/speeches/counterterrorism-risk-based-security-and-tsa%E2%80%99s-vision-future-aviation-security

Porter, Patrick. *The Global Village Myth: Distance, War, and the Limits of Power.* Washington, DC: Georgetown University Press, 2015.

Porter, Patrick. "Long Wars and Long Telegrams: Containing Al-Qaeda." *International Affairs* 85, no. 2 (March 2009): 283–305.

Preble, Christopher A. *John F. Kennedy and the Missile Gap.* DeKalb: Northern Illinois University Press, 2004.

Preble, Christopher A., and John Mueller, eds. *A Dangerous World? Threat Perception and U.S. National Security.* Washington, DC: Cato Institute.

Price, Michael. "National Security and Local Police." Brennan Center for Justice at New York University School of Law, New York, 2013.

Priest, Dana. "NSA Growth Fueled by Need to Target Terrorists." *Washington Post,* July 21, 2013.

Priest, Dana, and William M. Arkin. "Monitoring America." *Washington Post,* December 20, 2010.

Priest, Dana, and William M. Arkin. *Top Secret America: The Rise of the New American Security State.* New York: Little, Brown, 2011.

Priest, Dana, and Josh White. "War Helps Recruit Terrorists, Hill Told; Intelligence Officials Talk Of Growing Insurgency." *Washington Post*, February 17, 2005.

Privacy and Civil Liberties Oversight Board (PCLOB). Report on the Surveillance Program Operated Pursuant to Section 702 of the Foreign Intelligence Surveillance Act, Washington, DC, July 2, 2014.

Privacy and Civil Liberties Oversight Board (PCLOB). Report on the Telephone Records Program Conducted Under Section 215 of the U.S. Patriot Act and on the Operations of the Foreign Intelligence Surveillance Court, Washington, DC, January 23, 2014.

Puhl, Tyler. "Case 20: Bombing Transatlantic Airliners." In *Terrorism Since 9/11: The American Cases*, edited by John Mueller. Columbus: Mershon Center, Ohio State University, 2015.

Putin, Vladimir. "A Plea for Caution from Russia." *New York Times*, September 11, 2013.

Quindlen, Anna. "The Microwave War." *New York Times*, March 3, 1991.

Radio Technical Commission for Aeronautics (RTCA). "Aircraft Secondary Barriers and Alternative Flight Deck Security Procedures." Final Report, Special Committee 221, RTCA DO-329, Washington, DC, September 28, 2011.

Ramabhushanam, Ennala, and Marjorie Lynch. "Structural Assessment of Bomb Damage to World Trade Centre." *Journal of Performance of Constructed Facilities* 8, no. 4 (1994): 233–35.

RAND Database of Worldwide Terrorism Incidents. Santa Monica, CA: RAND Corporation. smapp.rand.org/rwtid/search_form.php

Rapoport, David C. "The Four Waves of Modern Terror: International Dimensions and Consequences." In *An International History of Terrorism: Western and Non-Western Experiences*, edited by Jussi Hanhimäki and Bernhard Blumenau, London: Routledge, 2013, 282–231.

Rapoport, David C. "Modern Terror: The Four Waves." In *Attacking Terrorism: Elements of a Grand Strategy*, edited by Audrey K. Cronin and James M. Ludes, 46–73. Washington, DC: Georgetown University Press, 2004.

Rapoport, David C. "Terrorists and Weapons of the Apocalypse." *National Security Studies Quarterly* 5, no. 1 (Summer 1999): 49–67.

Rashbaum, William K. "S.I. Man Describes Shattered Life, Then a Plot to Bomb a Subway Station." *New York Times*, May 10, 2006.

Ratnesar, Romesh. "The Myth of Homegrown Islamic Terrorism." *Time*, January 24, 2011.

Reagan, Ronald. *Public Papers of the Presidents of the United States*. Washington, DC: Government Publishing Office, 1983.

Reaves, Brian A. "Census of State and Local Law Enforcement Agencies, 2008." Office of Justice Programs, Bureau of Justice Statistics, Washington, DC, July 2011.

Reaves, Brian A. "Federal Law Enforcement Officers, 2008." Office of Justice Programs, Bureau of Justice Statistics, Washington, DC, June 2012.

Reaves, Brian A. "Local Police Departments, 2007." Office of Justice Programs, Bureau of Justice Statistics, Washington, DC, December 2010.

Reese, Shawn. "Department of Homeland Security Assistance to States and Localities: A Summary and Issues for the 111th Congress." Congressional Research Service, Washington, DC, December 1, 2009.

Reeve, Simon. *The New Jackals: Ramzi Yousef, Osama bin Laden, and the Future of Terrorism.* Boston: Northeastern University Press, 1999.

Reilly, Sean. "Poll Shows Alabamians Still Support President." *Mobile Register,* May 22, 2005.

Rice, Doyle. "USA Saw Fewest Lightning Deaths on Record in 2013." *USA Today,* January 11, 2014.

Richardson, Louise. "In Security." *New York Times Book Review,* October 26, 2014.

Risen, James. *Pay Any Price: Greed, Power, and Endless War.* Boston: Houghton, Mifflin, Harcourt, 2014.

Rittgers, David. "Abolish the Department of Homeland Security." Washington, DC, Cato Institute Policy Analysis no. 683, September 8, 2011.

Rizzo, Tony. "Terror Charges Filed Against Topeka Man Accused of Fort Riley Bomb Plot for Islamic State." *Kansas City Star,* April 10, 2015.

Robinson, Eugene. "We Can Handle the Truth on NSA Spying." *Washington Post,* July 3, 2013.

Robinson, Lisa A., James K. Hammitt, Joseph E. Aldy, Alan Krupnick, and Jennifer Baxter. "Valuing the Risk of Death from Terrorist Attacks." *Journal of Homeland Security and Emergency Management* 7, no. 1 (2010).

Roller, Emma. "This Is What Section 215 of the Patriot Act Does." *slate.com,* June 7, 2013.

Rollins, John. "Fusion Centers: Issues and Options for Congress." CRS Report for Congress, Congressional Research Service, Washington, DC, January 18, 2008.

Rosen, Jeffrey. *The Naked Crowd.* New York: Random House, 2004.

Ross, Brian. "Secret FBI Report Questions Al Qaeda Capabilities: No 'True' Al Qaeda Sleeper Agents Have Been Found in U.S." *ABC News,* March 9, 2005.

Ross, Brian, Aaron Katersky, James Gordon Meek, and Lee Ferran. "NSA Claim of Thwarted Plot Contradicted by Court Documents." *ABC News,* June 19, 2013.

Rotella, Sebastian. "Did NSA Surveillance Help Thwart Plotter of Mumbai Attack?" *Frontline* (PBS), June 12, 2013. Available at www.pbs.org/wgbh/pages/frontline.

Rubin, Jennifer. "Rubio and Others Run from Internationalism When It Matters." *washingtonpost.com,* September 8, 2013.

Russett, Bruce M. *No Clear and Present Danger.* New York: Harper and Row, 1972.

Sageman, Marc. *Leaderless Jihad.* Philadelphia: University of Pennsylvania Press, 2008.

Sageman, Marc. "The Stagnation in Terrorism Research." *Terrorism and Political Violence* 26, no. 4 (2014): 565–580.

Sageman, Marc. *The Turn to Political Violence.* New York: Free Press, forthcoming.

Sageman, Marc. *Understanding Terror Networks*. Philadelphia: University of Pennsylvania Press, 2004.

Sale, Richard. "U.S. al Qaida Cells Attacked." UPI, October 31, 2002.

Sanchez, Julian. "Decoding the Summer of Snowden." Cato Policy Report, November/December 2014.

Savage, Charlie. "F.B.I. Casts Wide Net Under Relaxed Rules for Terror Inquiries, Data Show." *New York Times*, March 26, 2011.

Savage, Charlie. "Manning Is Acquitted of Aiding the Enemy." *New York Times*, July 30, 2013.

Savage, Charlie. "N.S.A. Calls Violations of Privacy 'Minuscule.'" *nytimes.com*, August 16, 2013.

Savage, Charlie, and Scott Shane. "Secret Court Rebuked N.S.A. on Surveillance." *New York Times*, August 21, 2013.

Schanzer, David, Charles Kurzman, and Ebrahim Mooza. "Anti-Terror Lessons of Muslim-Americans." Triangle Center on Terrorism and Homeland Security, January 6, 2010.

Scherlen, Renee. "The Never-Ending Drug War: Obstacles to Drug War Policy Termination." *Political Science & Politics* 45, no. 1 (January 2012): 67–73.

Scheuer, Michael. *Imperial Hubris: Why the West Is Losing the War on Terror*. Dulles, VA: Brassey's, 2004.

Schneier, Bruce. *Beyond Fear: Thinking Sensibly About Security in an Uncertain World*. New York: Copernicus, 2003.

Schneier, Bruce. "The Efficacy of Post-9/11 Counterterrorism." *schneier.com*, September 2, 2011.

Schneier, Bruce. "Obama Says Terrorism Is Not an Existential Threat." *schneier.com*, February 3, 2015.

Schneier, Bruce. "Portrait of the Modern Terrorist as an Idiot." *schneier.com*, June 14, 2007.

Schneier, Bruce. "Why Are We Spending $7 Billion on TSA?" *cnn.com*, June 5, 2015.

Schuster, Henry. "Producer's Notebook: My Trip to Supermax." *CBS News*, October 13, 2007.

Schwartz, Mattathias. "Three Big Questions About the N.S.A.'s Patriot Act Powers." *newyorker.com*, June 2, 2015.

Schwartz, Mattathias. "'We're at Greater Risk': Q. & A. with General Keith Alexander." *newyorker.com*, May 15, 2014.

Schwartz, Mattathias. "The Whole Haystack: The N.S.A. Claims It Needs Access to All Our Phone Records. But Is That the Best Way to Catch a Terrorist?" *New Yorker*, January 26, 2015.

Scientific Committee on Emerging and Newly Identified Health Risks (SCENIHR). "Health Effects of Security Scanners for Passenger Screening." European Commission, Brussels, April 26, 2012.

Sedgwick, Mark. "The Concept of Radicalization as a Source of Confusion." *Terrorism and Political Violence* 22, no. 4 (2010): 479–94.

Seidenstat, Paul. "Federal Air Marshals: The Last Line of Defense." In *Protecting Airline Passengers in the Age of Terrorism*, edited by Paul Seidenstat and Francis X. Splane, 149–59. Santa Barbara, CA: Greenwood, 2009.

Seitz, Russell. "Weaker Than We Think." *American Conservative*, December 6, 2004.

Serrano, Richard A. "U.S. Faces 'Heightened' Threat Level." *Los Angeles Times*, February 10, 2011.

Shalal-Esa, Andrea, and Joseph Menn. "U.S. Domestic Spying Controversy Complicates Cybersecurity Efforts." Reuters, June 8, 2013.

Shane, Scott. "Bush's Speech on Iraq Echoes Analyst's Voice." *New York Times*, December 4, 2005.

Shane, Scott. "Court Upbraided N.S.A. on Its Use of Call-Log Data." *New York Times*, September 10, 2013.

Shane, Scott. "Pornography Is Found in Bin Laden Compound Files, U.S. Officials Say." *New York Times*, May 13, 2011.

Shapiro, Jacob B. *The Terrorist's Dilemma: Managing Violent Covert Organizations.* Princeton, NJ: Princeton University Press, 2013.

Shapiro, Jeremy. "Countering Violent Extremism: The Quixotic Quest for a Rational Policy on Terrorism." *brookings.edu/blogs*, February 16, 2015

Shatz, Howard. "To Defeat the Islamic State, Follow the Money." *politico.com*, September 10, 2004.

Sheehan, Michael A. *Crush the Cell: How to Defeat Terrorism Without Terrorizing Ourselves.* New York: Crown, 2008.

Sheridan, Mary Beth. "U.S. May Ease Anti-Terror Rules to Help Starving Somalis." *Washington Post*, August 2, 2011.

Sherrill, Kenneth. "The Political Power of Lesbians, Gays, and Bisexuals." *Political Science & Politics* 29, no. 3 (September 1996): 469–73.

Silber, Mitchell D. *The Al Qaeda Factor: Plots Against the West.* Philadelphia: University of Pennsylvania Press, 2012.

Silber, Mitchell D. "The Mutating al Qaeda Threat: Terrorists Are Adapting and Expanding." *Washington Times*, December 30, 2011.

Silber, Mitchell D., and Arvin Bhatt, *Radicalization in the West: The Homegrown Threat.* New York: New York City Police Department, 2007.

Silver, Nate. *The Signals and the Noise: Why So Many Predictions Fail—but Some Don't.* New York: Penguin, 2012.

Simon, Jeffrey D. *Lone Wolf Terrorism.* Amherst, NY: Prometheus, 2013.

Simon, Jeffrey D. *The Terrorist Trap: America's Experience with Terrorism.* 2nd ed. Bloomington: Indiana University Press, 2001.

Slovic, Paul, Baruch Fischhoff, and Sarah Lichtenstein. "Facts and Fears: Understanding Perceived Risk." In *Societal Risk Assessment: How Safe Is Safe Enough?* edited by R. C. Schwing and W. A. Albers, 181–216. New York: Plenum, 1980.

Sly, Liz. "Islamic State Appears to Be Fraying from Within." *washingtonpost.com*, March 8, 2015.

Sly, Liz. "The 'Islamic State' Is Failing at Being a State." *washingtonpost.com*, December 25, 2014.

Smeltz, Dana. "United in Goals, Divided in Means." Chicago: Chicago Council on Global Affairs, 2015.

Smeltz, Dana, and Ivo Daadler. "Foreign Policy in the Age of Retrenchment: Results of the 2014 Chicago Council Survey of American Public Opinion and U.S. Foreign Policy." Chicago: Chicago Council on Global Affairs, 2014.

Smith, Ben. "Public Documents Contradict Claim Email Spying Foiled Terror Plot." *buzzfeed.com*, June 7, 2013.

Smith, Patrick. "The Airport Security Follies." *nytimes.com*, December 28, 2007.

Smith, R. Jeffrey. "Senate Report Says National Intelligence Fusion Centers Have Been Useless." *foreignpolicy.com*, October 3, 2012.

Sofan, Ali. "Enemies Domestic." *Wall Street Journal*, January 23, 2013.

Stein, Jeff. "NYPD Intelligence Detectives Go Their Own Way." *Washington Post*, November 10, 2010.

Stenersen, Anne. *Al-Qaida's Quest for Weapons of Mass Destruction: The History Behind the Hype*. Saarbrücken, Germany: VDM Verlag Dr. Müller, 2008.

Stenersen, Anne. "Al-Qaeda's Thinking on CBRN: A Case Study." In *Unconventional Weapons and International Terrorism: Challenges and New Approaches*, edited by Magnus Ranstorp and Magnus Normark, 50–63. London: Routledge, 2009.

Stenersen, Anne. "The Internet: A Virtual Training Camp?" *Terrorism and Political Violence* 20, no. 2 (2008): 215–33.

Stephan, Alexander. *"Communazis": FBI Surveillance of German Émigré Writers*. New Haven, CT: Yale University Press, 2000.

Stevens, Donald, et al. "Near-Term Options for Improving Security at Los Angeles International Airport." Santa Monica, CA: RAND, 2004.

Stewart, Mark G., Bruce R. Ellingwood, and John Mueller. "Homeland Security: A Case Study in Risk Aversion for Public Decision-Making." *International Journal of Risk Assessment and Management* 15, nos. 5–6 (2011): 367–86.

Stewart, Mark G., and Robert E. Melchers. *Probabilistic Risk Assessment of Engineering Systems*. London: Chapman & Hall, 1997.

Stewart, Mark G., and John Mueller. "Aviation Security, Risk Assessment, and Risk Aversion for Public Decisionmaking." *Journal of Policy Analysis and Management* 32, no. 3 (2013): 615–33.

Stewart, Mark G., and John Mueller. "Cost-Benefit Analysis of Advanced Imaging Technology Full Body Scanners for Airline Passenger Security Screening." *Journal of Homeland Security and Emergency Management* 8, no. 1 (2011): Article 30.

Stewart, Mark G., and John Mueller. "Cost-Benefit Analysis of Airport Security: Are Airports Too Safe?" *Journal of Air Transport Management* 35 (March 2014): 19–28.

Stewart, Mark G., and John Mueller. "Responsible Policy Analysis in Aviation Security with an Evaluation of PreCheck." *Journal of Air Transport Management*, forthcoming.

Stewart, Mark G., and John Mueller. "Risk and Cost-Benefit Analysis of Police Counter-Terrorism Operations at Australian Airports." *Journal of Policing, Intelligence and Counter Terrorism* 9, no. 2 (2014): 98–116.

Stewart, Mark G., and John Mueller. "Terrorism Risks and Cost-Benefit Analysis of Aviation Security." *Risk Analysis* 33, no. 5 (2013): 893–908.

Stiglitz, Joseph E., and Linda J. Bilmes. *The Three Trillion Dollar War: The True Cost of the Iraq Conflict.* New York: W. W. Norton, 2008.

Stossel, John. *Give Me a Break.* New York: HarperCollins, 2004.

Stouffer, Samuel A. *Communism, Conformity, and Civil Liberties.* Garden City, NY: Doubleday, 1955.

Strom, Kevin, John Hollywood, Mark Pope, Garth Weintraub, Crystal Daye, and Don Gemeinhardt. "Building on Clues: Examining Successes and Failures in Detecting U.S. Terrorist Plots, 1999–2009." Institute for Homeland Security Solutions, October 2010.

Sunstein, Cass R. *The Cost-Benefit State: The Future of Regulatory Protection.* Chicago: American Bar Association, 2002.

Sunstein, Cass R. "Misfearing: A Reply." John M. Olin Program in Law and Economics, Working Paper no. 274, University of Chicago Law School, 2006.

Sunstein, Cass R. "Terrorism and Probability Neglect." *Journal of Risk and Uncertainty* 26, nos. 2–3 (March-May 2003): 121–136.

Swarts, Phillip. "Director Warns Shutdown Would Harm FBI." United Presss International, April 7, 2011.

Takeyh, Ray. "The Rogue Who Came in from the Cold." *Foreign Affairs,* May/June 2001, 62–72.

Tan, David. "Case 34: Times Square." In *Terrorism Since 9/11: The American Cases,* edited by John Mueller. Columbus: Mershon Center, Ohio State University, 2015.

Temple-Raston, Dina. "Terrorism Case Shows Range of Investigators' Tools." *NPR,* October 3, 2009.

Tenet, George, and Bill Harlow. *At the Center of the Storm: My Years at the CIA.* New York: HarperCollins, 2007.

Theoharis, Athan G., ed. *The FBI: A Comprehensive Reference Guide.* Phoenix, AZ: Oryx Press, 1999.

Theoharis, Athan. *The Quest for Absolute Security: The Failed Relations Among U.S. Intelligence Agencies.* Chicago: Dee, 2007.

Thrall, A. Trevor, and Jane K. Cramer. *American Foreign Policy and the Politics of Fear: Threat Inflation Since 9/11.* London: Routledge, 2009.

Thurston, Robert W. *The Witch Hunts: A History of the Witch Persecutions in Europe and North America.* Harlow, UK: Pearson, 2007.

Toner, Robin. "Democrats Don't Need a Sacrificial Lamb for '92." *New York Times,* March 11, 1991.

Transactonal Records Access Clearinghouse (TRAC). *As Terrorism Prosecutions Decline, Extent of Threat Remains Unclear,* TRAC Report 231, Syracuse University, May 18, 2010. Available at trac.syr.edu/tracreports/terrorism/231/.

Transactional Records Access Clearinghouse (TRAC). *Terrorism/National Internal Security Prosecutions for February 2013*, TRAC Report 316, Syracuse University, April 24, 2013. Available at trac.syr.edu/tracreports/terrorism/316/.

Travis, Curtis C., Samantha A. Richter, Edmund A. C. Crouch, Richard Wilson, and Ernest D. Klema. "Cancer Risk Management: A Review of 132 Federal Regulatory Decisions." *Environmental Science and Technology* 21, no. 5 (1987): 415–20.

Trevor-Roper, Hugh R. *The European Witch-Craze of the Sixteenth and Seventeenth Centuries and Other Essays.* New York: Harper & Row, 1969.

Ukman, Jason. "Are Muslim Americans Being Radicalized in U.S. Prisons?" *washingtonpost.com*, June 14, 2011.

U.S. v. Moussaoui. Substitution for the Testimony of Khalid Sheikh Mohammed, nd. Defendant's exhibit 941. Available at en.wikisource.org/wiki/Substitution_for_the_Testimony_of_Khalid_Sheikh_Mohammed.

U.S. v. John T. Booker Jr. U.S. District Court of Kansas, Criminal Complaint, April 10, 2015. Available at www.justice.gov/sites/default/files/opa/press-releases/attachments/2015/04/10/booker_complaint.pdf.

U.S. Coast Guard. "Always Ready." 2013 Performance Highlights and 2015 Budget in Brief. U.S. Coast Guard Headquarters, Washington, DC, n.d.

U.S. House of Representatives, Committee on Homeland Security Subcommittee on Oversight and Management Efficiency. Written testimony of DHS Management Directorate, U.S. Customs and Border Protection, U.S. Immigration and Customs Enforcement, and Transportation Security, April 12, 2013.

U.S. House of Representatives, Department of Homeland Security Appropriations Act, 2006, Amendment No. 10, by Ted Poe, May 17, 2005.

U.S. House of Representatives, Homeland Security Committee, Hearing on Fiscal 2013 Budget Proposal for the Homeland Security Department, February 15, 2012.

U.S. House of Representatives, Permanent Select Committee on Intelligence. "How Disclosed NSA Programs Protect Americans, and Why Disclosure Aids Our Adversaries." Washington, DC: Office of the Director of National Intelligence, June 18, 2013.

U.S. Senate, Committee on Commerce, Science, and Transportation. Written testimony of TSA Administrator John Pistole, April 30, 2014.

U.S. Senate, Committee on Homeland Security and Governmental Affairs. Statement by Marcus W. Flagg, president of the Federal Flight Deck Officers Association, November 1, 2011.

U.S. Senate, Committee on Homeland Security and Governmental Affairs. Testimony of DHS Secretary Janet Napolitano, September 30, 2009.

U.S. Senate, Committee on Homeland Security and Governmental Affairs. Written testimony by Michael O'Hanlon, Brookings Institution, July 14, 2005.

U.S. Senate, Committee on the Judiciary Hearing on Continued Oversight of the Foreign Intelligence Surveillance Act. Written Testimony of Edward W. Felten, professor of computer science and public affairs, Princeton University, October 2, 2013.

U.S. Senate, Permanent Subcommittee on Investigations. *Federal Support for and Involvement in State and Local Fusion Centers*, Majority and Minority Staff Report. Washington, DC: United States Senate Committee on Homeland Security and Governmental Affairs, October 3, 2012.

Van Linschoten, Alex, Strick Van Linschoten, and Felix Kuehn. *An Enemy We Created: The Myth of the Taliban–Al Qaeda Merger in Afghanistan*. New York: Oxford University Press, 2012.

Viscusi, W. Kip. "The Value of Life in Legal Contexts: Survey and Critique." *American Law and Economics Review* 2, no. 1 (2000): 195–222.

Vitka, Sean. "The Dragnet's Day in Court." *slate.com*, September 30, 2013.

Waller, Douglas. *Wild Bill Donovan*. New York: Free Press, 2011.

Walt, Stephen M. "Being a Neocon Means Never Having to Say You're Sorry." *foreignpolicy.com*, June 20, 2014.

Walt, Stephen M. "The Real Threat Behind the NSA Surveillance Programs." *foreignpolicy.com*, June 10, 2013.

Walt, Stephen M. "Why They Hate Us (II): How Many Muslims Has the U.S. Killed in the Past 30 Years?" *foreignpolicy.com*, November 30, 2009.

Warrick, Joby. "U.S. Cites Big Gains Against Al-Qaeda." *Washington Post*, May 30, 2008.

Wehrey, Frederic. "The Iraq War: Strategic Overreach by America—and Also by al Qaeda." In *The Long Shadow of 9/11: America's Response to Terrorism*, edited by Brian Michael Jenkins and John Paul Godges, 47–55. Santa Monica, CA: RAND, 2011.

Weimann, Gabriel. *Terror on the Internet: The New Arena, the New Challenges*. Washington, DC: United States Institute of Peace, 2006.

Weisburd, David, Thomas E. Feucht, Idit Hakimi, Lois Felson Mock, and Simon Perry, eds. *To Protect and to Serve: Policing in an Age of Terrorism*. New York: Springer, 2009.

Weiser, Benjamin. "3 Men Draw 25-Year Terms in Synagogue Bomb Plot." *New York Times*, June 29, 2011.

Weiss, Murray. "Posting NYPD Detectives Overseas Has Been a Waste, Federal Officials Say." *DNAinfo.com*, January 7, 2014.

Weisz, Rudy. "America's Lack of Airport Security." 2012 Critical Infrastructure Symposium, Arlington, VA, 2012.

Wells, Jane. "Has United Made Its 787 Less Safe?" *CNBC*, October 26, 2012.

Welsh-Huggins, Andrew. *Hatred at Home: Al-Qaida on Trial in the American Midwest*. Athens: Ohio University Press, 2011.

Western, Jon. *Selling Intervention and War: The Presidency, the Media, and the American Public*. Baltimore: Johns Hopkins University Press, 2005.

Wilber, Del Quentin. "Inside an FBI Anti-Terrorist Sting Operation." *Washington Post*, November 25, 2012.

Wilmott, H. P. *Empires in the Balance*. Annapolis, MD: Naval Institute Press, 1982.

Wilson, Michael. "From Smiling Coffee Vendor to Terror Suspect." *New York Times*, September 26, 2009.

Winter, Jana, and Cora Currier. "TSA's Secret Behavior Checklist to Spot Terrorists." *firstlook.org/theintercept*, March 27, 2015.

Witt, Griff. "Westerners Fighting in Syria Disillusioned with Islamic State but Can't Go Home." *washingtonpost.com*, September 12, 2014.

Wohlstetter, Roberta. *Pearl Harbor: Warning and Decision*. Stanford, CA: Stanford University Press, 1962.

Wolf, Charles Jr., K. C. Yeh, Edmund Brunner, Jr., Aaron Gurwitz, and Marilee Lawrence. *The Costs of Soviet Empire*. Santa Monica, CA: RAND, 1983.

Wood, Graeme. "What ISIS Really Wants." *Atlantic*, March 2015.

Woodward, Bob. "Why Did Violence Plummet? It Wasn't Just the Surge." *Washington Post*, September 8, 2008.

Wright, Lawrence. *The Looming Tower: Al-Qaeda and the Road to 9/11*. New York: Knopf, 2006.

Wright, Lawrence. "The Rebellion Within." *New Yorker*, June 2, 2008.

Wyden, Ron, and John Dickas. "Too Many Secrets: What Washington Should Stop Hiding." *Foreign Affairs*, May/June 2015, 114-19.

Yang, Alan S. "Trends: Attitudes Toward Homosexuality." *Public Opinion Quarterly* 61, no. 3 (Fall 1997): 477–507.

Yoo, John. "Conclusion." In *Confronting Terror: 9/11 and the Future of American National Security*, edited by Dean Reuter and John Yoo, 277–90. New York: Encounter, 2011.

Young, Mark D. "National Insecurity: The Impacts of Illegal Disclosures of Classified Information." *I/S: A Journal of Law and Policy for the Information Society* 10, no. 2 (Summer 2014): 368–406.

Zakaria, Fareed. Interview with President Barack Obama, *CNN*, February 1, 2015.

Zakaria, Fareed. "Post-9/11, We're Safer Than We Think." *Washington Post*, September 13, 2010.

Zenko, Micah. "Exaggeration Nation." *foreignpolicy.com*, November 12, 2014.

Zenko, Micah. "Mission Improbable." *foreignpolicy.com*, September 18, 2014.

Zenko, Micah. "Terrorists Among Us." *foreignpolicy.com*, October 12, 2014.

Ziliak, Stephen T., and Deirdre N. McCloskey. *The Cult of Statistical Significance: How the Standard Error Costs Us Jobs, Justice, and Lives*. Ann Arbor: University of Michigan Press, 2008.

Zubok, Vladislav. *A Failed Empire: The Soviet Union in the Cold War from Stalin to Gorbachev*. Chapel Hill: University of North Carolina Press, 2008.

ACKNOWLEDGMENTS

THIS BOOK HAS benefited from interviews of, or conversations with, Marc Sageman, Daniel Byman, Jeremy Shapiro, Mike German, Glenn Carle, Paul Pillar, Jonathan Rauch, Ed Folsom, Robert Pape, Richard Herrmann, David Rapoport, Richard Jackson, Paul Pillar, Benjamin Friedman, John Mearsheimer, Jim Harper, Jeffrey Simon, Karl Mueller, Jacques Hymans, Henry Willis, Robert Poole, Christopher Preble, Tim Legrand, Simon Bronitt, John McFarlane, Matthew Grant, and Michael Netherton.

Portions have been presented at talks and conference presentations at University of Chicago, Cato Institute, Oxford University, Ohio State University, University of Southern California, Peace Research Institute Oslo, Deakin University, Griffith University, Australian National University, University of Nantes, University of Durham, Tianjin University, University of Illinois, International Forum on Engineering Decision Making, Association of Private Enterprise Education, International Security Forum in Zurich, International Studies Association, Midwest Political Science Association, Carnegie Mellon University, American Political Science Association, Notre Dame University, Airports Council International—North America, RAND Corporation, Lawrence Livermore National Laboratory, Oakland University, Governors Homeland Security Advisors Council, ANSER, TASC, Ashland University, Syracuse University, International Conference of the Consortium for Comparative Research on Regional Integration and Social Cohesion, Strategic Studies Group of the Chief of Staff of the Army, Office of the Director of National Intelligence, U.S. Travel Association, Protection of Structures Against Hazards, International Conference on Applications of Statistics and Probability in Civil Engineering, Engineers Australia, Risk Engineering

Society, International Association of Protective Structures, International Air Transport Association, Australasian Conference on Materials and Structural Mechanics, International Conference on Reliable Engineering Computing, Safeguarding Australia Conference, International Conference on Shock and Impact Loads on Structures, Australian Explosive Ordnance Symposium, Border Security Conference, University of Warsaw, University of Otago, International Association for Bridge and Structural Engineering, Royal United Services Institute, Staffers of the Homeland Security Committee of the House of Representatives, Naval Postgraduate School, International Conference on Structural Safety and Reliability, Hammer Museum, Chatham House, Loyola University Chicago, Arizona State University, International Symposium on Aviation Security, University of St Andrews, and European Union's Framework Programme for Research, Technological Development, and Demonstration.

Various elements from this book have appeared in various ways and in various guises in *International Security, Journal of Economic Perspectives, Playboy, National Interest, International Journal of Human Rights, Journal of Risk Research, Journal of Air Transport Management, Time, Nation, The CIP Report, Cato Policy Analysis, I/S: A Journal of Law and Policy for the Information Society, Washington Post, Journal of Economic Perspectives, Journal of Policing, Intelligence and Counter Terrorism, Guardian, The Commentator, Breakthrough Journal, Huffington Post, Indian Express, Slate, Chronicle of Higher Education, Journal of Policy Analysis and Management, Risk Analysis, International Journal of Intelligent Defence Support Systems, Foreign Policy, Florida Real Estate Journal, Foreign Affairs, Public Perspective, Cato-at-liberty, Philadelphia Inquirer, Newcastle Herald, Global Post, Regulation, The Week, Australian Journal of Structural Engineering, Journal of Transportation Security, Los Angeles Times, American Conservative, Notre Dame Journal of International & Comparative Law, ABA Human Rights Magazine, Reason, International Journal of Risk Assessment and Management, CQ Researcher, Terrorism and Political Violence, International Studies Perspectives, Homeland Security Affairs, cnn.com, Lawfare. com, Dynamics of Asymmetric Conflict, Australian Financial Review, El Pais, American Interest, Nieman Watchdog Ask This, Policy Studies Journal, Canberra Times, Informed Comment, realcleardefense.com, cato-unbound.org, Journal of Homeland Security and Emergency Management,* and *Wilson Quarterly,* as well as in Patrick J. Carroll, Robert M. Arkin, and Aaron Wichman (eds.), *The Handbook of Personal Security*; Clive Walker (ed.), *Contingencies, Resilience and Legal Constitutionalism*; Benjamin Friedman, Jim Harper, and Christopher Preble (eds.), *Terrorizing Ourselves: Why U.S. Counterterrorism Policy Is Failing and How to Fix It*; Peter M. Haas and John A. Hird (eds.), *Controversies in Globalization*; Richard Jackson and Samuel Justin Sinclair (eds.), *Contemporary Debates on Terrorism*; Richard N. Rosecrance and Arthur A. Stein (eds.), *No More States?*; Robert Y. Shapiro and Lawrence R. Jacobs (eds.), *Oxford Handbook on American Public Opinion and the Media*; John Dumbrell and David Ryan (eds.), *Vietnam in Iraq*; Jean E. Rosenfeld (ed.), *Terrorism, Identity, and Legitimacy: The Four Waves Theory and Political Violence*; Rafael Reuveny and William R. Thompson (eds.), *Coping with Contemporary Terrorism*; George Kassimeris (ed.), *Playing Politics with Terrorism*; Stuart Gottlieb (ed.), *Debating Terrorism and Counterterrorism*; Matthew H. Morgan (ed.), *The Impact of 9/11: The Day That Changed Everything?*; James Pfiffner and Mark Phythian (eds.), *Intelligence and National Security Policy Making in Iraq*; and Jane K. Cramer and A. Trevor Thrall (eds.), *American Foreign Policy and the Politics of Fear.* There's a whole lot in this book, however, that is new.

Research assistance has been provided by Shurong Feng and Yue Li and by the writers of the terrorism case studies so essential to much of the analysis: Jolie Yang, Allison Barbo, Zachary Zaerr, Blaise Katter, Drew Herrick, Tessa Reinhart, Michael Spinosi, Rachel Cohen, Surili Sheth, Todd Ives, Andrew Ashbrook, Demetrius Daniels-Hill, Shannon Buckner, Andrew Braun, Zachary Karabatak, Lauren Brady, Tyler Puhl, David Bernstein, Jovan Galevski, Bryan Staub, David Dawson, Michael Coleman, Kelly Stritzinger, Justin Heilmann, Ronald Lieberman, Malgorzata Mrozek, Taylor Schmaltz, Matthew Spade, David Tan, Ruxton McClure, Chad Chessin, and Nicole Spaetzel at Ohio State University, and Jake Douglas, Alexander Hitchcock, and Leigh Stephens at Cato.

We are also grateful for support by the Mershon Center for International Security Studies at Ohio State University, the Cato Institute, the Centre for Infrastructure Performance and Reliability at the University of Newcastle, and the Australian Research Council.

And we'd like to thank the various movers and shakers at Oxford University Press including Dave McBride, Katie Weaver, and Peter Mavrikis.

AUTHOR BIOGRAPHIES

John Mueller is Woody Hayes Senior Research Scientist at the Mershon Center for International Security Studies and Professor of Political Science at Ohio State University, Columbus, Ohio, as well as a Senior Fellow at the Cato Institute. He is the author of over a dozen books, several of which have won prizes. Among the most recent of these are: *The Remnants of War* (2004), *Overblown* (2006), *Atomic Obsession: Nuclear Alarmism from Hiroshima to Al-Qaeda* (2010), and *War and Ideas* (2011). He has also edited the webbook *Terrorism Since 9/11: The American Cases* (2015). Earlier books include *Capitalism, Democracy, and Ralph's Pretty Good Grocery, Retreat from Doomsday, Astaire Dancing,* and *War, Presidents and Public Opinion*. He has published hundreds of articles in scholarly journals and general magazines and newspapers, is a member of the American Academy of Arts and Sciences, and has been a John Simon Guggenheim Fellow. politicalscience.osu.edu/faculty/jmueller/

Mark G. Stewart is Professor of Civil Engineering and Director of the Centre for Infrastructure Performance and Reliability at the University of Newcastle in Australia. He is co-author of *Probabilistic Risk Assessment of Engineering Systems* (Chapman & Hall, 1997), and has published more than 400 technical papers and reports. He has thirty years of experience in probabilistic risk and vulnerability assessment of infrastructure and security systems that are subject to man-made and natural hazards. Professor Stewart has received extensive Australian Research Council support to develop probabilistic risk-modeling techniques for infrastructure subject to military and terrorist explosive blasts, and cost-benefit assessments of aviation security, policing, and counter-terrorism protective measures for critical infrastructure. He is currently the recipient of an Australian Professorial Fellowship from the ARC to continue and to extend that work. www.newcastle.edu.au/research-and-innovation/centre/cipar/people

Mueller and Stewart are the authors of *Terror, Security, and Money: Balancing the Risks, Benefits, and Costs of Homeland Security* (Oxford University Press, 2011).

INDEX